A LEAF IN THE BITTER WIND

A MEMOIR

TING-XING YE

DOUBLEDAY

TORONTO NEW YORK LONDON SYDNEY AUCKLAND

Canadian Cataloguing in Publication Data

Ye, Ting-xing, 1952
A leaf in the bitter wind

ISBN (hardcover) 0-385-25603-5 (paperback) 0-385-25701-5
1. Ye, Ting-xing, 1952-   . 2. China - Social conditions -
1976-   . 3. China - Social conditions - 1949-1976.
4. Women - China - biography. I. Title.

DS779.29.Y4A3 1997   951.05'092   C96-032241-0

Jacket design by Tania Craan
Jacket photographs by Adriene Veninger
Jacket calligraphy by Zhong-xing Ye
Text design by Heather Hodgins
Maps by William Bell
Photo layout by Heidy Lawrance Associates

Published in Canada by
Doubleday Canada Limited
105 Bond Street
Toronto, Ontario
M5B 1Y3

BVG 10 9 8 7 6 5 4 3 2

This book is dedicated to the memory of

my mother, Li Xiu-feng
my father, Ye Rong-ting
my great-aunt, Chen Feng-mei

ACKNOWLEDGMENTS

Choosing the title was just a tiny part of William Bell's enormous contribution to this book. In a long, hard, sometimes tearful process, his gentle push and profound understanding helped me across the finish line. A writer himself, his love of words and solid knowledge of his craft inspired me to put down the first sentence, and his trust and confidence in me made this book possible.

I was fortunate to be befriended by John Pearce, who believed in, encouraged and guided this project. His judgment and expertise have been invaluable. My gratitude also goes to Gail Pearce for her careful reading of the manuscript and thoughtful advice.

I want to thank all my friends here in Canada for their support. My heart particularly goes to William Talbot, without whose assistance in bringing a stranger to this land in the first place this story would still be only a painful memory.

I also want to thank the Canada Council for assistance.

My last tribute is to my brothers and sisters in China, for their care and love, for their stories and research. I hope this book has done justice to the memory of our parents and great-aunt and to what the five of us have been through together.

A NOTE ON
CHINESE PRONUNCIATION

I have used the *han yu pin yin* system of romanization. A few names such as Yangtze and Chiang Kai-shek have been left in the older spelling because *pin yin* forms might be unfamiliar. English-speaking readers will find that most letters in *pin yin* are pronounced more or less the same as those in English. Some exceptions are:

c = ts, as in pe*ts*
q = ch, as in chur*ch*
x = *hss*
z = dz, as in a*dze*
zh = j, as in *j*uice

AUTHOR'S NOTE

The words *Lao* (Old, Venerable) and *Xiao* (Young) when used with a surname are common terms of respect in China. Thus, I was usually addressed as Xiao Ye by persons outside my family.

With the exception of public figures and members of my family, I have disguised the names of all Chinese persons in this book.

CHRONOLOGY

Year	My Family	China
1911	Great-Aunt Phoenix Sister born	
1921	Mother and Father born	
1935	Great-Aunt given to my family as free servant by her mother	
1937	Father goes to Shanghai to run family business; Great-Aunt goes along to look after Father	Japan invades China; the occupation of Shanghai
1938	Mother and Father marry	
1944	Mother joins Father in Shanghai	
1945		Japanese surrender
1946	Number 1 born	Civil War breaks out between Guomindang and Communists (–1949)
1948	Number 2 born	
1949	My two step-uncles leave for Taiwan	People's Republic established
1950	Number 3 born	Korean War; government issues People's Victory Bonds
1951		Three Antis Campaign
1952	Number 4 (me) born	Five Antis Campaign
1954	Number 5 born	First Five-Year Plan; State Economic Construction Bonds issued

1956	The government takes away Father's factory	Nationalization Movement
1957	Father's demotion from owner to laborer	Hundred Flowers Movement; Anti-Rightist Campaign
1958	I start elementary school	Great Leap Forward (–1959)
1959	Father's botched operation	Famine across China (–1962)
1962	Father dies	
1963	Number 2 forced to quit school to work to support family	
1964	Number 3 and I start middle school; Number 1 enrolls in Jiao Tong University in Shanghai	
1965	Mother dies	
1966	I am attacked by the Red Guards at school; the Red Guards come to our home; Grandfather severely beaten while trying to prevent my parents' grave from being leveled; I disguise myself as Red Guard on the pilgrimage to Beijing	Great Proletarian Cultural Revolution begins (–1976)
1967	I stay home from school with my siblings; Number 2 forced to fight in bloody battles against fellow workers	Shanghai "January Storm"; rebels take power at city hall; factional fights spread throughout the country; army's involvement in Cultural Revolution
1968	I am exiled to a prison labor farm in Jiangsu Province	

1969	Number 5 exiled to a farm in Jiangxi Province, Number 1 to Guizhou Province; I survive amoebic dysentery on the farm	Military clash with Russians; Ninth Party Congress formalizes the Cultural Revolution; Lin Biao becomes Mao's successor; PLA air force loyal to Lin Biao take over the prison farm
1970	I am denounced as a counter-revolutionary by army representatives on the farm; interrogation and humiliation, and my attempted suicide	Escalating war preparations against Russia; concubine selection on the farm for Lin Biao's son; construction on the farm to turn it into one of Lin's retreat bases
1971	I am sentenced; rehabilitated after death of Lin Biao; Universities reopened to "Worker-Peasant-Soldier" students	Lin Biao, his wife and son died in a plane crash while fleeing China; anti–Lin Biao Movement on the farm; army representatives leave the farm
1972	Number 1's marriage	Nixon visits China; withdrawal of army from all civilian duties across the country
1973	I am assigned to help young arrivals to the prison farm; studying English by myself	Deng Xiao-ping returns to power; "Suggestions for University Enrollment" announced; enrollment exams for Worker-Peasant-Soldier students set up
1974	I meet Xiao Zhao on the farm; enroll in Beijing University	"Criticizing Lin Biao and Confucius" movement
1975	Study English language and literature in countryside; return when first year ends	
1976	I am punished for attending Zhou En-lai's funeral; sent to Tangshan earthquake site in a rescue team	Zhou En-lai dies; Demonstrations in Tian An Men Square; Deng Xiao-ping ousted; Tangshan earthquake; Mao Ze-dong dies; the capture of the Gang of Four

1977	Early graduation announced	Nationwide restoration of university entrance exams
1978	I graduate from Beijing University and am recruited by the Chinese Secret Service; reassigned as an English interpreter for the government of Shanghai	Deng Xiao-ping returns to power; China's New Economic Policy and Open Door to the Outside World
1979	Number 5 returns home from farm; Number 1 enrolls in postgraduate studies in Shanghai; Great-Aunt suffers minor stroke	Deng Xiao-ping reinstitutes Four Modernizations Program
1980	I marry Xiao Zhao	The policy of "one child/one family" established
1981	My daughter, Qi-meng, born	
1984	I start postgraduate studies in Foreign Affairs College in Beijing	
1986	Postgraduate certificate from FAC	Large-scale student demonstrations in Shanghai
1987	I am accepted by York University in Toronto; leave for Canada	
1994	I return to Shanghai to look for Qi-meng	

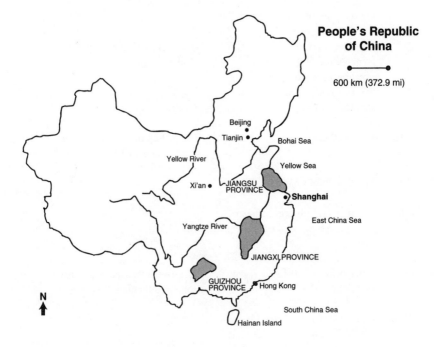

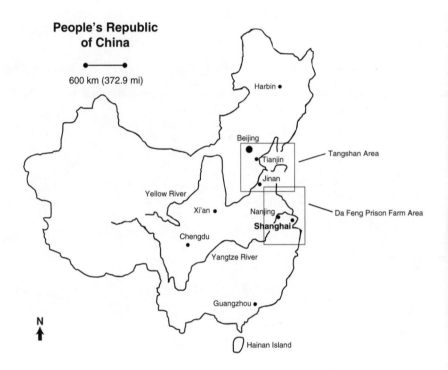

**People's Republic
of China**

600 km (372.9 mi)

Harbin ●

Beijing

● Tianjin

Tangshan Area

Jinan

Yellow River

Xi'an ●

Nanjing

Da Feng Prison Farm Area

Shanghai

Chengdu
●

Yangtze River

Guangzhou ●

N
↑

Hainan Island

DA FENG PRISON FARM AREA

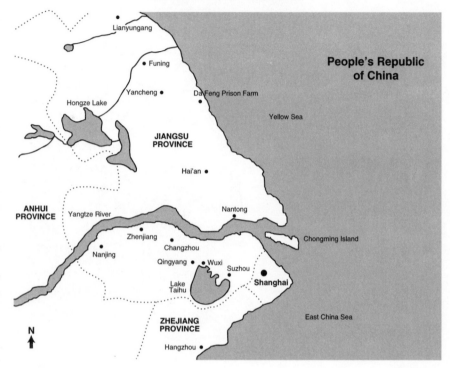

TANGSHAN AREA

INNER MONGOLIA

LIAONING
PROVINCE

to Harbin

HEBEI PROVINCE

Beijing

Tangshan

Fengtai ●

● ●

SHANXI
PROVINCE

Bohai Sea

Tianjin ●

**People's Republic
of China**

Baoding
●

Shijiazhuang
●

Yellow River

SHANDONG
PROVINCE

N

Jinan ●

to Shanghai

PROLOGUE

In my parents' silent bedroom I stand alone in my white mourning clothes, staring at the bed stripped down to its woven bamboo mat. The odor of incense hangs in the damp air, and outside the open window, spring rain hisses softly on terra-cotta roof tiles.

Father is dead: the empty bed in which he lay paralyzed for many years is proof. On his dresser, his spectacles gleam in the weak light; his calligraphy brush lies untouched. But where is Mother? It strikes me that I haven't seen her for — what is it? A few days? Months? Even years? My eldest brother, Number 1, has told me that Mother fled Shanghai because of me; she is living on a nameless island and doesn't want to be found.

"No, Mother, please! Don't punish me any more. I was only a child of nine and my wickedness just a split-second wish. Come back home!"

I wake in darkness to the sound of my own voice. My room is strangely quiet. The thrum of Shanghai's nighttime traffic has faded with the dream. Instead, the gentle sough of wind in the tall maples behind my home reminds me of my long journey to this small town in southern Ontario.

As they do each time I have the dream, my words echo inside my head and numbing, overwhelming guilt is the dreadful aftermath. It has been years since my defection in 1989, years since I began my new life in Canada, but the recurring nightmare has pursued me across the Pacific. For more than two decades my parents have been gone, yet, while I have accepted Father's death, Mother's passing haunts me still.

PART ONE

WIND OF TEARS
(1952–1966)

I WAS BORN IN SHANGHAI, late on a hot June afternoon in 1952, the fourth child in my family. So I was called Ah Si, Number 4.

My father decided to call it quits, but rather than rely on birth control, which was officially discouraged at that time, he put his faith in the power of words. A formal name for a child was no small matter: it required the weighing of tradition and precedent.

My surname, Ye, means Leaf. My generation name, Xing — Capable — had been decreed by my paternal grandfather after casting bamboo augury sticks in the family ancestral hall, so all Father's children were called Xing. My three older siblings Father had named after characteristics he admired; my brothers were Upright and Steadfast, my sister Diligent. For me he chose Ting, a homonym that means Graceful in writing but sounds like Stop when heard.

The magic didn't work. A year and a half later my sister Maple was born, mother's fifth and last child.

June was the beginning of the rainy season, a time of year abhorred by most people in the lower reaches of the Yangtze River. There was usually a solid month of drizzle and extreme humidity. Green mold grew on walls and floors; dampness seeped into people's bones. On the rare days when the sun appeared, courtyards and sidewalks were festooned with clothing, bedding and furniture. Everyone dreamt of living in a "zipper-roofed building."

As Great-Aunt never tired of telling anyone who would listen, my coming into the world was inauspicious, a girl born in the year of the dragon. She also said I was destined to a hard and unpredictable life, since June 1952 was uncharacteristically hot and dry, a sure sign of the King Dragon's disapproval, for he was the God of Rain. King Dragon, she said, dwelt in a crystal palace at the bottom of the Eastern Sea, where he was surrounded by crab generals and an army of shrimps, all of them male. I was often tempted to ask who did the household chores if there were no females like grandmother, mother and Great-Aunt herself around. But I had learned at an early age that there were two topics one should never question: the gods and the government.

Great-Aunt advised that, because of my unlucky birth, Tian Huang, the God of Heaven, should be enshrined for my protection, his statue placed in the center of a table along with one bowl of rice, three side dishes, two red candles and a bundle of incense sticks. This ceremony should be held once a year, on my birthday. Mother happily agreed. Like Father's selection of my name, this ritual proved ineffective.

🍃

A week after my birth, Mother took me from the Red House Hospital, so named because red paint covered its brick walls, wooden window-frames and doors, to my family's three-room apartment in the center of the city. Shaded by plane trees, Wuding (Violent Stability) Road ran east and west through the former International Settlement and many *long-tang* — lanes, some as wide as two carts abreast, some only shoulder-width — connected with it, forming a densely populated yet quiet neighborhood. We lived in Zi Yang Li — Purple Sunshine Lane. If you imagine a city ten miles wide and ten miles long with about six million people, you may have some idea of the population density of the central core around Purple Sunshine Lane.

Our two-story brick building was a traditional Shanghai-style stone-arched house, built around a courtyard or "sky-well" that served as the front entrance. This was guarded by two black-lacquer doors, heavy and tall, with brass door-knockers shaped like dragon heads with rings through their noses. Residents used the back door, however, reserving the front for occasions such as weddings and funerals.

In all, eight families lived in four apartments, two at each level. Two water taps in the tiny corridor at the back served all the families, and their use was strictly regulated and policed by our neighbor Granny Ningbo. The upper tap, with its brick sink, could be used only to wash food, clothing and dishes. The lower one was for cleaning chamber pots, rinsing mops and so on. On each floor, one small kitchen served four families. From the roof terrace I could see the chimney of Father's Zheng Tai Rubber Shoe Factory.

Where Purple Sunshine Lane intersected with Wuding Road was the *cai chang* — food market — whose two-tiered rough plank stalls stretched about thirty yards along both sides of the shady street. The center of our neighborhood, it opened at six o'clock in the morning, but lineups for food much in demand, like pork bones and fat, which were cheaper and required fewer ration coupons, began to form hours earlier. Some enterprising residents would rise early, take up spots near the front of the line and sell them for a few cents. By early afternoon the stalls were empty and the residents used them to make quilts on or to air their bedding.

For several years the sky-well, the lane and the busy market were my world.

In many ways, Shanghai of the 1950s was a city of faded glory. Once "the Paris of the East," with a foreign population of sixty thousand living in autonomous "concessions" that controlled the entire central portion of the city, Shanghai was the largest manufacturing center in Asia. But by the time the Communists took power three years before I was born, the foreigners had decamped, walking away from the child and slave labor, the massive prostitution, the opium trade and many of the businesses that had thrived and boosted the wealth of the city.

Most of the tall (higher than two-story) buildings in Shanghai were foreign-built remnants of the 1930s standing along the "Bund," or western embankment of the muddy Huangpu River, where its yellow waters were joined by the black and polluted Suzhou Creek. The entire city, whose name meant Above the Sea, rested on low, spongy ground, and its eighteen-mile-long harbor joined with the mighty Yangtze where it met the sea.

The weather reflected the dominance of river and sea. December and January were cold, dreary and damp. As all buildings were unheated, we wore our cotton-padded coats, trousers and shoes at all times, except when we went to bed. It was not unusual to see icicles hanging from our straw-wrapped water pipe in the morning. February brought back the sun and March the rains. May was the best month, with flowers blooming under sunny skies. July and August often saw the thermometer rise far above eighty-five Fahrenheit; on those scorching days, we would sit in the shade or inside, fanning ourselves and stewing in our own sweat, waiting for *tai-feng* to lash the city with wind and rain. In the autumn it was still warm enough to wear shorts, but we could finally enjoy a whole night's sleep, without being nudged awake by the insufferable heat.

The Ye family household was a busy place, with five children each born two years apart. So when I was ten months old, much of my care fell to Great-Aunt, who had been part of my father's family since long before he married Mother. The tragic story of how Great-Aunt, Chen Feng-mei (Chen Phoenix Sister), came into my family illustrates the way of life in rural China at that time.

Qingyang, a small town where my paternal grandfather lived, was an hour's bus ride from Wuxi, a city two hours by train north west of Shanghai. The area was known as "the Land of Fish and Rice" for its rich flat farmland criss-crossed by canals and dotted with ponds and lakes. The land was so fertile that locals claimed a seed spit from your mouth would grow into a watermelon in no time. Numerous villages surrounded Qingyang, each named after its dominant clan.

The matchmakers of Chen Family Village, in which Great-Aunt and her family lived, starting darkening her threshold as soon as she was seventeen. She had "quality of appearance" and, better, she had three-inch bound "lily feet," considered the most important indicator of female attractiveness. Within a year, she was engaged to a son of an upper-middle-class peasant family in a neighboring village. (An upper-middle- or middle-class peasant farmed his own lands and was able to hire laborers during the busy seasons.) The betrothal gifts were accepted and a wedding was planned for a year later. All these arrangements were made, as was the custom, without consulting the bride herself.

As the old expression said, "Marrying off a daughter is like throwing out a bucket of water." The gain for the bride's family was purely passive: getting rid of a burden. In Feng-mei's case her parents were especially anxious to be rid of her as she was the eldest of three and tradition dictated that the younger daughters could not be married before the eldest, or the family would lose face. The groom's family was the recipient and had the right to approve the bride. It was unnecessary for the bride to know much, if anything, about her husband-to-be, not even his appearance.

This particular wedding arrangement was a gamble because the groom was in the third stage of tuberculosis; while the matchmaker was wearing out her shoes rushing back and forth between the two families, the groom was on his deathbed. His family and the matchmaker hoped the engagement would undermine his deadly illness — a superstition based on the notion that the extreme propitiousness of a wedding would draw away the bad luck of the sickness, as if mixing the red of the wedding with the white of a funeral would neutralize the problem.

But things didn't turn pink at all. The groom died. However, his death did not free his fiancée. Feng-mei was required to stay in half-widowhood for a year after the wedding date, and for eighteen months after that she could not be rematched. The betrothal gifts were taken back, but what remained was the conviction that Feng-mei's life hadn't been good enough to save her fiancé's.

If she was originally a ten on the matchmaker's scale, the needle had dropped below five by the time her mother was approached again by a go-between. Feng-mei was now an old maid of twenty-two. This time there were no betrothal offerings and no engagement. She was taken by her mother and the matchmaker to her new home, accompanied by a hired man who toted her meager belongings on a shoulder-pole.

Feng-mei's new husband was not a handsome young man, but a widower twenty years her senior. Worse, he suffered from severe asthma that kept him bedridden. No wonder there was no wedding banquet or gathering of relatives to celebrate. The whole thing was a business deal: the groom's family gained free labor to care for the stricken patient while the bride's family saved face by expelling the unlucky eldest daughter.

Two months later the new bride was a real widow. Her husband's death was also, in a way, hers. Her in-laws were not even interested in taking her as free labor for life as the old tradition allowed; instead, they labeled her "a woman who should never be close to any man," one so unlucky that she had caused her husband's death. She was sent back to her family and the villagers called her "reheated bean curd soup," a woman rejected by her husband's family. Bean curd soup was the cheapest kind, so people never bothered to reheat the leftovers; they threw it out instead. Everyone was now totally convinced that Feng-mei's life was sharp as a knife to males.

One day Feng-mei's mother traveled from her family village to Qingyang to visit my great-grandmother. With tears in her eyes, the distraught woman asked Great-Grandmother if she would take in her eldest daughter as an unpaid live-in maid. On the one hand, Feng-mei would be a help around the house; on the other, the woman confided, it would bring shame on her family if her daughter lived at home. Feng-mei was twenty-three.

Feng-mei, who was never called by her name in Grandfather's house, was introduced to my father and his siblings as *Jie-Jie* — Elder Sister — a euphemism, for she was in fact a servant. Although Qingyang was only five miles away from Chen Family Village, she never saw her village again until she was an old woman.

🍃

Unlike his two stepbrothers who were running the family's rubber manufacturing business in Shanghai, Grandfather Ye had always considered the city a corrupt and evil place. But he had to face the fact that his son, Rong-ting, Prosperity, crippled in one leg by meningitis four years before, was not suited to live in the country, where physical strength was more than just an asset. Also, face was involved. How could he continue to rely on his stepbrothers and their sons to run his share of the business when he had a sixteen-year-old son old enough to take over? The family's three Shanghai factories had prospered and expanded over the years, particularly in the manufacture of tires and toys. "Forever" brand hot-water bottles hung from the walls of many thousands of Shanghai homes. So, after the Chinese New Year of 1937, Rong-Ting, my father, was packed off to Shanghai. Once he found accommodation, a 130-square-foot single room barely large enough for two single beds, five minutes' walk from the factory, he sent for *Jie-Jie* to keep house for him. It may seem strange that a young man of sixteen years would share a room with the family's maid ten years his senior, but in those days such a situation was not out of the ordinary.

In July that year the Japanese began their all-out war of aggression against China, and it spread to Shanghai the following month. The city was shelled, bombed and invaded as the Chinese fought back street by street. The foreign concessions were left intact, however, protected by barbed wire and barricades. In a fateful way the Japanese occupation led to the marriage of my father and mother.

Refugees fleeing into the area near Wuxi and Qingyang in advance of the Japanese army spread tales of atrocities: the enemy soldiers referred to unmarried young women as "flower girls," and "sleeping with flower girls" — a euphemism for brutal rape — seemed to be at the top of their agenda. It was the nightmare of every mother that the Japanese would rape her daughter, for, over and above the brutality and the suffering, a woman who had been raped was almost impossible to marry off. Young girls disguised themselves by wearing baggy clothing, smeared their faces with straw ash so as to appear ugly and uncouth, or cut their hair short pretending to be boys. Some mothers thought that finding husbands for their daughters would reduce the risk. That idea led my *Wai Po* (maternal grandmother) one October morning to my grandfather's grocery store in Qingyang.

A determined middle-class peasant woman who had refused to bind her daughters' feet, *Wai Po* had until then been well known in her Li Family Village for fending off matchmakers, having decided not to marry off her eldest of three daughters, Xiu-feng (Beautiful Phoenix), until she was eighteen. But with the horrific stories that preceded the coming of the Japanese, *Wai Po* decided she must act quickly.

"Boss Ye," she asked Grandfather, "do you want a wife for your son? Yes or no."

"Hold on there, Sister," Grandfather replied. "What are you talking about? My son is only seventeen. I haven't even thought of a wife for him yet."

At this, *Wai Po* burst into tears. "Boss Ye, I am not here to sell a piece of old furniture but to find a husband for my own flesh and blood. Xiu-feng is seventeen, healthy and beautiful. I can't allow her to be ruined at the hands of the Eastern Devils."

Grandfather, who had often claimed he could keep calm even if the Emperor himself were at the door, became noodles while facing a crying woman. "Give me a week to think about it," he told the distraught mother.

In truth, there was more here than met the eye. *Wai Po* was anxious to protect her daughter, but at the same time she must have known that she held a few cards herself. My father was certainly a good catch for a village girl: as the eldest son of a successful businessman and farmer, he had excellent prospects to inherit a store, land and a factory, even though there was a war on. He also lived in Shanghai, and not everyone shared Grandfather's prejudice about that city. Nevertheless, he was lame. *Wai Po* knew that. My father would be rejected by some mothers as a marriage prospect because of the superstitions surrounding any illness or disability.

Grandfather sent an urgent telegram to Shanghai. Five days after *Wai Po*'s visit, my mother and father, both seventeen, were married in Qingyang, and Mother moved into Grandfather's house. Two days after the wedding, Father returned to Shanghai without his bride, for he was too busy learning and running the business, Grandfather said, to devote time to a new wife. Besides, Shanghai was now totally under Japanese occupation, not a safe place to be. Father visited his wife and family once a year, during the New Year celebration.

2

I N THE SPRING OF 1944, six years after her marriage to a man she had never seen before she entered her father-in-law's house, Mother boarded the train to Shanghai. During that time, no child had been born and the family was worried. At that time and even now in China, the female partner was blamed for a couple's childlessness. Although the doctor had mentioned that father's childhood battle against meningitis might be an explanation, no one in the family wanted to think that way. Even though Shanghai was still under Japanese control, Grandfather now declared that the couple should be together. Perhaps that would help.

Time passed and nothing happened. Great-Aunt, who was not happy to be displaced by Father's wife, gossiped up and down the lane that Mother was barren and later even tried to match Father with another woman. Mother caught wind of Great-Aunt's plot and feared that Father would put her aside. Instead, Father told her that if there was a problem with their having children, he was to blame. He had accepted that due to his childhood illness he might not have an heir. And he would not have anything to do with another woman, he assured her. If she wanted to back away from the marriage, however, he was not going to stand in her way.

Father's loyalty to her won my mother's heart. Although she was choked with bitterness about *Jie-Jie*'s betrayal, she realized that leaving such a man would be the biggest mistake in the world.

A year later, in 1946, the Japanese surrendered and decamped. Life in Shanghai began to return to normal. Business flourished. And my eldest brother, Zheng-xing — Number 1 — was born.

My preschool years were mostly boring and lonely, but I vividly recall a day in late 1956, when I was four years old. Father came home from the factory with a big red silk flower pinned to the pocket of his Western-style sports jacket. Even at that age I knew that wearing a red flower, real or not, meant awards and honor. Posters with smiling soldiers and peasants wearing red flowers were everywhere.

Father was a handsome, gentle and scholarly-looking man, highly respected in the neighborhood, successful at business although by no means wealthy. Deeply intelligent, he was nonetheless politically naive. Before the Communists took over, his stepcousins had to advise him on how to keep good relations with Nationalist Party officials when they "inspected" his factory: by taking them to dinner and offering "gifts," the ubiquitous Chinese euphemism for bribes. These cousins fled to Taiwan upon Liberation.

But Father was not happy at all about his prize. He limped upstairs, walked past me, tossing the flower on the dinner table, and closed the door behind him. I stared longingly at the red blossom. From the other room I heard Father and Mother talking. It was only then I realized that Father had come home early. All my older siblings were still in school and two-year-old Number 5 was having a nap.

Mother saw me staring at the flower and said I could have it so long as I kept quiet. She helped me pin it to my jacket and I rushed joyfully downstairs to the sky-well, sporting my colorful prize. I didn't know that Father had been given the flower for handing over his factory — the enterprise his great-grandfather had established and he had operated for almost twenty years — to the state.

In 1951, one year before I was born, the government had launched the Three Antis campaign against waste, corruption and bureaucratic abuse of power in government. Shortly afterwards, in the spring of 1952, it started another one, the Five Antis, or as the more colloquial name had it, Anti Five Poisonous Creatures. This movement was aimed directly at private merchants and factory owners like Father. The five evils were bribery, tax evasion, theft of state property, cheating on government contracts and stealing "economic information," which "fattened private enterprise by sucking state blood, debauching revolutionary heroes whom the enemy's steel bullets didn't strike down but sugar-coated bullets did."

Father was an honest man and didn't suffer too much from these campaigns, but they had sent a clear message that China was ready for the nationalization of private enterprise. By 1956, with the Korean War over and the economy recovering, the time was right. Mao Ze-dong declared that the government was ready to "clean up inside the house."

The 1956 movement that took away Father's business in return for empty praise and a red silk flower was called *gong-si-he-ying* — public and private joint management. In the name of the "policy of redemption," the state expropriated the property at a price established by a committee of three: a government official, a factory worker (usually a Party member) and the owner. The appraisal was always an undervaluation, with the owner overruled by the other two. When the price was set, the proprietor received only 35 percent, paid in installments over seven years. The payments were a blend of cash and government bonds. Even so, in 1957, a year after the movement wound down, Mao Ze-dong published an article, "Correctly Treat the Contradictions Among the People," in which he criticized the method as a form of exploitation by the capitalists.

Father was kept on as "private representative" in his own factory, a nominal position, but he wasn't able to hold this post for long. A few months later another political movement, "Let a hundred flowers blossom; let a hundred schools of thought contend," was set in motion, a ruse of Mao's to encourage criticism so that he could jail those who spoke out. Innocent people, labeled rightists and "bad elements," were sent to prison or labor camps; many were executed. Father's managerial position was nullified because he insisted on claiming his "exploitation money." He was called a "hard-minded capitalist" who could be changed only through physical labor. Thus, by the time I was five, my father had fallen from a respected and prosperous businessman to a laborer with an uncertain future.

With all the worry and turmoil, no one appeared interested in me. I always seemed to be alone. I didn't want to play with Number 5; I preferred older kids, but they were all at school. Mother cautioned me not to go outside the building to play. "The streets are full of child-traders who will drug you and take you to the countryside, far from home, and sell you to the peasants for a laborer," she warned.

Great-Aunt would regale me with tales of devils who spirited away young children. I was too scared to ask who these mysterious kidnappers were, but the prospect of escaping the sky-well, seeing other neighborhoods and meeting new people still appealed to me, as long as I could come back home each night.

Even though I was too young to understand the momentous changes that worried Mother, Father and Great-Aunt, including the rapid fall in our standard of living, I was old enough to notice the differences. I saw much more of Father, and most of the time he came and went with Great-Aunt, who had begun working at the factory before Mother came to Shanghai. His attire was no longer the same. He had used to wear Western clothing, and every morning I would watch him knot his tie, marveling at all the twists and turns. Now he disappointed me by wearing a dark blue or black jacket buttoned up to the neck. He looked pale, old and troubled.

What I did not know was that nobody with any sense would wear a jacket and tie while pushing a heavy cart loaded with rubber shoe uppers, one of the most menial jobs in a factory of more than two hundred workers. He was being punished and degraded for collecting the money owed to him. It was "frost on snow" asking a person who walked with a cane to push a one-hundred-pound-plus cart between various workshops. It was the deep wound to his pride that would lead Father to make a decision that turned to tragedy.

Unaware of the implications of the changes in my family's fortunes, all I wanted was to go to kindergarten to learn singing, dancing and other things. Active and curious, I wanted to have friends and teachers. I was old enough to go to junior kindergarten, but my parents had not enrolled me. I missed Number 3 when she was not at home but I envied her more. When she described the exciting activities in her kindergarten I often pulled a sad face, looking at Mother to see if she noticed how hurt I was. None of the adults noticed, for they were struggling to cope with the political movements that were occurring one after the other.

Chief among these was the Great Leap Forward, in 1958. Its irrational mass behavior was symbolized for me by the War Against the Sparrows. When the government told us that sparrows devoured our precious grain, which was rationed strictly according to sex, age and a person's type of work, people joined the campaign without hesitation. Soon life-sized straw men with a banana-leaf fan in one hand and a white flag in the other stood everywhere in our neighborhood, in trees and on the roofs of buildings. Only a white flag, the instructions ran, would scare the sparrows. At the same time, real people would beat drums, gongs, aluminum cooking pots and anything else that would produce a lot of noise. I believed then that the constant din killed the birds, but the theory held that the racket would keep the poor birds in flight until they died from exhaustion. At six years of age I was an active sparrow hunter, running and jumping, climbing on walls, shouting and banging pot lids and spoons together, even though I was a little confused because Grandfather Ye had told me that sparrows were beneficial to the crops since they ate the insects that attacked the rice.

"Steel is as important as food to the people," said the new posters plastered on walls all over the lane; thus the nationwide steel-making frenzy, even more absurd and unrealistic than the sparrow war, was whipped up. With everyone's cooperation, Mao declared, China would surpass Britain in steel production within fifteen years. Government offices, factories, cooperatives, even schools were given a quota, with the result that inept and completely ineffective furnaces, large and small, stood everywhere

— in schoolyards, playgrounds, rally squares as well as farmland. They were built of house-grade brick and fueled by firewood and the soft powdery coal used for cooking. Our neighborhood committee built two furnaces on the playground of the elementary school attended by my three older siblings. The steel-making went on twenty-four hours a day, seven days a week.

Mother no longer stayed home to take care of Number 5 and me: she was ordered by the neighborhood committee first to collect bricks to construct furnaces, then to find fuel to burn, and later to scour the neighborhood for metal to make the steel. Door to door she went, asking for broken iron woks, candle holders, incense burners and cooking implements. If she didn't meet her quota, she would make it up by smashing one of our good woks with a brick. She told no one, afraid of being criticized for not making the quota, but equally terrified of being accused of waste or, worse, of being rich enough to be able to ruin good household utensils. Even the door-knockers on our front gate went into the fires.

In those days you never knew what would happen next. It was easier to predict the weather. One day Mother was collecting scrap iron; the next making coal balls, a scarf fully covering her permed hair, cloth strips tightly wrapped around her cuffs and pant legs to prevent the coal dust from seeping in; the day after that she might be helping out in the neighborhood canteen, dressed entirely in white, wearing a white hat.

This public canteen, set up in a warehouse, was another of the Great Leap's innovations. It came along with the propaganda that three meals in the canteen was the first step toward communism. "Why do people bother to shop, wash and cook? Let the public canteen serve your needs!" one poster advertised. My family life was totally disrupted. For the first few days I found it exciting and enjoyed the canteen food enormously. With me in charge of Number 5, not only was there no one nearby to rush me through my meal, but I could look around, talk to others and listen in on their conversations. Yet after a week had passed, the routine no longer interested me. I was not allowed to leave the canteen during the day, nor was I permitted in the canteen's working area. There were other children around, but all younger. I was frustrated, thinking continually of where I wanted to be: at school.

The war against the sparrows, the steel-making, and the canteen communism were short-lived. In Father's words they all "started like a tiger's head and ended as a snake's tail." The sleepless nights, the door-to-door search for scrap iron and the numerous accidents produced only heaps of useless iron ingots of poor quality. Residents were asked to cook their own meals again only to find that their utensils were gone. Broken gongs and drums, limbless scarecrows, hoarse voices and food stores filled with roasted birds, their little heads still on, were the legacy of the sparrow war.

3

ONE JULY EVENING IN 1958 I heard Mother telling Father that she was thinking of registering me for senior kindergarten because I had become "wild" in the recent campaigns. After weeks of climbing up onto rooftops and beating the drums and gongs, she said, there was no way I would settle down again and play alone in the sky-well. I knew that registration day was coming because I had heard Mother practicing with Number 3 for entry to elementary school. The quality of answers to such questions as "What is your name? Where do you live? What are your parents' names? What is your favorite song?" would determine where a child would spend his or her six years of school. Apart from connections (an open secret), these so-called academic results were the deciding factor.

Number 3, Shen-xing, was eight years old, and a publicly acknowledged beauty in Purple Sunshine Lane because of her large bright eyes and long dark brows. Though attractive, her eyes were weak. A year before, Mother had reluctantly acceded to Father's push to get glasses for her and from then on Number 3 was known as Little Four Eyes. Placid and slow-moving, with a kind-hearted disposition, my elder sister seemed to worry about nothing.

"Number 3 could fall asleep on top of a grave if she felt like it," Great-Aunt would say unkindly.

Mother was quite serious about this preparation and asked me to pay attention while Number 3 was rehearsing. There was a great shortage of schools and kindergartens, a situation that had led to a two-tiered system. A good performer could be enrolled in a *gong ban* ("Public") elementary school or kindergarten; a bad result meant a *min ban* ("People") school, run by the neighborhood committee and staffed by unqualified teachers. Father was the only one not surprised. He said that if the government could ask people who had never seen a furnace to make steel on the bare ground with their bare hands, why wouldn't it let the same people run schools?

That month I was registered, not in a *gong ban* kindergarten but as a grade one student in a *min ban* school. Mother said I could learn more in school than at kindergarten, and in this way I would be well prepared to enter a *gong ban* school in a year, when I reached school age. Great-Aunt was the only one who was unhappy about the whole arrangement, even though it was a temporary measure. Although she had never attended school and couldn't understand the two-school system, she said that a class held above a grain store and taught by the wife of the owner was anything but a school, and she repeated that I was an unlucky girl, born in the dragon year.

So in September I became a grade one student in the Jian Ban Yi Lian Elementary School run by the subdistrict committee. Mother never fulfilled her plan. Disaster struck and I remained in the *min ban* school for six years until my graduation.

Nicknamed Old Gun by colleagues at the factory for his heavy consumption of Great Front Gate cigarettes, Father was a man who enjoyed evenings at home. He would rise from the supper table and wash his hands and face in a basin of warm water set out for him by Mother, then retire to the bedroom to read in his old bamboo chair, sipping tea from a cup Mother replenished when necessary. Eschewing novels and other "light" literature, he preferred books on ethics and philosophy, written in the classic style. He was a skilled calligrapher who delighted in brushing Buddhist sutras and scriptures into a rice-paper copy-book, each elegant character no larger than a housefly.

Like many parents at that time, Father thought learning was mainly a male endeavor, and although he ensured that Number 3 and I completed our homework, he took special pains with my brothers, making them practice their own calligraphy every night. Once, Number 1 cheated by tracing characters from his book of models rather than writing them himself. Praised several nights running for his excellent writing, Number 1 was eventually found out when Father discovered Number 1's tell-tale marks in the calligraphy book. Father's disapproval was silent and effective; my brother never tried to fool him again.

I always felt ignored by my father and feared his rare wrath as much as I craved his attention. He seemed to favor my two brothers and ignore me. We three girls were clearly the responsibility of Mother and Great-Aunt. Father seldom spoke to us individually — when he instructed us it was "you girls," whereas my brothers were addressed as Ah Du and Ah Ni — but when he did speak to me alone I knew I was in trouble for some transgression, usually for fighting with my older sister. He spoke in a quiet, firm voice that allowed no contradiction.

Each morning, before getting us kids ready for school, Mother laid out Father's clothes, his shaving brush and razor, and I watched with fascination as he applied creamy soap to his face, stropped his razor and shaved. Before leaving for the factory with Great-Aunt, he carefully polished his spectacles.

Sometimes he wrote a large character on a piece of scrap paper and left it on the table for Mother — it was his way of supporting her struggle to learn to read. A Confucian saying held that an uneducated woman was especially virtuous, and both Mother and Great-Aunt had been brought up knowing only enough words to distinguish one denomination of paper money from another. Continually frustrated by an accumulation of small indignities, like having to ask Father or one of my brothers (she never asked me or Number 3) to help her tell one kind of ration coupon from another, Mother took advantage of the *Sao Mang* — "sweeping away illiteracy" — movement begun in the autumn of 1958, during the Great Leap Forward.

"Your mother has always been vain about her looks," Great-Aunt commented one night when we were in bed. "Now she wants to be an educated city lady."

For my part, I admired my mother's determination, harried as she was by the demands of both community and household — although I didn't appreciate her high-pitched scolding when I was underfoot or arguing with Number 3. While we children toiled at our endless homework assignments, Mother, her domestic tasks completed, bent over her book and chanted words to set them firmly in her memory. She glued Father's scraps of paper to the objects named by the word he had written until our household looked as if a paper blizzard had struck and left a bit of white on virtually every object. She was often impatient with her three noisy daughters, but to her learning she applied a fierce and admirable diligence.

One late afternoon in April 1959, a middle-aged woman from the public phone booth hammered her fist on our back door. "Telephone message for Ye family!" she called. "It's from Tong Ji Hospital. They want you to be there as soon as possible!"

Holding the message-slip in her shaking hand, Mother dashed to the kitchen and asked Great-Aunt what it could mean. Great-Aunt looked at the floor for a second before she answered, "You'd better hurry, Sister-in-Law. It must be about Brother."

"You still don't think I have the right to know what's going on in this house!" Mother said angrily. "He is my husband!"

"Listen, Sister-in-Law. Don't be mad at me. I'm only guessing, because I didn't see Brother at the factory today."

Mother grabbed her purse and flew out of the house in tears, leaving us children bewildered and frightened.

"It's a bad omen that your father kept it a secret," Great-Aunt mumbled.

Next morning as Mother got us ready for school and Great-Aunt prepared breakfast, our apartment was hushed. My two brothers quietly gathered their books; Number 3 finished up a bit of homework; Number 5, as uneasy as I, watched in wide-eyed silence. Although I had never seen Father in the kitchen and washing area, I searched there for him so that I could ask him what had happened. He wasn't there. Nor was he in the bedroom where he usually shaved before a three-sided mirror at a marble-topped dressing table. Today, his shaving things were not laid out for him.

"Where's Father?" I asked.

"In the hospital," Mother answered, her voice quavering. "He won't be home for a few weeks."

"What's wrong with him?" I demanded, tears in my eyes. "Why can't he come home?"

Great-Aunt pulled me aside and told me that Father had had surgery to cure his limp. Surgery? Why? Father was a sound and healthy man. True, his right leg was slimmer than his left and he limped, but he went to work every day just like other fathers. I had always liked the way he walked with the shining red stick in his hand. But what I didn't know was that the back-breaking work he was required to do and the pressure to meet the quotas had further damaged his leg.

Without telling anyone — not even Mother — Father had gone to the hospital and found out that a small operation could correct his limp. Neither Mother nor Great-Aunt was able to tell us more.

Three weeks later, when I turned into our lane on the way home from school, I saw an ambulance parked outside our building. Father had been brought home. I rushed up the stairs to his bedroom, pushed open the door and crept inside. Soft, shuttered light washed the room. On the mahogany bed Father lay on his chest, facing the wall. When he heard me come in he turned and smiled. His face was drawn and ashen.

"Are you in pain, Father?"

"No, Ah Si." He smiled. He pointed to his back, telling me to have a look, and flipped aside the quilt to reveal layers of bandages.

Why did he have dressings on his *back*?

During the weeks he had lain in hospital, no one had hinted at what the doctors must have known: that the operation had been botched, that Father was paralyzed from the waist down and would never walk again. All Mother knew was what she could see: Father's entire torso wrapped in bandages and a wide scar from the base of his neck to his pelvis.

Since I was at school for only half a day, I was able to help Mother care for Father by keeping an eye on him while she was cooking, cleaning or out at the market. Father looked over my homework, making me recopy it if I had made a mistake. In return, all I had to do was pass him his tea cup or puff up the pillows under his head. There was only one thing I couldn't do right — and I wished I didn't have to do at all — help him with his bed pan. Although Mother tried to keep her shopping trips short and made sure Father didn't drink too much tea before she went out, once in a while he needed assistance, and I always made a mess of it. The result was "mapping the sheet," as Father put it. His levity did not hide how badly he felt.

One day I overheard Mother talking to Mrs. Yan in the downstairs kitchen. "When I gave away the last of Number 5's diapers, I never thought I would use the drying rack over the coal stove again," she said. "My poor Rong-ting. What has he done to deserve this?"

I was looking forward to July, when school registration opened, so that I could go to a "normal" school. But July came and no one took me to line up and recite my memorized answers to the school officials. No one even mentioned it. When the new school year started, Father carefully wrapped my next textbooks with brown paper and I returned to the *min ban* school above Boss Tian's grain store.

Once in a while I came home with a red palm, thanks to Teacher Tian and her wooden ruler, for failing to answer questions correctly, for whispering to my seatmate during a lesson or for speaking to my friends in Shanghai dialect rather than the required *pu-tong-hua* — common language.

In the meantime, Mother had her own worries. Leaving me to care for Father in the afternoons, after dressing and applying lipstick with her usual care, she made innumerable pilgrimages to the hospital, hoping at first for a miracle, then, after she had been told again and again that no miracle would happen, trying to claim a malpractice settlement because Father could not work again. One of her friends had told her that the hospital was required to provide continuous medical care and support because of the malpractice, but at the hospital she spent many hours waiting in vain for a sympathetic hearing. Eventually she was refused admittance altogether. To make matters worse, Father's already reduced salary was cut by half — a further punishment for his refusal to give up his payments for the expropriation of his factory. Our family's economic status dropped dramatically.

At the same time the government put stricter rationing into effect. The official explanation was that there had been heavy floods in the southern provinces, plagues of locusts and drought in the northern parts. The Soviet Union, our "elder brother" and beloved friend, had turned against us and was forcing us to pay back our debts all at once, in every possible way, from rice and milk to new farm machinery and used factory equipment. It was rumored that apples sent across the border were checked one by one by the Russians for desired color and shape. The unwanted fruit was not sent back to China, where people were hungry, but dumped and left to rot in heaps. Eggs that failed the size test were smashed and discarded; in Shanghai's black market one egg cost more than a worker's daily salary. We did not realize then that food shortages were the direct result of peasants neglecting their crops because of the frantic drive to make steel.

In our family, meals were meager and unsatisfying. Soon bean dregs — the residue from making soybean milk — turned up on our dinner table. Father said we were now fighting the animals for food, since the awful stuff was usually fed to pigs. Mother mixed it with a bit of flour and baked it in the wok. It helped ease our hunger, but caused constant constipation.

The stricter Mother was in measuring our rice bowl, the hungrier we were. We all felt we had a hole in our stomachs. Even today I still have a special feeling about the twenty-fifth of each month. That was when the grain coupons for the next month became eligible. At home our rice jar and flour pot would be empty, and Great-Aunt would have a pot of hot water ready on the stove, waiting for Mother to return from the grain store. It was the only night she didn't carefully measure the flour, and we went to bed stuffed with green vegetable soup and dumplings.

Since Mother had worn out her welcome at the hospital, the only recourse for her and Father would be to pursue the malpractice through the legal system, but they realized that not only could their case not be won, it would not even get started, since Father would be seen as a hard-headed capitalist trying to frame the socialist hospital. Besides, there was a further deterrent. Father's friend Dr. Feng, a doctor of internal medicine in that hospital, was the person who had advised Father to try the operation and had taken Father to see the surgeon. In doing so, Mother was told by hospital officials, Dr. Feng had taken responsibility for the operation, even though he had not performed it. Father would therefore be forced to sue his own friend.

Dr. Feng was so devastated and guilt-ridden by the tragedy that he left the hospital a year later and returned to practice in his hometown, Hangzhou. To leave Shanghai was a great sacrifice and loss of face for him. Years later, after Father's funeral, he came to see Mother and offered to adopt two of us children. Mother refused his offer.

In September 1959, when I passed into grade two, the whole country was frantically preparing for the tenth anniversary of the People's Republic. There was to be a huge celebration, with rallies and parades. Far more relevant to my family were the extra ration coupons for pork, eggs and bean curd.

The day after the grandiose National Day fireworks display, Teacher Tian assigned a composition. At home that night I worked hard to describe our wonderful family dinner, the fireworks and the thick crowds on Nanjing Road. I took my finished piece to Father, who kept a book in which he recorded the grades he gave us for our work: fail, average, improved. There was no such word as good. For the first time he crossed out some of my writing and wrote his own sentence. Where I had used many words to convey the size and extent of the crowds, Father wrote, "The crowd surged like a wave moving through water."

I did not quite understand his metaphor, but when I got my exercise book back a few days later, Father's phrase was circled in red, which meant praise. I got a perfect five for my composition and I never forgot the simile.

One night near the end of November, Mother told me that Boss Tian had suffered a severe heart attack and consequently our classroom would have to move. The new location would be the old Buddhist temple at the entrance to our laneway, which had been there for years but which hardly anyone had been inside because it was always locked. It was said the temple had been built by two sons for their mother and abandoned when the family fled to Taiwan in 1949.

It had survived all the political movements of the 1950s, probably because it looked no different from the surrounding buildings; besides, there was a public urinal near the back door.

The next day on my way to school with Great-Aunt I saw a big truck parked outside the temple. She dragged me past the open door, ignoring my pleas to look inside. Great-Aunt was a Buddhist and didn't approve of meddling with a temple, especially filling it with noisy children. A week later, on a cool sunny day, I started classes in our temple school with a new teacher, named Li, who dressed stylishly and like Mother wore her hair permed.

I was happy to find that my new seatmate was Turnip Head, a "grain store school" veteran like me. His nickname sounds derogatory, but in Shanghai dialect *Lao Bo Tou* was an affectionate name, like Tiny Peas, Little Rabbit or Tiger Head. Turnip Head always got good marks in math and Chinese: it was believed that his intelligence came from his slightly bulb-shaped head, particularly his large forehead, which indicated he had a big brain.

When the temple was converted to school use, it seemed no one had thought about washroom facilities. On the first day, during recess, most of the boys rushed out the back door to try the public urinal. We girls were not so lucky. Pent up for a couple of hours, a few were in real trouble. Teacher Li anxiously inquired if any of us lived nearby and four or five hands went up. Quickly she organized us into groups. The next minute I was speeding home, closely followed by five girls desperate to have a pee. When we tumbled into our apartment, yelling and running around like a swarm of angry bees, Mother was speechless. Only when she saw one girl plop herself down on the chamber pot beside my father's bed did she understand. She grabbed the pot from under my brothers' bed, then rushed into Great-Aunt's room for a third. When she returned, the first round had almost ended and Father was laughing so hard he was in tears.

That night I made a list of the girls I wanted to bring home with me the next day. The next morning as we gathered at the school door, Teacher Li arrived carrying an old wooden chamber pot, its lid tightly in place. She announced that it would be placed in the back room for the girls to use. I was especially crestfallen. Mother will be too, I thought. She probably has all the chamber pots ready for our visit.

One afternoon the following spring, my friend Jian-feng and I were playing in the temple school's dirt courtyard and waiting for another friend, Ying-ying, who was on classroom clean-up duty.

"Look," Jian-feng exclaimed, pointing above the front door, where one of two tall cupboard doors had sprung ajar. "I never noticed that cupboard before."

"I wonder what's inside," I said.

Jian-feng ran into the classroom and returned with Teacher Li's pointing stick, made from a broken ruler. She stood on tiptoe, stretched, and slapped with the pointer. The door creaked open.

In the gloom of the cupboard I saw half a human face.

Jian-feng and I screamed. The face was larger than life and it glared down at us out of one intense eye.

Our cries brought Ying-ying rushing. While she and I cowered and backed away from the horrible face, Jian-feng mustered her courage and pried the second door open. There above us, his huge head shaved to the skin, his ears so enormous that the fleshy lobes rested on his shoulders, his bare tummy fat and round, was a Buddha. He was smiling, showing his dimples, and, now that my fright was gone, he looked pleasant.

Even though we vowed not to tell anyone, I knew I could not keep such a wondrous discovery secret. Bursting with news of my adventure, I told Mother as soon as I got home. Ying-ying must have done likewise, for her mother, "Mrs. Boss Wang," came to our apartment immediately.

"Ying-ying told me there was more than one statue, is that right?"

"Maybe," I answered, miffed that my friend had stolen my thunder.

Mother and Mrs. Boss Wang moved aside, whispering anxiously. After Ying-ying's mother left, Mother told me not to mention a word to anyone.

"That's not fair," I was about to protest, but no word came out of my mouth when I saw the worried look on Mother's face. Finally I had something special, even exotic, to make my brothers and sisters pay attention to me, and I was not allowed to tell it. How frustrating!

"Not even Father?" I tested.

"No. I'll tell him later."

All through supper I felt Mother's eye upon me. But I also realized that I would not be able to sleep if I didn't share my secret.

That night, after I had gone to bed with Great-Aunt (I shared her bed in the back room that was hers), I whispered my story. She listened without interruption, then began to mumble to herself. After a moment, she turned to me.

"A Buddha statue should never be in darkness but always enshrined in light. That's why temples are lit with candles and oil lamps, day and night, and the main figure, the Laughing Buddha, is usually kept separated in a huge glass box with its own candles. It is a sin to place them in such a dark and cold place as that cupboard. It's total madness."

I didn't understand her concern and soon fell asleep.

The next morning, Great-Aunt repeated my mother's warning as she helped me put on my shell-shaped cotton-padded shoes. "Keep your mouth shut. Believe me, no one will take you as a mute," she said. Using the excuse that she had to go to the grain store, Mother took me to school instead of Great-Aunt. We joined the crowd of kids waiting outside and Mother squeezed my hand, as if to hold my secret inside me, when Teacher Li arrived.

Once inside, Jian-feng began to tell everyone near her about the statue. Ying-ying and I, furious with our friend for one-upping us, joined in. By the time we had finished, the other kids thought there was a whole army of Buddhas with blue eyes and purple noses sitting in the cupboard. Some were curious and excited, others were frightened and wanted to go home.

Unable to make herself heard above the hubbub, Teacher Li herded us out, locked the door and went off to report to the neighborhood committee.

The next morning, reports ran up and down our lane that two *ping ban che* — flatbed tricycles — had been seen parked outside the temple school during the night. And when we got to school, the first thing Teacher Li did was open the cupboard and show us that it was empty. The Buddha with the huge ears, round belly and friendly face was gone.

4

FATHER'S CONDITION HAD ITS ups and downs. On the good days I would hear Mother singing and humming her favorite tunes from *Shaoxing* opera. But it seemed to me that good things were only teases, for they brought with them false hopes. Father's feet began to swell up, like two shiny shapeless balloons. He felt nothing, of course, but the swelling was life-threatening if not brought under control. Mother went around searching for cures, official or folk medicine, and trying every one. One week Father's feet were covered with white powder and wrapped in bandages; another they were soaked in hot herbal water until they turned red. Mother was constantly heating water and mixing herbs, and our apartment smelled like a medicine store.

Next, as the swelling crept above Father's ankles, came acupuncture and moxibustion. Each day a doctor from the neighborhood clinic twisted half a dozen needles into the doughy flesh of each foot, topping every needle with a mushroom-shaped ball of moxa. The material was then lit and began to smoke. The doctor would leave us to monitor the burning and to make sure the hot ash didn't fall on Father's numb skin. We would then pull out the needles for use the next day.

The acupuncture too was ineffective. By spring 1961, having used up his store of cures, the doctor said it was no use for him to come any more. Even the warm spring air couldn't entice Father out of his bed. He was so weak that moving to and from bed, even with our help, exhausted him. Mother was desperate but determined. She asked Mrs. Yan, our warm-hearted neighbor, for advice and was given the name of a folk doctor. The next day when I came home from school I saw Father sitting on his chair, pale as a ghost. His feet rested on tiny stools a few inches above the floor. They looked like bloody hornets' nests, pulpy and mottled with blood.

I covered my mouth with my hand, horrified. "Father, what has that doctor done to you?"

At that moment Mother bustled into the room with a steaming bowl of noodles. She explained that the doctor had said the cause of the swelling was bad blood. He had let it out by beating Father's feet with a little ivory hammer embedded with tiny nails.

I didn't understand. Did this mean that we all had bad blood and that someday I would have to have mine drained away? How could the doctor tell which blood was good and which was not? What I didn't know was that the term "bad blood" would come to haunt my siblings and me when the Red Guards told us that because we had been born into a capitalist family all we had was bad blood, and none of us could do anything about it.

After almost three years without touching his inkstone and brushes, one morning in late October, propped up against rolled bedding and pillows, with a small serving table across his legs, Father picked them up again. In his weakness it cost him a tremendous effort with ruler and pencil to mark more than five hundred squares on a piece of drawing paper before he could write with the brush. He wanted to record the forty-eight maxims on benevolence, righteousness, rites, loyalty, forbearance, virtue, filial piety and brotherly duty of Master Zhu Bo-lu, a Confucian scholar in the Qing dynasty. I couldn't understand what Father was up to, since he had given all of us children a hand-written copy when we started school.

Father practiced his calligraphy every day, getting ready to make the final copy, for one error would destroy the aesthetic appeal of the poster. He would write a few words, then rest for a while, rubbing his hands or warming them with a hot-water bottle, even though it was not cold in the apartment. "If you work hard enough," he would say, "even an iron rod can be ground down to a sewing needle."

By Mother's standard, good days meant no ink spilled on the sheet, seeping into the quilts.

On December 12, 1961, Father finished the poster. When he showed it to me, he seemed more relieved than satisfied. Mother couldn't afford a frame, so she covered it with a large piece of cellophane and pinned it on the wall. Father never touched his brush again.

Early one morning after the new year, I awoke alone in bed. I heard Mother crying and felt suddenly afraid. Since Father's operation I had often seen her weeping — on the terrace, in the kitchen and the washing area — but never inside the apartment. Her grief broke my heart and I would secretly blame Father for her sadness.

Mother's cries drew me to Father's bedside. "What sin did I commit to deserve this punishment?" I heard her say. Their bedroom was filled with the sharp odor of urine. Great-Aunt was holding my mother in her arms, the first time I had seen them so close together, and she too had tears in her eyes. My brothers stood, staring at the floor; Number 3 wept silently.

Until then, Father had had some control over his bowels and bladder. When he needed help, he would call Mother. But this morning a great change for the worse had taken place. When I too burst into tears, Father snapped, with eyes closed, "I am not dead yet, so stop crying." His humiliation had been worsened a thousandfold by Mother's outburst.

A thought passed through my mind, like the blink of an eye: if Father was dead, all this misery would end. Mother, her eyes red from crying, her hands raw from washing fouled sheets in cold water, would be free. Our life could return to normal. This unkind thought was followed by a flood of guilt so powerful that it haunted me for the rest of my life, and I feel it to this day.

After that morning I seldom saw Father sit up again. He seemed to sink inside himself. He ate and drank little. Gone were the talking and laughing in our cheerless apartment, the arguments and fighting among the five of us over the space at the table to do homework.

That whole winter I witnessed Mother working like a slave. She had to get up many times during the night to refill the hot-water bottles Father needed to fight off the chill only he felt. By the time we children rose in the morning she had already washed Father's stained bedding: because the building's washing area was small and public, she wanted to finish it before our neighbors could see what she was doing.

That was the longest winter of my life and the coldest in my heart.

With the coming of spring, Mother grew increasingly nervous and apprehensive. *Qing Ming*, the day of the dead, when ghosts would appear to lead the living into the afterlife, was approaching. Mother's superstition and fear were infectious, and I began to wish the day would arrive and pass quickly. But as April 5 came nearer, Father seemed to improve somewhat; he ate more and he began to talk to us again. The day of the dead passed without incident and our relief brought some cheer to our normally somber home.

One afternoon, a week later, we children were doing our homework around the table. My two brothers' pencils flew as they raced through their arithmetic problems. Number 3 chattered away to no one in particular in a running commentary that didn't appear to affect her Chinese lesson. Head bent over my work, I labored at another in what seemed like an endless list of composition topics while Number 5 looked on. Great-Aunt had not yet returned from the factory.

"Ah Du! Ah Ni!" Mother called sharply from the bedroom. "Come quickly!"

Number 1 and Number 2 threw down their pencils and rushed from the room with the three of us on their heels. Mother stood beside the mahogany bed, her eyes wide and pleading, her hands helplessly twisting a rag. Shrunken and pale, Father lay on his side, his chest rising and falling as if each breath was a burden. A thrill of fear ran through me as I saw Father's eyes flicker over us, as if memorizing our features. His chest rose and fell, and did not rise again. He closed his eyes and left us.

He was only forty-one years old.

When I put on my baggy and hastily sewn white mourning clothes, I said goodbye to my childhood. A slender and undersized girl of nine, I blamed Father's death on my sinful thought that if he were dead Mother would no longer be miserable. I had made him die. Whom could I tell? From whom could I beg forgiveness? I was convinced that I was an evil child. I left school each day as soon as I could, asking to be excused from study groups and other activities, to be with Mother. And when Mother asked me, a few days after the funeral, if I would go to the funeral home to see whether Father's coffin had been shipped by canal barge to Qingyang, where Grandfather had bought a piece of land as the family burial plot, I swallowed my terror and complied.

Mother's request caught me by surprise. It seemed a job my two brothers should do, since they were older and braver and the funeral home was on their way to school.

Nevertheless, I contained my fear and rushed out the door, drying my eyes on my sleeves. I ran all the way to the funeral home and explained to the kind old doorman why I was there. He showed me the way to the shed where the coffins were stored.

"You'll have to check yourself," he told me. "We don't keep a record of the comings and goings of the coffins. I would stay with you, but my replacement is not here yet and I can't leave my post."

It was about four o'clock and the last place I wanted to be when darkness fell was anywhere near this gloomy outbuilding populated by the dead, so I quietly crept into the storage shed, remembering all the ghost stories Great-Aunt loved to tell me.

Stacked in three rows, two high, the caskets had the names of the occupants on the ends in gold characters. I had no idea there were so many dead people waiting to be shipped out of Shanghai. I tiptoed past the stacks, terrified and grief-stricken, holding my breath and not daring to make a noise, looking for Father's name. I found him in the last row, with someone else on top of him. A heavy sigh came out of my throat as I made the quickest possible exit. I dashed out the gate and headed for home. When I reached our lane I ran into Great-Aunt. Out of breath, I told her what I had been doing.

"Don't mention to anyone that your father's casket is under a stranger," she cautioned me, drying my tears with her handkerchief. I promised Mother that night that I would go to the funeral home every day after school. With each visit to the dark, silent shed, familiarity diminished my terror. About ten days later I found Father's upstairs neighbor had left and I was suddenly seized with panic. What if I came tomorrow and saw Father's coffin was gone? The daily pilgrimage had made me feel, in a way, that I was visiting Father, pretending he was too sick to talk to me. I stayed longer than necessary and the other coffins somehow became invisible. At least he was still with me, close to home. The shed was quiet and peaceful, and sometimes helped me to forget what was going on at home — the whispering, the tears, the absence of smiles and laughter. Even out in the lane neighbors frequently stopped me, looked me over, sighed and asked questions, most of which — about what lay ahead of us — I couldn't answer.

Two days later there was an empty space where Father's coffin had lain. On my way home I found myself no longer conscious of, or embarrassed by, the staring of passersby at my white mourning outfit. Father had left me forever.

5

OTHER'S RELIANCE ON ME did not end with the daily trips to the funeral home. Time after time she took me with her to Father's factory, where she begged the officials to redeem some of the bonds Father had been paid when the factory was expropriated. The family had no income now, she argued. Her pleas and my tears had no effect. The bonds could not be redeemed for many years, she was reminded; we don't make the rules.

Mother had no job, thus no *dan wei* — work unit — so she swalloed what little pride circumstances had allowed her to keep and went to the neighborhood committee, asking for any kind of job that would bring in some money. Thanks to her efforts during the "Sweeping away illiteracy" movement, she landed a job collecting unpaid rent.

It sounded easy enough. She would be busy for the last two weeks of each month, not so busy at other times. But the job quickly began to wear her down, both emotionally and physically. She was not hard-hearted enough and soon became burdened with other people's problems. She felt guilty knocking on a door to demand unpaid rent only to find the family had no food for dinner. Sometimes, getting no answer when she knocked, she would push open the door and find a resident too sick to talk to her. She was shocked by the living conditions of some people and the poverty of most.

At the end of the day, after going through back alleys, climbing unlit staircases and sometimes enduring the loud abuse of angry residents, Mother would find that she had not collected much rent. No wonder, she concluded, she got this job so easily: no one else wanted it. Worse, the job did not pay enough. The poverty level at that time was considered nine yuan per month for each person. Mother, with six mouths to feed, received eighteen.

Great-Aunt, with a full-time job at the factory, helped Mother in every way except financially. Since Father had given her a job, she had fiercely defended her independence, for she no longer considered herself a servant of the Ye family. She paid her share of the rent and water and electricity bills; when she shopped, she took two purses, one for her purchases and one for our family's. She regularly sent money back to relatives in Chen Family Village.

Desperate for income, Mother sought to collect on some debts owed to Father when he was alive. Father had kept a book in which he carefully recorded his loans, and Mother was amazed to discover how many people he had helped — relatives, friends, friends of relatives and relatives of friends. She would never get the money from close relatives (if they hadn't paid voluntarily, it would be a loss of face for both parties to ask), but she wanted to try to collect from distant relatives and friends. After all, it was she who was now in need. Full of optimism, she took the train to Wuxi to see a distant relative who had borrowed money to start up a flour-processing factory. The family pushed her into the street and slammed the door in her face. The next day they disappeared.

Mother began to sell things for cash to buy food — her few remaining jewels, antique paintings, valuable clothes and fur coats, even furniture. But this measure brought only temporary respite. Mother knew there was something she had to do — and that it would shatter the dreams she and Father had held for many years.

When his factory was taken away, Father realized that his sons could not follow the traditional road and join him in the family business, so he had planned that both his sons would go to university. In this way they would become respected and important.

Mother now faced the fact that one of her sons would have to quit school and find a job.

My eldest brother, Zheng-xing, was seventeen. He was a fine-featured young man, quiet, unassuming and, unlike me, passive in the face of conflict. When concentrating, he would cock his head and look away into the distance. He was a brilliant student who had skipped a year in elementary school, won a spot in a key middle school and was now only a year away from being qualified to sit for university entrance exams. As *zhang-zi* — eldest son in a traditional family — he was the sun and the moon to Mother.

Number 2, Zhong-xing, was fifteen. He too was a shining student, his teacher's pride and joy: she said his marks were so high he would be exempted from writing the exams to enter senior high. Number 2 was stubborn and pig-headed at home but shy and retiring outside. His large eyes, set beneath thick brows in an oval face, gave him enviable good looks.

My brothers were inseparable: they walked to and from school together, did their homework as a pair, conducted scientific experiments as a team. They were polite and humble, constantly held up as model young men in our lane. "Look at Ye family brothers," people would say to their sons. "Why can't you act like them?" I looked up to them academically but thought them useless when it came to protecting me from neighborhood bullies. They avoided confrontation at any cost. But they always stuck together — until Mother's desperation drove her to ask one of them to make the sacrifice. Unable to bring herself to choose, she asked them to decide.

In the meantime Mother had to find out whether the factory her husband once owned would take a new worker. One morning in May 1963, a year after Father's death, she once again asked me to accompany her to the factory. She asked the director to take one of her sons on as an apprentice to help share her financial burden; if there was any way she could have avoided coming to him for help, she said, she wouldn't be sitting there begging him. We were sent away with uncertainty.

For weeks the atmosphere at home was so tense I could almost feel it: tense because my brothers were forced to make a decision neither of them wanted; tense because the factory director might turn down Mother's pleas. Finally the answer came: the Rubber

Industrial Department would take Number 1 on — not in Father's factory, but in the one that specialized in melting and refining raw rubber.

Mother was relieved but worried. She had wanted her son to work in Father's factory because it was nearby; more important, most of the workers knew our family and she hoped that their loyalty to Father would take care of her son. An added complication was that, although the director had specified a position for my eldest brother, Number 1 and Number 2 had decided differently. None of us knew how they had come to the conclusion that Number 2 was to be the one to quit school. When Number 2 told his teacher, she hid him in her home overnight, hoping that Mother would change her mind.

A week later, Mother and Number 2 appeared in the gate of Yi Shen Rubber Factory on Anyuan Road near the Jade Buddha Temple, thirty minutes' walk from home, and reported to its director. Number 2 filled in the required papers silently, putting down Number 1's birthdate. Since no one there knew my brothers, Number 2 became Number 1, and by the time the director of Father's factory found out, Number 2 was sixteen and already a skillful worker. "The rice was cooked."

But Number 2 was heart-broken and bitter, for his dreams of university were broken. We hardly saw him any more: he worked on revolving shifts week by week and when he was off work he did not eat with the family. He spent his free time at the district workers' library reading and studying. A wedge had been driven between him and his beloved older brother, and he felt the pain for many years.

While Number 2 was learning his trade, blackening his clothing and breathing in so much black powder that his handkerchiefs were stained, turning over to Mother his wages and the extra ration coupons that came with his job, I, Number 3, and especially Number 1 were locked in a frenzy of exam preparation. But my studies did not prevent Mother from attempting what I thought was a crazy scheme.

Two months before my middle-school entrance exams, Mother took me to audition for the People's Liberation Army song and dance troupe. If I was accepted I would be taken care of by the government. But I would have to leave home. When she heard of Mother's plan and saw my beautiful new light blue dress spotted with red flowers, Great-Aunt took me to her room.

"I did all a mother could possibly do for you except breast-feed you and I still don't have a say," she exclaimed, pointing at my forehead and venting her anger at me rather than Mother. "If she wants to get rid of you, I am willing to adopt you and she knows that. I have offered before."

Great-Aunt's fears proved to be premature, for Mother's plan didn't work. At the Army Club, she was yelled at by the soldiers: "She is too young, not even twelve yet. You're wasting our time."

"Ah Si," Mother said when we had escaped the building, "what kind of mother am I to even think about letting an eleven-year-old girl be on her own? What would your father think of me?" On the way home she bought me the biggest ice cream I had ever had.

The cramming continued. Great-Aunt moved out of her room, turning it over to Number 1, who suffered silently the enormous pressure of his family's hopes. I studied hard, too, because I wanted to go to university, a goal not given much credit by Mother and Great-Aunt, both of whom thought girls did not need higher education.

Meanwhile, Mother was still wearing herself out trying to make ends meet. Her health visibly deteriorated. Every night she went out on her rent-collecting rounds so that she could catch people at home. When she returned she seldom ate the dinner we kept warm for her. I often wondered if she was saving the food for us, but several times I overheard her say to Great-Aunt that she didn't care if she ever opened her eyes the next morning. In some ways things were getting better — the country's food shortage was waning, Number 2 was working and contributing greatly to the household — but obviously it was not so for Mother.

One sweltering mid-July morning, Number 3 and I woke to find sweet cakes and cookies on the dinner table instead of rice gruel. Mother had provided a treat for our exam day. Four hours later, my sister and I returned from the exam center. I knew I had done well in math but was worried about my essay: instead of writing a lot of nonsense and propaganda I had lost my head and described life as it really was. Failing to offer the official view would bring a low mark.

A week later it was Number 1's turn. We saw him off at the end of the lane, accompanied by Number 2, who had taken the day off to accompany his brother to the center. As they walked away on that hot, humid morning, I wondered what was going through Number 2's mind.

Our results arrived in mid-August. "I'm going to the new school!" my sister crowed, delighted that she would be near home — about five minutes away but "fifteen minutes of Number 3's walk," as Great-Aunt put it. My school, Ai Guo — Patriotism — a *gong ban* all-girl school in the former French concession, was forty-five minutes away. I had done well, but not as well as I had hoped.

A few days later, Mother's dream came true. Number 1 had scored extremely high on his exams, winning a place at the coveted Jiao Tong University in Shanghai, one of the key national universities that attracted the best talent from across the country. Within five years he would be an automotive engineer.

For the first time since Father's death had plunged her into a well of grief and struggle, I heard my mother laugh.

6

B Y THE TIME I WAS TWELVE, we had been on welfare for years. Where I had once worn a silk coat covered with a cotton smock, I now had on my brothers' hand-me-downs, and when I passed up or down our lane local busybodies, especially those on the neighborhood committee, would stop me and lift up my coat to check if I was wearing good clothing hidden beneath. When I became nearsighted in grade six, Mother ignored my pleas for glasses because she couldn't afford to buy me a pair. Instead she gave me a pair Number 2 had outgrown. They caused headaches, and I wore them only when necessary, or at night when I found it especially difficult to see.

However, I had become far from the modest and passive Chinese woman praised by the Confucians; in defending myself and my family's name against insult I was combative and argumentative, much to the chagrin of Mother and the delight of Great-Aunt. The degradation of poverty had left deep scars.

But I was going to a new school. I promised myself that I would never again feel the humiliation I had felt when some kids made fun of my mourning clothes. No longer a little girl, I planned to make a new start, study hard, and prepare for my future.

Listening to my new classmates complaining about the shabby look of our school, the size of the classrooms — even the blackboards were "not black enough" — I enjoyed every minute of my new adventure. Everything I saw, touched and shared was ten times better than what I had known. Even the washroom with its private, odorless stalls far surpassed the temple school's chamber pot in the corner. The biggest thrill was that I was going to have English lessons three times a week. I had never heard any language other than Chinese. I skipped home that day, ebullient and filled with hope.

But my joy was diminished on the second day. I had broken the teacher's rules and written Chinese in my English textbook to help me pronounce the letter Q. As she patrolled the aisles, examining our books as we worked, Teacher Zhu spotted my sin.

"Humph!" Her eyes brightened triumphantly. "It seems one of you can't even understand my Chinese, let alone English," she exclaimed, picking up my textbook and marching to the front of the class.

She held up my book so everyone could see the offending presence of Chinese characters. The whole class burst into laughter and ridicule. My face burned with embarrassment. I knew none of my classmates yet, and now it looked as if they would shun me. I managed to hold back my tears. Stupidity was bad enough, I thought; I will not add cowardice by crying. My book stayed on display for the entire day.

When I complained at home that night, Great-Aunt said my teacher was *sha-ji-gei-hou-kan* — killing a chicken to frighten the monkeys, but Mother said that a well-behaved monkey didn't need to be frightened. She seemed to forget that I was mimicking the technique she herself had used to memorize the words when she was learning to read.

One morning during recess in the first week, I spotted a crowd of students gathered around a bulletin board in the yard. Curious, I pushed close. The notice listed all the monthly recipients of *zhu-xiu-jin* — helping study fund, (a form of welfare) — and the amount they would receive. I was shocked to see the list posted in public, and horrified to notice that my name was on the top because I was to receive the most.

I had never imagined the school would be so insensitive as to put up this kind of information for all to see. Mortified, I turned around and walked away, sensing that all my schoolmates were talking about me, whispering that my father was dead, my family was poor, and I was a bad-luck girl. I wanted to run away and never come back, but my feet seemed made of lead.

For the rest of the day I spoke to no one and avoided any eye contact. I had expected the new environment to help me gain a fresh start; now I wasn't so sure. The hard-won confidence I had fashioned for myself, my three-year plan to ensure a good future, were broken. But soon I found more to worry about.

Our household had returned to normal. Number 1 was living on campus as required and sent home some of his monthly allowance to help out. Mother was especially happy to see Number 2 spending time at Father's desk; he had been admitted to a workers' night school and was taking senior-high-school courses to complete his education.

But throughout the autumn of 1964 Mother continued to lose weight. She insisted that everything was fine, but I frequently saw her holding a hot-water bottle to her stomach. When I told Number 2, he said, "Mother says she feels an emptiness in her stomach and the heat makes it better."

Then one day, Mother's pain drove her to the hospital. The diagnosis of cancer was devastating. A thick gloom fell on our house as Number 1 explained that Mother should never be told: the doctor subscribed to the common belief that a cancer patient who knew the nature of her illness would succumb more quickly.

Two-thirds of Mother's stomach was removed. The operation went well, the doctors assured us, and all the cancer was gone. We should hope for the best, but we should never tell her she had cancer.

Three weeks later, Mother came home, burdened by a list of "don'ts," mainly regarding food. She must eat only soft food like noodles or rice porridge, six or eight times a day, not three. Hot food, spicy dishes, ice cream, popsicles and, particularly, glutinous rice and pastries made from it were all forbidden. Yet the doctor had not told her why, so she ignored his instructions. I was worried sick seeing her eating proscribed food but had to hide my concerns.

My sisters and I quickly used up all our tricks when asked by Mother to buy "banned" food for her. We would come back from the market with the wrong thing. We forgot, we would say, or the store had run out of what she wanted. There was no gastronomic joy in our household during the New Year celebration. Every time I saw Mother putting forbidden food into her mouth I lost my own appetite and could hardly restrain myself from snatching her bowl away from her. But I didn't dare. It would not only be a sign of disrespect, but I would have to disobey the doctor's instructions.

At the beginning of the second semester I received my first mid-term report card. In the same envelope I was overjoyed to find an application for our district library card, a privilege that had to be earned; a student who didn't achieve good marks wasn't supposed to take time from her studies by reading books not on the school curriculum. The library card was valid for half a year. Another set of exam marks would determine if I would advance to the next grade and have my library card renewed. Meanwhile, I was the only student from all four classes of first-year girls invited to join a special math study group that met every Sunday at the district Children's Palace. Mother showed little enthusiasm when I breathlessly delivered the news to her. She was never keen on the academic achievements of her three daughters.

By the time summer vacation rolled around, Mother was on the mend and back at her part-time job collecting back-rents. I was excited to find that she had bought some printed cotton cloth for summer shorts and tops. Our three-year mourning period was finally over and I could cast off my somber white and gray clothing. What was more, it had been six months since Mother's operation and, according to the doctor, if the cancer was to reoccur it would show up either after three months or six.

My siblings and I cheered the good news, but one night at the end of July, Mother suddenly jumped up from the dinner table and ran outside. We could hear her retching. A few days later, while she was resting after an exhausting trip to the hospital, Number 1 told us that Mother's cancer had returned. Instantly, despite the heat, a cold chill raced through my body. The doctor hadn't bothered to order any tests; there was nothing he could do. He had instructed my brother that Mother could now eat anything she pleased, for it no longer mattered, and had given him a prescription for painkillers.

"Why? Why?" I cried out. "It's past the six-month period! Why is the cancer back?" Nobody could answer.

If it had been hard before to keep from Mother the nature of her illness, it became more difficult now to put on a happy face. I eyed her every swallow, hoping the doctor was wrong. But more and more she remained in bed, even for meals.

When the new school year started I was forced to leave Mother alone in the house. She was too weak to work any more. She blamed herself for not listening to the doctor's instructions and promised us she would never eat the taboo food again. What an irony, for now she could eat anything she wanted. How I wished the doctor had told her the truth from the beginning! How I wished I could push down the wall that had grown between us since her operation, a paper wall that could be punctured with my finger if only I had the courage. Then there would be no more deception on my part, no more self-reproach on hers.

While we children went to and from the druggist, renewing her prescription and returning with ever-larger bottles of pills that had little effect, Great-Aunt followed the path Mother herself had worn when Father was ill. She consulted Mrs. Yan, who put her in touch with a few families whose relatives had reportedly beaten cancer by taking unorthodox, traditional medicines. Great-Aunt dug out the old pots and began her campaign.

First, my brothers were asked to search the washing area in our building with flashlights for the fat slugs that crawled around, attracted by the dampness, when our neighbors were asleep. These disgusting creatures were washed and boiled in water for Mother to drink. Great-Aunt brought home peculiar ingredients in brown paper wrappings to start her battle of "combating poison with poison": orange peels, *Coptis chenensis*, rhizome Chinese goldthread, live earthworms, dried centipedes and so on. After she had brewed up these exotic liquors, she insisted that my sisters and I dump the dregs in the center of the laneway, believing that the more the dregs were walked on the greater the effect the cure would have. We were ashamed to litter the lane, for it was considered bad manners, so we dumped the stuff after dark. Although I was skeptical, I walked back and forth over the brownish dregs many times. Great-Aunt knew me too well. She admonished me that only a stranger's tread would help.

"So tell me how the dregs know whose feet are grinding them into the pavement," I wanted to say. Maybe she was right. We were constantly reminded that the spiciest gingerroots are the old and wrinkled ones; in other words, traditional thinking and practice shouldn't be questioned.

Weeks of stewing and boiling, and bitter odors in our apartment, only saw Mother's eyes darken and sink deeper into her face, but Great-Aunt would not give up. One night after everyone was asleep, she shook me awake and whispered, "Ah Si, will you get up and help me make medicine balls for your Mother?"

Wondering why she was being so secretive, I climbed out of bed and rubbed my eyes. Our door was closed and there was a mixing bowl on the table. Great-Aunt poured black powder from a paper bag into the bowl, adding a bit of arsenic. I was frightened but complied in silence. We made two hundred medicine balls, a week's dosage, each the size of a pea, and arranged them in a flat-bottomed basket to dry.

By the third day of treatment, Mother's lips had turned blue and her tongue was so swollen she could barely talk. She had to be rushed to the hospital. So much for folk medicine, I concluded.

But I was wrong. One evening after supper, Great-Aunt had a visitor, a stranger to all of us including her. The woman, in her thirties, was ushered into Great-Aunt's room and, ten minutes later, she departed by the back door. When Great-Aunt came back up the stairs, she drew all of us into her room. We were shown a new list of items given by the unknown woman whose mother, Great-Aunt reported, had been cured of inoperable stomach cancer by a foolproof method.

"Don't worry," she calmed us, "this cure is nothing like the others. Your mother will not have to swallow anything."

But what a bizarre mixture this new concoction was. As Number 2 read the ingredients, Number 3 and I looked at each other in wonder. We would have to make a paste of three kinds of herbs available in the local medicine store, along with a kilo of chopped fresh sunflower stalks. These were to be mixed together and put into the top of a turtle shell, no less than six inches in diameter, and the shell would be tied against the patient's abdomen with bandages! The turtle must be brought to the house live and killed and dismembered immediately before application. The theory was that the herbs and the shell would produce a drug whose heat would seep through to the tumor and slowly dissolve it.

Great-Aunt spent an entire day travelling to Pudong, on the east side of the Huangpu River, where she hoped to find a live turtle in the farmers' market. Number 2 volunteered to go to Nanhui County, southeast of the city, from where, after a day-long search, he brought home half a dozen sunflower stalks and farmers' good wishes.

Great-Aunt said the cure took five days, but after half that time the stench in our apartment was overpowering. "Phoenix Sister," Mother cried out early one morning, her face twisted in pain, "something as sharp as knives is sticking into my flesh! Take off the bandages. Get this thing away from me!"

Great-Aunt quickly took scissors to the reeking bandages. A disgusting stink filled the air and a horrible sight greeted me. Mother's skin was red, bubbled and spotted with blood, and in place of the hard dark shell were numerous fragments of fine bone mixed with her blood. I rushed from the room and vomited copiously into a spittoon. When I returned, Number 3 was helping Great-Aunt clean Mother up. I picked up the bucket containing the rotten shell, mashed herbs and bandages and lugged it out to the garbage pit, gagging at the stench.

As autumn wore on into winter frustration was my only emotion, and Mother's pain could be read in her face. Every time I heard her criticizing my brothers for not trying hard enough to get her into hospital, I walked out of the room. I hated to see them being blamed, but felt worse for Mother because I knew why the hospital had turned her down: not because my brothers wouldn't find the money to pay for her care, but because her cancer was terminal. If she knew the truth, she would never forgive herself for blaming her sons.

Mother's anger came to a head. One evening in late December, she called Number 1 and us girls into her room. Number 2 was at work. When we had gathered around her bed she glared at my brother. Hands shaking, she pulled off her ruby wedding ring and threw it at him.

"If money is what you're worried about, go and sell it!" she screamed.

Number 1 was stunned by Mother's uncharacteristic outburst.

"And the furniture in this house is not your inheritance yet. You could have sold a few pieces if you really cared about me!" She shook her head sadly. "What's the point of trying to raise children well if this is how they treat you?"

I had seen my mother angry at us before, but never had she treated Number 1 in this way. My brother's eyes were wide with shock and hurt. He picked up the ring and left the room. I followed him out and sat beside him at the dinner table. Lowering his head onto his arms, he sat there, quietly, with the ring in one hand. A moment or two later, he rose and led me back. We sat down on the edge of Mother's bed. Mother lay on her back, her face turned to the wall.

"Mother," Number 1 said quietly.

When she didn't respond, he took her hand in his and spoke again. Still she would not look at him. My brother began to sob.

"Mother, money was never an issue in your treatment. All the money in the world won't help. The hospital refused you over and over again because you have cancer!"

My sisters and I began to cry.

"Your cancer is in the late stage. That's why they won't take you."

Mother turned her head and looked at all of us in shock. She opened her mouth but no words came out. Then she started to beat herself on the chest, tears streaming from her eyes.

"How awful I have been," she moaned. "The way I treated you all. Why didn't you tell me in the first place?"

Number 1 gently took her hands into his to stop her striking herself. "The doctor told us it was best for you if you didn't know," he said.

For the rest of the evening the apartment was filled with sorrow. Great-Aunt reheated the dinner, and reheated it again when Number 2 came home from work, but no one ate anything.

For the first night in weeks we didn't hear Mother's moans of pain. In the morning she was peaceful and seemed completely free of anxiety. Her children, especially her sons whose love and loyalty she had doubted, were still hers. But her repose gave me an uneasy feeling. Number 1 must have shared my concern, for he sent a telegram to Mother's younger sister Yi-feng, who lived in Wang Family Village near Qingyang.

Since there were now no secrets between Mother and me, I had many things I wanted to explain to her — the lies I had told her about her illness, my "bad memory" when she sent me to the store to buy food she wasn't supposed to eat. Mother heard my confession without apparent interest. Her eyes remained closed most of the day.

At four o'clock in the morning Auntie Yi-feng knocked on the back door. She cried all the way up the stairs and went right to her sister's bedroom without even putting down her luggage. Mother's spirits seemed to rise with her sister's arrival. I wanted to stay by her side and it was easy to convince Auntie Yi-feng that missing a few days of school wouldn't hurt us much. She too strongly believed that girls had no business fooling with pens and books. On the last day of 1965, Number 1 asked my sisters and me to go back to school.

"At least take some homework back and find out what work you have missed," he insisted.

I hung back, dawdling after my sisters had left, and was glad when Auntie Yi-feng asked me to stay for a while so she could go to the market to buy some fresh noodles for lunch.

When Auntie Yi-feng returned, I went in to say goodbye to Mother.

"Mom," I said quietly, "is there anything you need? I'll be leaving in a few minutes."

Mother opened her eyes but seemed not to see me. I shifted my school bag on my shoulder and moved closer.

"Mom, can I get you anything?"

She didn't respond. Her eyes slowly closed. I felt panic. I dropped my bag on the floor and began to shake her.

"Mom, what's wrong? What's wrong?" I burst into tears, shaking her harder.

At that moment she opened her eyes. "Please, Ah Si, be quiet," she whispered. "I want to sleep."

Her eyes closed once more, and brown liquid streamed from the corner of her mouth as she died.

"How typical of your mother," Auntie Yi-feng wailed, "arranging to die at holiday time so her mourners wouldn't miss work or school."

When I went to the funeral home the next day I did not wear traditional mourning clothes. Auntie Yi-feng had insisted that times had changed and white cloth belts, black armbands and white shoes would be enough. I entered the parlor, surprised but pleased to see that the deputy director of the neighborhood committee was present, along with several other members. The housing department Mother had worked for was an organ of the committee. But I soon found that she was not there to pay Mother her respects.

At that time a family still had a choice of cremation or interment, but we were to be an exception. The reason was simple, the deputy director said. We were welfare recipients and earth burial was wasting money on the dead that was needed for the five orphan children. She did not mention what everyone knew: as in so many things connected with government policy, there was a quota. Each organization had to encourage as many families as possible to opt for cremation.

I felt everything close in on me. We all knew Mother wanted to be buried beside Father and had made Auntie Yi-feng promise not to cremate her. Mother had been utterly terrified of fire.

Number 1 remonstrated with the deputy director but she cut him off, announcing that delegations from his and Number 2's *dan wei* would arrive soon to "help solve the problem." She had told the funeral director that Mother's body was not to be put into the glass case for viewing until a paper had been signed guaranteeing cremation.

It was a horrible scene. My two sisters and I wept in grief and helplessness. My brothers were locked in heated discussion with the delegates sent by the university and the factory, who finally pressured them to agree. Great-Aunt kept out of it. My two uncles, Mother's older brothers, busied themselves arranging chairs and lining up tea cups.

When I saw that Number 1 was being tailed everywhere by a representative from the students' union, I could no longer contain myself. I cut in front of the young man and, with tears wet on my face, demanded in a shaky voice, "Would you let your mother be cremated against her wishes?"

Caught by surprise, the young man stuttered, but no words came out of his mouth. Number 1, to my astonishment, apologized for me. I wanted to hit him.

"What's the use having you for a brother?" I shouted. "What's the use having you as the eldest son, favored by Mother?"

I turned away to find Auntie Yi-feng had arrived. She had stayed behind to prepare for the visitation after the funeral. Sobbing with anger and frustration, I explained what was going on. Her face clouded with fury. With me in tow, she marched straight into the office of the funeral director. Before the startled man, who thought everything had been arranged, could open his mouth, she lit into him.

"Comrade, my *dan wei* is the Tongqi People's Commune, Zhongchun Brigade, Wang Family Village Production Team. Go, call my representative if you wish. He'll tell you I have his support to bury my sister according to her wishes."

Auntie Yi-feng knew that city dwellers looked down on farmers and always had, but she was also aware that, since the Communist takeover, Chinese peasants had become the most politically correct class of all.

"Aren't you ashamed of yourself," she continued, "putting these kids in this position, bullying five orphans?"

The director was at a loss, bowled over by her verbal attack, yet not quite understanding her every word because she was yelling at him in Wuxi dialect.

My aunt turned to me. "Let's go and find out where they're keeping your mother. We'll take her home and put her in the cedar chest!"

"Auntie, I know the place," I said, pushing the director aside. "I'll show you where they are hiding Mother!"

I ran down the hall, right into the arms of a worker, who in a kindly voice asked us to calm down and promised that everything would be all right. He led us back to the reception hall where Mother's body should have been on view by now.

The deputy director once again tried her persuasive powers on Auntie Yi-feng, but the conversation grew animated. This time Number 3 acted as interpreter for my aunt and soon Number 3 was shouting at the deputy director. My aunt was a formidable opponent, and eventually a deal was cut. Mother would be buried in a coffin, but only the cheapest kind.

When they finally placed Mother in the glass case I was so emotionally exhausted that I could cry no more. If my feelings for my mother could be interfered with in this way, what was left for me in the future? The world appeared a much harder and colder place from that day on. As I looked at Mother's body, I said the same words she had said to my father in the same place, not long ago: "What are we going to do without you?"

When one of the delegates discovered that Mother was still wearing her ruby wedding ring, she asked Auntie Yi-feng to have it removed, saying it should be sold to provide for the children, to ease the burden on the government. To my surprise, Auntie Yi-feng complied, but just before the coffin lid was closed for the last time I saw her put the ring back on Mother's finger.

That night, after our relatives and friends had left our apartment, Auntie Yi-feng took us girls to the public bathhouse, as Mother had done three years before after Father's funeral. It was an old custom to wash off the bad luck that attended a death. As a thirteen-year-old, I was fed up with such practices. So when Number 1 set about smashing Mother's rice bowl and tea cup according to tradition, I refused to help. I argued that after losing both parents already, I couldn't imagine how our luck could possibly become any worse.

I refused to go to school for the next few days. In fact, I wouldn't have minded if I never saw it again. The sight of my parents' silent room and empty bed frightened me. I was scared to stay home yet scared to go out.

I dropped out of my math interest group and felt like an odd duck among my classmates. All of us grieved and were disoriented, but Number 5 was hit the hardest. At eleven years old, she was totally withdrawn. With pretty eyes and delicate features, she appeared very fragile. She was always being sent home from school in the middle of the day because she couldn't stop crying in her classroom. She would spend the rest of the day with Mrs. Yan until Number 3 or I got home.

The spring passed slowly as each of us tried to face the fact of our parentless life. Great-Aunt was retired from the factory in March and was home all day. Her care and devotion to us made me miss my mother more than ever.

One morning, two months before my fourteenth birthday, I was busily working at my desk during a break between classes. When I stood up I felt something warm and sticky rushing down my thighs. One of the girls sitting behind me pointed to the floor and let out a cry. "Look! Blood!" The rest of my classmates craned their necks and whispered. I saw red spots on the floor and a pool of blood on the wooden seat.

Remembering how Great-Aunt's cousin had died from gastric bleeding, I was suddenly sick with terror. I snatched up my belongings, stuffed them into my bag, adjusted the strap so the bag would hang low and cover my bottom and fled home.

I ran all the way, my mind gripped with fear. First Father, then Mother. Now it was my turn to die. I would bleed to death. I burst into our apartment and found Great-Aunt darning Number 2's cotton socks. She looked up, startled, as I squeezed past her, ducked behind the curtain and plunked myself down on the chamber pot.

"Great Aunt," I cried, "I am bleeding to death, just like your cousin!"

"What are you talking about, Ah Si?" Through a gap in the curtain I noted that she hadn't even looked up from her mending.

"I have blood all over my pants and it's still coming!" I yelled. What's wrong with her, I thought. Can't she see I'm sick?

She put down the sock and needle and slowly rose to her feet, mumbling.

"What did you say?" I shouted, exasperated by her apparent calm.

"I really don't know what to tell you," she said, opening a dresser drawer. "It should be a mother's job to explain this."

I hated it when she said things like that, as she did often when Mother was alive. When I got on her nerves, she wouldn't criticize me but would blame Mother instead for spoiling me. If I complained about the ugliness of my clothes, she would say I had Mother's vanity in my blood. I had given up arguing years ago; she always got the last word.

Now here we go again, I thought. I'm dying and she makes remarks about my poor dead mother.

"Why can't you leave Mother alone? At least you're still alive."

I yanked the curtain closed, miserable and expecting criticism for my outburst. Instead she brought me a small paper parcel and a brown package with "Sanitary Paper" written on all four sides. Her placidity calmed me somewhat and I examined the parcel. I had seen ones like this displayed in store windows and had often wondered why there were two kinds of toilet paper, one called straw paper (an accurate description, since smashed straw pieces made a wrongful appearance here and there) and the other sanitary paper, which was sold in glued packages rather than stacks. Now that I thought of it, I had also seen it from time to time in our toilet paper basket at home.

But why was Great-Aunt handing me this stuff when I was in such danger? My very life was flowing down my legs. I recalled what the doctor had told us when he had diagnosed Mother's terminal cancer: "Let her eat what she likes." Was that why Great-Aunt was giving me such fancy toilet paper?

I turned the second packet over in my hand. "Sanitary Belt," it read. I thought, double sanitation. Inside was a pink beltlike contraption shaped like a T, made of soft rubber with white cotton bands.

"What's this?" I called out to Great-Aunt, who had returned to her work. "Why are you giving me these instead of pills?"

"Are you really as stupid as you sound? Can't you read?"

"Of course I can, but there's nothing here to tell me what they're for!"

"Don't try to fool me. I may not know how to read, but I can see there are words all over the packages," she insisted.

Knowing I had already gone too far, I softened a bit. Besides, I knew I could be left in this position all day if I opened my mouth again. In a moment Great-Aunt came back and showed me how to fit the paper inside the belt.

"Believe me, you are not going to die. Your parents wouldn't let that happen to you."

I put the strange contraption on and waited for Number 3 to come home for lunch. Maybe I could get some answers as well as sympathy from my elder sister.

"Number 3! I thought I was going to die this mor—"

"Cut your voice down, Ah Si," Great-Aunt interrupted.

"What's happened?"

I dragged Number 3 into the front room. "I have gastric bleeding, just like Great-Aunt's cousin. You can't imagine what a mess I made in the classroom."

Before I could go on my sister pushed me away. "It's a pity you only look smart," she sneered. "Didn't you read your textbook?" She walked out of the room, muttering, "As if there isn't enough death in this family."

Physiological Hygiene was a non-credit course at our school. We had one lecture a week and were supposed to study the textbook ourselves. But the lectures were often cancelled to make time for political study sessions, and I had avoided the book ever since a girl in my class had been accused of having dirty thoughts when she was spotted looking at the pictures of a naked man and woman.

That afternoon I hunted up the book. By the time I had finished reading it, I was weeping, for the relevant section emphasized that students should read it "under parental guidance."

As I closed the volume I felt Great-Aunt's hand on my shoulder. "Don't be sad, Ah Si. Every girl has to go through this, and believe it or not, some parents are happy for their daughters when it happens."

"Great-Aunt, you are right. The book says it's a mother's job to tell things like this to their daughters," I said without looking at her. "But Mother is gone. Who is going to tell me all the rest of the things I don't know?"

"Ah Si, I'll try, if you let me. I'll do my best to raise you, even though I'm not sure how."

I now felt sorry for the words I had thrown at her earlier. Probably nobody had ever told Great-Aunt herself about menstruation. And I was sure there had been no book available for her, even if she had been able to read. Considering her own life, how could she say that for a young girl to become a woman was a joy?

The harmony we had reached was short-lived, though. Before suppertime I asked her for another package of sanitary paper.

"Are you saying you used it all in less than half a day?" She sounded more shocked than angry.

"Well, I didn't eat it! It's paper, you know, not candy."

"Each package costs thirty cents," she rebuked me as she showed me how to extend the life of the paper by refolding it for a second use. "That was half a day's pay for your brother when he was an apprentice."

How nice it would be, I thought, if there was just one thing in life that didn't involve money. Only a few days before she had been complaining loudly about the rise in food prices. How could she save money for our winter clothes? I pictured our money flying away with all the sanitary paper for Number 3, Great-Aunt and me; and one day Number 5 would need it.

I sighed. "Great-Aunt, wouldn't it be wonderful if we were all boys?"

One dusty and windy afternoon toward the end of May, fifty classmates and I rode the bus for an hour and a half into Songjiang County to the Eastern Town Brigade, where we were met by representatives from the Number 2 Production Team. We had been sent there to help with the Three Summer Jobs, a policy that had more to do with politics than logic. In the space of two weeks we were to learn planting, harvesting and field management and to grow physically and mentally fit from hard labor. Our quarters were a large building with a swept dirt floor. Along the walls, boards had been laid on top of rice straw for our beds. I dropped my bedroll onto the boards and started to unpack.

There was not as much "real work" as we had been led to expect. First, we picked up loose ears of wheat in the fields and along the roads, an easy but tremendously tedious job. A few days later we carried bundles of rapeseed stalks, which had been harvested and tied loosely with straw. Since the seed pods were crisp and fell off easily, great care was needed when transporting them to the threshing ground.

The farmers instructed us to carry one bundle at a time, but we all burst out laughing after lifting them up: the large, awkward bundles seemed weightless. Ignoring the expert advice, we left with one bundle in each hand, struggling over the ridges in the plowed fields. A strong wind buffeted the bundles like kites, pulling me this way and that until I lost balance and fell to the dirt. Rapeseed scattered and rolled all around me. By the end of the day at least five of us had sprained our ankles. The next day we were back picking up wheat ears, a task that allowed for frequent afternoon naps.

Some villagers didn't hide their feelings about the whole business, calling our noble mission "lighting a candle for a blind person." But a few farmers did enjoy our visit, finally. One day, the team leader asked Teacher Zhang, my second-year English instructor, if some of the farmers could sit behind us during our evening English classes. The room was filled with giggling and mimicking. The farmers, who spoke a local dialect, found even the national language quite a challenge. They called the English words written on the blackboard "tadpoles."

When we stepped down from the bus into our schoolyard two weeks later I felt we had not gained much except our bundles of dirty laundry. Our principal greeted us with a long and boring speech, during which he constantly consulted his notebook as we stood baking in the sun.

"The physical achievement of your hard work is not nearly as important as your mental accomplishment through living with the peasants, the best teachers in life," he began.

As Principal Lin droned on, he kept glancing nervously at the school's party secretary, Fang, who stood to the side in the shadows. Something is up, I thought. Principal Lin continued that, contrary to custom, we would not have the next day off to rest. We must return to school. That was when Secretary Fang cut in.

In a sententious voice he announced that all our regular classes would be suspended until further notice. We had a lot of catching up to do in our political education. We would be studying documents from the Central Committee of the Communist Party — the May 7th Directive, the 16th Circular, and editorials from the People's Daily, the main mouthpiece of the Party. Drooping in the heat, I paid little attention when he declared that a new movement was about to start.

When I finally got home, Number 3 told me that her classes had been suspended also. Number 5, who had been cramming and beavering through exercises in preparation for her middle-school entrance exams, had been thrown into endless meetings and discussions as well. She was delighted. After watching her four siblings killing themselves with study on previous occasions, she wanted none of it.

"I feel great!" she crowed. "No more burning the night oil, no more nightmares. I'm liberated!"

Number 3 didn't look so relieved. She had been sent home to write a *biao tai* — a statement of belief, parroting the Party line — to make her position known in the new movement. I watched over her shoulder as she crossed out and revised her statement.

"I'd love to help, Ah Sei, but I have no idea what to suggest." I guess I didn't sound too sympathetic.

"Wait till it's your turn," she retorted.

Great-Aunt, too, was parroting new political terms, such as "a revolution that touches everyone's innermost being and purifies people's thinking." I laughed at her, for she clearly did not understand these soporifics.

We did not yet know it, but the Great Proletarian Cultural Revolution had started.

PART TWO

WIND OF CHAOS
(1966–1968)

7

"SUSPEND CLASSES TO make revolution!" was the first *da-zi-bao* — Big Character poster — I saw as soon as I walked through the front gate of my school the next morning. I had left my school bag and lunch at home because there would be no classes and the steam room where our rice was cooked would not be operating. A second poster read, "Long Live the Great Proletarian Cultural Revolution!" Each character on the blood-red paper was as tall as me.

Day after boring day our teachers read aloud to us government documents and newspaper editorials, which local and national papers were churning out with tedious regularity. This was the Party's method of disseminating information about new policies and denouncing or praising political figures, most of whom I had never heard of. Sometimes the teacher had us stand and read one paragraph each — a good method of keeping us awake. Soon we all sounded like Great-Aunt, spouting slogans and terms we didn't understand.

Like the other girls, I just went through the motions. This was not the first "movement" in which we had been forced to participate: a few days short of fourteen years old, I was already a veteran. We all assumed this campaign was directed mainly at those working in cultural fields — those who, in Great-Aunt's words, "drink ink and play with pens" — for it had been initiated by Mao's angry reaction to *Hai Rui Removed from Office*, a play by Hu Han, then the vice-mayor of Beijing, that told the story of an honest and courageous Ming dynasty official who had been sent into exile after confronting the emperor on behalf of ordinary people. Mao had taken the drama as an allegory of his purging of Marshal Peng De-huai, the former defense minister, who in 1959 had spoken out against the disastrous policies that had caused famine, laying the blame at Mao's feet. The attack on cultural figures like Hu Han would, we thought, be over in a few months. It was to rage for ten years.

One morning I heard the school's loudspeakers blasting long before I entered the gate. "Fellow comrades, wield your pens as swords and spears and aim your words like bullets against the reactionaries. Go to collect your weapons at the main office." The fervor of the movement was rising.

The office had been turned into a storehouse stacked with giant sheets of colored paper, boxes of bottled ink and writing brushes of all sizes. In one corner, Old Uncle Zhang, the gatekeeper, was making glue in a wooden barrel. His forehead shone with sweat and his shirt clung to his back. A chattering human stream flowed through the room, picking up supplies for the writing of *da-zi-bao* and *xiao zi bao* — small character posters written with pen rather than brush.

I left with a bottle of ink, two brushes and a sheaf of red paper under my arm. At the foot of the stairs leading to my classroom, two freshly hung posters, the ink still running, caught my eye. "Rebellion is justified!" screamed the first. The second filled me with confusion and dread: "If Lin Guang-min does not surrender, we will destroy him!" The three characters of our principal's name had been crossed over with Xs. Years before I had seen many caricatures of John F. Kennedy, whose name was transcribed into Chinese as *Ken Ni-di* — bite the dirt floor. On those posters, each character in Kennedy's name had been marked with an X to show he was an enemy.

I stood transfixed. Principal Lin, in his later fifties, was well respected by the teachers and students, a man who would "check the ground before taking a step, for fear of crushing an ant," as my geography teacher put it. What had he done to justify such extreme disrespect?

Shaken and confused, I spent the rest of the day filling my large red sheet with pointless sentences. While I was glueing my poster up on a wall I noticed that some of those already hung accused Principal Lin of "using ancient things to satirize the present" in his history classes. Most of them were signed by "Revolutionary Soldiers."

The next day I found my previous day's labor plastered over with new and more aggressive posters. The fervor had grown even more virulent. I had never seen the students in such high spirits: no classes, no school, no homework and, most of all, freedom to criticize teachers, an unprecedented phenomenon since the time of Confucius, who had emphasized that teachers should always be treated with honor and respect.

The colorful posters censured teachers for giving low marks or for writing critical remarks on report cards, and exposed their private lives through gossip and rumor. One related that a pretty young math teacher, Yao, had shared an egg with a bachelor teacher, Meng. Yao ate only the yolk and her colleague finished the rest. Therefore they were openly addressed as "Teacher Yolk" and "Teacher Egg-white" by the students. Another poster disclosed that the only son of Teacher Zhu, my first-year English instructor, was adopted. The cruelty and meanness of this act was enormous. Adoption within the extended family was not uncommon in China, yet adoption from outside was widely considered "fetching water with a bamboo-woven basket," owing to traditional attitudes toward blood lineage. As a result, adoptive parents never revealed the truth to the child and would often move to another neighborhood, even change jobs if possible, to keep the secret.

Not content with this, the poster writer also accused Teacher Zhu of refusing to have her own child out of vanity, "concerned that bearing a child will destroy her figure" — a rotten bourgeois way of thinking. I saw my former teacher standing in front of the poster, vainly trying to explain to the girls surrounding her that the charge was untrue. She could not have children, she said. She would show them her medical record.

Unable to witness her degradation, and sensing that even if there were mouths all over her body no one would listen to her, I stole away. All the way home I wished I could take back the unkind thoughts I had had about her when she pinned my English textbook to the board. What will come next? I thought. Whose turn will it be?

I arrived late the following day and saw a circle of screaming girls near the auditorium with Teacher Zhu in the center. She looked pale and exhausted.

"What did you mean," someone shouted, "when you taught us that 'Long live Chairman Mao' means 'Chairman Mao lives long'?" It was one of my own classmates, Tang, nicknamed "Super Flat" because of the unusual flatness of her head and face. In two years I had never heard her utter a word in class. Now here she was attacking our teacher over a point of grammar. None of us had been able to understand how to parse "Long live Chairman Mao" because we hadn't yet studied the subjunctive mood, so Teacher Zhu had suggested that for the time being we take it as "Chairman Mao lives long."

"We all wish that Chairman Mao will live forever, but you said he just lives for a long time," my classmate shrieked. "How long did you have in mind? What was your real purpose? Confess!"

The girls immediately broke into a chant. "*Wan shou wu jiang! Wan shou wu jiang!* — May our great leader Chairman Mao live forever!" They waved a little book as they chased the mortified teacher across the schoolyard.

The book was wrapped in red plastic, about 5" by 4". I realized that almost everyone around me had one except me, and, frightened by the attacks on Teacher Zhu, I figured I'd better get one quickly. I headed for the main office, where two students sat behind a desk piled high with the little red books, which had the title *Quotations of Chairman Mao* embossed on the cover. I gave them my class number and grade.

"What is your class background?" the heaviest of the two demanded.

All the political turmoil that had swirled through my school, all the personal attacks on teachers, should have made me more careful, but I was still naive. I answered.

"*Zi chan jie ji* — capitalist class."

"Then you don't deserve one," came the angry reply. "The 'red treasure books' are for students who are from the Five Reds, not for your stinking shit-smelling class, who exploit the workers!"

I couldn't believe my ears. I looked around for a teacher to help or at least tell me what was going on, but none was in sight. What were the Five Reds? What could they mean calling me an exploiter and member of a shit-smelling class? My family was poor and I was living on government welfare. I felt the tears sting my eyes, but refused to let them out.

"You don't need to insult me," I said. "If you don't want to give me the book, I'll be fine without it." And I ran from the office and the school. When I got home I broke down. I had thought that I would never cry like that again, never after my parents died. Great-Aunt listened without interruption, then went to her dresser and returned with a red book in her hand.

"Ah Si, take mine," she offered. "When the neighborhood committee gave it to me I didn't know what it was. All I can recognize is the portrait of Chairman Mao."

"You don't understand!" I shot back. "I'm not crying because I don't have this book. It's the insult. I don't deserve to be degraded like that. Calling me 'shit'!" I threw down the book and stormed out of the room.

As if I was not upset enough, Number 3 arrived home with a copy of the red book. When I retold my tale of woe, she burst out laughing, saying I was "brainless" and lacked "flexible thinking."

"Why did you tell them the truth?" she sneered. "Did you think they would bother to check? These books come by the truck-load! I told them I am a daughter of an office clerk, not totally untrue. Father did work in an office and did clerical and accounting work, didn't he? It all depends on your point of view. Grow up, Ah Si! Don't be so naive."

I must have looked astonished. Was this what she meant when she said I was not "flexible"?

That night, Number 2 explained to me who the Five Reds were: factory workers, poor and lower-middle-class peasants, soldiers and officers of the People's Liberation Army, Party officials, and revolutionary martyrs. The families of these five categories were therefore "red" also. In contrast, the Five Blacks included former landlords, rich peasants, counter-revolutionaries, rightists, and former capitalists. Until now, capitalists had been treated differently from the other four categories, depending on the ups and downs of the political thermometer. They had been urged to "transform themselves into working people through labor" in the early 1950s, then accused of "dragging the weak-willed Communists into the mire" in the '60s.

I was puzzled yet furious that my family was included in the Five Blacks. How could we be capitalists? We had been born and had grown up under the Communist flag, and we were poor. Our so-called capitalist parents were dead. We didn't own anything.

I made up my mind before I went to bed that I was not going back to school the next day no matter what Great-Aunt said. To my surprise, she didn't object, and I passed a peaceful day at home, reading and snoozing. After that I had many more. Each day Number 3 told me what was going on in her school. More teachers were publicly denounced and locked up in "cow-sheds," so named from the term "cow-demon" in classical literature. Students belonging to the Five Reds were calling for "making revolution around the clock" and had turned the classrooms into dorms, refusing to go home. A "work team" composed of factory workers and government officials had been stationed in her school and was encouraging the students to "blast the lid off the class struggle."

"I don't know how long you can stay home like this, Ah Si," Number 3 warned. "They have a name for students like you now — idlers — and you won't be able to get away with it for long."

8

ABOUT TWO WEEKS LATER, at the beginning of August, Number 5 burst through the door in tears.

"My classmates called me dirty names and told me that our father was an exploiter!" she wept. "Ah Si, I can't even remember what Father looked like; I was so young when he died. I didn't even know what he did for a living. How come the others know all that?"

She had cried all the way home because she had been rejected by the *Hong Xiao Bing* — Little Red Guards — because of her family background. I was unable to comfort her.

I myself was worried about the summons signed by Red Guards ordering me to report to them at my school. Great-Aunt had often said that if you have done nothing wrong you needn't be frightened by a pounding on your door in the middle of the night. I repeated the saying to myself as I walked along. If attacked for being an idler, I planned to admit my "lack of revolutionary spirit" to deflect the criticism.

The street outside the school was ablaze with Big Character posters. "Smash So-and-so's dog head!" "Flog the cur that has fallen into the water!" (Be merciless with bad people even if they are down.) One poster declared the establishment of the school's Red Guards, ending with, "It is right to rebel against reactionaries!"

Old Uncle Zhang was not in the gatehouse. His bed had been replaced by benches and chairs. I recognized all of the occupants except two young women dressed in faded army fatigues with red armbands. *Hong Wei Bing* — Red Guards — was written in yellow, along with smaller characters underneath.

I was challenged by a knot of girls at the gate. "State your class background," one of them shouted. There was no time to use the ruse Number 3 had suggested, for one of the girls recognized me and pointed her finger. "She's the one who told me she could get along just fine without the treasure book!"

One of the strangers strutted over and stood in front of me. She was much taller than me and solidly built.

"You son-of-a-bitch capitalist!" she hissed. Her accent told me she was a Northerner. I hung my head, hoping not too many of my schoolmates had heard. She punched my shoulder to straighten me up. "Go to the side gate. We will deal with you later."

Frightened, I did as I was told. As soon as I entered the side gate I was confronted by three Red Guards. My name and class background were taken down and I was directed to a Red Guard whose armband indicated that she was from Dong Chen District, Beijing. She stood, sweating in her ill-fitting army uniform, cap pulled down tightly, armpits mapped with perspiration, thumbs in her belt in a pose praised by Mao, who had written that Chinese women preferred battle array to silk. She ordered me to join six other students facing a brick wall. I knew all of them. They were always well dressed and a few were members of the students' council, a prestigious position in most people's eyes, including mine. Not one of them said a word. I got the feeling that it was not their first experience staring at the wall, so I followed their lead, and stood still, looking down at my white cotton shoes.

Although it was not yet nine o'clock, the heat was stifling, beating down on us and radiating from the wall. By noon — I could tell the hour by the slow progress of our shadows — there were about two dozen of us wilting in line. Finally the Beijing Red Guard led us away toward the schoolyard. There weren't many students there; most had been driven indoors by the sweltering heat. The dirt yard was like a laundry with crisp, faded paper sheets hung from numerous clotheslines strung from side to side.

"You are ordered to read all the *da-zi-bao* and then report to me before you go home," she shouted. "Maybe we can drive some capitalist ideas from your stinking heads."

Walking between the rows of hanging posters, I not only found many duplicates and copied newspaper articles, I noticed that some of the writers had inadvertently omitted half sentences or entire paragraphs, making the poster nothing but a joke. They were all signed "East Is Red" or "Defending the East" or "Revolutionary Masses" or "Red Rebels." How ridiculous, I thought.

But I felt a chill when I saw that Teacher Zhang, my second-year English instructor, had been denounced. Someone had listed the names of her and her five siblings, circling the middle character of each name. The linked characters read "Long Live the Republic of China."

I knew Teacher Zhang was in big trouble. The Republic of China, not the People's Republic of China, was how the Guomindang — Chiang Kai-shek's Nationalist Party — referred to my country before the Communists took over. To show the slightest loyalty to the Guomindang was treason. But why blame Teacher Zhang? Why not blame her father?

Number 1 was at home a lot, since the university too was in turmoil and all classes were suspended in favor of endless political study. That night I asked him about Teacher Zhang's case. He said that obviously all the children in her family had been born when the Nationalists were still in power and her father had found a smart way to show loyalty to the regime. It was difficult to get a legal name change, he explained; there were as many procedures as hairs on an ox.

When I told him about the Beijing Red Guards, he grew agitated.

"Listen, Ah Si, do whatever you're told and never, ever argue or talk back. I know you too well. Your sharp tongue will get you in trouble. The Beijing Red Guards are the children of high Party officials. They have received Chairman Mao's support and they can be very dangerous if they get angry at you."

"There are no imported Red Guards at my school," Number 3 said. "They are probably punishing you for staying away from school, Ah Si."

Great-Aunt had stayed out of the conversation. When she and I were in bed she began to talk, staring at the ceiling. "It's you again, Ah Si, bullied by the Red Guards. Why does bad luck always follow you around? If that isn't Fate, what is it?" She let out a heavy sigh. "Your mother should have let me adopt you when I offered. Then you would be the daughter of a working-class woman and you would be safe."

I kept telling myself I would not be cowed, but as I got closer to school the next day I could feel softness in my legs. For the first time I was grateful that none of my classmates lived in my lane and that the school was so far away. No one in my neighborhood would witness my humiliation.

That thought brought to my mind one of Mao's sayings that had until recently begun our daily sessions: "Good things can turn to bad things and vice versa." I had always wondered why this inane statement was the object of reverence, but maybe it had some truth after all. Before I reached the school I decided what I would put in my thought-report to the Red Guards. I would tell them that I now understood the Chairman's saying and that I had learned from my own experience how correct he was.

But I never got the chance. My group had apparently been treated "too leniently," walking around and reading posters. One of the Beijing Red Guards spouted from her red book: "Revolution is not a dinner party, nor is it writing articles, drawing pictures or doing embroidery; revolution is a class struggle of life and death." She divided us into work groups and set us to our "life and death struggle" — cleaning toilets and sweeping out the classrooms.

I knew that this assignment was not an effort to help the custodian and Old Uncle Zhang, who had been under house arrest in the cow-shed along with the principal because the Red Guards claimed that he was a spy for his former employer, the Christian mission school. As far as I could see, he was good only at matching our faces to the photos on our student cards. I couldn't imagine poor illiterate Old Uncle Zhang spying for anyone.

So the hot days of August crept by. I had thought I would never sweep dirt floors again after I left the temple school, but I soon considered the time I spent sweeping the back alley, mopping wooden floors and stairs and cleaning out the washrooms to be my good days. The bad days were those when I was yelled at and forced to write self-criticisms, complying with the Red Guards' shrill demands without hesitation. More than once I wondered what Mother would think, seeing her fourteen-year-old girl treated like an old-hand criminal.

9

S O FAR THE RED GUARDS had wreaked havoc largely inside the schools and universities, but an incident in Beijing changed their status dramatically. On August 18, Chairman Mao, wearing an army uniform, appeared at the Gate of the Heavenly Peace. There he was formally presented with a Red Guard armband by a young woman named Song Bin-bin. Bin-bin — Genteel — is a fairly common name for a girl. Mao asked her, "*Yao-wu-ma?*" ("Do you want violence?")

At that moment, said the newspaper reports, the young woman accepted Mao's suggestion and changed her name to Song Yao-wu — Song Wants Violence. Song confessed years later that, once "a girl who would panic at seeing a dead cockroach," she turned into a revolutionary "who wouldn't even blink while beating someone to death."

Hundreds of thousands of young people throughout the country rushed to change their names to respond to Mao's call. And from that day the Red Guard movement, blessed by the Chairman himself, spread into the streets, its targets no longer limited to teachers and students with bad class backgrounds. Mao Ze-dong had unleashed a violent windstorm that would engulf me and my siblings because we had been born to a capitalist father and mother who were no longer around to be attacked.

"Long live Chairman Mao! Long live the red sun in our hearts!" screamed the weeping Red Guards in my school when the news about Mao's blessing was announced. Armed with carte blanche for violence and chaos, they swept from the school to "smash the Four Olds." This vague category of new enemies comprised old culture, old customs, old habits and old ways of thinking.

A few nights later a deafening racket of gongs, drums and strident voices drew my sisters and me into the streets. Wuding Road was a turmoil of milling crowds, bonfires, shouted slogans. My memory of the hysterical steel-making campaign contained nothing like this. Number 3 and I walked uneasily with Number 5 between us.

We watched the Guards rename our street: Wuding became Yaowu, to echo Mao's call. We felt the heat of bonfires fed by books, paintings, embroideries and other "bourgeois goods" confiscated by the Red Guards when they raided local homes. Women with "bourgeois" hairstyles had their tresses hacked off in the street; men with hairdos that "looked like Kennedy" suffered the same humiliation. People wearing trousers with narrow legs were held down while the Red Guards took scissors and slashed the pants open. Those who wore pointed-toed leather shoes had them torn off their feet and hurled into the fire. Such "rotten Western" styles, the Guards screamed, must be driven out of China.

🍃

A few days later I was stopped on my way home from school by two girls who were not of the Five Reds nor Five Blacks, but were "Grays," children of shopkeepers, office clerks and elementary and middle-school teachers. They belonged to a peripheral Red Guard unit, as they were not pure enough for the real thing.

I was fortunate, the girls brusquely informed me. I had been allowed to join an overnight parade to show Shanghai's support for the Great Proletarian Cultural Revolution. "Allowed" meant that

I'd better turn up and take the opportunity to "educate and reform" myself. I resented their arrogance, but was secretly glad of the opportunity because I was sick of being the object of scorn and abuse at school. Maybe if I took part in the demonstration they wouldn't call me a shit-smelling capitalist any more.

But I was worried that I could not endure a night-long parade. My period had started the day before. What would I do if the Guards did not let me leave the parade to visit a washroom?

To make matters worse, the hot, humid weather was producing powerful winds and thunder, declaring the arrival of a typhoon. But the word came down: even if it rained knives, the parade would go on. The demonstration would show "our true revolutionary spirit as well as our determination to carry on the Cultural Revolution to the end."

As evening came on, Great-Aunt helped me prepare. She filled my school bag with sanitary paper, adding two extra pairs of underpants in case I needed them. By the time I fought my way through the wind and driving rain to the school, my umbrella had been pulled inside out and I was drenched. I was assigned to the tail end of our school parade along with my "brick inspector" sisters, a name we had given ourselves after spending so many hours under the scalding sun, staring at the wall.

We began the slow march along dark streets in pounding rain. It took half an hour to get to the main road, where the congestion of thousands of converging marchers forced us to halt. By now the rain had stopped but the wind had ripped our flimsy paper flags away and we were left holding naked bamboo sticks. Larger red flags rippled and snapped; the black ink characters on the red cotton banners dissolved into meaningless blotches.

Still sodden, we stood buffeted by the gale for more than an hour. I was becoming desperate for a washroom so I could change my sanitary pad. I finally got the attention of a Red Guard and received her permission to leave the parade and go home with a girl who lived nearby. You-mei — Plum Blossom — took me to her family's opulent apartment, which had a huge carved steel door at the lane entrance. Her elderly parents were sitting in the living room, reading, oblivious to the political and atmospheric storms outside. You-mei showed me to a luxurious bathroom with a flush toilet, bathtub and sink. Embarrassed by the visit, I thanked them on my way out, turning my face away quickly so they would not recognize me if I met them again.

When we rejoined the still noisy parade it hadn't advanced an inch. The downpour began again. I wished I had a raincoat like most of the others, for it was hard to keep my bedraggled umbrella over my head in the wind. Time dragged. Still we remained rooted in the middle of the dark street. I began to think my daily sweating confinement at school was preferable to this cold and hungry vigil.

After midnight cramps gripped my abdomen again and I was in need of a change, but all the sanitary packages laboriously prepared by Great-Aunt were soaked. You-mei had disappeared and I could find no one else to take me to their home. Luckily it was dark and the stains on my soaking wet trousers would not show.

By now the crowd's enthusiasm had diminished. The flags had been rolled up and the banners put away. The chanting of slogans and shaking of fists and bamboo clubs had died down. Finally the word was passed down the stationary parade that our destination was People's Square downtown, where we would be greeted by the mayor and other municipal officials. The news caused an enthusiastic stir, since being received by high officials was like being blessed by the Emperor in the old time.

But to me nothing would be more exciting than finding a toilet. I began to understand the meaning of the word pilgrimage, which I had learned from reading the classic novel *Journey to the West*. The night crept on; the rain beat down; the wind howled. My blood flow was heavy and I was growing weak. My teeth began to chatter and tremors shook my body.

At last, the parade began to move. We inched forward until pale light showed in the sky.

As dawn arrived we entered the square. In the distance, so small I could hardly see them, three or four figures waved at us from a raised — and roofed — reviewing stand. No standing in the wind and rain for them. Moments later, the Red Guards ran up and down the ranks, telling us that the parade was over and we could go home.

The grateful crowd rapidly dispersed in all directions to bus and streetcar stops, but the transportation system had shut down for the parade. The hordes of marchers, like deflated rubber balls filling the streets, reminded me of the words Father had added to my composition six years before: "The crowd surged like a wave moving through water." Only now the water was a violent and bitter sea.

Exhausted by miles of marching and standing all through the rainy windy night, I began the two-mile walk home, drained by fatigue and loss of blood. I do not remember my arrival home. When I awoke it was late afternoon and I was lying half on, half off Great-Aunt's bed in a pool of blood, my clothes still drenched with rain and blood from the night before. I dragged myself from the bed in a panic. It was no use: the blood had long since seeped through the straw mat and stained the bedding.

"Never mind, Ah Si," Great-Aunt waved off my apologies. "You have a hot bath and I'll take care of this."

Number 1 carried the water from downstairs and Number 3 brought me dry clothes. The hot bath was heavenly. After I had finished soaking, Great-Aunt prepared a cup of boiled ginger soup with brown sugar. I did not tell her about the wasted sanitary paper.

When I returned to school in the first week of September, the Red Guards from Beijing had vanished. Nevertheless, the schoolyard looked uninviting, for the typhoon had swept almost all the posters to the ground, blocking the sewers with them, leaving puddles here and there dyed black with ink. This institution that should have been filled with happy schoolgirls at the beginning of a new school year had, in the past few months, been turned into a hateful vindictive place. And now it resembled a ghost town.

I turned and went home. Now, all of us except Number 2 had become idlers, and our lane was full of schoolkids trifling around with nothing to do. I was glad to stay at home. But good things never last long. Late one afternoon when most families were preparing supper, we were once again drawn from our kitchens by the clamor of gongs and the racket of drums.

Some Beijing Red Guards led a group of a dozen local youths into our lane, marching slowly, checking the building numbers. Many of the onlookers — among them Boss Luo's wife from the building next to us, and my friend Ying-ying's mother — slunk away, no doubt hoping the raid would not be aimed at them. As the Guards passed me, beating their drums and gongs, shouting slogans against capitalists and counter-revolutionaries, I fell in behind them. To my relief, the noisy procession passed our door and stopped in front of Building Number 45. "Yao family! Show yourselves!" the leader shouted.

Some Guards began to paste *da-zi-bao* on the laneway walls; others pushed into the Yaos' apartment.

The raids on our lane had been launched. In the days that followed, the neighborhood was thronged with Red Guards. Old Yang, a worker at home with an injury, served as our information source, continuously updating his statistics. "So far, eighteen families have been searched. In Building 75 the Red Guards have taken the roof-drains apart to see if gold bars were hidden there. Now they are going through the roof tiles, looking for guns."

The residents were terrified. Even a toy drum beating could halt a conversation. The raids spread to the houses near us, then next door. Through Great-Aunt's bedroom window I watched the attack as she sat on the bed mending socks. The Guards poured bottles of ink into dresser drawers and over chesterfields, enraged because they hadn't found the gold they thought would be there. They built a bonfire in the sky-well and burned books and paintings, old and new, hurling them into the flames from the upper windows. The senseless destruction terrified me. I wondered whether Great-Aunt still believed that if a person had done nothing wrong she had nothing to fear.

"Ah Si! Ah Si!" Number 1 shouted behind me, bursting in and slamming the windows shut before my eyes. "Come with me, now!"

In the front room, my two sisters stood silently. My parents' pride and joy had been our five antique Ming dynasty paintings. No one had ever thought about selling them for much-needed cash. For my entire life they had hung on our walls, mounted on fine silk, with rosewood scrolls at the bottom. Four of them, landscape scrolls of spring, summer, autumn and winter, were more than two yards long and half a yard wide, done in traditional Chinese style. The fifth, the centerpiece, depicted three tigers so fierce and realistic they looked as though they might climb down from the wall and prowl the room.

Now the paintings were spread out on the floor. I looked questioningly at my brother. He was twenty years old now, the head of the family.

"These are the only things the Red Guards could punish us for," Number 1 said, his face grim, his voice flat and determined.

We looked at each other.

"What would the Red Guards come here for? To look for gold?" I scoffed.

"If they do look for gold and jewels in the home of a welfare family it will show their stupidity," he responded, "but these paintings are antiques. They belong to the Four Olds. We have to show them a clean house because if they get angry at us, there is no telling what might happen. People have been beaten to death for less."

Suddenly, I knew what we were going to do. Nobody wanted to say the first word, nor make the first move.

Great-Aunt broke the tense silence. "I will dump the pieces into the garbage bins after dark." She did not say what we all knew: as a life-long worker, technically independent and separate from us children of capitalists, she was relatively safe from attack. "Be careful," she added. "The Red Guards will not let you off easily. Do what you must and let me know when you're finished." She returned to her room and waited there.

"All right," Number 1 said, "one painting for each. Number 2 will be home soon to help."

I had little sense of what an antique was, but I loved the paintings, their beauty, power and poetic calligraphy. Now here we were ready to cut them into strips with scissors, as if we were doing some sort of craftwork. I chose "Winter," thinking that my dislike of the cold damp season would make my task easier. But I was wrong. Soon tears fell onto the painting as I worked. I looked over at my baby sister, struggling with a pair of oversize scissors, scraping holes here and there in "Summer," and my tears came faster.

"Stop, you're ruining it!" I yelled, immediately realizing the stupidity of my words. I took her into my arms as she wept. The last time we had all cried like this was when Mother died, eight months earlier.

"Go on," Number 1 urged. "Hurry!" Once more we set about our horrible task.

Seeing Great-Aunt leave, her sewing bag stuffed with strips of painting, while my two brothers swept the wall with dirty brooms to hide the marks left by the pictures, my fear intensified. Any marks or indication of a new paint job would lead to accusation of trying to hide evidence.

Our building was one of the few in the lane that had not yet been searched. Granny Ningbo was utterly terrified, jumping at every footstep. The Guards had hacked off Granny Yao's hair in Building 45, making her look like a crazy woman, and she was under close watch by her three grandchildren for she had already tried to kill herself. Mrs. Qiao was in worse shape after having talked back to the Red Guards when one of them insulted her children: they had shaved half her hair off, creating what they mockingly called a yin-yang style. In the Ye family apartment, we waited for the inevitable.

At last, one hot night soon after, we heard footsteps on our stairs followed by a knocking on our door. There were no gongs or drums, no yelling of slogans or insults. Tentatively, Number 1 pulled the door open. It was Uncle Yu, a worker from Father's factory, whom Father had employed as a cook years before because he was from Wuxi and could prepare the kind of food Father liked. Uncle Yu pressed his index finger to his lips and quickly shut the door. He was a short, plump man, with a chubby, youthful face, though he was over fifty.

"Ah Du," he whispered to Number 1, "I came to warn you children. I overheard the Red Guards talking at the factory. They plan to raid your house tomorrow."

He went on to explain that the workers had split into two factions: the Loyalists, who still supported the city government, and the Shanghai Workers Revolutionary Rebels, who wanted to overthrow it. Number 2 had joined the Loyalists, for it was impossible to remain impartial. Uncle Yu went on to tell us in hushed, apologetic tones that there were a number of da-zi-bao in the factory calling Father insulting names and saying that his soul refused to leave the factory.

"There's no such thing as a ghost, the Communists claim," I said, "so what are they doing, putting up such nonsensical posters?"

"What are they coming here for, Uncle Yu?" Number 3 cut in.

The old man looked as troubled as we felt. "I have no idea. But don't give anyone an excuse to hurt you." He pulled open the door, glanced out into the hall, and slipped away.

All of us were touched by Uncle Yu's courage. Out of loyalty to Father, he put himself at great risk to warn us. That was the last time we saw this kind old man. After vindictive Red Guards revealed that his daughter had been adopted, she left Shanghai, taking Uncle Yu's grandchildren with her. He killed himself a few months later.

That night I could not sleep. Neither could Great-Aunt, who tossed and sighed beside me in the heat. She had said nothing after Uncle Yu had left. When I thought about it, I realized she had been uncharacteristically silent since the raids had begun.

All her life Great-Aunt had made a living by her own hands. She had envied Mother and others like her who were also country girls but had lived a better life through a good marriage. While she herself had been cursed with bad luck, Great-Aunt had watched Mother start a new life, surrounded by children. Now, ironically, her bad luck had made her safe from attack.

We waited all the next day, all six of us huddled in our three-room apartment, and when dusk fell our building was hit a double score. Granny Ningbo's place was raided first. Then, after half an hour of shouting and crashing, it was our turn.

The insistent banging on our door was accompanied by bawled orders to open up. Seven people burst into the room — six Red Guards, two female and four male, all in their late teens or early twenties, all sporting the sinister red armbands. With them a young male worker from Father's factory. The leader, who was from Beijing, ordered us into my parents' bedroom.

"Form a line in the center of the room!" he shouted. We stood with heads bowed as he read us several items from Mao's treasure book.

"Whoever lives in this society is branded by the class he or she was born into!" one of the women Guards exclaimed when he had finished.

The Beijinger and the worker sat at Father's desk and examined our *hu-kou* — registration book — checking against a list in his hand and ordering us to stand still, face forward and answer as our names were called. The Beijinger, about Number 1's age, had puffy red cheeks. His interrogation was continually interrupted by shouts from the other Guards who had fanned out and begun a systematic search of our two rooms. Great-Aunt's room was left alone once the worker pointed out that she was a retired working-class woman. She remained inside with the door closed.

One of the women searching a dresser waved a pair of cotton socks with frequently mended soles and jeered, "Are these socks or shoes? It seems this family has iron soles!"

The Guards scouring the bedroom burst into laughter, but our interrogator kept his attention on his list. I stood silently, thinking of one of Mao's quotations: "The poorer people are, the better revolutionaries they will be." Another of his famous lines said that poverty was like a piece of new white paper on which one could write the finest calligraphy and draw the most beautiful pictures. Yet at the same time we were humiliated, first because we were the offspring of a capitalist, second because we were so poor we walked in mended socks.

A sudden movement interrupted my thoughts as the Beijinger pounded his fist on the desk.

"I knew it! I knew it!" he crowed. "Reactionaries are never straightforward in their evil ways. Look, everyone!" he shouted, bringing the ransacking of our meager belongings to a temporary halt. "See what I have found."

He stood and strutted around the desk, pushing his finger into Number 2's face. "Tell me your name again."

"Ye Zhong-xing," answered my brother, his voice shaking.

"How old are you?"

"Eighteen."

"And you?" He pointed to Number 1.

"Ye Zheng-xing. Twenty."

"You see!" he looked around at his comrades and then suddenly punched Number 2 on the shoulder as he hissed, "Now you can tell me how your dead father was a supporter of the Guomindang reactionaries!"

I was dumbfounded. Beside me, Number 3 caught her breath.

"We all know that Chiang Kai-shek's other name, given by his mother, is Chiang Zhong-zheng, the one he prefers but doesn't deserve!"

Number 1's name, Zheng — Upright — is a good name for a boy though uncommon. Number 2's, Zhong, means, in the context of a name, Steadfast. These were names a scholar like my father would think appropriate for his male children.

But there was something wrong with the Red Guard's theory. "That can't be true," I spoke up, earning a warning glance from my eldest brother. "As you said, Chiang's name is Zhong-zheng. If Father had been a Nationalist sympathizer he would have named Number 1 Zhong instead of Number 2. The word order is wrong!"

"Shut up!" screamed the Guard, spit flying from his mouth. "That just shows your ghost-father's cunning! He reversed the order to fool people. But our Red Guards' eyes are much cleverer, thanks to Mao Ze-dong Thought!"

I felt helpless in the face of his twisted logic. I had never so much as seen a photo of Chiang Kai-shek. The caricatures in our textbooks depicted a skinny, stiff man wearing a crossed bandage on his right temple. The Guomindang was described as rotten to its roots; Chiang Kai-shek's army had been full of "playboys" and all his soldiers had "rabbit legs" because they constantly ran away from battle during the wars against Japan and the Communists.

Our apartment pulsated with booming voices as the Red Guards began to vilify my father, shouting in unison, "Down with Ye Rong-ting! Down with the Guomindang running-dog, Ye Rong-ting!"

Despite everything, I couldn't help smiling inwardly at the fools shrieking around me. The literal translation of down with in Chinese — da-dao — is to knock someone down physically. They seemed to forget that my father was dead.

As if reading my thoughts, the fools changed the chant. "Ten thousand deaths will not expiate Ye Rong-ting's crime! Feed his dead body to the dogs! And the dogs won't want it because it stinks too much!"

I stole a glance at my brothers and sisters. Their eyes were wide with fear. We had been badly enough off as children of the hated capitalist class; now the blood of a traitor supposedly ran in our veins. Yet, despite all the vindictive yelling and screaming, I felt strangely calm. The anxiety and panic of the past weeks and the endless waiting for the dreaded raid were over. Number 5, though, was shaking in terror, and I put my arm around her shoulders. I glanced at the door of Great-Aunt's room but it remained closed and there was no noise from within. Our neighbors, who in the past would always stick their noses into our apartment at the slightest provocation, were silent, as if they had suddenly lost their hearing.

When the shouting died down, Number 1 began to speak. Calmly he tried to reason with the Guards, telling them how my father's stepcousins had left for Taiwan before the liberation, but Father had remained. Why would he stay in Shanghai if he were a running-dog of Chiang Kai-shek?

"Aha, an overseas relationship!" one of the Guards exclaimed.

"Having illicit relations with foreign countries!" piped a second.

Another stupidity, I thought. Even at fourteen I knew clearly China's stern policy that Taiwan was a province of China. It was strictly prohibited to refer to it as a foreign country and the punishment for violation ranged from "reforming through labor" to imprisonment.

"But we have no contact with —"

"Shut up, traitor!" yelled the Beijing Red Guard.

"Make them change their names!" a thin woman with a long face and protruding teeth suggested. The rest of the Guards shouted agreement.

While the search resumed, my brothers were given five minutes to think of new names. One male Guard approached the Beijinger and presented him with a thick sheaf of papers.

"You can have them if you want," Number 1 offered without delay. "We don't want them."

"These are stock certificates and government bonds. Capitalist trash. Destroy them," the Beijinger sneered, handing them over to Number 1.

Without hesitation my brother tore the securities to bits while three of the Red Guards nodded their approval. As far as I was concerned the fancily printed bonds and certificates, the expropriation payments for Father's factory, were useless, just stacks of paper gathering dust in a drawer for years. The Red Guards, who thought the documents were valuable, praised Number 1's actions. (In the late 1970s, these securities became redeemable again.)

"Please," Number 2 spoke up. "I'd like to change my name to Loyalty." The character for loyalty was turning up more and more in *da-zi-bao* on walls and in store windows. The Red Guards accepted it right away. Number 2's choice was brilliant, because his new name was a homonym of "steadfast," his original name.

The Red Guards were starting to lose interest. Our two rooms offered nothing of note or value except a few items of furniture. But they did confiscate our family photos, claiming that they were "of the Four Olds" because in one grandfather had on an old-style "half melon" hat and in others Father wore a Western-style suit coat and tie and Mother had permed hair and makeup. Led by the Beijinger, the Red Guards left, chanting slogans as they thumped down the stairs and into the sky-well. Again I smiled inwardly. They had forgotten that Number 1 had not changed his name.

No one said a word. Number 5 wept quietly, shoulders hunched, hands shaking. Number 3 stood apart with her hands crossed across her chest, eyes wide. My two brothers looked at each other and nodded. We had survived.

After a few moments, Great-Aunt shuffled from her room, looking sheepish and guilty, but none of us blamed her for failing to come out and stick up for us. We all knew that would only have made things bad for her and worse for us. She immediately set about making tea and preparing us a late supper, which we ate in silence.

Over the next few weeks, trucks came and went through our lane loaded with goods: sofas, paintings, silk hangings, clothes, record players and records, even some cooking utensils — all were labeled "bourgeois" and appropriated by the Red Guards. What could not be seen were the jewelry and money they confiscated. And what they couldn't take away with them, they wrecked, leaving smashed roof tiles, holed walls, splintered floorboards and ripped chairs and chesterfields.

I realized then how wise Number 1 had been in voluntarily tearing up the securities. And I smiled whenever I thought about Number 2, whom Great-Aunt called slow and stubborn, brilliantly choosing his new name.

10

MID-SEPTEMBER BROUGHT REPORTS from Beijing. Another massive Red Guard rally had been reviewed by Chairman Mao and Lin Biao, minister of national defense, who had praised the Guards' nationwide beatings, lootings and burnings. "The direction of your action has always been correct," Lin Biao said. He applauded their revolutionary battles against reactionary scholastic authorities, "bourgeois blood-suckers" and "capitalist roaders who operated in a socialist environment but took the capitalist path in their thinking and policies."

Within a week the attacks of the Red Guards had veered in the new direction, aiming at capitalist roaders. Families in our lane, whose goods had been put under seal to be hauled away, waited for weeks, but the trucks didn't arrive. The guards had lost interest. Some of the braver neighbors began to unpack their "confiscated" belongings.

Meanwhile the railway station in downtown Shanghai was jammed with trains from other provinces, each car crammed with enthusiasts who had come to "exchange revolutionary experience" in a city they would otherwise never have had a chance to visit. These interlopers demanded free food and accommodation as well as unrestricted access to public buses, school campuses, office buildings and even some private homes. Neighborhood committees supplied thousands of steamed buns to the young travelers. At the same time the Red Guards from Shanghai boarded every available train and ship bound for Beijing, leaving paid passengers stranded in stations and on docks. The city authorities met every request laid down by the Guards lest they be branded as capitalist roaders.

With Mao and Lin Biao fanning the flames, the Cultural Revolution began to burn like a fire out of control. Authorities in offices and factories who had provided the Red Guards with information on the class backgrounds of their employees now found themselves sweeping floors and scraping out toilets with those they had helped to denounce. Abandoning their livestock and neglecting their crops, peasants flooded into the cities demanding bonuses and benefits. The supply of produce in our local market dwindled and I began to fear that the "three hungry years" we had barely survived would return. Workers took to the streets. While the rest of us idled at home, Number 2 struggled in factional battles with the Rebels who had vowed to seize power from the city government. All across the city, factory production declined rapidly.

In mid-October I walked to school to collect my monthly ¥9 welfare allowance, worried that the collapse of the school system would paralyze my stipend. Except for a few girls skipping in the yard, there was nothing going on. Nervously, I entered the office and asked the accountant, a pleasant, gray-haired woman in her fifties, about my stipend.

"Don't worry, Xiao Ye, the teachers are still getting paid even though there are no classes, so why shouldn't you get your welfare allowance?"

As she counted out the cash she added, her voice low, "Did you hear? Poor Old Uncle Zhang's ashes are still in a box in the cow-shed where he hung himself. No one has claimed them."

Old Uncle Zhang was not the only one. In those days, if I was surprised at the speed with which my neighbors adapted to the many suicides, I was totally shocked by the way they talked about them in public. They sounded as if they were telling a thrilling story or describing a scene from the movies. Our neighbor Big Fatty calmly related one day that he had almost become a "cushion for a flying-down person" who had thrown himself from a highrise on Nanjing Road. Bloated corpses were fished out of the Huangpu River; people gassed themselves; others jumped from high windows, leaving their blood and guts hanging on windowframes or ledges that projected from the buildings.

All suicides were condemned by the authorities as "alienating oneself from the Party and the people." The papers announced that the victims deserved to be dead, in a messy way. At fourteen I could hardly imagine what would drive a person to take his or her own life. But I soon discovered.

Even though the new political wind had put capitalist roaders at the top of the hate list, relegating bourgeois families like ours to second place, I was still shocked when Number 1 announced one evening that he and seven other students at the university had formed a musical band, Spreading Mao Ze-dong Thought Group, and planned to go to Beijing. "We've even made ourselves red armbands," he added.

Their choice of name, he explained, would keep them safe from harm. All of them were from capitalist families, so they could not call themselves Red Guards. But the name of their band was ideal. It echoed the ubiquitous posters: "Making Mao Ze-dong Thought known to everyone and every household is a sacred duty of each Chinese citizen."

He had somehow managed to save his clarinet from the fire at the university — Western musical instruments were destroyed by the Guards — and that night I heard him practising out on the terrace. The clarinet stopped; and he started to sing.

The vast universe and boundless land
Are not as great as the kindness of the Communist Party.
The love of your mother and father
Is not as deep as that of Chairman Mao for you.

"How can you possibly utter those words after all we've been through?" I yelled through the open window. "What has Chairman Mao's love done for us?"

Number 3 rushed over and dragged me away. "Are you out of your mind, Ah Si? Someone might hear you! Why are you angry at him? They're just songs, empty words. They don't mean any more than anything else nowadays. Come on, you'll get us all in trouble."

That was typical of my elder sister. Nothing mattered to her as long as the sky didn't fall down. Number 1 left for Beijing the next day with his clarinet hidden in his bag.

At home, life was dull, the days long and uneventful. Only Number 2 and Great-Aunt came and went. There was no school to attend, no homework to do. We three girls were too young to attend the neigborhood meetings with Great-Aunt, and because of the factional wars, the streets were dangerous and unpredictable. Libraries and movie houses (which we couldn't afford to go to in any case) were shut down. Even the radio offered no relief — only incessant propaganda announcements echoing the bulletins that blasted from loudspeakers mounted on poles along our lane.

We received no news from Number 1, even after a few weeks. I was worried about him — he was not street-smart — but I envied him his adventure. Desperate for something to do, I asked Great-Aunt to teach me needlepoint. I slept in mornings and took naps each afternoon.

Beijing continued to be a sea of political turmoil, with rallies so massive that they had to be divided between Tian An Men Square and the capital's airport while Mao, along with his wife, Jiang Qing, and Lin Biao, scuttled back and forth to "review" the waves of Red Guards from every province except Tibet. Hearing all this, I felt even more envious. All those teenage and young-adult Red Guards were able to travel to Beijing and see the country along the route. Never having traveled farther than Wuxi, I fantasized about taking the train to Beijing and visiting the palaces and temples I had heard so much about in school.

Late one night at the beginning of November, about three weeks after Number 1 had left, I heard someone calling my name from the lane. "Ah Si, Ah Si." Then another voice. "Ye Ting-xing!"

Great-Aunt sat up, startled. "The Red Guards!" she whispered. "What do they want?"

She scrambled to her feet and tottered to the window, throwing it open. Terrified, I squeezed in beside her, peering down into the darkness. I was barely able to make out two girls from my school, Xiu-fang and Guo-zheng, standing in the back-door lane.

"I know them," I said, relieved. "They're all right."

Both girls were members of the Peripheral Red Guards in my school because their parents had owned small stores, which made them capitalists of a sort. We had not been close before the Cultural Revolution but circumstances had given us something in common and they were among the few who had not been hostile to me.

I headed out of our apartment and downstairs before Great-Aunt had a chance to object, and as soon as I opened the back door, Xiu-fang said excitedly, "We thought you might want to join us." Each of them had a small bundle slung over her shoulder. "We're on our way to the railway station to catch a train to Beijing," said Guo-zheng.

I pulled them inside and closed the door. "How can I go to Beijing if I'm not even allowed to use the front gate at school?" I asked, knowing that you had to be "pure" to make the pilgrimage to the capital.

"There aren't many Red Guards at the station at this time of night," said Guo-zheng, pulling strips of red cloth from her pocket. "We can wear these until we get on the train. As soon as we are out of Shanghai, we'll be just as good as anyone else. Who'll know what our parents used to be?"

"Brilliant!" I exclaimed, excitement surging through me. I poked Guo-zheng's bundle. "What do you have in here?"

"Not much. My winter stuff and a change of clothes. My mother said it's much colder in Beijing."

Mention of her mother made me remember I had left Great-Aunt standing on her bed. How would I be able to convince her?

"Come upstairs," I said, "but wait for me in the hall."

Great-Aunt was sitting up in bed, and as soon as I entered the room she gave me a look that was only too familiar — the corners of her eyes curved downwards at the same degree as her mouth. Ignoring her scowl, I took a direct approach.

"Great-Aunt, I am going to Beijing. I am going no matter what you say."

"Is that what they are here for?" she shouted. "Are they missing an arm or a leg that they need you to help them travel? Or are they anxious to see you lose one of your limbs?"

Her outcry brought my two sisters rushing. "What's the matter?" Number 3 cried. "Have the Red Guards come back?"

"Your foolish sister wants to join them! She wants to go to Beijing! With two other brainless girls!"

Number 3 grabbed me by the shoulders and shook me hard. "Which one of your bones is itching, Ah Si?"

"I know where you should go," Number 5 piped up. "To the hospital, to get your head examined. Have you forgotten what Number 1 told us? It isn't safe for us to go out."

"And where is Number 1 now?" I countered.

All the remonstrations that followed brought to mind the scene when the five of us saw Auntie Yi-feng off at the bus stop after Mother's funeral. We couldn't afford even one train ticket to Wuxi, so Mother had had none of her children by her side when she was put into the ground. Now, here I was, able to travel all the way to Beijing with no need to pay a cent.

Great-Aunt began to recycle the washing-area gossip — the turmoil in the streets, the beatings, the suicides — in an attempt to scare my decision out of my head. She refused to provide me with winter clothes, warning that I would freeze to death in the frigid northern city she had never visited.

"That will be just fine with me," I told her stubbornly. "People in Beijing will not allow me to freeze to death. Didn't your newspaper readers tell you that the student-pilgrims are treated royally, as 'Chairman Mao's guests'?"

To support my point I called in Guo-zheng and Xiu-fang, who had been cooling their heels in the hall. Ignoring the embarrassed looks on their faces, I pointed at them. "Ask them if I need to take anything with me." Guo-zheng's mouth opened, then closed again without a sound. "You don't think their parents would let them go if it isn't safe, do you?" I argued, knowing I had scored a hit.

My two sisters fell silent as Great-Aunt got out of bed and hobbled to her dresser, saying nothing. That was typical of her. She knew that silence was the best medicine for my temper. When I saw her remove from a drawer her long woolen scarf and a pair of wool gloves I instantly wished I could take back everything I had said, even half of it, or that she would criticize my impertinence. I had never in my life acted like this, full of denial and allowing no discussion.

My eyes followed her every move, hoping she would ask me to help her. Silently she squeezed past me to the attic, where we stored our winter clothes. Number 3 helped her up the ladder. She let me stew in my own juice as she packed, playing her best game on me. Finally she spoke.

"Ah Si, take off your undershirt so I can sew a pocket on it."

She put one ¥5 note into the pocket along with some special food coupons that could be used anywhere in the country and secured it with two large safety pins. (Normal coupons could be used only in the area in which they were issued, a measure to prevent people from moving outside their designated area.)

"Don't ever take this shirt off," she warned. "And use the money and coupons only when necessary." She then took out her purse and gave me some small money and local food coupons. "Buy some bread at the train-station store in case you can't get food when you're traveling."

If anyone at that moment had said so much as a word to persuade me to stay I would have called the whole thing off. I had won the argument but didn't want the reward. Ashamed as I was, I would have traded anything for a hug from Great-Aunt. But it didn't happen. I couldn't remember a single occasion when Great-Aunt showed me any physical affection, though I knew she had deep feelings for me. Showing emotion even among family members was criticized as non-proletarian.

As I said goodbye to Great-Aunt and my sisters, I pledged to myself that as soon as I arrived in Beijing I would jump on a return train. I missed them already and held back tears, determined they would not see me cry. In the lane, I walked backwards, until the windows of our apartment disappeared.

The North Station square was almost empty, washed with pale fluorescent light, forbidding and cold. Boldly we marched into the unguarded waiting room, passed the long rows of benches occupied by hundreds of sleeping men, women and children, and made our way to the platform. There the scene was totally different. People milled around in a hubbub. Loudspeakers pumped out train numbers, schedules and advice to travelers. Passengers hung out of train windows talking to those on the platform. No wonder the streets and the square are empty, I thought: everyone is here.

Guo-zheng stopped. She fished in her pocket and pulled out three red armbands. "Here, let's put these on now before we get to the train."

Mine said *Hong Wei Dong* — Red Defending the East, a suitably ambiguous slogan. East symbolized Chairman Mao, from the song "The East Is Red." I pocketed my black mourning band. The less personal information, the better.

We pushed our way the length of the platform, searching for the Beijing train, but were unable to find it. Every train was so packed that the doors could not be opened. The passengers seemed to have set up camp in the cars. Heads protruded from windows. Some people busily brushed their teeth, spitting onto the tracks, which were littered with garbage. Some of the trains had been stranded in the station for days because the railway lines were all blocked, particularly north of Nanjing. The railroad was trying in vain to accommodate the mammoth flow of traffic to the capital as factional wars among the railroad workers added to the chaos. Their posters covered the walls of the station. Some were even glued to the ceilings.

We continued to stroll around, now willing to take any train so long as it was heading north. We found one and begged the passengers to let us in through the windows. Some rejected us, telling us there was no room, even the aisles were full. Some asked us to fetch fresh water as the price of entry, then refused us after we had complied. We were not strong enough to force our way in and, being very small for my age, I had to stand on my toes just to reach the windowsill of the train. The air was punctuated by screams as people attempted to climb through the narrow windows, which were no bigger than one foot high and two feet wide.

Xiu-fang's constant complaining got on my nerves. By this time I wanted nothing more than to go to sleep. When we all sat down around one of the pillars, I put my head on my knees and drifted off.

"Ah Si, wake up!" I awoke, startled, cold and disoriented, and heard a shrill whistle nearby. I jumped to my feet. It was four o'clock in the morning.

"A train is leaving!" Guo-zheng too jumped up. Suddenly the area became a war zone as those around us snatched up their belongings and surged toward the departing train.

"Quick! This is our chance!" Guo-zheng shouted above the din, pointing to a stationary train on the other side of the platform. Passengers were rushing out of the coaches and heading for the moving train.

Xiu-fang crouched down and I got onto her shoulders. When she struggled to her feet, lifting me higher, I was clutched by hands stretched from the window, then turned horizontal and passed like a small plank into the train. My two schoolmates were hauled in after me.

We found ourselves in a car jammed to the walls with bodies. All the benches were full, the aisles were blocked with seated passengers, recumbent forms occupied the spaces under the seats. The only space left for me was the luggage rack. I climbed up and lay on my back, my face inches from the curved ceiling. The train was hot, the air a stew of odors: unwashed bodies, cigarette smoke, urine. Wrinkling my nose and reflecting that Great-Aunt would have a fit in this fetid air, I made a pillow of my bundle and fell asleep.

When I awoke it was light, and the train was in motion. I panicked, unaware of where I was, and banged my head. Stars spun before my eyes.

"We're moving!" I yelled. "Where are we?"

"Why shouldn't we be moving?" a gruff voice below me responded. "We're in a train." Laughter followed. "We'll be in Wuxi soon."

Wuxi! I lay back, staring at the ceiling, and began to think. I was already so homesick I would gladly have jumped down from the train and walked back home. Then a thought struck me. Why couldn't I detrain at Wuxi and make my way to my grandparents' house in Qingyang? I could visit my parents' grave. I hadn't seen my grandparents for more than seven mostly bad years.

Clutching the bars of the luggage rack and poking my head downwards, I caught the attention of an older, tough-looking girl sitting next to the window.

"Is it possible to get off at Wuxi station?"

"Why?" she frowned at me. "Don't you want to go to Beijing and see Chairman Mao?"

Her tone of voice and red armband reminded me of the purpose of my mission. My instinct warned me to be careful.

"Of course," I said. "But I understand this train is only going to Nanjing and —"

"So? That doesn't mean we can't get to Beijing." She stood up and looked at me closely, her voice softer. "How old are you? Are you traveling alone?"

"Fourteen," I answered. "I am in the third year of middle school."

"I'm seventeen, from Yang Pu District. Which district are you from?"

"Jing An. I'm from Ai Guo Girls' School."

I felt someone tapping my feet. It was Guo-zheng, who glared meaningfully. Yang Pu was a working-class district. Most of its residents originally came from Su Bei, a poverty-stricken section of Jiangsu Province, and were looked down upon by other Shanghainese. This girl would thus be a genuine Red Guard. I had blabbed that I came from Jing An District, an area full of people with bad-class background. No wonder Guo-zheng had tried to stop me. All troubles came from the mouth, Great-Aunt would have said.

"Yes, I have heard of your district." I wished I had bumped my head harder so I wouldn't have started this conversation.

"I want to trade places with you," Guo-zheng interrupted.

I climbed down, stepped across the seat backs and was directed to the rack across the aisle. Obviously moving me was Guo-zheng's way of shutting me up. I would not tell her of my plan to get off the train far short of our destination.

If it had not been for the sign I would never have recognized Wuxi station, even though I had seen it many times in my early childhood years. As we drew slowly to a halt people swarmed onto the platform and began to pound at the doors and windows, screaming that they wanted to get in. The chaotic scene frightened me. Nobody dared to open the windows, even though, with the train still and no ventilation, the coach became so stifling that it was difficult to draw a breath. To open the window would be like breaching a dike. I changed my plan, horrified at the thought of trying to climb down into that desperate crowd, and made up my mind to detrain in Wuxi on my way back from Beijing.

An hour or so later, the besieged train inched out of the station.

I dozed the rest of the afternoon away and it was almost dark when we reached Nanjing. The railway workers told us to dismount: it was the end of the line and the train needed to be serviced.

Guo-zheng, Xiu-fang and I decided to stick around the station rather than follow the other pilgrims into the city to see the sights, rest in free accommodations and eat free meals. We were joined by the girl I had spoken to earlier. She had had herself named Yang-yang — Bright Sun — a stylish appellation at the time. Her father had originally called her Zhao Di — Waiting for Brothers. Compared with me, she was tall, at least five-foot-eight, and she outweighed me three times over.

Before I did anything else I had to visit the washroom. The four of us pushed through the wall of clamorous travelers, and when we finally made it, I realized one of the unpleasant results of hundreds of thousands of human beings in a confined space. Unlike most public bathrooms, this one was large, with one sink and two rows of cubicles separated from one another by waist-high walls. The "toilet" was a wide slot in the floor, periodically sluiced by water that flowed under all the cubicles and emptied into a cistern. There was no water in the tap in this stinking and fly-infested place and every toilet was plugged by a pile of human dung that rose above the level of the floor, which was wet with urine. When I stepped carefully into a cubicle, I gagged at the sight and the putrid smell. But desperate times call for desperate measures.

Back outside, we walked along the rails beside the coaches, begging entry to the northbound train, bribing the occupants with what little food we had and fetching water for them. At last we met a sympathetic Red Guard who helped drag me in through the window after Yang-yang lifted me up. But Xiu-fang was heavy and clumsy, and after numerous pushings and pullings she fell in a heap onto the track, screaming in pain and clutching her right ankle.

One of the passengers gave Guo-zheng directions to the station's clinic. I tried to climb down to join them.

"No, no. You stay," Guo-zheng shouted up to me. "Keep a place for us when we get back."

She returned half an hour later, but without Xiu-fang. After Yang-yang and I had hauled her in through the window, she gave us her report.

"The doctor said Xiu-fang has to have her ankle x-rayed because it's probably broken. He assured me that the clinic will treat her as one of Chairman Mao's guests."

It was far past midnight when our train was severed into parts and shunted onto the ferry for the ride across the Yangtze River. By then I had stretched out on the luggage rack. When dawn broke, I awoke to find we were still in Jiangsu Province. By then my feet had swelled so badly my shoelaces had burst and the coach was so crowded I could not climb down to relieve the pressure.

Yang-yang became our big sister. Her long legs and strong arms served us well. When the train stopped at a station, she would jump down onto the platform, fetch water for us and collect a few of the steamed buns the locals had made to show their support for the Red Guards. Whenever she praised me in front of the other passengers, calling me a "tiny pea full of mountain-high revolutionary spirit and steel-iron determination to see Chairman Mao," I felt guilty, for I had lied to her, telling her my parents were workers at Number 13 Textile Factory near our home. Flat on my back on the hardwood racks, I wondered if I was going to live the rest of my life telling fibs.

I began to lose track of time on the slow, endless journey, frequently interrupted by stops. Every part of my body ached. My pigtails had absorbed the odor of urine in the car and I feared I could never wash my hair clean again. At long last the train drew to a halt and someone yelled, "We're here! We're in Beijing!"

A deafening cheer followed and people began to gather their belongings, bumping and banging into one another in pandemonium. I was for the first time glad to be up on the racks, above the crush. Windows were thrown up. Bundles were tossed out, followed by bodies, crawling, jumping, falling from the train. But there were no gongs and drums to greet us as I had expected.

It was shortly after midnight, and Yang-yang, practical as always, suggested we stay on the train until morning. But the train workers ordered us off, telling us PLA soldiers were waiting to take us to our destination. We were not in the center depot as I had presumed, but in the southern suburb at Yong Ding Men station. But I was in Beijing! Only momentarily did I reflect on the irony that it was the hated Cultural Revolution that had given me the opportunity for unpaid travel to the ancient capital, a place I might otherwise never have seen.

II

OR THE FIRST TIME in our journey, I used the door of the train. Shivering in the cold, I made my way through the station, exhausted, hungry and aching in every limb, my laceless cotton shoes flapping on the cement. Outside stood long lines of army men, silent in their long cotton-padded coats and hats with long earflaps.

We marched to a nearby park where we stood a long time in the dark, some jumping up and down to keep warm, until army trucks arrived to carry us away and deposit us before a complex of large, mostly unlit buildings. There we were herded into a spacious, dimly lit room, and instructed to sleep on the floor. I did so gladly.

I dreamt I was at my school, standing before a brick wall under the relentless midday sun. But I awoke to find myself wrapped in a blanket, though fully clothed in my cotton-padded pants and coat with Great-Aunt's knitted wool scarf around my head and neck. I was sandwiched between two shapeless forms, motionless under green blankets.

"Yang-yang? Guo-zheng?" I whispered, shaking the body beside me.

The body turned my way. I jumped to my feet in terror. I had been sleeping with a man! I looked around in a panic. I knew nothing about where babies came from — except that even as a child I understood the significance of men and women "sleeping together." I had overheard adults' conversations and had listened as kids at school related stories in which rape was referred to as "sleeping with flower girls." Babies were the result. I had never asked Great-Aunt for details because I knew she would not provide them and I dared not ask others for fear of being accused of having dirty thoughts, the worst kind of criticism for a girl. So I pictured the process as some kind of chemical reaction, like the one I studied in physics where a dog salivated when shown food. Was I going to have a baby?

Terrified, I yelled for Yang-yang and Guo-zheng. All over the room heads popped up; eyes stared; caustic voices shushed me.

"I'm sorry," I announced to no one in particular as I stepped over the sleeping forms between me and my friends. After a few moments of whispering, they assuaged my fear.

A little while later an officer strode into the warehouse. PLA officers did not distinguish themselves from enlisted personnel by wearing insignia, braided ropes, medals or epaulets — just by four pockets on their olive drab Sun Zhong-shan jackets (named after Dr. Sun Yat-sen) as opposed to the regular two. This officer was in his thirties, tall and bulky, and when he saw me a string of words rolled off his "tightly curved tongue," as southerners describe northerners' speech.

"What did you say?" I asked in my Shanghai-flavored *pu-tong-hua*.

He smiled and spoke more slowly. We were in the compound of the General Political Department of the PLA, he said, and were requested to attend a meeting in the canteen across the basketball ground. Breakfast would be ready when we got there.

The name of the army unit rang a bell. It was the same unit Mother had tried to get me into three years earlier as a singer and dancer. Thinking of Mother sent a pang of homesickness through me.

With my two friends, I made my way across the courtyard toward the canteen, shadowed by the biggest buildings I had ever seen. In those days a five-story structure was considered a highrise in China. We were given two enamel bowls, one for hot rice gruel, the other for steamed buns. To my amazement I didn't have to show any identification to get my food. No money, no coupons were required. No wonder those around me stuffed themselves so full they could hardly walk around. It reminded me of what I had been taught at school about real communism: from each according to his ability to each according to his need.

Cheered by the hot food, we listened as the officer formally welcomed us and then, inevitably, set down rules. Once a person had participated in a rally, he or she had to vacate the capital within forty-eight hours because of the overwhelming number of youngsters arriving in Beijing each day. We were here to "exchange revolutionary experience," the officer admonished, not to sightsee and stuff ourselves with free food. Each of us was issued a free bus pass, good for the whole city.

I was overpowered by the feeling that, at fourteen, I was in control of my own life for the first time. Food and lodgings were free; I could go anywhere I wanted in our nation's capital, a place my parents had talked about but never seen. I decided to enjoy this freedom as long as it lasted. Awed by my sense of independence and discovery, I walked out the gate with my two friends. It was a bright sunny day, but without an overcoat I was chilly, even in the sun. The streets, lined with leafless trees, seemed empty compared to crowded Shanghai.

Yang-yang said goodbye to me and Guo-zheng at the corner of Hongguang Road, which on the map was Baiguang Road. "White" had been replaced by the favored "Red." All over China the Red Guards had renamed the streets. I had even heard stories about attempts to alter traffic lights so that red meant go and green meant stop.

Guo-zheng and I wanted to visit Tian An Men Square to see the Gate of Heavenly Peace, which was described in one of my nursery rhymes as "red brick walls and yellow glazed tiles; tall and gigantic, beautiful and magnificent."

Hunching our shoulders against the chill, we followed the twists and turns of the alleyways and found ourselves on Changan Avenue. I felt like a fish swimming in a sea of red and yellow. The citizens of Beijing had responded to the call to make the capital a "sea of red" by writing Mao's quotations in red paint on a yellow background, plastering walls and buildings with slogans and exhortations. As I walked along past the roughly painted walls and hastily written slogans, I wondered whether people in the city had ever run out of red and yellow paint.

China's broadest and most elegant avenue was lined with bare trees and temporary latrines, constructed of bamboo poles with woven bamboo mats wired to them to the height of my head. Inside the bamboo enclosures, cement paving squares had been lifted and pits dug. These were the revolutionary toilets. When full, they were covered over with earth and the squares put back where they belonged. The area was slick with frozen urine. Clearly the influx of millions of Red Guards created more than just political problems.

The red walls of the Forbidden City were papered over with *da-zi-bao*. The Palace Museum itself was, to my disappointment, closed, because sightseeing was discouraged as unrevolutionary. Guo-zheng and I sat on the broad steps of the Great Hall of the People and rested in the sun. Later, tired, we returned to the barracks.

Our newly assigned room had once been someone's office. Six bunks lined one wall. After another hot and generous meal, the officer in charge asked us all to state our class background and report on our day's activity in the "heart city" of our country. I prepared myself to lie again when my turn came. I was stunned when one girl told the group that she was from a shopkeeper's family. How could she be so stupid? I thought. Surely she would have trouble heaped upon her?

But no one showed any resentment. I realized that here, too, the "capitalist roader" had taken over as the number-one class enemy. I began to relax a little, but lied anyway when it was my turn, reporting that I had spent the entire day closely studying the *da-zi-bao* on the walls of the Forbidden City.

Yang-yang, fervent as she was, read out the accusations she had copied down at Qinghua University. The most dramatic and shocking of these attacked Liu Shao-qi, president and second man after Chairman Mao. He was declared the number-one capitalist roader, China's Khrushchev (a caustic insult), a revisionist who aimed to change the nature of communism. Worse than all this political denunciation was the information from his private life.

According to Yang-yang's notes, Liu Shao-qi had married five times. She had written down the details of each failed marriage. There were even cartoons of Liu and his latest wife on the posters. I listened, gaping, as she gave out information that until then had been treated almost as a military secret. Any gossip about the personal life of any of our leaders was a sure road to severe criticism and punishment. It had been revealed only recently that Mao Ze-dong himself had a young wife named Jiang Qing and, although people were naturally curious about her, no one dared speculate about Mao's personal life. Ordinary citizens like me lived in an environment where we had to provide every detail of our personal and family history for several generations back, yet in this society where the word privacy did not, literally, exist, the impression had been given that state leaders led the life of nuns or monks. But if the president's life could now be turned inside out like a dirty sock, I wondered, who would be safe?

The afternoon following Yang-yang's scathing report, the women's bathhouses opened. It had been almost a week since I had washed in warm water and I rushed to line up. Two hours later, after a long shower in gloriously hot water, Guo-zheng and I decided to go out and have a treat: candied haw berries, famous in Beijing. My hair was still wet, and soon I had icicles clicking at my ears. I paid dearly for this foolishness. That night I developed a high fever and ran from one nightmare to another. My own screaming woke me up, and in the morning Guo-zheng fetched a doctor. My temperature was around forty degrees and I was taken to the infirmary on a stretcher.

If the plentiful food at the canteen was a luxury, the hospital was paradise. The ward was much brighter and cleaner than those I had seen when visiting Mother. There were five beds in the room besides mine, all filled. My bed was like a cloud. I lay on a spring mattress and bounced up and down on it. The nurses were friendly and kind, so different from people in the outside world where it seemed to me that, perhaps because the army had kept out of the political movements, yelling and shouting filled our everyday life.

When I had recovered several days later and began to eat again, I was even offered a choice of food. What an easy life. Great-Aunt would have said, "Hold out your arms and you will be dressed; open your mouth and you will be fed." At night we patients were entertained by a song and dance troupe.

One day after I had left the infirmary I learned at the evening meeting that there would be a big rally at the airport the next day. We would see Chairman Mao with our own eyes, the officer enthused. Preparations must be made and, of course, new rules laid down.

First, we were paired up at random, each partner under the other's responsibility and scrutiny — a common surveillance technique. No one was allowed to leave the compound until the morning, when we would all depart for the rally together. No pocketknives or sharp metal tools were permitted. And while marching we should never, ever try to pick up anything we had dropped, or we might never stand up again. Each of us was issued a pair of extra-long shoelaces and instructed on how to bind them tightly around the insteps, since the thousands of trampling feet around us might grind our heels and pull off our shoes. Not only would the lacing technique prevent us from injury or even death, it would aid the cleaners who usually faced mountains of lost shoes when the rally was over. On the way out of the canteen everyone was to be given a paper bag holding two boiled eggs and two fat steamed buns stuffed with pickled vegetables.

To my surprise, I could barely contain my excitement. I was going to see Chairman Mao in person! I had seen his picture all my life, staring at me from walls, buses and store windows. In real life I saw people aging or even dying, most of them much younger than Mao; but he, in my eyes, was like the immortals I read about in fairy tales, never one day older, with the same smile and the same mole under his mouth. The songs and slogans called him the sun, the rescuing star of our universe. I wondered if my fate would change after I saw him in person. I concluded, before I fell asleep with all the singing and excited talk around me, that this rally was going to make a difference in my life.

Before we were allowed to climb into the military trucks early the next morning, my partner and I, a girl from Anhui Province, searched each other in front of another pair, then reversed roles with them. After an hour's jouncing along the cold streets, we were dropped off about three miles from the airport and ordered to form ranks. We marched eight in a row under a cloudy sky, scrutinized by PLA soldiers and officers, singing our revolutionary songs. Even the fierce wind from the northwest wasn't too bad. Compared to my night parade in Shanghai months before, this one was a picnic.

Bright chalk lines divided the tarmac at the airport into squares. There wasn't an airplane in sight. Each square could hold at least thirty rows of twelve spectators. The sun was peeking from behind the clouds when we sat down, according to instruction, on the icy cement, cross-legged, like the soldiers in front of us. Because of my short stature I was in the second row, so I should get a good view. We were required to remain seated throughout the rally so everyone could see, and under no circumstances were we to rush the motorcade.

At noon, I broke out my food, peeling chilled eggs under the envious eyes of those who had eaten theirs earlier. Although the steamed buns were now hard as a rock, I didn't dare drink too much water to soften them. There were toilets, but they were far from us and no one knew exactly when Chairman Mao would appear.

It got colder. My bottom was like a block of ice and my legs grew numb. I received permission from a soldier in front of me to kneel to ease my cramped limbs. Hours of singing and reading from the Red Book crept by. I yawned and shifted my position, my enthusiasm dampened by boredom.

Suddenly, from far away, came the rumble of engines, then hysterical chanting — "Long live Chairman Mao!" — roared in the sky. One minute I was slapping my numb legs to warm them, the next I was on my feet yelling at the top of my lungs like everyone else.

"Long live Chairman Mao!" I shouted, my voice lost in the waves of sound.

Tears streamed from my eyes. The motorcade was moving toward us. Peering between the soldiers in front of me, I got a brief glimpse of a jeep. There was Mao's wife, Jiang Qing! And Lin Biao stood beside her! They were waving their Red Books, but their faces were pale and unsmiling. Frantically I searched for Chairman Mao. In another jeep I saw Liu Shao-qi, dressed in army fatigues, looking worn down and disturbed. I recalled what Yang-yang had told us about him. My eyes followed his grim form until it disappeared, and I wondered how such a powerful man could be attacked just like the teachers in my school and the neighbors in my lane back home.

It was then that I realized I had missed Chairman Mao. I closed my eyes and covered my face with my hands, feeling cheated and lost.

On the way back through streets jammed with marching youngsters and loaded trucks, although exhausted from ten hours of walking and waiting in the cold, I hid my disappointment. Everyone was excited, telling each other how clearly he or she had seen Chairman Mao, how healthy he looked, how kind he appeared, how lucky they were. Some could not wait to get back to the barracks: they wrote down their impressions as the truck bounced through the streets, overwhelmed by the sense that they had participated in the making of history.

I joined them enthusiastically, using my imagination, unwilling to admit that I hadn't seen the Chairman at all even though I had been in the second row. If everyone else had seen him, so had I. That was what I was going to say to everyone, including my siblings and Great-Aunt. That night when I told Guo-zheng that I had also seen Liu Shao-qi, she covered my mouth with her hand, fearing I would cause trouble again. Yang-yang pointed out that he had been in the last jeep. We all knew what that meant.

Early the next morning after our last free meal, we were trucked to the train station. I had already changed my plan to stop at Wuxi. I never thought I could miss Great-Aunt so much.

12

JANUARY 1967, THE FIRST anniversary of Mother's death, ushered in another year of turmoil. More state leaders were denounced and detained, and Chairman Mao urged the whole nation to seize power from the capitalist roaders who "were still in the bourgeois headquarters across the country." Confused as they were by Mao's inexact call to arms, the people of Shanghai took a lead. On January 4, the Shanghai Workers Revolutionary Rebels overthrew the municipal government, which had, so the radio broadcast, "turned rotten to its roots." The coup was headed by a textile-factory security officer named Wang Hong-wen, who in turn was directed by Zhang Chun-qiao. Zhang was a longtime associate of Jiang Qing from her early days in the theatre and ultimately head of the Cultural Revolution Authority for the entire country. Jiang Qing, Wang and Zhang, joined by a well-known left-wing writer, Yao Wen-yuan, later formed the notorious "Gang of Four."

The "January Storm" in Shanghai brought great trouble to our doorstep. Number 2, being a member of the defeated Loyalist faction, was swept up in the subsequent purge. The newly ensconced Shanghai Revolutionary Committee had received the blessing of the Chairman himself and it went about housecleaning with a vengeance. Soon the majority of Loyalists, after criticism and self-criticism, were identified as "good people but misled" due to their "simple but pure class feeling toward the Party." But that was not the case for Number 2. He was set up as an example of those who were "secretly supporting the old municipal government while showing their resentment of the Cultural Revolution led by our great Chairman Mao" — in other words, my brother was labeled anti-Mao, a deadly charge. He was forced to sweep the floor and scrub toilets alongside former factory authorities during the day and to submit to merciless condemnation at evening rallies. The cleaning during the day was actually easier than his job dyeing rubber, and he continued to receive his salary; it was the public humiliation of the "struggle meetings" that hurt most.

One night when he had been allowed to come home for clean clothes, I could tell that Number 2 was scared.

"Some people," he said, "have been beaten to death by their fellow workers in the struggle meetings, especially in factories involved in military projects."

I was horror-struck. "You mean the same might happen to you?"

He shrugged his thin shoulders. "I don't know."

The Red Terror ushered in the spring. Fighting among the factions broke out everywhere, each group claiming to be more revolutionary than the next. Factories, government offices, research institutions and communes had turned into battlegrounds of hatred. The streets on the outskirts of Shanghai rang with gunfire. The history I learned at school was no longer a theoretical study: the Communists' struggle to eliminate all classes other than the proletarian had escalated. Chairman Mao continuously harangued us that this last fight was *Ni-si-wo-huo* — You die; I live. The bare fists and bronze belt buckles used by the Red Guards were now replaced by iron rods, steel bars and bullets. The entire nation was in an uproar, and cruelty ruled.

And then Chairman Mao did what many thought he would never do. Until now the PLA had remained neutral, kept out of the

Cultural Revolution. But when Mao was notified that in some areas of the country the rebels had not been successful, while in others the fighting was out of control, he relented and ordered in the army. The army's involvement made the muddy waters muddier. And it brought Commander-in-Chief Lin Biao into prominence as Mao's number-two man.

Was this how I was going to spend the rest of my life — hiding at home, fearing for the safety of myself and my family, watching my future dissolve? The days dragged by, but my sleep was filled with nightmares, especially when Number 2 was forced to fight in the streets again, for the PLA had at last moved into Shanghai to oust a powerful faction in the Shanghai Diesel Engine Factory. The battle raged for three days. This time, the losers were not simply arrested or set to humiliating tasks; they were killed.

A week or so later a letter arrived from Auntie Yi-feng. As we deciphered her unpunctuated sentences and characters with bits missing, we had our worst fears confirmed. The fighting had spread strife throughout the countryside, the peasants were at war, and my paternal grandfather was right in the middle. He was attacked because he used to be a businessman and had owned a plot of land. First his house in Qingyang was confiscated and he and Grandmother were left with only one room while other families moved in. Next the rebels slaughtered his chickens, rabbits and goats to "cut off his capitalist tail," that is, deprive him of his sideline. When he tried to stop the crazed rebels from flattening the "bourgeois" grave mounds of his mother, his first wife and my parents, he was so badly beaten that he had to be carried home on a door, and had been confined to bed ever since. Not long after, Grandfather died of his injuries.

He was cremated against his and Grandmother's will. The rosewood coffin he had had made when he was fifty was broken up by the rebels and sold for making furniture. Preparing one's own funeral long ahead was traditional, and many believed that the better provided you were, the later the funeral would occur. I had seen Great-Aunt making her tiny red silk burial shoes even before she retired, each with a ladder stitched on the sole to help her climb to heaven. The Red Guards had labeled this tradition both feudalistic and bourgeois — such contradictory labeling didn't seem to bother them — and punished it severely. Granny Ningbo had been made to walk down our lane wearing all her burial outfit, followed by jeering children, then to burn the clothing in a bonfire. She died soon after the humiliation. I wondered, in Grandfather's case, how great a part humiliation had played in his death, as he was a well-known and highly respected resident of Qingyang before the rebels attacked him.

By 1968 the country's productivity had dropped alarmingly. In the countryside, Auntie Yi-feng wrote, crops were neglected or not sown at all. "Better to have proletarian weeds than capitalist seeds," screamed the posters. Hunger began to stalk the country again.

No doubt prompted by the chaos across China, Mao declaimed, "Grasp revolution in one hand, boost productivity with the other," and called upon youths to "resume classes while continuing to make revolution." In May, after two years of idleness, I received a letter authorized by the Mao Ze-dong Thought Propaganda Team calling me back to school.

I did as ordered, full of apprehension that the Red Guards would harass me again. The school was then in the hands of the Propaganda Team, composed of workers, none of them qualified to run a school. Their leader asked the teachers and students to address her as Master Ma. There was no sign whatever that classes would resume as the letter had said. The teachers who had survived the cruel attacks from their own students and colleagues did not care to work. The students, after two years of challenging authority and humiliating their teachers, found it hard to sit down again. Most of our textbooks had been labeled "poisonous weeds," but there were no new ones to replace them.

So, despairing that I would never get an education and try the university exams, I fell into my old practice of reading newspapers and studying Mao's quotations. Not long after the recall, I found out the real reason for it: we were all — the entire school population — being graduated in July! There were to be no exams: they had been abolished as "bourgeois tools" used to eliminate working-class children by barring them from higher learning. We had to leave the school to make room for younger ones like my little sister, who had never been to a middle school but was going to be a second-year student as soon as she walked in the door, and graduate a year later. "I won't even have time to warm my seat in my new school," she scoffed.

After barely two years of proper middle-school education, I graduated, two years ahead of schedule, at sixteen. My dream of going to university went up in smoke, for I would not be able to apply. To make things even more ridiculous, while I and others were "waiting for work," we were required to report to our school every day, but there were no classes! We sat around talking and playing cards.

I was now confronted with a harsh and unexpected reality and it frightened me: I must become a worker.

Since all jobs were filled according to the government's design, there was no such thing as applying for a position. A graduate of secondary school who did not go to university simply waited until the government assigned him or her a job. Those with connections "used the back door" to land favorable assignments, the most coveted of all being in the army because of its social status and security. Sick at heart, I filled out the official form, at the top of which, of course, was "political fitness," that is, class background. I also had to list all my siblings, with their ages, occupations and addresses.

What terrified me most was a new government policy, supposedly an effort to relieve the burden of urban population: one child from each family must move to the countryside and remain there for the rest of his or her life. Students who were the only child in their family were safe, guaranteed a job in the city, and those with siblings already working outside Shanghai had winners' smiles on their faces.

If the government had wanted to cause conflict in families, it couldn't have picked a better method. No one born in an urban area would ever voluntarily give up his or her city residency and live in the country, for country living in China was a life of hardship and deprivation. Now, long before we expected, both Number 3 and I had become middle-school graduates. Since Number 1 was still at university, Number 2 already had a job in Shanghai and Number 5 had just become a middle-school student, either my older sister or I would have to leave the city and live the life of a peasant until she died.

How I wished time would stop. I counted every hour until October when the ax would fall on the "graduates" of my year. I reminded myself of Great-Aunt's saying that a boat carried in the river's current would always straighten itself out before it came to the bridge. But I wasn't so sure. The battles in families intensified as siblings fought like enemies. One of my classmates, who had walked out on her adoptive parents and denounced them as capitalist blood-suckers, now realized that when she returned to her biological family, where she had siblings, she had given up her "only child" status for an uncertain future. She feared she would be the one chosen to go to the countryside. She begged forgiveness from her adoptive parents, but they were brokenhearted and refused to take her back.

I had no one to share my troubles with or to advise me. Great-Aunt never liked to talk over problems; she relied on her homily about the boat. My older brothers had replaced my parents in so many ways, but I didn't want to burden them. Whatever they decided between Number 3 and me would leave one of us bitter and disappointed. They had been through that kind of anguish themselves. Some of my classmates came to school with horror stories of their parents' suffering, wracked with guilt and indecision when they had to pick one of their children to send away. I desperately missed my father's guidance, and yet I couldn't forget Mother's agony when she had to choose which of her sons was going to sacrifice his university education.

The tension in our home grew to be unbearable. No one would discuss our dilemma. More than once I wished that a big fight would break out to clear the air. Maybe family conflict could be helpful at times. But after many years of growing closer together because of the death of our parents and our suffering in political storms, we could not face a clash.

In mid-October I was called back to the office and confronted by Master Wang, a worker from a nearby refrigeration-equipment factory who was part of the Propaganda Team. He informed me officially that it was time for me to give an answer. Would I or my elder sister be the one to leave? I begged him to make an exception for us, saying that both I and Number 3 were needed at home to take care of our baby sister, as we had no parents.

"As far as I am concerned," he said firmly, "all three of you should go. Children like you, spoiled rotten by your bourgeois parents, ought to be sent away to see the real world. Yes, that is what I am going to recommend."

His pen hovered over the official form.

I stood there crying, stung by every word and terrified by this threat, my mind numbed with panic.

"I'll go," I stammered. "I'll be the one. But please leave my two sisters in Shanghai!"

"You'll go at the first opportunity?"

"Yes!"

With that one word, I sealed my fate.

I rushed from the school and ran to Number 3's school, more than a mile away, frantic to get there before she too was forced to "agree" to go to the countryside. There I signed a paper in front of Number 3's teacher and a member of her school's Propaganda Team, saying I was willing to go to the countryside. Number 3 knew nothing about it.

As I walked home I felt relieved, as if a heavy burden had dropped from my shoulders. Finally the tension that had been oppressing us would be broken. Many would have thought that Number 3 should have been the one to go because she was two years older. Certainly that was what Great-Aunt was hoping for, although she never said a word.

I had always felt guilty about Great-Aunt's favoritism and had occasionally hurt her feelings as a result. I wished she would treat us all equally, or show more concern to Number 5, who needed more help. My leaving Shanghai would hurt Great-Aunt deeply, and she would inevitably resent Number 3, but I was also aware that if I stayed and let Number 3 go, my conscience would give me no rest. The unspoken conviction that I was a bad person continued to haunt me and played no small part in my decision. I had wished for my Father's death; I was the least worthy of all his children and as such should be the first to leave home.

All the way home I tried to think up reasons to convince Great-Aunt that I should go to the countryside, hoping to reduce her resentment toward Number 3. That evening at dinner, when I announced my decision, I was greeted by silence. I didn't tell them about Master Wang's threats because I thought I would look stupid. Later I talked to Great-Aunt alone in her room.

"I should have known it would be you," she sighed, using her sleeve to wipe away a tear. "Ah Si, the dragon-year girl. If your mother had let me adopt you, you would be an only child and you could stay with me."

I tried to persuade her by saying that Number 3 would not be safe away from home because she was accident-prone. Hadn't she hurt herself three times in one year in her physical education class? The first time, she had chipped a front tooth; the second ended with five stitches in the chin; the third brought cerebral concussion and a trip to the hospital. How would she survive in the countryside? I argued.

As usual, reason was lost on Great-Aunt. "A clumsy person will be well taken care of," she said, "maybe even exempted from physical labor. But who will look after you, Ah Si?"

Master Wang wasted no time in getting me out of Shanghai. Two weeks later and in front of my fellow "graduates" he gave me two options: I could go to a rubber plantation on Hainan Island in the South China Sea, a place I had heard of but knew nothing about, or to a prison farm, far north of Shanghai in Jiangsu Province. I was shocked by the news no less than by his insistence on announcing it publicly.

He added acerbically, "Probably your father the 'capitalist rubber manufacturer' would have loved to see you working in a rubber plantation." His remark drew hoots of laughter from other girls. Before he left he said, "You have forty-eight hours to decide, or I will decide for you."

Though angered, what I felt most was panic. Why a prison farm? As far as I knew, all the graduates in the city were sent to the civilian farms on Chong Ming Island, a two-hour boat trip from the city. And why was I the only student in the school given forty-eight hours to come to a decision?

Our phys. ed. instructor, Teacher Chen, took me aside and said quietly that the reason I had become the first target was because my name was first on the school's welfare list. She added that if I refused to comply (as some others, backed by their parents, would), my monthly allowance would be cut off immediately. Even worse, Number 3 would not be assigned a job until I left the city.

For the first time in my sixteen years, I wished I had never been born into this world. I called the university and left an urgent message for Number 1 to come home. I needed his counsel badly. That night I told him I thought I should go to Hainan Island, my reason being that since it was tropical I would be spared the expense of winter clothing. Most of all, though, I was terrified at the thought of living with hardened criminals at the other place. While speaking to him, I lost control, where earlier I had refused to shed a single tear at school.

"Why would they want to send me to a prison farm?" I cried. "What have I done to deserve this?"

My family kept silent, not knowing what to say, and we all went to bed before dinner.

The next morning Number 1 told me to stay at home while he tried to find out more information. My other siblings went out too, leaving me alone with Great-Aunt, who had cried quietly the whole night through. Now she bustled around, pretending to be busy. Watching her, I realized how much I was going to miss her. I wished she would tell me how much she loved me and how she didn't want me to leave her.

By lunchtime Number 1 had returned with news. He had visited the Farm Management Bureau of East China Region and talked to a clerk there. The rubber plantation, he said, was in one of the poorest areas in China and had long suffered a devastating outbreak of hepatitis. That was one of the reasons new workers were being recruited. The prison farm was called Da Feng, Big Harvest, and was near the coast of the Yellow Sea. The farm had been established in the early 1950s to put away Guomindang prisoners; later it also became a labor camp for criminals.

"They are all minor offenders, Ah Si," Number 1 tried to reassure me. "And some of them have been sent there because of their dissolute lifestyle. They won't harm you so long as you keep away from them."

I had learnt from *da-zi-bao* that "dissolute lifestyle" referred to men who, like my great-grandfather, had had more than one wife, or to those who messed around with others' husbands and wives. Unmarried persons who had been caught "sleeping together" were also in this category.

I felt only slightly better on hearing this. It seemed that either choice would be hell on earth. Being sixteen was supposed to be like opening the first page to a bright future. To me it was as if someone had shut the book of life in my face. I chose the prison farm.

13

ONE WEEK LATER, Teacher Chen came to our home and brought with her the official notice of my assignment. It announced my departure on November 20, less than two weeks away. Only after I had left Shanghai would Number 3 be assigned a job.

"Ah Si! I don't want you to go!" wailed Number 5.

Everyone, even Great-Aunt, began to cry except me. I kept reminding myself that tears would only make everyone feel worse. Besides, in two weeks, totally alone and cut off, I would have all the time in the world to weep.

When we had all calmed down a bit, Teacher Chen pointed out that the notice contained a number of rules and regulations. First and most important, I had to terminate my *hu-kou*, the most vital thing I had next to life itself. In China at that time only about 20 percent of the population had urban *hu-kou* and thus enjoyed the best food and other supplies, because the city industries provided more than three-fifths of the nation's revenue; not to mention the fact that Shanghai was one of only three cities directly under the central government. (Beijing and Tianjin were the others.) Even my younger sister was aware that if the Shanghainese had to tighten their belts, it meant farmers were starving. Once I lost my *hu-kou* I could never get it back again. It was the symbol of exile.

Second, the winter was cold there, the notice said. There was no heating system. Bring warm clothes and extra bedding.

Early next morning I left the house, glad to escape the funereal silence. I turned in my *hu-kou* and ration coupons at the local police station and was issued food coupons valid anywhere in the country; special certificates for raw cotton and for fabric to make clothes and bedding; a pair of rubber shoes; one cotton-blend blanket, and a mosquito net.

When I got home, Number 2 was waiting for me. We sat down at the dinner table and he handed me one hundred yuan, a king's ransom, more money than any of us had ever seen in our lives.

"I borrowed it from my factory," he said, "so you can buy anything you need or want."

I was moved to tears. It would take him years to pay back such a huge sum. I didn't know how to thank him. And at the same time, staring at the money through tear-filled eyes, I realized with an awful finality that I was going away from my family, from the house where I was born and raised, for the rest of my life.

"Don't cry, Ah Si," he said. "Everything will be all right. Come on, Number 1 is waiting to take you to the stores."

Throughout the shopping trip with my eldest brother I hardly paid attention as he led me through crowded stores and purchased warm clothing and cotton and cloth. But as we passed one store window what caught my eye, of all things, was a pair of colorful nylon socks, smooth and stretchy and looking like they would fit comfortably. After years of wearing socks mended so often that I had to wear shoes at least a size too large, they seemed to me the height of luxury. I asked Number 1 to buy me a pair. He bought me two.

Mother used to say that "far away relatives are not as dear as close neighbors," and she was absolutely right, for our neighbors pitched in to help me prepare for my exile. Mrs. Yan was burning the midnight oil making my padded coat and pants.

"The farm is called Da Feng, isn't it?" she said. "It must be bloody cold there!" She thought Da Feng meant Big Wind because feng, meaning wind, sounds the same as feng, for harvest.

Ying-ying's mother was as practical in her support. She gave me two rolls of high-quality toilet paper, white as snow and soft as cotton, which she had bought in the special Overseas Chinese store before the Cultural Revolution. She told me that when I had my period, if I had to walk a lot I should wrap this paper around the rough sanitary paper.

Great-Aunt kept herself busy all the time, so busy she said she didn't have time to talk to me. That was typical. Whenever she was sad or angry, silence was her response. She sat in front of the stove hour after hour, day after day, roasting flour in a wok, stirring it carefully so it wouldn't burn. Roast flour was cheap and handy, and when mixed with boiled water it swelled up and filled the stomach. If a little sugar was added, it became a treat. But the procedure took tremendous time and patience and I was shocked to see how much Great-Aunt had prepared for me. She had used up all her food coupons, plus some she had borrowed from neighbors, to buy the flour. That too was typical.

In the following days and at nights as we lay side by side, I waited for Great-Aunt to tell me to watch out for myself because I would be alone, and that she would miss me. I fantasized that she would suddenly announce that I wouldn't have to go, that somehow we would make do without my welfare stipend or a job for Number 3. None of it happened.

The departure day arrived, a characteristic November day in Shanghai, damp and chilly with an overcast sky. My two brothers silently wrapped my wooden suitcase and bedroll with thick straw ropes against the long rough journey. For lunch Great-Aunt made my favorite meal: pork chops Shanghai-style, with green onions. I ate hardly a mouthful, nor did my brothers and sisters. After the dishes were cleaned up, Great-Aunt told us she was going to her regular newspaper-reading meeting and, without saying goodbye or wishing me a safe journey, without looking at me, she left and closed the door behind her.

An hour later, I left my home, wondering if I would ever again walk in those three rooms, sleep in Great-Aunt's bed or stand in the sky-well and look up at the room where my parents had lived and died. My sisters and brothers and I trudged down Purple Sunshine Lane where I had played and chased sparrows, where I had walked white-clad in two funeral processions. We passed the temple school and the market where I had diligently lined up to buy rice and pork bones. On the way to the bus stop we had to pass the building where Great-Aunt had her meeting. I saw her sitting in the doorway, weeping. I stopped and tried to speak. I wanted to tell her how much I loved her, but she looked away.

When we arrived at the district sports center, where the outbound "graduates" were to assemble, my brothers set down my luggage and they and my two sisters stood awkwardly, at a loss for words. Number 5 was crying; Number 3 stared at the damp sidewalk. I discovered that only those going to the farm could enter the building. My final moment with my family had come. I let out a loud cry.

"Why can't they stay with me until I have to leave?" I begged. It was no use.

At that moment someone shouted my name and through my tears I saw Teacher Chen running toward me. She had come to see me off. She assured my brothers and sisters that she would stay with me. I said a solemn goodbye to each of them, picked up my suitcases and walked to the stadium door.

Teacher Chen persuaded the guard to let her accompany me inside, saying she represented the school. There were more than three hundred unhappy teenagers gathered there, with bundles tightly packed and tied. Four other graduates from my school were also going, Teacher Chen told me, but I didn't know them.

We sat down to wait. My teacher gave me some bread she had brought for me, but it stayed untouched. "Be proud of yourself, Xiao Ye," she said, trying to cheer me up, "because you are not a coward."

I didn't feel brave at all.

It was getting dark when the loudspeakers called us to the waiting buses. As I was about to board, Teacher Chen held my hands in hers, in front of her chest. "Xiao Ye," she whispered, "remember the old saying, 'When at home, depend on your parents; when away from home, rely on your friends.' Make friends on the farm. They will help you."

I knew that in repeating this familiar old saying she was taking a risk, because most of the old proverbs had been denounced as feudal rubbish and she might be overheard. Everything is against me, I thought, even this proverb. I had no parents at home, and the Cultural Revolution, which encouraged friends to denounce one another, had destroyed friendship. There seemed nothing left to depend on, not even my shadow.

When I got on my bus, the fifth in line, there were no seats left. After stowing my luggage in the overhead racks, I stood in the aisle, wiping my eyes with my sleeve, as others were doing, and stared out the window. The bus passed through the gate into a street thronged with families and relatives who had been waiting for hours. Horns from passing vehicles honked. Bicycle bells rang out. People ran alongside the buses, shouting names and crying. When the buses came to a halt, dozens of hands were thrust into the windows, clutching the hands of loved ones. I searched the crowd for my sisters and brothers.

The bus began to move again. The hands at the windows gradually fell away. Then I heard desperate shouting. "Ah Si! Ah Si! Where are you?"

I pushed and squeezed my way to a window, ignoring the protests of those in the seats.

"Here! Here!" I yelled.

Then I saw Number 1 checking the buses ahead of me, waving and calling out my name as each one passed him.

"Number 1, I'm here!" I cried out.

The bus sped up. My brother ran alongside, stretching his hand to the window. More than anything I wanted that one last touch. I reached out the window as far as I could, opening and closing my hand, but Number 1 fell back and I felt only cold air.

PART THREE

BITTER WIND
(1968-1974)

14

A FTER AN OVERNIGHT PASSAGE on the ship *The East Is Red, Number 8*, a flaking hulk crammed with miserable teenagers, I climbed aboard a decrepit bus to begin the long ride to the farm. The fields around the city of Nangtong in Jiangsu Province soon fell away behind our convoy and we entered a flat and not quite believable landscape, swept by wind so strong it forced its way around the edges of the windows into the buses. Mile after mile there was not a tree, a building or a human being to be seen under the gray sky. Raised in one of the country's largest cities, I had never seen a street empty of people, not even in the middle of the night. I was no expert in country living, but in the countryside surrounding Qingyang, where, before Father's operation, we had traveled every year to visit Grandfather, I had always seen farmers working the green fields, traversing them on narrow paddy dikes, or walking the dirt roads. There, even in winter, the densely populated land was green and the air heavy with humidity and the rich odors of growing plants.

This emptiness could mean only one thing: the soil was no good for farming.

"House, house!" someone yelled from the front of the bus. We had been rattling along for five hours. Through the dust-coated window I saw a cluster of thatch-roofed houses. The bus turned off the road and bumped through a village on a rutted track. It turned onto a wider road blanketed with white powder. The unfamiliar substance also lined the fields, and seemed like a permanent feature.

The buses ahead of us began to peel off onto narrow dirt roads to the left and right. Mine rumbled across a wooden bridge and pulled up in the midst of a cluster of wattle buildings thatched with rice straw. Everyone fell silent, staring. Around the buildings, desolation: flat, dry, empty fields. I told myself that this must be just a temporary stop.

When the door flapped open, letting in the chill November wind, a middle-aged man stepped up into the bus. "Hello, revolutionary comrades," he greeted us in a Su Bei accent, using a term that had been out of date since the beginning of the Cultural Revolution, for it lacked precision. "Welcome to the Number One Brigade of Xi Min sub-farm of Da Feng Labor Camp ... er, Da Feng Farm," he corrected himself hastily. "My name is Chang Wen, and I am the leader of this brigade."

Reluctantly I stepped down from the bus with the others. The welcoming team consisted of Chang's assistant, Lao Deng — a short old man whose mouth and eye-corners pointed up, even when he wasn't smiling; their wives; the doctor, and the accountant. The latter, a tall skinny man, shook hands with each of us, bowing deeply as he did so and smiling, showing his cigarette-stained teeth. Shaking hands was a novel experience for me, as it suggested I was now an adult.

I looked around, searching for some sign of scar-faced criminals, high walls or stout buildings with barred windows, but saw nothing out of the ordinary, just a tiny village with dirt roads and pathways. Dr. Wang, the youngest of the greeting party, whose sharp and bright eyes reminded me of my grandfather, asked the male students to follow him to their dormitory. Lao Bai, Lao Chang's wife, a chubby middle-aged woman with a piercing voice, called for the females.

"Is this where we're going to stay?" someone shouted from the men's dorm.

Our dorm was, like all the buildings, single-story, made of wattle — woven sticks and straw plastered with clay and mud — with a thatched roof and dirt floor. On the south side of the village, it was separated from the men's dorm by a pathway on the left and from the empty fields by the ditch at its right.

"Come on," Lao Bai said. "Pay no attention to him. Come in and have a look."

We filed through the narrow door. My first impression was the heavy odors of dampness, lime, smoke and rotten rice straw. The building was like an oversized train coach, about fifteen yards long but only six wide. Though it was midafternoon, three naked bulbs fought to dispel the gloom. There was a door at each end and three small windows on each side. The dirt floor had been packed hard by many feet; the walls were newly whitewashed, but brown clay was already oozing through. Along each wall ran a low platform of undressed boards supported by sharpened tree branches driven into the dirt and covered with malodorous straw. This was our bed.

As if she had seen into my mind, Lao Bai said cheerfully, "It won't look so bad when you've all spread out your bedding. You city girls are good at decorating, aren't you? Soon this place will look like home."

After a short but determined tussle during which many angled to be with their schoolmates or near the windows and everybody fought to stay away from the doors, territory was marked out by our carrying bags. Lao Bai then led us to the canteen on the north edge of the village for a late lunch. Before entering, I looked around for a tap to wash my hands. I spied half a dozen water jars outside a small building, each one as high as my chest and as wide as my outstretched arms. Every one of them was filled with clean water, though it smelled of mud. This shack must be a pump house, I thought, and wondered how I could wash my hands without contaminating the whole jar.

A white-haired man appeared from behind a hut, where he had evidently been working, for his hands were black.

"Can I help you, young miss?"

I explained my predicament.

"Come with me," he said quietly, and led me through the door of the shack. On the floor was a basin with soap and a towel beside it. He motioned me to use them, then left me alone. Outside again, I scooped a basin full of water from one of the jars, thinking that this was the village's fresh water supply.

Once inside the canteen I was asked by several students how I had managed to wash, since none of our luggage had arrived. I told them, adding that the basin, towel and soap could be used by them too, for the old uncle seemed kind enough.

"Young lady, be careful of what you are saying," Lao Bai cut in, scowling. "You should call no one here uncle or aunt, nor go to their places and use their things. Only those who greeted you should be addressed. You must have no contact with anyone else." She lowered her voice dramatically. "You wouldn't want to be anywhere near that 'old uncle' if you knew what he had done before Liberation."

Her words sent a bolt of fear through me. Had I been speaking to one of the criminals? Was he a murderer?

"You, all of you," Lao Bai went on, "stay away from them. You are all young girls. You never know what those curs are up to. If you have to, just call them Wei, nothing else."

Wei means "Hey, you!" in Chinese, or "Hello" while talking on the telephone. We had been taught all our lives to call a man Uncle or Old Uncle, depending on his age; a woman was Auntie or Old Auntie. To address anyone older than you, even a stranger, by saying only "Wei" was disrespectful.

Lao Bai's warning had destroyed my appetite. I repeatedly stole glances at the men standing behind the counter, the ones who had served up our food. No wonder they stood there like blocks of wood, expressionless. No wonder they had said nothing to us and avoided eye contact. But if they were as dangerous and untrustworthy as Lao Bai said, why should we trust the food they prepared?

That evening Lao Chang cautioned us never to use the public toilet at night. He didn't specify whether he was afraid we would fall into the open manure pit beside the unlit latrine or be molested by prisoners. His warning didn't help my attempts to fall asleep. Around me the other girls talked, cried or screamed in their sleep. I was utterly discouraged. I felt as if we were all little lambs in the jungle, waiting to be slaughtered.

When I awoke I found myself encroaching on my neighbor's space. It would take us a while, I thought, to get used to sleeping together on the long bench. Her name was Liu Lan-lan — Orchid — a senior-high graduate of Xiang Yang middle school in the same district as my school. From her puffed eyes I gathered that her night's sleep had been no better than mine. As soon as we were out of bed she began to clean and tidy her spot, her long thin body a bundle of nervous energy as she tried in vain to arrange her sheet neatly on the straw.

My neighbor to my right turned out to be one of my schoolmates, although I didn't know her well. Jia-ying was a pretty nineteen-year-old with big dark eyes and a pale oval face, her hair trimmed stylishly. When she introduced me to my other three schoolmates in her soft voice, she sounded like an organizer at a social event. In fact, organization was not her strong suit: there were unwashed bowls under her bed, jumbled clothing piled on her open luggage. A little later she asked shyly if I would hold up a sheet so that she could huddle behind it to change her clothes.

Standing on her bed with the sheet in my hands, I had a good view of the long narrow dorm, filled with young women — all of them at least two years older than I — walking to and fro in their underwear while others squatted on the spittoons, used for chamber pots, a scene I knew would be repeated endlessly in the weeks, months and years to come.

The opening of the day was a parade to the latrine, with many carrying their chamber pots amid giggles and sarcastic remarks from the male students and the prisoners. When I saw the women's latrine I repeated to myself the overpraised expression "Everything is hard at the beginning," but suspected that in this case the difficulty would never diminish. The walls were of reed mats, the ceiling thatched with straw and obviously not waterproof. The dirt floor was slotted by a series of ditches, over which we would squat, one foot on each side. The inside wall, no more than three yards high, separated our latrine from the men's, from which laughter and the smell of cigarettes came clearly.

I had grown up in an environment in which emphasizing personal needs was criticized as bourgeois garbage; nevertheless, I had always nourished my sense of privacy. Although this was not my first experience of relieving myself in such an open and exposed way — the Beijing trip had given me a startling awakening — I found it hard to cope. I walked gingerly to a corner ditch, farthest from the men's side, amazed at how casual some of the women were, chatting to one another, calling out to new arrivals, saying goodbye to those departing.

Before breakfast I stole off by myself and inspected the village. It didn't take long. The camp was made up of four rows of buildings: the first two residences and dorms, the others, on the north side of the central road, housed the clinic, administration offices, canteens and pump houses, and the warehouse for storing tools and farm equipment. The perimeter on three sides was a wide ditch, partly filled with sluggish water and littered with garbage, which converged on a river on the fourth side. It was a desolate and featureless place.

I got to the canteen just in time to hear Lao Chang's first lecture, arms behind his back, to the new arrivals. He had stuffed himself into a faded army uniform, complete with a cap, and made every effort to sound official and important. Each ponderous sentence was broken up by "*zhe-ge...na-ge,*" bureaucratic punctuation demonstrating self-importance. My eyes were drawn to the strained stitches on his sleeves and the five buttons of his jacket, which were making their valiant effort to hold the coat together.

Lao Chang was a "Thirty-eighter," one of those who had joined the Communist Party in 1938 and taken part in the war against the Japanese invaders. Being a Thirty-eighter meant high status and prestige. There were other honorifics, such as Long Marcher (one who endured the famous 7,750-mile trek with Mao Ze-dong in 1934); White Area Underground Activist (a Communist undercover agent in a Guomindang-controlled area), and Soviet-area Worker (one who worked in the Communist bases established during the Second Revolutionary Civil War against the Guomindang from 1927 to 1937). In my understanding, these designations were like expensive liquor: the earlier bottled, the better.

Lao Chang opened his speech with good news. Each of us would earn ¥18 per month. I was ecstatic. Finally, after nearly a lifetime of poverty and humiliation as a welfare recipient, I would be earning a wage. I would be able to send money to help my family.

Next, with his hands still clasped behind him, rocking as he spoke, Lao Chang told us about the prisoners. There were eighty-seven of them in the brigade, all males from Shanghai.

"Where are the female prisoners?" one woman interrupted.

"Does that mean they can go back home to Shanghai when they have served their time?" a man asked. "Why can't we go home, then?"

Lao Chang made no attempt to hide his annoyance at having his speech pushed off the rails. "All the female prisoners are at the Chuan Dong Sub-farm," he said sternly. "So far as I am concerned, mixing males and females spells one word: trouble."

Years later I learned that Lao Chang's bitterness about women came from experience. He had been punished for having an affair with a married woman in his work unit and banished to the farm for his "rotten lifestyle." His wife and family had accompanied him, and his "assignment" was indefinite.

"As for you, young man," he continued, "I will not reply to your ill-mannered interruption." His voice became shrill. "When I was your age I was laying my life on the line for our motherland so that you could live the easy life you have now. Don't take your own fortune for granted."

He then stood aside for Lao Deng, who informed us in his quavering voice that this farm had been reclaimed from the Yellow Sea, and that every winter there was a massive labor campaign to repair and strengthen the dikes along the seashore. The farm's soil, he went on to say, was so alkaline that, after a summer shower the heat would form salt rocks around the village. As a matter of fact, the closest town, about thirty miles to the northwest, was called Yan Cheng — Salt City. Because of the quality of the soil, the main crops of the area had been cotton and peanuts, along with some vegetables. Since the inception of the National Program for Agricultural Development, great efforts had been made in the last few years to grow rice, but without much success. Nevertheless, he said ominously, these efforts would continue.

Most of his words went in one ear and out the other. I was a city girl. Surely one crop was the same as another. Soon I would learn the hard way how wrong I was.

Lao Deng finally left off speaking and we lined up to get our breakfast. Afterwards we had to run a gauntlet of prisoners who had been standing outside the canteen waiting for their turn. Most were shabbily dressed, their coats held closed by the braided rice-straw belts, and wore padded hats with hang-dog earflaps. They banged their enamel bowls and yelled and laughed at us, making rude remarks to some of the female students.

"First you steal our house and now our food!" one of them hollered above the racket.

Apparently the dorms we had moved into the night before had been theirs and they had been forced to live in even less-inviting quarters. I didn't blame them for their anger; but they still frightened me as I hurried past holding my two bowls.

That first day my new farm-mates, who were almost all "non-red" students, and I began our hard labor. It soon became evident that Mrs. Yan's mistake about the name of the farm — calling it Big Wind instead of Big Harvest — was grimly appropriate, for all day and night an icy-cold wind swept out of the northwest. A local rhyme described it: on odd days the wind rolled up the land like a rug; on even days it unrolled it again. Although the water in the river and the jars outside the pump house seldom froze, our proximity to the sea ensured that the almost freezing air was heavy and damp.

The first thing I learned was to pick cotton — not to harvest the puffy white balls, for the prisoners had picked them more than a month before, in October, but rather to go from bush to bush and strip the bare brown branches of the unripened pods. These had to be torn open by hand so that the sticky black substance inside could be collected and later shipped to a mill to be pressed for cooking oil. Before long my hands were raw and red from cold and the abrasive pods. When that job was complete we had to pull the cotton plants from the ground, a back-breaking task since Lao Deng was determined that rice would be planted there the next season.

One night several weeks after we had begun working in the fields, I found Jia-ying weeping silently in bed.

"What's wrong?" I asked.

She showed me her swollen fingers, her raw and scratched skin. "How can I ever play the piano again with hands like these?"

I picked up my pillow cover, a small towel, and wrapped it around her hands. "They will heal, Jia-ying. Don't worry. Our work in the cotton fields will be over soon."

"Over?" she scoffed. "It will never be over." She threw the towel at me and crawled under her quilt.

Even though I believed in the healing of wounds, I doubted that our invisible wounds would ever be remedied.

Our long days in the cold, desolate fields did not earn us any free time: between dinner and lights-out we had political study in the dorm. Usually one of the two Laos would join us to lead the obligatory readings and discussions as we sat on the end of our trestle bed and went through the motions. Tired and aching all over, I would try in vain to find a comfortable position. On those occasions when the Laos failed to appear, the study session was run by our team leader. We would climb into bed and wrap ourselves in our cotton-ticked quilts and soon our discussions would go off topic. At these times, driven by cold and boredom, I was prone to make jokes and kid around.

My sense of humor was honed by hardship. I always seemed keenly aware of ironies, and the Cultural Revolution provided an endless supply. The hated Little Red Book, linked in my mind to suffering, nevertheless reminded me of the world I knew back home. Yet, even while the mere contemplation of spending my life on the farm plunged me into depression, letters from home made me realize how peaceful it was here, a forgotten corner in a crazy world, free of the strife that was still sweeping over Shanghai.

And so, in silence and loneliness, the year 1969 arrived.

15

To celebrate the New Year, Lao Chang ordered that a pig be slaughtered, which put broad smiles on our faces. For many weeks we had had nothing to eat with our rice but preserved vegetables and dried fish so loaded with salt that they reminded me of the Red Army, half-starved on the Long March, having to lick salt blocks for strength.

All of us arrived at the canteen half an hour early. As I waited in line with the others, anticipating the savory odor and rich taste of pork, I recalled the many times when Mrs. Yan would wake me up at four in the morning so we could go to the market to queue up for a bit of pork fat. The fat required fewer coupons than meat, and Great-Aunt found it valuable as a flavoring for freshly cooked rice, with a bit of salt or soybean sauce. My hunger also reminded me of the day when I discovered Jia-ying had brought a can of chicken fat from home and I tried not to show my jealousy.

When our meal began, I ate one thin piece of pork, cooked in soybean sauce and edged with fat and skin, as slowly as possible, relishing every bite. It was heavenly.

After dinner, while I was rinsing my dishes with Jia-ying, we were castigated by several gaunt and bedraggled prisoners. For the first time at New Year they had been denied meat; instead, they had been fed bones, intestines and nameless organs.

"You useless city brats have ripped the food from our mouths," they snarled. We ran off with our dirty dishes, followed by their curses.

Two days later they got their revenge. Although we had been repeatedly warned not to move around by ourselves, not even during the day, I insisted on going to the latrine on my own, for I had my period and didn't want to change my napkins with others around. The rest of us had gone to the rice-threshing ground to fetch new straw for our beds. I was gratified to find the latrine empty.

A few moments later I heard rustling. Thinking there must be a bat in the thatched roof — a fairly common occurrence — I covered my ears, for I had been told that bats like to try to enter human heads. At the same time I closed my eyes and bent my head between my knees, hoping no one would come in and see me in such a ridiculous position, pants around my ankles, squatting over the trench.

"How are you, my dear?"

Startled, I opened my eyes and saw a man's hand waving at me over the top of the partition.

"Why don't you come over here, young lady? From what I can see, we'll be friends in no time."

I tried to scream but no sound came out. I jumped up and ran all the way to the dorm, which was, luckily, unlocked that day because two girls were in bed with the flu.

With tears of fear running down my face I told them what had happened. Not long after I began to wish I had never opened my mouth. An investigation started. I was interviewed twice by Lao Chang and each time I had to repeat my embarrassing tale. I was questioned by the two Laos' wives, the doctor and the accountant. When they returned from their work, my dorm-mates badgered me for details. Soon everyone, even the men, knew about the incident, including the fact that I had made a mess on my clothes in my hasty exit.

My relatively peaceful but lonely life was disturbed one bitterly cold day in mid-January when I got a letter from Number 2. Number 3 had finally been assigned a job, he wrote, but not in Shanghai. She had been sent to a factory in Songjiang County that made small electronic meter parts. It was near where I had spent two weeks in a commune before the Cultural Revolution working with the peasants. Despite my sacrifice in volunteering to go to the countryside so that my elder sister could remain in Shanghai and look after our little sister, Number 3 had had to move outside the city and could go home only on weekends.

"Number 3 did not protest," my brother wrote. "She knew it would be useless." And a good thing she didn't, he went on.

Just one week after Number 3's assignment, in late December 1968, Mao Ze-dong issued a new call, ordering all city middle-school graduates to the countryside, which he described as "a vast world where much can be accomplished; a boundless field for youngsters to use their talents." If Number 3 hadn't accepted the job, she too would have been sent to the countryside.

"The whole city," wrote Number 2, "is like a funeral home for the living. Mao has cast a net instead of catching fish one by one, as in your case, Ah Si."

Obviously, letters received by others spread the same news, for the result was vengeful laughter and grim satisfaction. Usually the arrival of the mail brought tears of homesickness, but not this time. All of us had been banished to this remote farm rather than to the much more civilized farms on Chong Ming Island because of our "bad class background"; now those who had harassed and humiliated us at school and on the streets would suffer the same fate! Lan-lan told me that two of her classmates who had shaved her mother's head during a raid on their house were being sent far north to Heilongjiang Province near the Russian border, a place where, according to legend, black bears would knock at your door and your breath turned to icicles.

"It serves them right!" she said bitterly. "I hope their noses and ears turn to ice and fall off!"

The next morning we were called again to the warehouse for a mass meeting so that Lao Chang could "brief us on the new government documents." Lao Chang, I had noticed, loved these gatherings because in his eyes his prestige among his colleagues and their families, as well as the prisoners, was enhanced when he was addressing more than sixty middle-school graduates. He had held meetings on the importance of cotton plants, the making of straw mattresses and the twisting of straw into ropes.

In order to respond to Chairman Mao's call to make rice the key crop and to ensure year-round planting to build China's self-reliance, we would be converting most of the cotton fields to rice paddies, he announced pompously. This was hardly news; we had been pulling the cotton plants out of the unyielding ground for ages and most of us had bandaged hands to prove it. Our accountant, Lao Shi, assured us that as long as we could harvest rice once a year we would have a surplus, and he shook his abacus to confirm his speculation. With the others, I applauded this announcement, thinking that any crop must be easier than cotton.

"More city kids are coming!" Lao Chang crowed excitedly when he regained the floor. "We must build new houses for them. They'll be here in four weeks."

All the male laborers, including the prisoners, were to go to the dike to cut reeds and haul them back to the village on wagons drawn by water buffalo. The females were to construct walls and roofs from the reeds, after binding them into stalks.

I was less enthusiastic than Lao Chang about the arrival of more students. They would be politically correct "reds," not like us, and that meant only one thing — conflict and persecution.

16

IN MARCH, FIFTY-SIX WIDE-EYED youths stepped down from the old buses to the beating of gongs and drums. They did not seem as cowed as we had been when we first set foot on the alkaline soil of the prison farm.

Awaiting them were two brand-new dorms, still smelling of fresh reeds and the lime coating on the inner walls. We had hoped we might move into the new dorms ourselves: the early spring rains and subsequent dampness had covered our walls with green mold. So many evenings I had awakened to damp bedding and the *plink-plunk* of rain dropping through the roof into the rice bowls and washbasins we had scattered around. More often, I was startled by sudden screams from myself or others after discovering unrecognized creatures crawling inside our bedding. But Lao Chang said no; we were "veterans" now and should yield the new dorms to the novices.

These fresh arrivals were not the scared and compliant beings we had been (and still were). Within a week Lao Chang was confronted by a newly formed committee of students and informed that he was no longer in charge of the welfare of the school youngsters; his connection to us from that day on was only as a production consultant. The self-appointed committee consisted of two women and three men. At the first meeting, each stood up and claimed to be *san-dai-hong* — three generations red — working-class as far back as their grandfathers. Their leadership of the brigade was thus legitimized and changes began immediately, from the reappointment of canteen staff to the reorganization of our living arrangements. Half of my original dorm-mates were replaced by red students, so as to "break up the stiff soil by mixing it with sand"; it seemed that the reform of those with bad class backgrounds was to continue.

This plan was promoted by Xu Gang, a handsome man in his early twenties, a senior graduate from a key middle school. Although I held no sympathy for him, I was aware that his being sent to this farm was not an auspicious event in his life. He could have been at university now, a glory for him and his family. In the past, students like him from the working class were rare at universities. Their parents couldn't afford tutors, as the rich could, and they often had duties around the house, whereas the better-off students could, and were expected to, devote all their time to study. Just when the old ways were being gradually reversed and people like Xu Gang could get into university, the Cultural Revolution broke out and Chairman Mao sent them down to the countryside.

Xu Gang's bitterness was evident in his speech and manner. As he regaled the audience, he punctuated his words with a waving fist — so much so that before the meeting was over he had earned the nickname Five Past Twelve for the position of his raised fist during his speech.

Each regrouped dorm was to be called a platoon, comprising three squads. My squad leader, Yu Hua, a pretty young eighteen-year-old, was, of course, one of the newcomers. She announced to us proudly that one of her sisters was a veteran in the air force in Guangzhou Province. To be in the services had been a glory since Liberation. It was even more prestigious now. For those who had political connections and didn't want their children to go to the countryside, joining the PLA had been the only way out. The "glory and honor" part was propaganda to justify the end-run around Mao's call. From the time they put on their uniforms, these people looked forward to the day three years later when they would be demobilized and return home with the promise of a lifetime career and a high salary.

The new committee's big plans for numerous meetings, political study and the assignment of self-reports and self-criticism met their first resistance: physical exhaustion.

Converting cotton fields to rice paddies was a tremendous undertaking and the process was slow and laborious. First, the land was divided into paddies by building low dikes to hold the water that would be pumped in. Each paddy was then flushed two or three times to wash away as much of the alkaline salt as possible. The next stage was to enrich the soil by plowing vegetation and composted nightsoil into it. The vegetation consisted of grass and any other green plants that could be found in the vicinity, cut down and carried by shoulder-pole to the paddies. The first problem was that, even though the lunar calendar said spring had arrived, it was anything but spring on our farm and there wasn't much new vegetation around yet. "The cleverest housewife cannot make a meal without rice," the old saying puts it, but the red students claimed that man could and would conquer nature.

For weeks, each day saw us leaving the village with shoulder-poles and straw-rope net bags, searching for anything green except reeds, for they would not decompose quickly enough. Each of us had a daily quota, which rose as weather warmed. No matter how hard I worked, yanking and ripping weeds, grass and even some leaves with my bare hands, I couldn't get my name off the "failure" list posted in the canteen every day, accompanied by a red minus sign.

One night when I was washing my blistered feet and complaining worriedly to Jia-ying about my predicament, she laughed. "Isn't it about time you grew up and understood this world better, Xiao Ye? Do you really think we are working harder than you? The answer is no, but we know how to play with the rules. We not only bring back the green stuff, but dirt besides." She smiled sweetly, showing her dimples. "If the dirt is good for growing grass, it must be good for rice too!"

From that day on I met my quota.

But I overdid it. Typical, Great-Aunt, whom I missed greatly, would have said. I not only made sure the vegetation I harvested had clumps of dirt on the roots, I soaked the load with water. The mushy bottoms were glued to the ground and I could hardly lift the mess up.

One day at the end of April we were called back from the fields and ordered to gather around the loudspeaker mounted on a pole in the central road. In my utter physical exhaustion and mental dullness I welcomed the command and sprawled on the dirt with the others to listen to the radio broadcast. At the Ninth Party Congress under way in Beijing, the "biggest political event in everyone's life," as the announcer intoned, there were more than fifteen hundred delegates, "elected" by ordinary citizens. Not since 1956 had a congress like this been held. Sitting there, my shoulders and back aching, my skinny thigh muscles burning from the weight of my burden, I couldn't have cared less.

But in listening to the speeches over the following days I was spared the increasingly futile search for greens and the strain of toting them back. At night I listened to committee members read documents and news bulletins, participated (on orders) in discussions, made personal "statements of belief."

The report on Lin Biao's speech opened my wounds. Any hope I had harbored that the Cultural Revolution might begin to wind down was smashed by his testimony that "its merits are the greatest while its losses the smallest." His words forecast more political commotion. The Congress "accepted" Mao's recommendation and appointed Lin Biao as his successor. This fact further enhanced the PLA's status in the Cultural Revolution and laid the foundation for the army to take over almost all key structures across the country — public security organizations, procuratorial and people's courts, institutions of higher learning, even the jails and prison farms.

The list of newly elected members of the Central Committee was shocking by virtue of those names not mentioned, including President Liu Shao-qi. Among those elected was Mao's wife, Jiang Qing.

To everyone's surprise we were organized for a celebration on the closing day of the Congress. Trucks rolled into the compound before supper bringing red cloth banners, paper flags and boxes of firecrackers of all sizes. In spite of myself I found the diversion exciting. We marched four abreast to the sub-farm nearly five miles away under a starless April sky, guided by diesel-fuel torches. It was the most enjoyable night I had passed since my arrival at the farm.

When the shouting of slogans and singing of propaganda songs died down we filled the darkness with talking and laughing, shrieking delightedly with the detonation of every firecracker. Great-Aunt had once told me that firecrackers were traditionally used to drive devils away. For centuries they had been a part of New Year's celebrations. That night, with every cracker that exploded in the sky, I wished hard for good luck.

The next morning the figurative worship of Mao Ze-dong became literal. Each dorm was issued two plaster statues, along with pieces of red cloth and yellow paper hearts with the character *zhong* — loyalty — embossed on them, the same word Number 2 had cleverly selected as his new name. We set up a *zhong-zhi-tai* — loyalty shrine — at each doorway. Every morning thereafter we stood before the shrine and held our Little Red Books in front of our chests, requesting instruction and greeting Chairman Mao with rehearsed shouts, wishing him life "forever and ever" and his successor Lin Biao, "our beloved vice-chairman, good health, always, always." We could not even fully dress or wash ourselves first, because, we were told, the adoration exercise was the first and most important political matter in our daily life.

As I stood there on the dirt floor or on my unmade bed, surrounded by waving arms, my thoughts went back to my childhood when my siblings and I accompanied Grandfather to our ancestral hall in Qingyang. Never in my life had I seen or heard of people erecting a shrine for someone still alive. Even I knew that worshipping the living guaranteed bad luck. Less than half an hour later we repeated the same words in the canteen while we waited in line for breakfast.

One day the female students were commanded to the rice-threshing ground and taught the "loyalty dance" by professionals sent out by the Shanghai city government. While we struggled to learn the steps, we sang, "Our beloved Chairman Mao, you are the sun which will never set and we are sunflowers always swirling around you . . ."

Our dancing won us the title "Flowers on the Cow Shit" among the prisoners, who witnessed us dancing during a work-break from spreading cow dung to dry before it was hauled to the paddies.

My genuine effort to meet my daily vegetation quota touched my squad leader, Yu Hua, who offered to pair up with me to help me out. At that time I was only about four-foot-three and weighed no more than eighty pounds, and I needed all the help I could get. Yu Hua was a strong, sturdy woman of eighteen, with short hair and a no-nonsense manner. Her kindness moved me deeply. It was the beginning of the first real friendship of my life.

We worked together well. I was quick with my sickle; she toted cuttings to the weigh station. We met our quota regularly. But the newly formed paddies were insatiable monsters, eating up everything we cut. The vegetation near the farm had long since been stripped away and we had to go farther and farther afield.

One day Yu Hua and I packed some steamed buns and pickled vegetables and left right after breakfast to search for vegetation. Our shoulder-poles bounced with each step as we headed north along the main road, gathering weeds and grass as we went. After a few hours' work we spied a swampy pit in which new shoots had sprung up where the reeds had been cut. We made our way over the spongy ground to relieve ourselves. A moment later Yu Hua called out to me. She had found a pathway leading over a bank into a stand of plane trees. I followed her, curious to see where the path led.

Yu Hua stopped. "Look, Xiao Ye!"

I couldn't believe my eyes. Among the trees, newly in leaf, tall grass grew, uncut and undisturbed.

"We will be able to meet our quota for weeks," I said, "if we keep this secret."

We fell to work immediately and by noon had our four mesh bags full. After a lunch of hardened buns and pickled vegetables washed down with water, Yu Hua shuffled off under the weight of her shoulder-pole, leaving me busy with my sickle.

After months of living day and night in a crowd of students and amongst the circus of Mao worship and dancing, I found myself alone. I worked steadily, enjoying the solitude. The breeze stirred the grass and whispered in the branches of the surrounding trees. After a while I sat down to rest, leaning against a tree, and closed my eyes. Strangely, the isolation began to make me uneasy. Why had Yu Hua been gone so long? I decided it would be better to get back to work than to think of bad things that could happen to a girl left alone. Gathering my cuttings into piles, I bent to pick up a bundle of grass and found myself staring into the empty eye sockets of a human skull.

I screamed and dropped my burden. Stumbling down the embankment into the reeds, running and falling over the soggy ground, feet and arms torn by the brittle reed stubble, I finally gained the road. Blood ran down my legs and arms. My heart pounding and my chest heaving, I set off toward the village.

When I met Yu Hua I burst into tears, breathlessly describing the horror of the skull. Only after she had calmed me down did I realize that I had left my sickle and shoulder-pole behind and would not be able to meet the day's quota.

"Never mind that for now," Yu Hua said. "You need a doctor."

The doctor dressed my wounds, tut-tutting and wondering under his breath how such a slight young woman could have done such damage to herself. Then Lao Deng came into the clinic with Yu Hua. I braced myself for criticism for losing my tools and for the usual remarks that we spoiled bourgeois youngsters were lazy and incapable of hard work.

"Now, Xiao Ye," he began. "Let's hear your report."

When I told him where Yu Hua and I had been cutting grass and what I had seen, his reaction surprised and confused me. He seemed amused.

"You two are quite the detectives, aren't you?" he said. "How did you find that graveyard? What —"

"Graveyard?" I interrupted him. "Is that what I found? Why is it unmarked, and where are the burial mounds? The skull was just lying on the ground."

"Listen, girl, that's *Wu Mao Yu* — Number Five Unmarked Burial Ground, an execution site. You'd better keep your discovery and all your questions to yourself. That's an order. And don't ever go back there again!"

For the first time since I had come to Da Feng Prison Farm, I eagerly embraced a command.

Before Lao Deng left, he wrote out a chit for a new sickle and shoulder-pole and sent me away.

17

THE INTENSIFYING CONFLICT BETWEEN prisoners and students was brought to a head by two events. The first was the disparity in work assignments. While we foraged for vegetation, the prisoners had the more difficult assignment of tilling the paddies with plows drawn behind water buffalo, mixing the vegetation and composted nightsoil into the mud. They also constructed seedbeds, a laborious and exacting task since the mud had to be smoothed by hand before the seeds were sown. The prisoners' discontent was made worse by shortages of food and cooking oil, over which there were often fights with their canteen staff.

With the arrival of the busy season at the beginning of June, when the emerald seedlings were ready to be transplanted to the flooded paddies, a compromise was reached under which we students had to work the same hours, with the same quotas, as the prisoners. If we didn't succeed, Lao Chang warned us, there would be ugly consequences.

Each day, when dawn broke, we were whistled awake and, after our Mao worship, we headed to the fields. We carefully pulled the rice shoots from the seedbeds, shook them to free the roots of soil, bundled them in straw, and carried them to the paddies, on each of which a grid had been laid out with straw ropes pegged into the dikes. Wading up to our knees between the parallel ropes, we transplanted the seedlings. It was an arduous, precise job, six seedlings across making a straight column, about four inches separating the rows. The precision, Lao Chang instructed us, made for the most efficient weeding and harvesting. He waved a ruler, warning us that any deviation from the measurements would lead to punishment.

Our daily quota was seven twenty-five-yard columns a day. It was a backbreaking job, bending down constantly, even for someone like me, so small, the others said, that I didn't have a waist. The only relief came with the short walk from the seedbeds to the paddy and back. When the day ended I could hardly straighten my back. Before long I had worn my elbows raw from resting them on my knees as I worked. My hands swelled and developed cysts from pulling out the seedlings and plunging them into the cold water. Leeches were a frightening menace. They crawled up and hung on to my legs, and I had to slap the skin hard enough to make them go. Thin streams of blood flowed from the wounds. The disgusting creatures startled me so much that I often fell back onto my bottom in the cold, muddy water.

Lao Chang said timing was the key point in growing rice and no delay could be tolerated. Swollen hands and feet met with no sympathy. He even went so far as to have his wife check the girls who claimed to have their periods, because, according to the rules, they were allowed two days of dry land work at such times. For the first time in my life I welcomed my period, wishing it would come weekly rather than once a month.

I lost count of the times I slept in my clothes after returning from the fields, too exhausted to clean up first, my two mud-covered calves poking out from under the mosquito net. Yu Hua continued to look out for me, particularly after I told her I was an orphan. "I will be your *Jie-Jie* — elder sister," she said. Although I was conscious of my daily mounting unpaid debt to her, I often thought how true was Teacher Chen's advice that a friend was a treasure beyond price.

When the summer arrived, one wave of suffocating heat followed another, bringing thick clouds of mosquitoes, which made sitting outside at night impossible. The living conditions inside the ovenlike dorm were horrible. Our windows stayed open but, afraid of the prisoners, we locked the doors when we were sleeping so that there was little air circulation. Although we had managed to persuade the committee to allow us to break up the long trestle bed into separate doubles so that we could more easily hang our separate mosquito nets, nothing relieved the heat. Almost everyone was covered with heat rash as well as skin afflictions caused by the fertilizers we spread by hand in the paddies.

There was no bath- or shower-house, but I was able to wash in the nearby river. Not everyone was so lucky; the others feared the river because they couldn't swim. Bathing in the warm water reminded me of the day in July 1966 when the news came to Shanghai that seventy-three-year-old Chairman Mao had swum in the Yangtze River. The city government had organized the citizens on numerous occasions to emulate Mao by swimming in the polluted Huangpu River. I had joined Number 2 and his factory team, but suffered severe diarrhea after swallowing a couple of mouthfuls of river water. On the farm, I was more careful.

The second event that exacerbated the precarious student-prisoner relationship was an act of revenge. As a reward for their work in rice transplanting, Lao Chang had always allowed the prisoners to catch fish by blocking off a section of the sluggish river. In early August that year, they built dikes to partition the river and began to clear the water out of the section in wooden barrels. It was a round-the-clock operation for a day or so until the water was shallow enough to wade in and catch the fish. This year, instead of handing the catch over to the canteen immediately, they secretly stored the fish in barrels until it began to rot.

Then, to our surprise, one day our canteen was presented with a load of cleaned fish covered with salt. The salt was to keep the fish fresh, the prisoners explained. Inexperienced and ignorant, the staff washed off the salt and sent out the news that we were to receive a treat that night. We were delighted. Fish is always a delicacy; to us, living as we did on boring and often inadequate fare, it was a gift from the gods. There was a long lineup before the canteen opened; some people even managed to buy extra to keep for future meals.

By midnight the doctor and his assistant were run ragged making trips from dorm to dorm, cleaning up vomit and caring for those who rolled on the floor clutching their abdomens. Everyone was on the move, either to or from the latrines or helping out the doctors and patients. When the morning arrived, hardly a student was able to get out of bed.

I was hit hard. After a night of violent cramps, vomiting and running to the latrine, my whole body felt like a cotton ball, totally without energy. I craved water but was afraid to drink. By noon the sub-farm medical team had arrived, bringing large quantities of antibiotics. But they were too late. The latrines soon contaminated our water supply, and before we recovered from the food poisoning, we were in deeper trouble with severe diarrhea. On the fifth day I and three other girls were so dehydrated that we were taken to the farm hospital ten miles away in a flatbed wagon pulled by a water buffalo. Because I passed out, I remember nothing of the trip. My condition worsened. My body was wracked with pain and I was continuously voiding bloody stool.

Diagnosed with amoebic dysentery by a mobile medical team from Shanghai Number 1 People's Hospital, I was rushed by jeep to the ship, then to Shanghai dock, and from there directly to hospital. I was told my life was in danger unless I received proper medical treatment immediately. After two days in hospital the doctor said, "You have escaped Death's hand, but barely. Your disease will likely recur." For the next week I continued my frequent visits to the toilet, but could not eat. Instead I received glucose injections. When I was released, I weighed less than seventy pounds.

Great-Aunt and Number 2 came to take me home in a taxi, an unheard-of luxury and the first such experience of my life. I had every reason to be cheerful, considering that I was still alive, but I found myself pensive and sad. The city had become a huge construction site, with clouds of dust in the air and piles of dirt along every road. As the taxi passed through the streets, my brother told me that after the military clashes with the Soviet Union over

Zhenbao — Treasure — Island in the Heilongjiang River separating the two countries, the whole nation was on a war-preparation footing. Every work unit, every neighborhood committee, was responsible for its own air-raid shelters. Mao's call had been for "deep digging [shelters], massive saving [of grain] and no truck with the superpowers [since the U.S. and Russia were both against us]." While the young continued to be sent out to the countryside, tens of thousands of government employees were "evacuated" to rural areas and remote provinces to decentralize industry so that it would not all be destroyed if the cities were hit with air raids.

Both Number 1 and Number 5 had left the city in July, and I had been unable to come home to see them off. Number 5, after spending less than a year at middle school, left as a "graduate" and was sent to an army reclamation farm in Jiangxi Province, southeast of Shanghai. My eldest brother, a student of motor vehicle engineering, was assigned to a tool-repair shop in a small town in Guizhou Province, then and now one of the poorest and most backward areas of the country. His letters confirmed the frequent rumor that "some people in Guizhou are so destitute that the whole family shares one pair of pants."

Thinking about Number 5 and Number 1 added to my depression. Our family was scattered now, their intelligence and abilities wasted. When I thought of my mother's anguish at having to decide which one of her sons would be denied a university education, my heart was heavy. Number 1 had gone to university only to be banished to a wasteland.

As if that was not enough, when we had a chance to talk alone Number 2 informed me that Number 3 had not been home from Songjiang for months.

"I have to explain this to you before you ask after her," he began. "For the past months Great-Aunt's resentment toward Number 3's letting you go to the countryside has made Great-Aunt hostile and abusive. She accused Number 3 of being a coward and the worst kind of elder sister. Ah Si, we all are aware that you made a huge sacrifice for the family, but Number 3 has not had an easy time since you left. She could hardly keep a dry eye whenever you were mentioned and the tremendous burden will go with her for the rest of her life, even without Great-Aunt's blame. What a time!" he sighed. "You have a home that you are not free to visit, and Number 3 has one that she is afraid to visit!"

How could Great-Aunt say things like that to someone who had spent her entire first month's salary to buy me a fashionable polyester shirt, much prized in China at that time? But my resentment toward Great-Aunt — whom I had missed greatly — was, as usual, tinged with guilt. I understood why she treated my sister badly. I wished she could treat all of us equally, but it was not in her nature.

Lying in the darkness on my first night at home after almost a year, I was torn apart with conflicting loyalties, and my tears ran down onto the pillow. After living in pretense for the past ten months mouthing political slogans, now I must hide my feelings at home too.

Number 3 came home a few days later. She burst into tears when I opened the door, skinny and wasted from my illness and all the hard work. "Great-Aunt was right," she exclaimed. "This is my fault!" She asked me a thousand questions and I tried my best to answer them without including the grim details. I turned the food-poisoning into a humorous episode; the dysentery I reported as a character-building life-experience. Telling the truth would do no one good, I concluded.

I tried to reconcile Number 3 and Great-Aunt but the effort was in vain. Great-Aunt ignored my sister but doted on me, doing my laundry, cooking my favorite dishes, offering me money to see a movie or go shopping. But she never sat and talked with me. She kept herself busy all the time, playing her part in the massive earth-digging campaign during the day, distributing mosquito pesticide among the neighbors for the committee at night. "The worst year for mosquitoes I have ever experienced," she said.

After four weeks, during which I spent most of my time alone in our apartment, the doctor stopped my sick leave and Great-Aunt took to her flour roasting again. Number 2 and Number 3 saw me off at the dock, and I was on my way to the Da Feng Prison Farm once more.

18

I RETURNED TO THE FARM early in October to find that the PLA had moved in — specifically, the air force, which was loyal to Mao's successor, Lin Biao, and his son, Lin Li-guo, who, in his late twenties, had been made deputy commander. The PLA representatives had established themselves at leading levels of the farm, sub-farm and brigade.

Our brigade's two reps made an interesting team. They were both officers, but there the similarity ended. Cui was in his thirties, slim, average height, appearing reasonable and well-spoken. Zhao was in his forties, chunky and strong. Everything about him was short, from his arms and legs to his almost invisible neck. After only a few days I concluded that the big head that sat on that neck was hollow.

If Cui had earned his four officer's pockets by his charm and elementary-school education, the unschooled and illiterate Zhao had acquired his by sweating, and even shedding blood for twenty years. The two of them reminded me of the "red face" and "white face" characters in classical plays, such as the traditional Beijing

Opera, in which a red-painted face represents a good person while the white denotes its opposite, though quite often they worked together. From the beginning Cui and Zhao worked that way.

Zhao described himself to us as *lao-da-cu* — old, big and inelegant. Unlike us, he pointed out, who had "drunk a few bottles of ink" so that we had "more twists in our minds than in our guts," making us hard to deal with, he was simple and straight. Red-face Cui would then take over, saying that he himself had a mind no different from ours, so we would get along just fine. Zhao liked to yell and shout to emphasize his remarks; Cui spoke in a low voice and sometimes joked around while conveying the same message.

Some of us felt they were a two-man comic show, but their routine filled me with ill feeling. Why did they act that way instead of being straightforward?

At that time I and others held the PLA in the highest possible esteem. They were the heroic "uncles" who had brought Liberation: self-sacrificing men and women who loved China and Chairman Mao. Even the Cultural Revolution had not smeared them. Their rigid "Three Main Rules and Eight Points of Attention" were well known to every schoolchild. (Obey orders in all actions; take not even a single needle or piece of thread from the citizens; turn in everything captured — these were the three rules. Speak politely; pay fairly for what you buy; return everything you borrow; compensate for anything you damage; swear at or hit no one; damage no crops; take no liberties with women; mistreat no captives — these were the eight points.) Mao had recently called upon the whole nation to learn from the revered PLA. In the days to come I would have a hard time relating what I had been taught at school to what I saw with my own eyes.

A brick house was under construction on the south side of our village to house Cui and Zhao and their office. No wattle and thatch for them. We female laborers were divided into teams of four, given a cart and sent to the sub-farm for bricks. The long flatbed cart with projecting handles and a straw pull-rope bounced easily over the deep ruts left by the typhoons. But once loaded with bricks it became as difficult to handle as an angry water buffalo. With one person on each handle, one shouldering the pull-rope and the last one pushing from the rear, we were barely able to move the cart and wept with frustration when the two lost control of the handles and the rear of the cart slammed to the ground, throwing the bricks into the road. Our vexation intensified when we finally reached our destination only to be scoffed at by the bricklayers for bringing hardly enough bricks to make a thin pillar.

The very day that our PLA reps moved into their eye-catching new house, Lao Chang rushed us back to the paddies, where the rice stalks had turned golden yellow. Although our paddies were nothing like the "rolling waves of golden ears" described in songs, we were excited because we knew that every single plant had been touched by our hands, from gently tugging the seedlings from their beds, to planting them in straight rows, to endless weedings and applications of fertilizer. Now the rice would be cut down, by hand.

The paddies had been drained and harvesting could begin; once again Lao Chang reminded us that timing was everything. For two weeks we worked from dawn until dark. Our lunches were brought to the fields so that we would lose no time. Wearing boots (the paddies were still muddy) and a long-sleeved shirt to protect my forearms from the rough stalks, I wielded my sickle, bent at the waist, hour after hour, chopping the plants off at ground level and piling them carefully so that they could be bundled up and hauled away to the threshing ground.

After each day of bone-weary labor we still had to endure political study at night. Although we never saw Cui and Zhao during the day — they were rushing between meetings in their jeep, often accompanied by two lucky and usually good-looking female students chosen to take notes for them — they always showed up for political study. And both of them had "elephant bottoms," for when the endless meetings finally drew to a close, they seemed reluctant to leave our dorm. None of us could get ready for bed while they were there. They never seemed interested in conducting political study with the men.

In November the threshing began. This was a new experience for me and it soon proved horrifying. This year the women had no help, for all the male laborers, including the prisoners, had been commandeered to rebuild the main road. "Order Number 1" had reached the farm, Zhao told us at the meeting: "Our great leader

Chairman Mao teaches us to 'be prepared for war and natural disaster.' The original road is not adequate for military vehicles."

While trucks loaded with gravel and cement came and went, we worked at the threshing ground, a large flat area trampled hard and free of vegetation. Six horizontal thresher barrels were turned by long belts attached to an electric motor. From the surface of the barrels projected long, sharp metal teeth. As the drum turned, I held a bundle of rice against the top so that the teeth could tear the ears free. One careless move and my hand would be ripped to shreds. It would be even worse if I fell against the swiftly revolving barrel.

Once threshed, the bundles of rice stalks were stacked for later use in building, rope making and so on. On the other side of the barrels, where the ears fell, workers raked away the chaff. It would be used for fuel. Everyone wore a cotton mask against the cloud of dust that hung in the air so thickly that it almost obscured the lights set up for the evening shifts.

I found it impossible to hold the bundle of rice stalks against the barrel in the prescribed manner because my "kindling arms" were not strong enough and the bundle was often yanked from my hands. I tried to compensate by wrapping my arms around the bundle and pressing it against my chest. This method required that I lean closer to the whirling, flashing teeth. Even worse, since I was too short, Lao Chang ordered me to stand on a pile of straw, making balance all the more difficult to maintain.

For the first few nights I had nightmares about falling against the barrel and being shredded to bloody bits. I wasn't sure whether it was my pleas or the fact that I would often lose my hold on the bundle and watch it be torn away from me and pulled under the barrel, causing the whole production line to come to a halt, but Lao Chang eventually reassigned me to piling up the threshed bundles.

Thus the first anniversary of my coming to the farm rolled around. It was Jia-ying who reminded me of the date. But what use was it to remember?

I had never bought Great-Aunt's theory that I was a girl born with bad luck, but occasionally I wondered. One sunny day during our lunch break, I fell to the threshing ground with a sharp pain in my abdomen. The pain grew and I was soaked in sweat, curled up like a shrimp. Yu Hua immediately sent someone to the road-construction site for Dr. Wang. Lao Chang arrived but could do nothing except stand there and make guesses. A while later Dr. Wang ran up with two young men, Xiao Zhu and Xiao Qian, who carried a stretcher between them. It took the doctor only a few moments of prodding my stomach to diagnose acute appendicitis.

"You need an operation," he urged. "Immediately. We must get you to a hospital."

Xiao Zhu and Xiao Qian wrapped me in quilts and put me onto a cart, the kind we had used to haul bricks. There were no proper medical facilities in our village nor in the sub-farm; worse, because the main road was under construction, the farm hospital couldn't send its ambulance over. So Dr. Wang took the lead and the two young men pulled and pushed the cart along the rutted country road to the Sanlong — Three Dragon — River, which bordered a commune just over a mile away. The distance seemed like the Long March as every bump and jiggle of the cart sent a searing arrow of pain through my belly. Yu Hua periodically mopped the cold sweat off my brow as she jogged alongside the cart.

The Sanlong River was about fifty yards wide, broader and cleaner than the tributary that flowed beside our road, and marked the boundary of the commune. That village, because of constant raids by prisoners who stole crops and animals to supplement their meager diets, was like an armed camp surrounded by a wire fence.

It was about two o'clock when we reached the river. Dr. Wang and the two men called out for help. There was no response. Yu Hua began to run along the dike, jumping and shouting in her surprisingly deep voice. "It's an emergency! Please help us!"

Sweat bathed my face and soaked my clothes. Scared, still curled tight, knees to my chest and chin tucked in, I fought the nausea and piercing jabs of pain. Yu Hua's frantic calls and the doctor's urgent commands did little to dispel my anxiety.

Finally a voice floated across the river. "Wait a bit. We're sending a boat over."

Xiao Qian and Xiao Zhu carried my stretcher onto a cement barge. The doctor and Yu Hua scrambled aboard and we were poled across. Another cart was found and the painful jouncing began again.

By the time I was in the operating room night had fallen. Dr. Wang was beside me. I wished desperately that someone from my family were present. I knew nothing about appendicitis and its possible complications. All I knew was that Dr. Wang was going to cut me open and I might die.

I had been put under only local anesthetic, so was fully aware of what was happening. I could see nothing but the ceiling. There were two other doctors, constantly asking Dr. Wang questions and remonstrating with him about the delay. No one wanted to talk to me, apparently.

After a while, everything went black. Literally.

Curses rang out in the pitch darkness. Feet shuffled.

"Doctor, I've lost my sight!" I cried out.

"No, no, Xiao Ye," Dr. Wang said. "The power went off. Don't worry, the nurses are out looking for flashlights. Thank goodness I have already removed your inflamed appendix."

Losing electricity was not new to me or to anyone else in China. Even in Shanghai, power was regularly cut off in residential areas on certain days to conserve energy. Factories sometimes sent a shift home, especially during the summer, a time of peak consumption. But there was usually a warning.

The nurses soon returned, barely visible behind the bobbing circles of their flashlights. I closed my eyes again, completely spent, only to open them wide when a sharp pain shot through my stomach, causing my right leg to recoil. The anesthetic had worn off. Someone pushed my leg down and I realized the operation was still going on. I screamed when another bolt of pain went through me.

"What's wrong! What are you doing to me?"

"It's all right," one of the nurses said calmly, "the doctor is sewing you up. He shouldn't be long."

I screamed for more anesthetic.

"Not possible," Dr. Wang said. "The needle would have to be administered in your spine and we can't turn you over."

Holding her flashlight to illuminate her Little Red Book, a nurse started to read me quotations from Chairman Mao. "Do not fear hardship; do not fear death," she exhorted.

When Chairman Mao penned that advice, I doubted he was

being repeatedly punctured by a sewing needle. I gritted my teeth against the pain.

I was carried on a stretcher into the dimly lit ward, completely drained but out of danger. Yu Hua and the two young men who had brought me all that way were waiting to see how I had fared in the operation. I was deeply touched by their kindness and I wanted to thank them, but all I could manage was a weak smile.

19

I WAS RELEASED FROM the hospital a week later and given light duty cleaning up in the canteen. I felt lucky to be working indoors, for the northwest wind had turned sharply cold again and dampness chilled to the bone. The male students were still laboring to complete the road and the women were building paddy dikes with heavy iron-toothed rakes. If the dikes were not made properly, Cui or Zhao squashed them flat and ordered them redone.

Failure to reach quotas was no longer a simple minus sign on the posted list; it was now assumed to be politically motivated, and that meant trouble. After the PLA's arrival, everything was done the army way. We were no longer allowed to walk to the canteen individually, "like a plate of loose sand," as Cui put it. As "real soldiers" we marched together, bowls in our left hands, swinging our right hands in unison. Students with good family backgrounds were formed into a militia with daily training, including rifle practice, led by Zhao. The militia was on call twenty-four hours a day.

On call for what? Although I had never been a "news digger," since coming to the farm I had never been so ill informed. There was no newspaper available, and transistor radios, at that time rare and expensive, provided only repetitive propaganda. Needless to say, the camp's loudspeakers offered the same. Even though mail was delivered twice a week, everyone knew that putting things down in black and white in such dangerous times was not a good idea. I was aware only of what was going on in our little village.

As I had seen during my medical leave in Shanghai a few months earlier, the whole country was building air-raid shelters against a widening of the conflict with Russia, but why did our farm need a "ready for war" road, broad and strong enough, in Zhao's words, for two tanks to travel side by side? And why did we need a militia? What strategic importance could our village have, out in the middle of nowhere, surrounded by flat land that produced poor crops?

When the winter deepened, we looked forward to a few relatively easy months before spring brought back the intensive heavy labor of growing rice. The temperature dropped so low that on some mornings we found the water jars sealed with ice. To stay warm at night when the wind hissed through the wattle walls of our unheated dorm, Yu Hua and I put our bedding together, as did others.

But many was the time we were torn from our sleep by the sharp ringing of bells calling us to military exercises. Militia members or not, we all had to go, jumping out of our beds into the freezing darkness, fumbling into our clothes, dashing to the threshing grounds to be harangued by Cui and Zhao, snug and warm in their army greatcoats, peering at their stopwatches. I had accepted hard labor long ago, but I hated the "war preparation."

One night at our regular political study meeting a few women were talking about the cost of building the road, trading rumors and passing on gossip.

"All that effort and expense to build a road nobody uses," I joked. "Too bad we couldn't put half the time and money into building dorms with thicker walls."

That joke would come back to haunt me.

When February rolled around the students' spirits lifted, for it was time for *tan-qin* — home visit — the national government policy of a two-week paid holiday each year for employees who worked away from home. Travel costs were picked up by one's work unit. Lao Chang had told us long ago that we could take our *tan-qin* at any time during the year, except busy seasons, but Cui had changed that, saying we must all go home at the same time.

I had long been worried about Number 5. In her correspondence she sounded so despondent that I feared she was heading for a nervous breakdown. Each letter ripped my heart to pieces. I had planned to wait and take my *tan-qin* in July to coincide with hers so that I could meet her at home. Cui's new policy ruined my plans.

When I asked Yu Hua what I should do, she suggested I explain things to Cui and Zhao. "You have reasonable grounds for an exception," she said. "I am your group leader. I'll go with you to talk to them."

That night we went to the brick building. The reps' office was lit by two bare bulbs hanging from the ceiling. Cui and Zhao sat at their respective desks, sipping tea, their faces blank.

I was so nervous that I tripped over my words, so Yu Hua stepped in to explain that both my parents were dead and that I had hoped to take my vacation at the same time as my siblings. "They have been scattered," she finished, "and want to see each other when they can."

"If I can take my two weeks later on," I said weakly, "I promise to work all the harder when I return."

Cui and Zhao sat silent, as if we were not there, as if neither of us had said a word. I recalled the humiliation I felt on my many visits with Mother to uncaring factory officials who offered no help. Suddenly I missed both my parents terribly and began to cry.

Cui stood up and came around to the front of his desk. A cold smile crossed his face. "What are you crying for," he said harshly. "We haven't said a word yet, have we?"

He smirked at Zhao, who was leafing through the registration book that held all our names and family histories.

"*Tan-qin* is for comrades who are married and working away from their spouses, or for unmarried ones to visit their parents. Isn't it?"

"Yes, Representative Zhao," I muttered.

"Are you married?" he asked with phony politeness. Cui smirked.

"No, Representative Zhao."

"Then you have no spouse to visit, do you? And your parents are dead. So it seems," he concluded, "that you are not eligible for *tan-qin* at all."

I turned cold with fear. I would never see my brothers and sisters or Great-Aunt again.

Zhao stood up, his face still calm, his voice restrained. "There are millions of brothers and sisters sent to different places to serve our motherland. Why should you get special treatment? You of all people," he added, making reference to my bad class background.

My lips trembled. I looked at my friend. Yu Hua's expression told me she was as astonished as I.

"Please," I managed, but Cui cut me off, laughing.

"We'll let you know. You're not in a hurry, of course. You said you wanted to delay your visit. And your parents won't be in a hurry, will they?" He laughed even louder. "The two of you are dismissed."

I was so scared I couldn't sleep that night, and the next morning, Yu Hua tried to console me, but failed. Then she brightened. "Xiao Ye, I have an idea. Let's go to the sub-farm administrative office and get this cleared up. Cui and Zhao are PLA reps, after all. They shouldn't be interfering in this matter."

Once again I was grateful for my friend's clear head. After we hurried to finish our quota of new paddy dikes, we asked Jia-ying to fetch our supper for us and keep it in the dorm, then headed for the sub-farm. By the time we arrived, it was dark. My heart fell when I saw the office was closed for the day.

"Don't give up," Yu Hua urged. "Maybe they're having supper."

We found the canteen and, after questioning a number of people, were directed toward a tall, middle-aged man eating alone at one of the tables. Representative Huang had a kindly face and large, intelligent eyes. Hearing the reason for our visit, he led us to his office.

His accent placed him from Zhejiang Province. He invited us to sit down, and his politeness gave me confidence. I omitted my original request to delay my *tan-qin*; I explained my concern that the reps would not allow me to go home at all. Representative

Huang took out his copy of the farm personnel registration book, leafed through it, turned it toward me, and asked me to point out my name. I did so, with a shaking finger. He read the information about my family, then closed the book and looked up.

"There will be no problem," he said. He went on to explain that the government policy applied to everyone. As he spoke, an angry edge crept into his voice. "It is tragic enough that you lost both your parents. How could those two —" and he stopped himself.

I left the office, filled with relief.

On our way back to our village, we met Xiao Zhu, Xiao Qian and and Xiao Jian, three male friends of Yu Hua. Zhu and Qian were the ones who had helped during my attack of appendicitis, and all three of them, along with Yu Hua, had visited me in the hospital. I had always appreciated their friendliness. Like Yu Hua, they were all older than me, but despite their correct political backgrounds, none of them looked down on me.

Xiao Jian — our accountant — suggested we all go to his tiny office next to the canteen where he could heat up our supper. While I ate, I talked and laughed, happy that my problem had been solved and delighting in their camaraderie.

The next evening Yu Hua and I were summoned to Cui and Zhao's office. As soon as we entered, Zhao began to shout at us.

"How dare you two play tricks behind our backs!" he screamed, his face red with anger. "How dare you go over our heads!"

Swearing and cursing, his army cap crooked on his head, he accused us of trying to undermine the PLA. When we tried to speak he cut us off, became angrier, screamed louder. Cui sat at his desk playing with a pencil, not saying a word through the entire tirade, until he finally dismissed us with a wave of his hand.

"Fuck your mothers!" Zhao shouted as we left. "Fuck both of them!"

We slunk away. I had no idea what kind of a mistake we had made, but when I boarded the ship for Shanghai a week later, my heart was full of foreboding. I knew I had not heard the last from Cui and Zhao.

20

THE DOCK AT SHANGHAI Number 16 Pier was awash in people. Shouts of joy swirled around me as my farm-mates threw themselves into the arms of weeping mothers and fathers. No one from my family was there to greet me. Great-Aunt, now almost sixty, was too old to fight the crowds; on her three-inch lily feet she would have been thrown off balance and trampled in no time. Number 1's and Number 5's *tan-qin* did not coincide with mine. Number 2 would be home soon, but this day he was digging air-raid shelters in the suburbs with his fellow workers. Number 3 couldn't get to the city until Sunday, her day off.

Since I knew I would find the apartment that once rang with the noise and bustle of eight people empty and quiet, I was in no hurry to get on one of the overcrowded buses. I also knew that as soon as I walked in the door I would start to dissemble, for I couldn't burden anyone with my true experiences and loneliness on the farm. I stood in the cold February rain waiting for the next bus.

Number 3's arrival in Purple Sunshine Lane lifted my heart.

"Ah Si, you look wonderful," she exclaimed as soon as she came in the door. "The last time I saw you, you were as thin as a stick!"

A pretty young woman, now nineteen, she lived in a one-room factory dorm with three other unmarried female workers — not an ideal arrangement, but her job meant she was secure from assignment to the countryside and could think about settling down.

Over tea prepared by Great-Aunt, we chatted happily.

"I haven't found a boyfriend yet, but I've got my eye open," Number 3 joked. "Look," she added proudly, handing me a photograph that showed her in an army uniform, a gun slung in her shoulder.

"You're in the militia?" I asked, passing the photo to Great-Aunt.

"I'm a leader."

"By the time Number 3 gets around to pointing her gun," Great-Aunt put in caustically, "the Russians will have taken over the factory."

"I'm surprised they accepted the daughter of a capitalist," I said.

"Oh, they don't care. I don't give them any trouble. Eat, sleep and work, that's my motto."

A few days later, when I told Number 2 about almost having had my *tan-qin* taken away, he explained the new political climate to me, and some of the strange things on the farm began to make sense. When Mao had ordered the PLA into the work units to stabilize them against further upheavals and civil strife, the plan had been to establish "three-in-one" authority, composed of representatives from the masses, the revolutionary cadres and the PLA. Since then the PLA had accrued more and more power in farms, factories and bureaucracies. It had then launched a purge of those who were against the involvement of the armed forces. The strongest anti-PLA voices came from universities and academic institutes; consequently, a "counter-revolutionary" group was "discovered" at the famous Fudan University in Shanghai. A wide-ranging witch-hunt ensued.

This situation was further complicated, as I learned many years later, because Lin Biao had long been quietly preparing to unseat

Mao and take over the country. In total control of the air force and much of the rest of the armed services, Lin Biao was putting men loyal to him into key positions. When the time was right, he planned to assassinate Mao Ze-dong and take power. In retrospect, the reason for the new road on our farm became clear. The road was not there to prepare for a Russian invasion at all; it was there to support a possible retreat of Lin Biao's forces.

None of us then knew of Lin Biao's plot, of course. All Number 2 understood was that the PLA had achieved new power in China and was ferreting out all opposition. He warned me to steer clear of any conflict, particularly where the PLA reps were concerned.

Neither he nor I knew the full significance of my visit with Yu Hua to see Representative Huang at the sub-farm, nor of that kind man's intervention on my behalf. The sub-farm administration office was, like all units, assigned PLA representatives: that was Huang's function. But the sub-farm PLA reps were from the Shanghai Garrison, which in turn was controlled by the Nanjing Military Region, a force loyal to Chairman Mao, and therefore inimical to Lin Biao. Thus, by going over Cui's and Zhao's heads, Yu Hua and I had gone to their enemy.

🌿

The evening after my return to the farm at the beginning of March, an urgent meeting was called in the warehouse. We were instructed not to bring our pens, notebooks and stools — an unprecedented announcement that made me nervous. In those days anything out of the ordinary was a bad omen, and Yu Hua and I were already in the reps' bad books.

The warehouse was festooned with political slogans. "Never Forget the Class Struggle!" "Forgetting Means Betrayal!" "Long Live the People's Liberation Army!" "We Will Smash the Heads of Anyone Who Dares to Oppose the Army!" I was well used to the strident tone of posters, but this last seemed unusually threatening.

Once inside the cold, damp warehouse, we were directed to sit on the freezing cement floor, not to squat on our heels. Cui was in his glory. Fist in the air, he led the recitation of Chairman Mao's slogan, "Grasp class struggle and all problems can be solved!" It grew louder with each repetition. As the room boomed and echoed with the well-worn words, two white-clad canteen staff walked slowly to the front, a huge wok held between them. Ceremoniously, they placed the wok on the ground at Cui's feet.

Cui motioned for silence, tugged at the tails of his jacket, and began to speak. "Representative Zhao and I feel that there is a lack of class-struggle consciousness in our brigade. Chairman Mao has taught us that the class struggle must continue! In order to carry the Great Proletarian Cultural Revolution through to the end, it is necessary for all of us to be reminded of the proletariat's hardships before Liberation."

I eyed the wok as an unpleasant smell spread through the chill of the warehouse.

"We are going to have a special meal," Cui went on, pointing at the wok, "to recall the suffering of the past so that we can appreciate the good life of the present. I warn you, Representative Zhao and I will be watching carefully to make sure all of you take part. Any cheating will be considered politically motivated."

One by one we filed to the front to get our share of the "meal." When it was my turn I was handed a fist-sized ball of malodorous, lukewarm green stuff. I returned to my place, sat down and regarded the repulsive object that was to put me in touch with the pre-Liberation poor. The ball was heavy and smelled of earth and grass. I glanced at Yu Hua, who shrugged her shoulders and tried not to show her disgust. I broke it in half, but long green stringy stuff bound the halves together.

"Come on!" came Zhao's voice. "Don't be cowardly. Remember some of your former generations had even less to eat. Of course, others had an easy life sucking the blood of the poor!"

I held my breath, closed my eyes and took a bite. The ball had a sandy, rubbery consistency and tasted of hot bitter grass and foul dirt. It seemed to be made of weeds mixed with wheat chaff. The stringy texture and horrible odor made me gag.

Poor Jia-ying, who sat near me, threw up hard, soiling her jacket and the cement floor in front of her. The smell of her vomit didn't make my task any easier.

Yu Hua leaned over. "Break it into pieces with your fingernails and swallow the bits. Don't chew it."

Jia-ying was weeping in frustration. Each time she put the putrid green ball to her mouth she vomited again. She begged Zhao for some water, but he walked away without answering. For me Yu Hua's method worked, and in a few moments I had forced the pieces down my throat. I slipped closer to Jia-ying and told her what to do. Finally, she too succeeded and, through her tears, she smiled with relief.

As we left the warehouse we passed two inspectors who made us open our mouths, lift up our tongues, and then turn out our pockets. I was convinced the sadistic display by Cui and Zhao had one purpose only: to show us they could do whatever they wanted with us.

I tossed and turned all night, my stomach aching, until dawn was ushered in by a voice blasting from the loudspeakers, commanding the entire camp to another meeting after dinner. Marching to the canteen, we passed a bunch of prisoners who had gathered to torment us. With bits of grass and straw protruding from their mouths, they laughed and jeered at us. One lay on the ground, twitching, as if seized by epilepsy.

"Ignore them," Cui warned us. "When you look at them, you see nothing."

In many ways I felt that the prisoners had more freedom than us and their lives were easier, since they were not required to participate in the Cultural Revolution. And when they had served their time, they would go back to their families. My sentence was final, for life. Some of the male students on the farm had run away, hoping they would be caught and sent over to the prisoners, but they were returned to the brigade. It was, to me, part of the madness of the Cultural Revolution that lawbreakers were better off than pepole who had done nothing wrong.

That night, Cui took a different tack at the meeting. He cajoled us, humbly asking for our help. "Representative Zhao and I are relatively new here and inexperienced at this kind of work," he said with false sincerity. "We are unfamiliar with sophisticated city youth. Please help us by writing your criticisms and suggestions. Be open and honest; in this way you can show your support for the PLA."

Remembering Number 2's warnings, I determined to do and say nothing. I advised Yu Hua to act the same way. But she was taken in. She wrote a criticism of Cui and Zhao, saying that, in dealing with my request to reschedule my *tan-qin*, they had behaved unfairly.

Three days later, the two PLA reps proved they had learned well from the "Hundred Flowers" movement in 1957 when Mao had rounded up those who had naively penned the criticisms he had requested. The reps even used Mao's words in their posters: "The Snake Has Poked Its Head Out of the Hole: What Shall We Do About It?" "Those Who Try to Overthrow the PLA Will Have No Good End!" Other *da-zi-bao* encouraged the students to expose those who opposed Cui and Zhao behind each other's backs.

Depressed and disheartened, I tried to prepare my mind for the attacks, the suspicion and the betrayals to come. Outside the dorm, a bitter northwest wind howled.

21

A WITCH-HUNT WAS LAUNCHED in our brigade. From among the "red" students an eight-member "clarifying and checking team" was formed, its members relieved of all other duties. They were to help Cui and Zhao carry out the purge. The three chosen women were Loaf, Fatty and Leggy, nicknamed, like many of us, according to their appearance. Loaf, whose eyeglasses were the thickest I had ever seen, was proud that her father, a tailor, was making costumes for the modern ballet "The White Haired Girls," one of only eight plays Jiang Qing allowed to be publicly performed. Fatty often voiced the Revolution's blood-line theory that "a dragon's son is a dragon." Needless to say, her blood ran pure. Tall and slender, with a large, flat head, Leggy was a hard worker who kept to herself. She had denounced her whole family after her father was labeled a rightist in the 1950s and had since been chosen as a model youth. Leggy even gave up her *tan-qin*, refusing to visit her "muddle-headed mother." I did not know the rest of the team well, but soon found that they were equally malevolent.

I was horrified to learn that the "snake's head" that had, according to Cui and Zhao, shown itself by coming partway out of its hole was the foursome who had befriended me when I was ill and when I returned from the sub-farm office to inquire about my home leave. They were Yu Hua, my friend and protector, Xiao Zhu, Xiao Qian and Xiao Jian. All four were from correct class backgrounds, and all were leaders. But all four were naive. They had, as requested by Cui, written and turned in their criticisms and suggestions.

At the struggle meeting that followed, my four friends were forced to stand before us as Cui led the crowd in shouting and waving fists, demanding that they confess their crimes.

"They have been hiding behind a curtain!" he screamed. "They and anyone who is part of their counter-revolutionary plot must be exposed!"

The din created by the hollering, in which I did not participate, almost split my eardrums. My friends stood with heads bowed, looking humiliated and guilty. It was too ridiculous to think that these four young people had plotted to undermine the revolution and the PLA.

After more bellowed slogans, more urgings to expose the snakes and all who trafficked with them, Cui ended the meeting by announcing that the four were now under house arrest. The crowd dutifully cheered and stamped their feet. The downcast youngsters were led out of the warehouse, each followed by a "watcher" whose job was to stay with the person at all times.

I rushed back to my dorm to find Yu Hua packing her belongings. "Yu Hua, where are they taking you?"

"Shut up or you'll have to bear the consequences of talking to a counter-revolutionary!" shouted Fatty, her watcher.

Yu Hua, her eyes bright with fear, shook her head to indicate I should be quiet. I turned and asked the others in the dorm where my friend was being taken, but they had been intimidated into silence. I watched as Yu Hua was led to the brick house.

Jia-ying appeared beside me. "Don't cry, Xiao Ye," she whispered. "The reps are simply killing a chicken to scare the monkey. When you wake up, Yu Hua will be back." I wished I could share her confidence.

I was shaken violently from a troubled sleep.

"Ye Ting-xing! Wake up! Get out of bed right now!"

Leggy and Fatty stood beside my bed, barely recognizable in the dim light.

"What's the matter? What time is it?"

Up and down the row, heads popped up; some girls leaned on their arms, staring.

"It's one o'clock," Jia-ying answered as Fatty threw my padded jacket into my face.

"Hurry up," Leggy commanded. "You're wanted by the reps. Right now!"

I struggled into my padded trousers, pulled on my socks and grabbed my coat. "Why do they want me, in the middle of the night?"

"Hurry up," Leggy said again. "There is no palanquin waiting for you, Miss! Stop dragging your feet."

The two of them bustled me out into the cold darkness. I tripped and stumbled repeatedly, for in my panic and haste I hadn't brought Number 2's glasses with me. There were a few people standing on the porch when we got to the brick house. Every light was on and the radio blared songs and Mao quotations. Leggy pushed me in.

Cui and Zhao were at their usual places behind their desks. I stood before them, shaking with fear.

"Do you know why you are here?" Zhao began.

I shook my head, squinting as my eyes accustomed themselves to the bright lights.

Zhao spoke calmly. "We have uncovered a counter-revolutionary group in this brigade, as you learned earlier tonight," he said. "We want to know about the meetings you have had with them. Every gathering, every word, times and locations."

"I don't understand what you mean," I stammered.

"Don't play games with us," Zhao responded, maintaining his calm. "We know what's been going on. As a matter of fact, we are doing you a favor, giving you this chance to clear yourself."

My fear deepened. "Clear myself from what? I don't know about any meetings."

In a flash Zhao slammed his hands on the desk and leapt to his feet, his face twisted. "Our patience is limited," he shouted, saliva flying. "Don't try to stall. This is your only chance. Cooperate, or it will be too late for you!"

Cui too got to his feet, stepped around his desk and patted Zhao on the shoulder. Zhao took his seat.

With a phony smile on his face, Cui said patiently, "You see, your friends are under house arrest. We are treating you differently because we're confident that you'll help us. Think about it," he urged, pointing at the filing cabinets behind him. "You know your dossier is in there, and you know what it contains: three generations and more of your family's history. A family of landlords and capitalists."

I saw what Cui was implying. Everyone in China had a dossier; its influence was one of the first things I had learned as a young girl. Besides being used to brand you, the dossier contained every bit of damaging information anyone had said about you. The Red Guards had filled hundreds of thousands of dossiers with hatred and false information.

Cui and Zhao's plan now became clear to me. They considered me a member of the counter-revolutionary group — a group of five, not four. But because I was the only one with a bad class background, because I was the youngest, least experienced and most vulnerable, they thought I would break first and seize the opportunity to save myself by informing against the others.

Trembling, I clenched my fists and pressed my lips together. Cui ordered Fatty to take me into an adjoining room and guard me while I wrote a confession.

"No confession, no sleep," he screamed as Fatty led me out.

In the small room, poorly illuminated by a single bulb hanging from the ceiling, were two desks and two stools. On one of the desks was a stack of paper and a pen. Fatty pushed me down on a stool.

"Write down everything you remember about your meetings with the others, as well as your own bad thoughts. Remember Chairman Mao's teachings, 'Leniency to those who confess their crimes, but severity to those who refuse to do so.'"

She left the room, slamming the door. I sat there shaking, then for what seemed like hours just stared at the pen and paper.

The next thing I knew, Fatty was shouting, her face inches from mine. I must have fallen asleep. Others from the "clarifying and checking" team were also yelling at me, denouncing my lack of cooperation. Finally, after repeated warnings, all but Fatty and Leggy left the room.

Until daylight showed in the window they took turns at waking me each time I put my head down on the desk. I would stare at the blank paper until my eyes closed, then be punched on the shoulder and violently shaken alert.

Finally I wrote one sentence. "I, Ye Ting-xing, am sorry for being disrespectful to reps Cui and Zhao and I am willing to accept their punishment."

Fatty snatched the paper from my hands and led me to breakfast. Mechanically I pushed food into my mouth while my watcher looked on silently. Immediately after, I was turned over to Loaf so that Fatty could catch some sleep, and escorted to the field. I was not permitted to sleep.

By this time I was like a zombie. A lost night of sleep was debilitating enough, but the fear and tension had drained all my energy. Once again I found myself the object of criticism and ridicule. I remembered Great-Aunt's expression: "We escaped the bitter sea only to fall into the mouth of a tiger." I worked alongside Yu Hua, building paddy dikes with a long heavy rake in the chilly late-March rain as our watchers sat chatting under umbrellas. We were not allowed to work with others, nor could we talk to each other. I was worried about Yu Hua. She was withdrawn, her eyes were puffy, and she seemed to have aged overnight. I wondered if I looked as bad.

That night yet another struggle meeting was held in the warehouse. When I walked in, trailed by Fatty, no one spoke to me. People looked away when I passed them. As soon as I sat down in the front row, someone yelled from the back, "Bring up the counter-revolutionaries!" Only then did I notice two cells made of bamboo poles and reed mats newly installed at each end of the warehouse. Yu Hua emerged from behind one of them. Xiao Jian, Xiao Qian and Xiao Zhu were led to sit behind me.

The same voice at the back began to chant slogans, and the mass of students joined in. "Down with the counter-revolutionaries! Down with anyone who dares to oppose the PLA! Those who oppose the PLA are against the Communist Party!" With each deafening shout, my shoulders hunched a little more, as if the bitter words were being piled on my head. I glanced at my friends, who looked miserable and terrified. The whole scene brought back memories of attacks by Red Guards bellowing in the streets.

The next stage of the struggle meeting was an open invitation for people to stand up and report on "crimes" committed by the five of us. One by one my friends were accused of betraying their class and of setting up a secret counter-revolutionary group.

When it came my turn, from behind me I heard, "Ye Ting-xing has no respect for the motherland! She makes fun of everything!" "Ye Ting-xing looks down on the PLA," a second woman blurted out, referring to my mimicking of Zhao's Sichuan accent in the dorm at night. My joke about the new road, charged another, proved that my "hatred of our beloved PLA was rooted in my bad blood, which had been growing since the day I was born." "Her parents were capitalists who sucked the blood of the working class," screamed a fourth.

The imprecations, curses and insults went on and on, and my humiliation deepened with every cruel lie or false accusation. How could all of them hate me so? These were the women with whom I worked, ate and shared a dorm. If I could, I would have ended my life there and then.

Finally Zhao stood up. He informed the crowd that the five of us had held secret meetings in Xiao Jian's tiny accounting office. "You all know the size of that room," he sneered. "Just imagine how closely the five of them would have been jammed together. Do you really believe that they were just eating supper and talking?" He smirked, then suddenly pointed at Yu Hua and me. "And you two! You are constantly seen sharing the same bedding at night." He turned to the audience. "I wonder if staying warm was the only reason!"

His remark brought an uproar of laughter. From the corner of my eye I saw that Yu Hua had begun to cry. I knew nothing about lesbians, but Zhao's remark was clearly meant to be low and obscene, and I felt I would never hold up my head again.

22

TWO DAYS LATER I WAS put under house arrest. Zhao had not been satisfied with my one-sentence confession. Loaf shoved me into the same room in which I had written the sentence, pushed me behind the same desk and ordered me once again to confess all my crimes and report on the counter-revolutionary thoughts, words and actions of my four friends.

At first I didn't care. For the past two days I had not been shadowed because, as Cui put it, I was "under surveillance of the mobilized masses." The prisoners mocked me, the students lowered their eyes when I passed or openly criticized me. I felt like a leper.

There were two beds in the room, I noticed, one for me and one for Loaf. The first night was a repetition of my initial interrogation, shouting, punching, slapping whenever fatigue seemed to remove all the strength from my neck muscles. Fatty, Leggy and Loaf took turns: when one grew tired of the attack, another took over.

I wrote a few more sentences. I admitted to going over the heads of our PLA reps and criticized myself for doing so. At midnight I was allowed to lie down on the bed, fully clothed. Only minutes later, it seemed, I was shaken awake and dragged back to the desk.

"Not good enough," Loaf asserted. "Stop stalling. The reps say this is not enough. You must give a full confession."

"But I did nothing wrong," I repeated so often that it became a litany. "My friends did nothing wrong. We're not counter-revolutionaries!"

Shouting, slaps on the face, criticism, insults. Back to bed. Shaken awake again. Pulled to the desk. More yelling, more demands.

Each morning I went to the paddies. Every evening there was another struggle meeting to vilify me and the other four "counter-revolutionaries" before I was dragged back to the room. Exhausted, disoriented and deprived of sleep, I finally wrote a full self-criticism, telling how I went to the sub-farm and what I said to Representative Huang about my *tan-qin*. I filled several pages, writing as much as I could to satisfy them. Anything to be allowed to sleep.

It wasn't enough. I was kicked awake again. By now I could no longer tell how long I had been allowed to doze. Was it four hours or four minutes? I lost track of how many days had passed since the interrogation had begun. Loaf hauled me to my seat. Then Zhao came in, his military coat unbuttoned, his plastic slippers dragging. He sat beside me, very close, and ran his hand down the back of my head. I could smell green tea and cigarettes on his breath.

"Your hair needs a wash," he observed. Speaking softly, almost politely, in complete contrast to my watchers' vituperative abuse, he explained that my confession was a good start, very good indeed — but it didn't go far enough.

"You've told us what you did. But you must examine your thinking. What motivated you? What were you really attempting to do? Not simply talk about your home leave, surely? Wasn't there more to it? Think about it."

He left, closing the door quietly. I stared at the sheet of paper, struggling to keep my eyes open. The slam of a hand on the wood beside my ear startled me.

"Wake up, parentless bitch! Who gave you permission to sleep?"

"Leave me alone!" I shouted.

Loaf slapped me across the face. My cheek burned with pain and tears of mortification ran down my cheeks.

"Your dead capitalist parents can't help you now."

"Leave my parents out of it," I said, earning another stinging blow.

It took them fourteen days to break me: two weeks of laboring ten hours a day, tilling corners of the paddy missed by the plows, two weeks of struggle meetings, two weeks of night-long interrogation sessions in which Loaf's angry shouts blended with Zhao's soft inducements. Two weeks without rest. I was not allowed to wash or change my clothes. My body stank; my hair was matted with mud; my pantlegs rotted off from the alkaline water that soaked into them in the paddies. Sometimes I did not know in which room I was, or what time it was. I was profoundly disoriented.

When I was older I learned that I had been subjected to the kind of sleep-deprivation torture Stalin had used during the Terror. It was frequently practised by interrogators during the Cultural Revolution and is still employed in some countries.

Finally, one night, Zhao spoke again. "Wouldn't you like to sleep, Xiao Ye? Wouldn't you like this to be over?"

"Tell me what you want me to write," I said, "and I'll do it."

To my everlasting shame, I filled two pages with untruths and exaggerations. I wrote that Representative Huang had criticized Cui and Zhao, which was true. I said that my friends and I had held meetings and criticized the PLA, which was false. My pages were sent back and forth to Cui and Zhao that night. They crossed things out, wrote comments in the margin, and I would rewrite the confession according to their wishes. Then, when it seemed I would finally be able to lie down, Cui insisted that I report everything that Yu Hua's sister, who was in the air force, had said to her about life in the military. Yu Hua had told me her sister frequently complained about the poor quality of the newly enlisted men and women and said that Lin Biao's son was a womanizer. At dawn they ordered me to sign the papers.

Even today I have never forgiven myself for informing on the only four colleagues in the village who showed any friendship to me. We were singled out so that Cui and Zhao could prove that they had found and rooted out a counter-revolutionary conspiracy in their midst. Why had they chosen us over others? I had no way of knowing, though in retrospect I see that my visit with Yu Hua to the sub-farm provided a means for Cui and Zhao, who were in the air force loyal to Lin Biao, to undermine the Shanghai Garrison by finding fault with Representative Huang.

After my confession was signed, my friends were released. But we were kept apart. Cui and Zhao told me they had sent their recommendation for punishment to higher authorites. We would certainly go to prison, they said; only the length of the sentence remained to be decided.

I was no longer shadowed by Loaf or anyone else; however, every morning I was forced to bow my head before a life-sized statue of Chairman Mao set up in the middle of the village at the crossroads. Although I kept telling myself not to take it too hard, I was always in tears when I finished. Until my house arrest and interrogation I had regarded myself as an old hand at dealing with mortification, after the years of wearing my brothers' cast-off clothes and Number 2's unfitted glasses, after the begging trips with Mother, after living on welfare and enduring the insults of Red Guards. But nothing matched the inhuman treatment by Cui, Zhao and those whom they corrupted to do their work.

One very hot night in July, several days after my eighteenth birthday, I passed hour after hour of sleeplessness and depression. I decided there was only one way out. I pushed aside the mosquito netting, rose quietly from my bed and stole from the dorm. I crept through the humid darkness as if in a trance, heading for the Sanlong River, where I scrambled down the bank and waded in.

The river was deep, its surface like an inkstone, smooth and black. Between my toes, the cool bottom mud squashed, and the strong current tugged at my knees. I stood, taking in the silence and the heavy odor of water and earth from the paddies.

I need only push off into the current, I thought, immerse my head, and suck the water deep into my lungs. It would be over quickly.

I was up to my waist when I heard disembodied voices floating toward me. The hot night must have driven others out. As I prepared to plunge, a memory came to me. Several years before I had seen a drowned body pulled from the Suzhou Creek near my home, so bloated that the shirt had split up the back and the trouser legs had parted at the seams.

I imagined my corpse lying like a piece of driftwood on the riverbank, limbs puffed like sausages, my face doughy. Strangers would manhandle my body and throw me into a wagon for disposal.

I turned and fought the current to the riverbank, convinced that life was a prison, that even death offered no escape.

If at the beginning of my interrogation the prisoners had been mean and cruel to me, some of them now tried to make things right. They looked at me with sympathy. Whenever I was washing or doing laundry, the stooped, white-haired old uncle who worked at the pump house would give me a rubber hose connected directly to the pump so that I didn't have to fetch water from the jars. I thanked him each time, but never learned his name. When I was too late to get my vacuum bottle filled with boiled water at the supply hut, a prisoner would take it over and have it filled in their hut. He always refused my penny. "You are no better off than us now," he would say. Though I appreciated his kindness, I often cried to think that I was on the same level as a criminal.

The busy rice-planting season was over and still no word came down about my jail sentence. No one seemed to care too much. Some students were friendly enough, but distant. I hadn't talked to Yu Hua since we were arrested, not even when we bumped into one another. We were forbidden to talk, but we could have got around that. Things had changed between us. Our friendship had become a casualty of the purge. I wanted more than anything to tell her what I had done and to ask her forgiveness.

So I became withdrawn. When I was not working in the paddies, I kept to my bed, isolated under my mosquito netting. In early August, when our workload abated somewhat and I could breathe a little easier, I came down with malaria, a disease as common as colds in winter. Jia-ying added her blanket to mine, but the chill crept into my bones and I lay curled up in a ball until sweat soaked my clothes. In the breaks between attacks I lay feeble and exhausted, waiting for another onslaught. So many of us fell ill that a medical team was sent to the farm from Shanghai before the malaria got out of hand, and we were all admonished to kill every mosquito under our nets before going to sleep.

The summer dragged on. In the fall, Cui and Zhao called a meeting to announce the sentences meted out to us "counter-revolutionary conspirators." We got two years each. We should consider ourselves lucky, Cui said, because he and Zhao had recommended five years. The sentencing was "semi-final," awaiting approval by the Shanghai Labor Reform Bureau, then under the Number Four Air Force Command.

That same night, while I was writing home to tell my family the news that their Ah Si was going to jail, the girls in the dorm were all chattering about a greater tragedy. Xiao Jian, one of the three young men also sentenced, was the son of a man who had participated in the legendary Long March. When he learned that his son had been branded a counter-revolutionary, he told everyone in the family to sever all relations with him. It was Xiao Jian who had "blinded his left eye," he claimed, referring to an injury he had sustained in the March. In her grief and shame, Xiao Jian's mother hung herself in a closet.

Soon after, I learned how my "crimes" affected my family. Number 2 had spent two years trying to join the Communist Party. He was grateful to the Party because of their help during the factional battles among the workers in Shanghai, when he had barely escaped the rope. His application had been at long last accepted; finally, he thought, he would get away from the shadow of our bad class background. But when it was discovered that he had a counter-revolutionary sister, his bubble of hope burst. The Party rejected him. He was furious with me, and said so in his letter.

"I warned you to stay out of trouble," he wrote. "Obviously you didn't listen, and I must pay for your errors." If my own brother and adviser could blame me in that way, believing my accusers instead of me, what would my "revolutionary" Great-Aunt say? I felt abandoned by my own family.

My *tan-qin* was canceled that February because I was still awaiting final word on my sentence. "I'm afraid that Representative Huang can't help you this time," Cui sneered as I left his office.

I dreaded the idea of going to prison, and kept the news away from Number 1 and Number 5. Until my arrival at the farm, I had never seen a real convict. In my childhood I had pictured criminals as green-faced, long-toothed monsters. How could I tell my eldest brother and my baby sister, who had their own problems, that I would soon be behind bars?

23

WHEN THE SPRING OF 1971 arrived, I was strangely at peace. To people like Loaf, Leggy and Fatty I was now a non-person. To others I was invisible. To many more I was an example, a reminder of the rule, "Obey or be destroyed."

That spring a whisper circulated around the farm. Three female students from our brigade, well groomed and well dressed, were swept away in a military jeep. Under the guise of recruiting talented young women for song and dance troupes, the air force was rounding up attractive young women as *fei-zhi* — imperial concubines — for Lin Li-guo, Lin Biao's only son. Like an emperor and, as I learned many years later, like Mao himself, Lin Li-guo liked to surround himself with young virgins.

It was a form of beauty contest. The candidates from each brigade were selected by the PLA reps, after their political backgrounds had been investigated. Political purity was the first criterion; next came beauty. The three women from our brigade returned the next afternoon, downcast. They had failed.

That evening, as soon as political study had been concluded, the women in my dorm swirled around one of them, Xiao Hong, like a flock of sparrows. Where had the soldiers taken her? What had happened? Had she actually seen Lin Li-guo?

There had been a panel of seven judges to examine her. "All in uniform," she said. "They told me I was too big and tall, and that my feet were too long and wide! How can they expect us to have small feet when they know we work barefoot in the paddies for over six months a year?" she whined. "Why do they prefer small feet, anyway? Isn't that a feudal idea that was condemned a long time ago? Look at the women in the posters everywhere. Aren't they all big and strong?"

Xiao Hong went on to confirm the rumor that the recruitment had nothing to do with singing and dancing. "How could our leaders be enlisting concubines?" the women around her whispered. "How could the glorious PLA allow itself to be used in this manner?"

I overheard this conversation as I lay in my bed. At one time I too would have been shocked to learn that the PLA would involve itself in seamy practices, but Cui and Zhao had taught me otherwise. But the leaders — that was a blow to what little idealism I may have retained. If the leaders were so corrupt, so hypocritical, how could anyone be safe?

"Do you know something, Xiao Ye?" Jia-ying confided from the bed beside mine. "If you had been from a 'red' background, you would be a perfect candidate."

"Don't be silly!" I shot back, though I was half flattered.

I wondered how many of the women at the prison farm would have jumped at the chance to escape the farm and return to civilization, wear elegant and costly clothing, eat rich and carefully prepared food, enjoy sumptuous surroundings and, most important, live without politically motivated harassment. A *fei-zhi* was not the same as a mistress kept in secret. Historically, a man with sufficient wealth might have a Number One Wife, his official and most powerful spouse, but also secondary wives or concubines who had high and enviable status in the household. My great-grandfather had had three wives. This custom had ended with Liberation, and men who had relations with more than one woman were officially dissolute and repugnant. Or so we had been taught.

"If you ever had the chance, would you go?" Jia-ying pressed.

Although I was eighteen, I knew nothing about relations between the sexes. Like many women my age, I was ignorant about sexual intercourse, or how babies were conceived or born. I was aware that to be Lin Li-guo's concubine was dissolute, but had no idea what such a role entailed.

"Well, would you?"

There were, as I knew now, only three ways to escape a lifetime of exile in this desolate and strife-ridden place: suicide, prison or selection as a *fei-zhi*. I had tried the first. The second loomed over me.

"Yes," I whispered.

"So would I," said Jia-ying.

Since her return from her home visit the previous February, Jia-ying had changed. She was bolder now — the only one who would speak to me directly — and nothing seemed to intimidate her, not even Cui and Zhao. I surmised that something was in the air when she was transferred to the vegetable-growing team, an assignment we all considered heaven. Usually only the two PLA reps' favorites were given this privilege.

A couple of months later Jia-ying's mother showed up at the farm, shocking everyone, since parental visits were unheard of. She soon let it be known that her younger sister, Jia-ying's aunt, was married to Li Zheng-dao (Lee Tsung-dao, as he is known in the West), a Chinese-American scientist who had won the 1957 Nobel Prize in Physics along with another Chinese-American, Yang Chen-ning. During the early phase of the Cultural Revolution, this "foreign connection" had worked against Jia-ying's family, causing them untold misery; but now that China–U.S. relations were improving with President Nixon's impending visit, the family fortunes had been reversed and they had returned to their original residence, from which they had been evicted several years before.

The same government that had encouraged Red Guards to pillage, beat and kill families like Jia-ying's was now "looking forward and forgetting the past" because of the change in relations with the United States. Although she was my friend and I was happy for her, I envied her unexpected good luck.

A week or so later word came that a woman from Number Two Brigade had been chosen by the panel selecting young virgins for Lin Li-guo. After a big farewell meeting she was paraded in a jeep from one village to another, waving to the crowds like a queen, then sent to the city of Guangzhou, where the young Lin lived.

"I told you so," Jia-ying said to me as we watched the procession. "Only in the Tang dynasty were big and tall women considered beautiful. That's why they turned down Xiao Hong."

I wished I had brought Number 2's glasses with me so that I could see what all the fuss was about. All I could make out was a petite young woman in a blue Mao jacket, squeezed between two officers in the back seat of a jeep. In a society where beauty was officially labeled bourgeois, where femininity was condemned and where women and girls wore blue, brown or gray Mao suits, cut their hair short (unless they were young) and tried hard to look revolutionary, many women did not carry mirrors. I used the window glass to braid my pigtails.

Great-Aunt had once said, "A human being needs fine clothes the way a Buddha statue needs gold paint to enhance its glory." But I had grown up wearing my brothers' shabby clothes. How could I be good-looking, as Jia-ying had told me? No one else had ever even hinted that I was attractive. Until my friend made that remark I had never really thought much about how I looked to others, especially boys.

That evening I borrowed Jia-ying's mirror. Outside, in the fading light, careful that I was not observed, I had a long look at myself. I saw a young woman with jet-black braids, an oval face with even teeth and large eyes with folded lids. Folded eyelids were considered more beautiful than unfolded in both China and Japan.

The woman who looked back at me from the little mirror was not beautiful, I thought. Pleasant-looking, perhaps, and certainly not ugly, like Fatty or Loaf. But not lovely.

I recalled my first trip to the farm on the bus. Because I knew no one and I had sat alone on a seat for two, the boys had vied with each other to fall "accidentally" into the seat beside me. Absorbed in my feelings about leaving my family, I had paid no attention at the time, but now I wondered if they too had found me attractive. Was that why they had shyly offered me candy and cookies? Even after some people in my brigade had started to call me "Mila" after a pretty woman in an Albanian movie, I never took it seriously. But at least I didn't have a thick rump and ugly big breasts like Mila. Chinese standards of beauty preferred a small bosom and a flat bottom.

I turned the mirror over. What did it matter anyway? A woman with my bad blood could be as beautiful as a goddess and no one would give her the time of day.

By the time I walked into my nineteenth year, in the summer of 1971, Lin Li-guo's vice had spread among the PLA reps.

Lao Chang had warned us when we first arrived at the farm that dating was prohibited; under Cui and Zhao any kind of relationship, even friendship, was persecuted. Men and women could not visit one another in their dorms. When the hot weather drove us outdoors at night, the reps would lead search parties under the bridge piers and through the bushes, looking for couples. Any they found Cui and Zhao then put on display, humiliating and criticizing them in front of the entire brigade.

At one special criticism meeting, Cui read out a letter from Zhen Bao to her boyfriend, Wang Hua-shan, whose brother was married to Zhen's sister. The letter had been stolen from Wang and handed over to Cui, who read Zhen Bao's words out loud in a falsetto voice, leering and mimicking, drawing sneers and laughter from some of the crowd. "'Thank god my period came yesterday,'" he read. The women near me shied away from this embarrassing declaration, but soon all of us, as expected and required, were shouting in unison, "Down with the hooligan Wang Hua-shan!" The next day, Wang was transferred to another sub-farm.

A few weeks later we were called together again and, on the way into the warehouse, forced to walk in single file past a table on which a dish and a Do Not Touch sign sat side by side. In the dish I saw a small shapeless object like a collapsed balloon. Next to the table, Yang, the tallest man in the village, stood with his head bowed. At the meeting, Zhao called Yang a dirty bastard for possessing a condom. Yang's girlfriend was then named and vilified. The next day she failed in her attempted suicide.

All this moral rectitude on the part of Cui and Zhao was pretense. We often saw them through the open windows and doors of the brick house, lying on their backs while girls, using two aluminum penny coins, pulled the hairs from their chins. Both reps openly petted and fondled willing female students. On more than one occasion a woman was sent packing. We learned later that these women had regained their city *hu-kou* as a "reward" for having an abortion and keeping their mouths shut.

Meanwhile I was still living in suspense, wondering what my jail sentence would be. Then one day the decision was handed down. The five of us counter-revolutionary plotters were called before the reps. It was a hot, humid July day, and the oscillating fan on Cui's desk clattered in vain. Yu, Zhu, Qian, Jian and I stood with our heads bowed as Zhao read sententiously from the paper in his hand.

"For forming a counter-revolutionary clique and attempting to undermine the PLA, you are sentenced to two years. Sentence to be served supervised by the masses."

I could hardly believe my ears. I clamped my lips shut to hold back any expression of relief and fought to keep myself from glancing at my friends. It was an anti-climax, after all. I would not be shipped off to a prison. The charge and sentence would be recorded in my dossier. I would lose my *tan-qin* for two years and that hurt me deeply. But "supervised by the masses" meant that I would continue as I had been since my release from interrogation — working as normal under the nominal scrutiny of everyone. The reps' recommendation for our imprisonment had been repudiated at a higher level.

My four friends were sent away to different brigades. I was not even allowed to say goodbye to them. If not for Jia-ying, I would have felt completely alone.

24

CUI OFTEN SAID THAT IT was better to "reap proletarian weeds than sow capitalist seeds." That autumn he got what he wanted. The rice harvest was so meager that Lao Chang said it would have cost the government less money to have us sit around and do nothing, for the yield hardly repaid the investment of seed, equipment and fertilizer, let alone our wages and months of labor.

But for me, the poor harvest was more than balanced by good news. September 24, 1971, was a typical crisp fall day, a welcome relief after the long season of heat and humidity. When I awoke that morning I heard someone shouting outside the dorm.

I rushed outside, rubbing the sleep from my eyes. A young man stood in front of the reps' brick house, hands cupped around his mouth, yelling, "They're gone! They're gone!"

People began to run toward him. I hung back, afraid of a trick. But when everyone converged on the house, I joined them. The structure was empty, stripped bare of furniture, posters, even the photo of Mao and Lin Biao. "Where have they gone?" everyone asked, but no one knew. Many made guesses. I kept my mouth firmly closed.

The speculation and gossip continued for a week until one day, as we made our way to the fields, Representative Huang of the Shanghai Garrison pulled up in a jeep with an officer I had never seen. Huang asked all of us, except the prisoners, to go to the warehouse immediately for an important meeting.

When we were all assembled Huang wasted no time.

"The traitor Lin Biao, his wife and son are dead. The plane they had commandeered for their escape to the Soviet Union crashed in Outer Mongolia."

No one spoke. We were stunned. Once again someone we had been taught to revere was now being called a stinking heap of animal dung.

More than three weeks before, we learned, Lin had fled when his plot to assassinate Mao and take over the government by military coup was unearthed.

Huang went on to admonish us not to speak of these events. An official investigation conducted by Premier Zhou En-lai himself was under way, and since our farm had been under the authority of Lin Biao and had figured largely in his plans as a base, some people's political lives were at stake. When he spoke these words, many turned their eyes toward me. I stared straight ahead, numb with fear.

And so yet another movement began, a rectification campaign criticizing Lin Biao. Our nights were filled with political study, reading and discussing documents denouncing Lin Biao and his counter-revolutionary activities. Now, all the evil stupidities of the Cultural Revolution carried out on our farm — from the neglect of the fields to friends informing on each other — were blamed on Lin Biao and our departed PLA reps. Even Leggy bragged that she had harbored doubts about the reps as she took part in the interrogation of me and my friends. I seethed at the hypocrisy. It wasn't Lin Biao but the people around me who had persecuted me.

In the end, my four friends and I were brought together for a rehabilitation meeting at the sub-farm. Our malicious treatment was blamed on the dead. But exoneration tasted like ashes in my mouth. Our innocence, friendship and trust had been lost. None of us talked about what had happened or what we had said and written under torture. None of us discussed our detention. More than ever I wanted to tell Yu Hua, Xiao Jian, Xiao Qian and Xiao Zhu what I had said and done, to clear the air. I craved their forgiveness even though I could hardly remember the things I had "admitted."

On my visit home that winter, Number 2 bought me a new short-wave radio and a set of recently published English textbooks. The gifts were his way of showing his concern for my suffering and apologizing for the letter in which he had criticized me for ruining his chances to join the Party.

"Shanghai Radio Station has started broadcasting English lessons as a positive signal to the United States," he said. "You always liked English, Ah Si, so maybe you can continue learning it."

Holding the books in my hand, I could not speak, for my throat was thick with emotion. I was touched by his generosity. I knew he was still paying off the loans he had taken out to help Number 5 and me prepare to go to the countryside.

But I was also filled with sadness because I could not bring myself to tell him the details of my ordeal or what I had done to my friends. Nor would Great-Aunt be a help. Even she was saying how she had always had a bad feeling about Lin Biao's "conspiratory nature." "He had ghostlike features," she claimed, "with those tiny triangle eyes under bushy brows. That pale smiling face always gave me goosebumps."

Hindsight can be blinding.

Two months after I returned to the farm, news came that there was a shortage of manpower in Shanghai, from salesclerks to street-sweepers, from prison guards to teachers. The chaos of the Cultural Revolution had killed many by suicide, beatings or battles, and hundreds of thousands had been sent to the countryside. Some of us would be chosen to return to the city to fill some of the jobs, and the farm buzzed with excitement and speculation as everyone tried in vain to keep their hopes in check. Hope, we all knew to our cost, was mother to disappointment. People around me thought I might have a chance to become a teacher because, ironically, a pure class background was not necessary for that role. To avoid frustration, I fought hard to remain unenthusiastic about my chances. Yu Hua was selected to be a prison guard. When Jian, Qian and Zhu were assigned teaching posts I began to hope in earnest. Delirious with joy, they packed up and left the farm for good.

But all four of them were "red" students and I was not. Our new rep, Meng, said that I must remain on the farm. He explained that I needed more hardship to overcome my "bourgeois weakness."

During 1972 a newly formed civilian leadership took control of the farm, replacing PLA reps and self-appointed students' committees. We moved across the bridge into houses with brick walls and thatched roofs — a great improvement over the damp wattle buildings in which I had spent the last four years.

I passed what little free time we were allowed on my bed, listening to my new radio and studying English. Although I was hurt and extremely bitter, as well as lonely, I reached a separate peace. My roommates pitied me and left me alone or jeered at me for "drawing water with a bamboo basket" — wasting my time studying a useless language. They could not understand that I wanted to be by myself and stay out of trouble. Nor did they know how much I thirsted for love and friendship.

A month or so after my four friends left, I got a letter from Xiao Qian, who was training to be a physical education teacher. It was a love letter. He had loved me for years, he said, and now that he was fortunate enough to be back in Shanghai with his city *hu-kou* returned, he felt he could tell me. On the one hand, I was confused, especially when I remembered the horrible things that had happened when relationships had come to light on the farm; on the other, my state of mind was so twisted that I instinctively took his declaration as a kind of chauvinism. Only now that he was better off than me, both economically and socially, could he reveal his love for me. I didn't need his pity. I didn't reply, yet I kept the letter.

On my visit home in January 1973, Xiao Qian came to see me at home and urged me again to become his fiancée. I said we could still be friends, but that was all. He was willing to give up his teaching position, he assured me, and his city *hu-kou* and return to live on the farm if that would satisfy me. Still I said no. I was not ready for a relationship.

"What more do you want?" he demanded.

"I don't know what I want."

After Xiao Qian had left, Great-Aunt criticized me. She thought he was a great guy. He had visited her twice since his arrival back in Shanghai, bringing her the sweetest dates she had tasted in years.

"What's wrong with you, Ah Si?" she asked. "Where can you find that kind of man nowadays — good-looking, polite? Think of the sacrifice he is willing to make for you."

She nagged me day and night, calling me a strange creature who couldn't tell right from wrong, bad from good. Finally I had had enough.

"If you like him so much, why don't you keep him for yourself?" I shouted.

"I knew it, I knew it. The minute you stepped out the door five years ago, I knew I would lose you forever. That farm did nothing but fill you with misery and hatred and now you think it's your turn to treat others in the same way. See if I care if you end up an old maid like —"

She stopped. Great-Aunt was called "the old maid" behind her back in our lane, and she was painfully aware of the insult.

Maybe she's right, I thought. I have changed. I've become a cold and insensitive creature not fit for this world. After all the persecution, insults, lies and betrayals, I didn't know how to deal with matters of the heart like love and trust.

When I met Number 5 at the train station a few days later, both of us were at a low point of our lives: trapped on our respective farms, watching in helpless frustration as our farm-mates left for city jobs and gained a city *hu-kou* through connections or "earned" it through good political background. Nevertheless, we agreed that we would try to make our two-week visit a cheerful event, especially since Number 1 was to be married. It was to be our first gathering as a family since I had been sent into exile in 1968.

Number 1's marriage was the fruit of matchmaking and the postal service. I was sad to see my eldest brother give up his belief in love. I remembered, during his first year at university, his conversation with Mother, who had been secretly arranging a marriage for him. Number 1 had become very upset and told her that times had changed, that the government encouraged the abandonment of feudal customs like arranged marriages. He would choose his own wife, he vowed, and marry her for love.

But in the meantime Number 1, a deeply intelligent man with a once promising future, had been stripped of his Shanghai *hu-kou* and sent to a remote and backward mountainous area in Guizhou Province to work in a tool repair shop. There he had been confronted with reality. If he married a local woman, he would have to spend the rest of his life there, and so would his children. He would not see us again because the home-visit policy would no longer apply. So he agreed to exchange letters and photos with a young woman named Yu-qin, who lived in Shanghai. The whole arrangement was a gamble. No one knew when the young couple would be able to live together, if ever. But marrying a Shanghai resident was Number 1's only hope.

The wedding ceremony was held at home, with the two families having dinner together. (In China it is the groom's responsibility to pay for and host the wedding.) I couldn't remember the last time there had been so much food on the table at our house in Purple Sunshine Lane. There was chicken stewed in soup, duck simmered in soybean sauce, steamed fish and braised pig's legs, along with stir-fried vegetables, much of it bought by Number 3 in the Songjiang black market. The duck and chicken must be cooked and served whole, Great-Aunt had insisted, to symbolize the unity of the new family. It was a happy moment, but my heart was loaded with sorrow and contradiction. Number 1 had given up his dream and married for advantage. What advantage was there for Yu-qin, his new wife? I wondered. She seemed pleasant enough, but was also loud and brash.

It seemed that history was repeating itself. Father and Mother had lived apart for a long time after their marriage. Looking at my smiling eldest brother, I was overwhelmed with sadness. I found Great-Aunt in the kitchen and told her I was going for a walk to get some fresh air. My face must have signaled my thought, for she didn't argue. It was dark and cold outside and the streets were almost deserted. Probably everyone was feasting, I thought, the main activity of the New Year celebrations.

With nowhere to go, no friends to visit, I wandered the streets for hours and was shocked to find myself standing before Xiao

Qian's house, the last place I wanted to be. In panic I ran out of his lane.

A couple of months later Number 1 wrote to me with good and bad news. Yu-qin was pregnant, but she had been listed as one of those to be sent to work in a small town in Anhui Province, northwest of Shanghai, another undeveloped area of the country. This kind of assignment, called a "third line project," was very common (the first two lines were factories in major and medium-sized cities).

As with so many people in those days, Fate had played a trick on my new sister-in-law. Both Yu-qin's parents were workers. When she had graduated from junior-high school, she had chosen to enroll in a trade school attached to a factory. Such a choice was a last resort, made by those who couldn't get into a normal high school, and involved a major loss of face for student and family. But subsequently the humiliation was paid back when Yu-qin saw her contemporaries, who had it made into good schools sent to the countryside, while she, a worker, and therefore exalted, remained in Shanghai.

But the blessing was short-lived. Now married and pregnant, and with her husband in Guizhou, she was transferred to a third-line factory. She was able to postpone her departure until her baby was born, but then she left for Anhui, taking her son, Ye Xiang, with her. Ten months later, after he had been weaned, she brought him back to Shanghai and left him in Great-Aunt's care. Number 1 still had not seen his son.

And so Great-Aunt, at sixty-three, suffering from high blood pressure, began to care for the fourth generation of the Ye family, who had taken her in and given her a place to live more than forty years before. But now the Ye family was scattered, and she cared for the baby alone.

25

IN MARCH 1973, DENG XIAO-PING was brought back to power as vice-premier, after years of disgrace. Within a month the "Suggestions for University Enrollment" was issued by the Party's Central Committee. Deng realized the need for educated people after years of turmoil throughout the school system. Until then a person who had worked in a unit for at least two years and had a recommendation from his or her unit leaders and co-workers could get into university without taking entrance exams. These were the "Worker-Peasant-Soldier" students. Deng's declaration stated that Worker-Peasant-Soldier candidates must sit for exams, although their scores would not be the sole criteria; for university entrance political correctness would also count.

I took this as a sign that things might be returning to normal and was encouraged in my English study, though I dared not hope that I would ever get a chance at university. Just a couple of weeks before, my application to be a taxi driver in Shanghai had been refused. The farm's new civilian leader, Sun, told me that as the youngest of the experienced hands in the brigade I should let the older men and women go back to the city first to plan their future. Instead I was assigned as "elder sister" to a batch of newly arrived seventeen-year-old girls, to show them the ropes. For days and nights I was like a fire-fighter, running out one door and in another, except that I put out tears instead of flames. My heart went out to the miserable teenagers. They were about the same age as I had been when I first came to the farm and they were depressed, scared and homesick. I did the best I could to teach them everything, from the differences between rice seedlings and grass to the best way to hang clothing to avoid insect contamination. Using my five years of experience to help them gave me great satisfaction.

In May of the following year I learned that our farm had been allotted ten slots for university enrollment. One of them was for an English major.

My heart leapt. Was this my chance? Or was it nonsense to even consider that I would get the support of the brigade to take the exam, even though I had been studying English alone for two years? The summer before, I had applied to go to Fudan University to study Spanish, but the unit had turned me down, once again citing seniority.

But this seemed to be a more auspicious time. I had now been on the farm for almost six years and, according to the regulations, if I was successful I could take my salary with me to university. I would not need to ask my family for support. I filled out the application.

The votes of the young women to whom I had acted as an elder sister tipped the count in my direction. My unexpected success at getting over this first hurdle gave me sleepless nights. The next obstacle was another selection: the farm was made up of thirty brigades, and each had elected a candidate. Now the administration would select fifteen from the thirty to take the medical exam. Those who passed would sit the entrance exam.

I was encouraged that Representative Huang, who had quashed my attempt to return to Shanghai as a teacher (probably because he found out I had written something about him in my confession), had nothing to do with the present selection process.

So I waited, trying not to think about it as I bent double in the paddies. One afternoon, as I washed the mud from my legs and feet, I heard that the medical team had arrived at the sub-farm. I entered the dorm and sat on my bed, afraid to move, and asked someone to bring back my supper from the canteen: I didn't want to be away from my dorm in case I was sent for. Hours passed by and no one came. The village got darker and quieter, and my heartbeat soared each time I heard passing footsteps. But there was no news.

I woke up in the morning fully clothed, with a severe headache. I had failed again. I tried to put it out of my mind, but it was hard. I dragged myself out of bed and to the paddies.

I was lugging bundles of seedlings on my shoulder-pole when I was hailed by a man out of breath from running.

"Xiao Ye, someone has telephoned from the sub-farm," he blurted, stopping to gulp down some air. "They're asking why you didn't show up for your medical checkup. The doctors are about to leave and —"

I threw down my shoulder-pole, scattering the green seedlings on the dike, and ran toward the paddy where brigade leader Sun was working. As soon as he caught sight of me he shrieked.

"*Ai yah!* I forgot to tell you —"

"How could you forget such a thing? How could you!" I cried.

Sun and I rushed back to his office, where he snatched up the phone and frantically wound the handle. He spoke to the operator and asked her to tell the doctors to wait.

"We're on our way," he said, hanging up. "Come on, Xiao Ye, we'll take my bike!"

After bumping along the dirt roads, side-saddle on the rat-trap carrier of Sun's bike, I found myself in the clinic, feet, legs and hands still caked with paddy mud, talking to a group of white-clothed doctors. They did their best to calm me down, then conducted the examination.

The next day I was to have a blood test for hepatitis. This was another hurdle. Hepatitis was widespread throughout the country and our farm was no exception. The number of cases had climbed in the past few years because of contaminated water and poor and crowded living conditions. When I got up early the next morning, having eaten or drunk nothing overnight as ordered, I was showered with advice.

"My mother said sugar makes the liver softer," said Xiao Jiang, one of the newer girls. "That's why hepatitis patients get extra sugar coupons."

I drank the proffered cup of sugar-water and immediately felt guilty for cheating. Later, as the doctor drew my blood, I confessed.

"Don't worry," he said. "I have two daughters and one of them is your age. She is working on a farm in Heilongjiang Province. I hope someday she will get a chance like yours." He didn't tell me, though, whether the sugar-water would help me or not.

So, more waiting. I was anxious about the coming exam. I felt confident I could pass, given all my studying of textbooks and the English lessons on the radio; but nothing was ever simple or clear. I had heard the story of Zhang Tie-sheng, a young man who had, as a protest, handed in a blank sheet at his exam the year before. Since then there had been articles and editorials praising his action and condemning the newly reinstituted exam system as a "bourgeois counter-attack" against the Cultural Revolution that precluded true peasants and proletarians from higher learning. (With support from Jiang Qing, Zhang later became a high official in the education bureaucracy in his area. When Jiang Qing fell from power, he was removed.)

One afternoon in August I was called from the paddies once more and told to go to the sub-farm administration office. This time I remembered to wash off the mud in a ditch. Xiao Zhao, a young man who worked in the canteen, took me on his bike. All I had with me was a ballpoint pen.

The sub-farm was quiet, a usual weekday afternoon. I hopped down from the bike, thanked Xiao Zhao, and went to the office. There I was directed to a room down the hall. I remembered the day of my middle-school entrance exams. There were flags snapping in the breeze outside the buildings, hundreds of students and their families milling around on the sidewalks, row upon row of desks in the sultry classroom. Mother had been alive then, and the most important issue challenging my young mind had been which middle school I would go to. Now, at twenty-two, I faced the most important test of my life. Success meant a brighter future; failure more of the same misery.

I stepped into the small room, where two middle-aged women, with their hair cut plainly at earlobe length, sat behind desks, fanning themselves. It was hot and stuffy. An armchair sat forlornly in a corner; a single desk and chair had been placed before the two women; the bamboo curtains were drawn against the afternoon sun. The examiners rose.

"There is no one else here," said one, who looked to be in her fifties. She smiled. "Yours is the only exam."

In my nervousness I completely missed the significance of her words.

"I am Teacher Chen from Beijing University," she went on. "Teacher Xu is from Qinghua University."

I nodded at the younger, stern-looking woman.

"We are recruiting students from East China," Teacher Chen explained.

My brain began to function. "Do you mean that you came down here just for one candidate?"

"This by no means suggests that you will be successful," Teacher Xu cut in, indicating that I should sit down. "Now, let's begin."

She handed me a piece of paper on which a few passages in classical Chinese were printed. "Please translate them into vernacular."

I took out my pen and began. It was not difficult; my first semester in middle school had been devoted to this kind of work. Classical Chinese is cryptic and condensed, idiomatic and metaphorical. A word contains a phrase; a phrase may take several sentences in modern Chinese. For example, *zou-ma-kan-hua*, "ride horse, look at flowers" or "looking at flowers from the back of a horse," means "going through the motions" or "failing to give the matter the necessary attention." About an hour later, I completed the passages.

My second test was oral. Teacher Chen gave me a text in English called "We Have Friends All Over the World" and asked me to read it out loud. I didn't need to translate, just read. It was a piece I had read over many times at night under my mosquito net, for it was in one of the books Number 2 had given me.

Now all my studying in isolation, while my dorm-mates played cards, chatted or crocheted, paid off. I read out the text, clear and loud. Teacher Chen could barely contain her pleasure. Teacher Xu maintained her serious demeanor and reminded me that, although I had done well, that didn't mean I would be selected.

"One red heart, two preparations," she admonished me — a good person should be prepared for failure as well as success — a common expression around exam time at school.

I stood up and forced myself to look her straight in the eye. "Please," I stammered, "please let me go to university. I have been here for six years, working in the paddies the whole time. Don't you think I have got enough education from the peasants, as Chairman Mao wishes? I promise you, if you accept me, I'll never let you down."

When I turned around and left the room, Teacher Chen followed me. As we shook hands, she looked into my eyes and squeezed my hand.

On the way back to the village I was deep in thought. I had done my best and said what I wanted to the two teachers. Now I would have to let Fate take care of the rest. And yet, why was there only one person to take the exam? And what was Teacher Chen trying to tell me when she squeezed my hand?

26

BY THAT TIME I HAD BEEN "dating" Xiao Zhao, the young man in the canteen, for a few months — the old prohibitions had been relaxed. It was the first relationship for both of us, although he was much sought after by the pretty women in our village. Nicknamed *Wang Di* — King — for his good looks, Xiao Zhao was three years older than me, the seventh of eight children in his family. His mother had died of a heart attack when he was seven and his father had remarried.

Like mine, his parents had been Shanghai businesspeople. Though we came from the same background and had arrived at the farm on the same day, we had walked different paths. While the majority struggled in the paddies, buffeted by the northwest wind, he had worked in the canteen from the beginning — one of the plum jobs in the village. Xiao Zhao hadn't suffered persecution like the rest of us with tainted blood. In fact, under Representatives Zhao and Ciu he had been designated a "Five Goods" Worker — outstanding in five stated areas of political correctness — every year.

My first contact with Xiao Zhao had come after I was released from house arrest. I had been summoned to the brick house and told by Cui to prepare for another struggle meeting that night. By the time he let me go, supper was over. I took my food tin to the canteen, entered the darkened dining room and knocked on one of the serving windows. Xiao Zhao opened the window, took my tin and returned a few moments later, having gone to the trouble of heating up the food for me. I was grateful for the kindness and thanked him.

"Do you really think what you are going through is worth the trouble?" he asked, handing me the food through the serving window. "Why not just go along with them? Take my advice, don't push against the wind."

I had no further contact with him for two years, then a very strange thing happened. I was at home and my two-week *tan-qin* was drawing to an end. Number 3 found me in a nearby store where I was doing some last-minute shopping for my return.

"There is an old man in our apartment," she exclaimed, "and he has a big parcel with him. He says he wants you to take it back to the farm and give it to his son."

I was at a loss. No one had asked me for a favor.

"He's well dressed," Number 3 went on, "with a heavy Ningbo accent. Judging by the way he talked, I bet he used to be a boss."

I hurried home to find a man exactly as Number 3 had described. Showing me a piece of paper with my address on it, he said that his son, Xiao Zhao, had written and asked him to come and request the favor. He knew his son had said nothing to me.

On the day I arrived back at the farm, Xiao Zhao came to my dorm to pick up his package. He apologized for not asking me ahead of time for the favor. I was confused and too shy to ask him where he had acquired my address.

One day the following spring when I came back from the paddies for lunch, Xiao Zhao met me at my door.

"Do you have any fresh water?" he asked. "The pump is not working."

From then on, he would visit our dorm on a couple of nights each week. Many of the girls were happy to see him. He would say

"Hello, everyone!" and be entertained by hopeful females, plied with cookies and tea. But gradually he spent more and more time talking to me, and it soon became clear that I was the one he had come to visit.

For the first time, I had someone to talk to. Tentatively, Xiao Zhao asked me about my house arrest, but I gave him no details. I was still ashamed of myself and had decided to take my shame to the grave. Most people didn't want to relive those days. "Look to the future," they would say, "there's no use refrying old rice." Nevertheless, I was thankful for his concern.

Xiao Zhao was a kind and sympathetic listener, and our talks were the start of our relationship. I was flattered that he had chosen me when so many women were attracted to him, but at first I was reluctant to begin dating him, and said so.

"Is it because you haven't written back to Qian yet?"

"How did you know about that?"

He laughed. "Oh, I have friends in the post office."

He kept our relationship from his family. He was worried that his parents, especially his father, would reject it. Boss Zhao, a strict traditional Chinese father whose authority extended to every aspect of his children's lives, especially their choice of partner, had insisted that Xiao Zhao not involve himself in any relationship until he left the farm. That was why Xiao Zhao had resisted all the women who would have loved to be his girlfriend.

"It was you I was interested in," he told me, "ever since I saw you the first time."

"Why did you wait so long to let me know?"

"Well," he answered, "you always seemed to be in trouble of one kind or another."

Although it was not the answer I wanted to hear, I accepted it. At least he was frank with me.

I didn't tell anyone in my family about him, either. I didn't know how long our relationship would last; most of those on the farm were short-lived. Besides, I didn't want another reason for Great-Aunt to get stirred up.

On the day I took my exam, Xiao Zhao came to see me in the evening. We sat outside the dorm, as usual. I was utterly exhausted, but peaceful. Xiao Zhao was unusually quiet. Finally he spoke.

"Tell me. Will you drop me like a sack of potatoes if you get into university?"

"Of course not!" I answered. "Why are you talking about this? You shouldn't. It's bad luck to talk about events in advance." Great-Aunt's superstitions had had an effect on me and I thought for a moment he was trying to put a curse on my chance by predicting success before the results were known. I hoped my quick response would make him drop the subject.

But he ignored me. "You are going to be a student at Bei Da" — the short form for Beijing University — "one of the best in China. And I probably will stay here for the rest of my life, being a peasant." He emphasized the last word, although strictly speaking he was not a peasant; he did not work in the fields.

"Just drop it," I said. "I don't want to talk about it any more. We can discuss it when the time comes."

"No," he insisted again. "It will be too late then. I want you to promise now, tonight. Will you abandon me or not?"

"You've got your answer." I got up and went inside the dorm.

I didn't sleep that night. With no preparation, suddenly Xiao Zhao had forced me to make a serious commitment. I had often heard the heartbroken sobbing of those who had been abandoned by their "city *hu-kou*" lovers and had joined in condemning their lovers' unfaithfulness. It became clear to me that I would have no option if I was accepted at Bei Da, at least if Xiao Zhao was still on the farm. Duty would now prohibit me from breaking off with him.

It was ten long days later that the news came. I was in my dorm after the day's work, fetching my food tin, when Sun knocked on the door and stepped inside.

"Xiao Ye. I just got a phone call."

My tin dropped from my hands, my throat went dry and my temples pounded. "What did they say?"

A smile broke across Sun's narrow face. "You've been accepted. Go to the sub-farm tomorrow and fill out the enrollment forms."

My hands began to shake. Soon my whole body was trembling and I had to sit down. I laid my head on the table and covered it with my arms. I was going to be a university student. Suddenly, unbelievably, a bright ray of sunshine lit up my future. I wished my parents could know, and, thinking of them, I began to weep quietly. Now Great-Aunt could be proud of me. Now the burden of guilt at my replacing her on the farm would lift itself from Number 3's shoulders. Now I could help my little sister.

"Congratulations, Xiao Ye," Sun said, pulling the door closed as he left.

The word spread quickly and I was showered with plaudits. I was the first ever in our brigade to go to university since we had arrived here six years before. The next morning, after a night without rest, I went to the sub-farm office. My hand shook as I filled out the enrollment paper with my name on it. I learned that my acceptance notice had been sitting in a desk drawer since my exams took place, but no one had bothered to tell me.

It was difficult to grasp the fact that my days as a peasant laborer in the unyielding paddies were over. Except for Xiao Zhao and a few supportive friends, I had no one to say goodbye to. Certainly I would not miss the stark, unfriendly landscape or the northwest wind. I remembered poor Jia-ying. Soon after she had been transferred to the vegetable-growing team, her brother came to visit her and the two of them spent the afternoon together in the dorm with no others around, causing some women to gossip behind her back and men to laugh at her in front of her face, accusing her of incest. The shame and humiliation drove her to mental instability and she was sent back to Shanghai. I remembered my four "counter-revolutionary" friends and the ordeal that shattered our unity; the days of unearned ostracism and disgrace; the struggle meetings; and always, the thousands of hours of backbreaking labor.

I had entered my twenty-second year. Up till now my existence had been controlled by fate, political storm, and loss. Maybe now I could lay my hand on the rudder of my own life and steer out of the bitter wind.

🌿

I planned, when I arrived in Shanghai, to organize a family gathering to celebrate my good news, and I looked forward to having my whole family together again in my parents' home. But when I arrived in our lane and ran up the stairs to see Great-Aunt,

I found an empty apartment: Number 2 was in hospital and Great-Aunt was with him.

A few days before, Number 2 had been riding on the back of a carelessly loaded truck. The load had shifted when the driver turned a corner, throwing Number 2 off and breaking his leg in several places. By the time I arrived at the hospital, he had just had his third operation and was in agony. He had lost a lot of blood.

I wanted to tell him my good news and thank him, for it was his gift of the radio and the English textbooks that had given me my opportunity, but when I saw his leg suspended on a rack over the bed and his handsome face pale with pain, I kept quiet.

Every morning Great-Aunt got up before dawn to line up for pork bones, which she boiled to make a milky-colored soup for me to take to Number 2. She said it would help his bones heal.

In the meantime I had only ten days to prepare for my journey to Beijing. Xiao Zhao and I had parted with a solemn pledge to love each other, *shan-meng-hai-shi* — witnessed by the mountains and the sea. He had given me a letter to post when I got to Shanghai in which he revealed to his father his relationship with me, a university student-to-be. It was apparently all right to disclose the truth now. He also set a date for me to visit his father and stepmother, taking two live chickens as a gift from him to his parents.

Xiao Zhao had bought the chickens from the farmers in Sanlong People's Commune and the two fowl had accompanied me on my journey home, riding on the top of a bus, in the cabin of a ship, then in the aisle of a city bus before they took up temporary residence in Purple Sunshine Lane. Handing them over to Xiao Zhao's parents would give me more relief than pleasure.

On the appointed day I stood in the hall outside their apartment — the Red Guards had forced them to give up the house they owned and move their belongings into quarters much like ours. I was a bundle of nerves: I knew Xiao Zhao's family had been wealthy and was afraid they would look down on me, and I was conscious of Boss Zhao's having warned his son to avoid a relationship while he was on the farm.

In each hand I held an unruly, squawking chicken upside down by the feet. The door opened before I had a chance to knock and a stylishly dressed attractive woman in her late thirties let me in. I

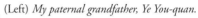

(Left) *My paternal grandfather, Ye You-quan.*

My great-aunt, Chen Feng-mei, given to my family as a housemaid by her mother after two arranged marriages didn't work out.

The main street of Qingyang in Jiangsu Province, where my father was born and raised.

My mother, Li Xiu-feng, Shanghai, 1948, just before the Communist takeover.

My father, Ye Rong-ting, Shanghai, 1948.

My four siblings and I in 1956. Back row, left to right: second eldest brother, Number 2; eldest brother, Number 1. Front row, left to right: me; younger sister, Number 5; elder sister, Number 3.

The "stone arched" house in Purple Sunshine Lane, downtown Shanghai, where I was born and raised.

Number 3 and I, autumn 1957.

Purple Sunshine Lane, showing laundry drying on bamboo poles overhead.

The alley leading to my "temple classroom," where I spent five years in elementary school. A public urinal marks the entrance.

(Right) My father's calligraphy, presenting the 48 maxims of Master Zhu Bo-lu (a Confucian scholar in the Qing Dynasty), on benevolence, righteousness, loyalty and filial piety.

(Left) *Number 1 disguised as a Red Guard in the "Great Travels," 1966, in front of the Yangtze River Bridge in Wuhan.*

(Right) *Number 3, an enthusiastic member of her factory militia, in Songjiang County, 1969.*

(Left) *My ID photo for the prison farm where I labored for six years (1968–74) and was persecuted as a "counter-revolutionary," Jiangsu Province.*

Number 1 (with clarinet) rehearsing with the Spreading Mao Ze-dong Thought Band, 1966.

My friend Rainbow (left) *and I in front of the new library of Beijing University.*

My Beijing University ID photo, autumn 1974.

My daughter, Qi-meng, on her first birthday.

One Child/One Family certificate for my daughter, Qi-meng, born in June 1981.

Great Aunt with the fourth generation of the Ye family – one child from each of my siblings, (Qi-meng wearing the scarf), 1986.

Working as an interpreter for the Foreign Affairs Department of the Shanghai Municipal Government, inside the office building, 1984.

Qi-meng and I, taken two days before I left China, August 1987.

My post-graduate class with our Canadian teacher, Bill (William Bell),
at the Foreign Affairs College, 1986.

My first trip back to China after my
defection in 1989. With Number 1's
family in Daishan County, Zhejiang
Province, 1994.
From left, front row: Bill; me; my sister-
in-law, Yu-qing; my brother, Number 1;
in back: my nephew Ye Xiang.

My Auntie Yi-feng, Mother's youngest sister, in
Wang Family Village near Qingyang, 1994.

My parents' grave site, with the re-installed gravestone, Qingyang.

Number 2, Shanghai, 1996.

Number 3 (left) and I, Shanghai, 1996.

Number 5, Shanghai, 1996.

took a quick look around the apartment, which seemed jammed with expensive furniture.

"You must be Xiao Ye," she said. "I am Xiao Di's eldest sister. Mother is out on an errand but Father is here."

Xiao Zhao was called Xiao Di — Youngest Brother — by his family. His white-haired father was still a handsome man with a stern, commanding manner. He welcomed me formally and we made small talk for a few minutes before Lao Zhao said I must be tired from my journey across the city — a signal that the visit was over. I had hardly touched my tea.

Weeks later, after I arrived in Beijing, Xiao Zhao told me in a letter that his father had had a favorable impression of me. "Not beautiful, but good-looking enough; good-mannered but not refined or ladylike; appeared to be intelligent and quick in her response; and her clear enunciation seemed to promise success as a language student. But be aware," Xiao Zhao continued to quote his father with a startling insensitivity, "that, unlike the spouses of your siblings, her family can provide nothing so far as financial assistance is concerned."

In fact, the chicken errand had been a setup so that Xiao Zhao's parents could meet me and render a judgment. Reading the letter, I felt as if I had been sent to auction without my consent. Recalling the stilted conversation with his father, I thought bitterly that I should have opened my mouth and let him count my teeth; I should have told him how the barefoot dentist on the farm had mistakenly removed a healthy molar instead of the one giving me trouble. I was stung also by the remark about my family's financial status. I made up my mind that someday I would show the Zhao family that there were things better and more valuable than money.

"Ah Si of the Ye family is going to Bei Da to learn to speak a foreign language." The news was running up and down Purple Sunshine Lane. Old neighbors came to the house to congratulate me and new ones marveled at what a lucky creature I was. One old woman in the next building, whom everyone called "old chamber-pot cleaning lady," claimed that she had always known from the shape of my forehead that I had a bright future.

The only one not thrilled by the news was Great-Aunt. Having always believed that reading and writing were the business of men, she was unimpressed with the prospect of my being a university student. She was getting older and weaker, and all she wanted was for the daughter she had never had to be home again with her after six years.

I went to the hospital to see Number 2 before I left. Smiling weakly, he handed me a used copy of the *Oxford English-Chinese Dictionary*.

"I fished it out of a garbage pail years ago when the Red Guards were on a book-burning spree."

How typical of my brother, who loved learning, to put himself in danger over a dictionary.

Number 3 saw me off at the station. I hugged her for the first time in our lives.

"I am no longer on the farm, Ah Sei," I told her. "That means you are free now, too."

Weeping freely, Number 3 embraced me again.

When the train stopped at Wuxi station to discharge and take on passengers, I thought sadly about my parents. I hadn't been able to visit their grave on my way to Beijing; Auntie Yi-feng had written to me that since the Red Guards had toppled and broken the headstone, the peasants had carted away the pieces and used them for construction, then sowed the land, obscuring the gravesite. I wondered if my parents would be proud of me now, and vowed that some day I would return to the land of fish and rice to find their grave and raise a stone again in their memory.

PART FOUR

WIND OF CHANGE
(1974–1978)

27

IN LATE AUGUST 1974 I set foot in Beijing for the second time in my life. Where my mode of travel in 1966 as a slight, underfed girl of fourteen had been to lie prone atop a luggage rack for days on end in various crowded and slow-moving trains, now, my body toughened by six years of toil, I had just spent twenty hours in third class, sitting on a wooden bench in comparative comfort. It was a warm day and, toting a duffle and school bag, I set off by bus across the city on a two-hour ride to the northwest outskirts. I was no less excited — or scared — when I approahced the main gate of Beijing University than I had been when I travelled to the capital in 1966. I was still hardly able to believe that my dream had come true. Would I be able to keep up with the academic work assigned? Had the six years on the farm put me so far behind that trying to study at this level would be useless?

The campus of the famous university was different from the pictures I had seen as a child. The Nameless Lake presented the reflection of a tower, lifeless under a bright autumn sky. The exquisite vermilion buildings with their graceful roofs and sweeping eaves looked like wounded soldiers, patched up and down with posters. Even the majestic stone lions guarding the main entrance had lost their heroic bearing and appeared sad and defenseless.

The registration hall near the south gate was like the inside of a laundromat, festooned with row after row of slogan-bearing banners on ropes. Down a newly paved road lined with French plane trees and *da-zi-bao* I found the building that housed the Western Language and Literature Department. My dorm was right across the road. Outside the door a huge poster read, "Attend university; run the university; transform the university with Marxist-Leninist-Mao Ze-dong Thought!"

The dorm was in no better repair than the other buildings. The glass had been broken out of the front doors and replaced with plywood sheets. Inside, pungent lime wash barely covered the political graffiti on the walls. On the third floor where the female students lived there were ten rooms and one washroom with toilet stalls, cold-water taps and cement sinks. My billet was long and narrow, with four two-tiered bunks against the walls. In the aisle between, six small desks were lined up. Two of the bunks were used to store luggage, books and other belongings. A small window looked out the back of the building over an empty patch of weedy ground.

I went inside and squeezed between the beds and desks and threw my bedroll onto a top bunk next to the window, as all the lower ones had been taken. I looked around, pleased with my new home. The unpainted cement floor, drab walls and tiny radiator seemed like heaven compared to my quarters on the farm.

I took a look around. Near our dorm I noticed one building that stood out because the facade was completely clear of posters. Curious, I pushed open the door, in which the glass was intact, and was immediately confronted by a guard. "No entry," he said curtly. This was the foreign students' residence, and no one could get in without permission. I was excited by the news that there were foreigners on campus. I had never seen a foreigner, much less heard English spoken by a native speaker.

Full of hope and enthusiasm to learn, I began my studies a few days later. There were about sixty new students in the English

Language and Literature Section, divided into four classes. As was normal in China, each class had a monitor, who served as liaison with the department administration, and a Party secretary, leader of the Party members in the class, who reported to the Party officials on campus. This long-standing "parallel organization" system was used in every work and academic unit across the country. The Party secretary was higher in rank than the monitor.

About half of our grade were Worker-Peasant-Soldier students from local factories, government offices and communes, and would return to the same units when they graduated. The rest of us had been recruited from all parts of China. Our future job assignments had also been decided, but we would not be informed what they were until we graduated.

Although anxious to study hard and make up for the years lost on the farm, to honor my family and do my small part in putting the country back on a sane course, I was deeply disappointed to realize that I had merely transferred from one battlefield to another. The campaign of "Criticizing Lin Biao and Confucius" was roaring across the campus, part of the power struggle between those like Deng Xiao-ping and Zhou En-lai who wanted to restore order to China, and the forces led by Jiang Qing, who, having started the Cultural Revolution, wanted it to continue so they could remain in power. Education was the front line. The universities were the cradles of the Great Proletarian Cultural Revolution, and foremost among them was Beijing University.

I had no idea why an educator and scholar like Confucius, who had been dead for over two thousand years, had been linked with the conspirator Lin Biao. Confucius had advocated obeying rulers and doing one's civic duty; Lin Biao had supported Mao's theory that political power came from the barrel of a gun, then had attempted to seize power by the same method. Nevertheless, classes were frequently canceled for meetings, announcements and discussions, and I spent a great deal of time wandering the campus, assigned to read the *da-zi-bao* — I had eyeglasses of my own now — and put bits and pieces together to make one of my own.

My initial hope that I would be able to meet and talk to the foreign students was merely an illusion. Most of them were from other socialist countries, either "brother and comrade" nations like

Albania, North Korea and Yugoslavia or third-world African countries cultivated by China to keep them dissociated from the Soviet Union. Allies or not, we had little to do with any of them.

One morning Lao Lu, a French teacher in charge of foreign students, introduced our class to Alina, a niece of Cambodia's exiled Prince Sihanouk. He and his family had been living in China since his overthrow in 1970. Alina was going to study English with us, Lao Lu said.

Among the women in the class, dressed in genderless Mao jackets and pants of gray, blue or PLA green, Alina looked like an alien. Her long black hair fell freely to her shoulders, a style most girls would have adopted had it not been politically incorrect. She wore a bright, tight blouse with a large, pointed collar and curious bellbottom slacks so long that the cuffs swept the floor as she walked.

One of us was to be chosen to move into Alina's room with her, as required by the Chinese *pei-zhu* — keeping company — system, a euphemism for watching and reporting. I hoped I would be a candidate. My thirst for knowledge about the world and people outside was one of the reasons I had been attracted to studying English.

But I should have known better. Xiao Shi, our monitor, announced that Xiao Guo, a peasant all her life, had been selected. The "unhealthy bourgeois style of life" of a foreign student was tempting, she explained, so only a student with impeccable political credentials could resist it.

However, I did manage to be part of the team who helped Xiao Guo move into Alina's dorm that night. All I wanted was to look around and maybe talk with some foreigners. When she opened the door and found us standing in the hall holding Guo's bedroll, suitcase and books, Alina's face betrayed her shock. Using hand gestures, she refused to let us enter the room, which she had had all to herself. A crowd gathered in the hall as the futile gesture-negotiations went on, until Lao Lu arrived and spoke to Alina alone in her room. Moments later, Xiao Guo was allowed in and we dispersed.

The next day Xiao Guo showed us the note Alina had written to her in English: "I want privacy." Xiao Guo asked me to translate it for her and I searched my brain for the proper Chinese expression, for there is no word for privacy in our language.

"She wants to be by herself," I tried.

The note was regarded as rude and unfriendly, from a spoiled young foreign woman. Alina remained distant and aloof, speaking to no one, sitting in class by herself. Another of my foreign classmates, the daughter of the Albanian ambassador to China, quietly moved away from the campus and was chauffeured to and from her classes.

28

MY FEAR THAT I WOULD not be able to keep up with my classmates proved unfounded, not because I had any special talent, but because many in my class had had much less education than I. Most of them had had less than a year of high school, some hadn't finished elementary school, and a few were almost illiterate. Deng's entrance-exam system, which I had passed, had obviously broken down, especially in the countryside.

"Don't Let One Single Class Brother or Sister Fall Behind" was the new slogan — an ironic exhortation, since our studies were constantly interrupted for political meetings. We were paired off, according to ability, so that one person could help the other. I was partnered with Xiao Shi, the monitor. As our Party secretary, Xiao Liu, explained to me, "Xiao Shi is a veteran Party member from a poor peasant's family. She will help you grow politically and you can give her a hand with her English study."

I was ready to help, but I resented having no choice in the matter. What was worse, Teacher Chen, who had examined me back on the farm, had added to my record that I had studied English on my own there. I was branded as interested only in academic learning, not in politics — a great sin during the Cultural Revolution. As the weeks passed, I was criticized for doing extra reading, and my "unnecessary" trips to the library were recorded. I was frequently interrupted by Xiao Shi and others, who would pull off my earphones to make sure I wasn't listening to "enemy broadcasting" — the Voice of America or the BBC. Although listening to these stations was no longer illegal or considered counter-revolutionary, it was still not encouraged. Xiao Shi had swallowed the Party line that academic achievement was suspect and that staying ignorant was virtuous. "Better Red than Expert" was a common slogan.

Xiao Shi's attitude was soon reflected by the university administration. A few weeks later the head of our department, Representative Gao, made this point clearer. Gao was a former PLA officer who had been sent to the university to support the "Leftists" and had become "first-hand" of the department when the universities were reopened in 1971. (The term "department head" had been dropped to show revolutionary egalitarianism.)

In his speech to welcome us new students, Gao warned us against "wearing new shoes but following old paths" and urged us to remember that he would rather have us walk out of the campus in four years as revolutionaries than as "slaves to knowledge." To these platitudes he added, "Without a strong proletarian consciousness, you could do great harm to this country, for if you decided to betray it, you would not need an interpreter." The unstated message here was frightening and far-reaching: teachers were reluctant to teach, and students to learn, for fear of criticism.

I was forced to be devious. During the week I tried to stay together with my fellow students, taking part in the endless political discussions, spending little time in the library studying. But on the weekend, when the Beijing students went home, I spent every waking moment in the library to make up for lost time. To keep up with my reading, I often took risks by covering my books with the red plastic jacket of the Selected Works of Mao Ze-dong. These guerrilla techniques, as I liked to think of them, worked. In front of the whole class I was praised by my partner, Xiao Shi, for my improved political awareness.

That autumn an agricultural college in Liaoning Province, in the northeast of China, moved its campus to the countryside to be close to, learn from and help the peasants. This highly "correct" act was pounced upon and applauded across the country by Jiang Qing and the radicals and they called for a national movement to follow this example. First-Hand Gao began to plan, and soon he announced that our "imperialist language and literature" department would relocate to the mountains outside the city and make "a historical impact on modern Chinese education history."

Gao named the place, but provided few details. He didn't need to: it was known to most of our teachers because they had been sent there for "re-education" during the years when the university was closed, and had lived a nightmare. It was a mountain valley, no more than a gully, with a few thatched-roofed houses and a small apple orchard.

I was crushed and felt helpless. The whole thing made no sense to me. How could we study in a labor camp? Why did the university even offer to teach foreign languages if they were so evil? It was absurd.

It turned out that the camp was too small to accommodate the whole department, and for a few days I dared to hope that the whole ridiculous scheme would be abandoned. But Gao was determined. For now, only the first-year students and our teachers would go, and we would expand the place to accommodate the rest. Meanwhile the foreign students would be put into second-year classes exempt from farm labor. We would march there on foot, to "renew the spirit of the Long March." A marching-practice schedule was posted.

When the moving date was near, I came down with pneumonia and was hospitalized. A new friend I had made, Chang-hong — Rainbow — came to see me to tell me that I would not be required to participate in the march.

"I wish I could be exempted from the whole stupid enterprise," I said.

Since meeting that fall, Rainbow and I had become very close. She was a year older than I and had been sent to Bai Da by the Beijing Tourist Bureau, where she worked. Her parents were veteran Communists, and her father was a high official of the city

Public Security Bureau — the police. Rainbow was a caring and generous person, especially to those of us not from Beijing. She spent hours helping students whose educational background was not strong. Though my family background was politically unsound, Rainbow ignored the fact. Unlike most others who seized any opportunity to lord it over people like me, she was nonjudgmental in that respect. She reminded me of my four friends on the farm.

A few evenings after my release from hospital, First-Hand Gao harangued the assembled teachers and students, each of whom carried a shoulder bag holding enough water and food for the march to the village.

"Comrades," he shouted, "our great leader, Chairman Mao, teaches us that it is people who create history, and tonight we are going to write a new page." And off they tramped into the dark streets. They had to leave at midnight, for during the day and early evening the streets were far too crowded to accommodate a parade.

I and the others who were too old or weak to march left the next morning with the farm tools and classroom equipment. The bus took us into the barren foothills east of the city and set us down two hours later in the small village of Tai Ping. The road to our camp, Beijing University Cadres Labor School, had been washed out by heavy rains.

The camp comprised five one-room, single-story brick buildings scattered over the brow of a rocky, treeless hill and linked by a narrow dirt path. All the buildings were in poor repair, with blackened thatch on the roofs. Behind the hill, the mountains reared up to the sky. I found the building where the female English teachers and students were billeted and gently pushed the door open. The sleeping women lay fully clothed on the wooden cots, their suitcases, bedrolls and boxes piled on the hard-packed dirt floor.

My heart sank, for the desolate scene brought back memories of the farm. I closed the door and climbed the path farther up the hill to an unkempt orchard. I sat down on a rock, surrounded by fallen apples rotting in the uncut grass. The tragic irony of a neglected orchard and unharvested fruit near a village of peasants living at the starvation level threw me into a deep depression. Absurdity was piled on absurdity. I had been accepted into a university where I was encouraged not to study; enrolled in a foreign-language department when anyone who could speak or read another tongue was suspected of subterfuge; sent to a village where the peasants were forced to make politics and disregard their crops.

I missed my sisters and brothers and wondered if Great-Aunt's blood pressure was giving her trouble. I wished Xiao Zhao, with whom I had been corresponding regularly since I left the farm, was there to listen to my troubles, doubts and fears. Ironically, the fact that I was engaged to a "farmer" — one of the latest items recorded in my dossier — won me revolutionary merit in the eyes of my radical fellow students. I wondered if Xiao Zhao's father, who had "approved" of my being a language student, would change his tune when he found out I was once again in exile.

Thinking of Xiao Zhao reinforced my conviction that Fate was playing tricks on me. Just before leaving the campus I had received a letter from him. He had been transferred from the farm back to Shanghai and now had a job as a coal carrier in the harbor. It was the hardest work he had ever known, he had written, dusty and dirty, but he was happy. He was home with his family and had regained his city *hu-kou*. Almost all of our farm-mates were back, and some had married and begun a family.

Maybe I should have turned down the chance to go to Beijing University, I thought. If I had, maybe I'd be home by now, taking care of Great-Aunt.

Gao had set up a half-day system of study and physical labor. Under the guidance of the local peasants, we English students began pruning and cultivating the six dozen or so neglected apple trees. We toted water and manure up the steep hill in buckets suspended from shoulder-poles. The students of other languages were making terraced fields to grow vegetables, digging dirt from uncultivated places in the hills, hauling it to the new fields and mixing it with composted nightsoil. Gao's goal was to make us self-sufficient in vegetables within two years. I doubted we would succeed, since every rainfall washed away most of the newly formed fields and the work had to be done over again.

There were no classrooms, of course. Our lessons were conducted either in the dorm, with our bedding rolled up so that we could sit on our beds, or in the open, when weather permitted, sitting on the ground.

Our teachers gave us sheets of vocabulary reflecting our daily work and surroundings. But as the old saying goes, "Once bitten by a snake, a man will regard even a coiled rope with suspicion." Our teachers followed no overall plan or program: they had learned that a written course of study could be turned against them. They were reluctant to put any pressure on the slow students, and those of us who wanted to learn more and progress quickly were actively discouraged. Gao had allowed only one tape recorder — used to practice listening and speaking — for each class of fifteen students; ours was in such demand that we had to keep a damp towel draped over it to prevent it from overheating.

My class was divided into three smaller groups, each with a mixture of class backgrounds and of Party members and nonmembers. These groups were for *fang-pin-wen-kuo* — visiting the peasants' homes to share their hardships. My group was assigned to the Hai family.

Tai Ping Village was one of the oldest in this part of China. Long ago, the inhabitants had served as forced laborers in the building of the Great Wall. Later they were stone-cutters and craftsmen for the tombs built by the emperors. The eighty or so families had more or less survived the battles between the Nationalists and Communists.

The attempt to have us learn from the poor and lower-middle-class peasants was a dismal failure. The truth was that the farmers resented us. Our presence was "taking away their rice bowls," they claimed, meaning that it was hard enough to eke food from the barren soil without having to share it with interlopers. They considered our visits to chat with them a waste of their time. I didn't blame them. Here, then, was another absurdity: we didn't want to be there; they didn't want us. But First-Hand Gao, encouraged by Jiang Qing's faction, continued his plans.

The Beijing students were allowed to go home every weekend and I was often invited to go home with Rainbow. Her parents treated me with great kindness. They not only ignored my family background but evinced deep sympathy for my family tragedies. Even so, when I was in Rainbow's house I couldn't help but feel jealous, so I visited only occasionally. Her being with her family, prosperous and happy together, filled me with painful memories and unrealistic longing.

I therefore stayed back when the others boarded the truck, even though there was no library, not much to study, and only two meals on Sunday. I had long since become used to being alone.

In June the apple trees blossomed and I looked forward to a break in the labor and more class time, for the trees had to be left alone when in bloom. No break came, though. We were divided into two shifts and began to build a new road to the camp. The two-shift system was used because there was a shortage of tools and equipment. One group worked in the cool morning hours, the second in the evening, for the days were extremely hot and dry. Study was conducted at midday.

Once again, political fervor attempted to make up for incompetence. Gao knew nothing about road-making; the rocks and stones we gathered and arranged to form a roadway had nothing to bind them together, and when a truck passed by, the road collapsed beneath the tires.

29

A T THE END OF JULY, I boarded the train for Shanghai,
looking forward to the longest holiday I had experienced
in many years, to being with Great-Aunt and my new
nephew, to talking with Number 2 and asking his advice. I wanted
to see Xiao Zhao and fill up his ears with my troubles and problems.

We had been writing regularly. He often repeated his own
philosophy of life: drift with the stream; when in Rome do as the
Romans do. This outlook had worked well for him all his life, but I
was unable to make myself so passive.

Xiao Zhao had written that, when I got home and met his
parents, I should not mention my relocation and the half-day study
system. I should act as though I was still at Bei Da studying full
time. This seemed to confirm that, to his parents, I was a university
student who would someday have a good job that would benefit
their youngest son, a goal that could not be achieved if I was
tending apple trees. Xiao Zhao was also afraid that I would talk
politics. I resented his admonition and wished he had not tried to
tell me what to say and to do. As the train pushed south I wondered

if this meant that from now on I had to live up to his parents' standards.

It turned out that meeting both Xiao Zhao's parents didn't make me as nervous as I thought. I had a good conversation with his stepmother, and learned that she herself had gone to college, a rare choice for a woman at that time. She had become a businesswoman in her own right, involved in the stock market, like "snow in June," she said, in that man's world, shocking both her family and herself. She had stayed single until she married Lao Zhao in her early forties. During the Red Guard raids, she had been humiliated and attacked, forced to open her safe-deposit box at the Bank of China and hand over all her jewelry, foreign stocks, bonds and currency. She had suffered even more than her husband.

During that summer my relationship with Xiao Zhao was officially approved by his parents. For days after I introduced Xiao Zhao to her, Great-Aunt couldn't hide her smile. Given his city *hukou*, there was a good chance that her Ah Si might return to her side again.

When I returned to the camp at the end of August to help harvest the apples, it was a good feeling to see that our hard labor had paid off. We were the first to taste the delicious fruit, free of charge. Gao had reminded us of the PLA's Three Main Rules and Eight Points of Attention, but everyone, Party members and teachers included, ignored him. When someone chomped away at an apple, the others would simply turn their backs. In his speech after our return to the campus, Gao praised the iron discipline of the English language students. I could hardly contain my laughter.

At Bei Da, instead of moving back to our original dorms, we were settled in a four-story building near the old south gate, a building constructed from preformed concrete slabs. There were twelve rooms on each side of the long, damp hallways, with toilets and washing areas at each end. It was a dark and dreary interior, but after living with thirty people in one dirt-floored hut, I thought it a paradise.

One of the achievements of the Cultural Revolution was to allow the Chinese people to witness their leaders rising and falling like horses on a merry-go-round. In November of that year, Jiang Qing's faction lashed back and Deng Xiao-ping was once again denounced.

As usual we were forced to participate in the rhetoric and recrimination, but by then the Revolution was entering its ninth year, and, after about ten months of relative peace and stability, people were more than fed up with it. At political study meetings some read openly, chatted, even dozed. I used the opportunity to memorize new vocabulary. This loosening-up spread throughout the student body and we became more considerate with one another. The constant tension began to ease. I remembered one of Newton's laws of motion: for every action there is an equal and opposite reaction.

It seemed even the weather wanted a change. The winter of 1975 came early and cold, with freezing winds sweeping in from Siberia and tearing down the *da-zi-bao* stands that had been in place since the beginning of the Cultural Revolution. The temperature remained far below zero for weeks on end. While I was at Rainbow's home wrapping dumplings in preparation for the arrival of 1976, her grandmother complained that she couldn't remember the last time Beijing had been so cold; she had an eerie feeling that the new year, the year of the dragon, would bring hardship. Her words brought to mind Great-Aunt's frequent reference to my inauspicious birth.

The misgivings of Rainbow's grandmother were borne out a week later. I had just finished the obligatory group exercise on the sports ground and had dashed into my dorm, my breath forming frost clouds as I ran. The hallways were strangely empty, but I could hear voices and a radio broadcast coming from the rooms. The cold must have kept a lot of students from their morning exercises, I thought as I climbed the stairs. A burst of funeral music stopped me in my tracks.

Premier Zhou En-lai, highly regarded by most people, had passed away after a long struggle with cancer. My own feelings toward him were mixed. I was often angry when I saw him in newspapers and TV documentaries, meeting Red Guards and rebels, giving them instructions and praising their fervor. While other state leaders rode the merry-go-round, he always seemed stable. However, I was also aware that if Premier Zhou hadn't been there to pick up the pieces, the country would have suffered even more and we could have been enmeshed in a civil war. I wondered naively if the premier had been aware that he had been dealing with devils and that the biggest one was Chairman Mao himself.

Zhou's death cast an even darker shadow of doubt over the future. In my lifetime I had never seen such an outpouring of public grief. The government, fearful that Zhou's demise would provide a focus for opposition, moved quickly to set out regulations, and the campus loudspeakers announced restrictions on mourning procedures. No private mourning was allowed; no one was permitted to wear black armbands. TV and radio coverage were circumscribed. Jiang Qing had many followers at Bei Da and they had been very active in the recent campaign against Deng Xiaoping. Jiang Qing herself had paid frequent visits to the campus, claiming she did so on Chairman Mao's behalf. It was she who was behind the attempt to minimize the response to Premier Zhou's death.

Nevertheless, no one seemed to care any more. Classes were canceled, despite an order to the contrary from the university authorities. Rainbow and a few others collected cotton ration coupons from the students from Beijing and went to a nearby fabric store to buy black cloth for mourning bands. Others made paper-flower wreaths and wrote poster poems expressing their grief. A lecture room was turned into a mourning hall.

Each evening I went to the TV room, which was always jammed with students, and watched the coverage of citizens waiting outside the hospital to pay their last respects to the premier and later of the state leaders filing up to Zhou's bier in a pavilion west of the Forbidden City. Mao was not to be seen. Standing before the bier was the premier's widow, Zhou's beloved companion for the many years of their childless marriage.

When the camera showed Jiang Qing approaching the bier, an outburst of anger filled the room as we saw that she was still wearing her army cap, a sign of disrespect. Some students left to avoid trouble but others yelled and waved their fists, a dangerous action at a time when the mere hint of disapproval of Jiang Qing meant imprisonment.

An extremely important department meeting was called for January 15, and all of us were commanded to attend. Posters around the campus issued the same order to all departments. Then we found out why: January 15 was the day Premier Zhou's funeral procession would pass through the city to the crematorium. Despite my mixed feelings, I wanted to pay my respects to the man who had said in his will that he wanted his ashes scattered over China's rivers and mountains, not buried with his revolutionary comrades in the Eight Treasures Hill Cemetery.

Rainbow and I worked out a plan that night, and the next morning we left separately for our morning run. Instead of jogging through the campus as we normally did, we ran into the street. We skipped two bus stops, for we saw student officials posted there to turn back those who were disobeying the university's orders. It took us almost three hours on the unusually overcrowded buses to reach Changan Avenue.

Already tens of thousands had gathered along the sidewalks under a cold cloudy sky. Among them were toddlers cuddled in their mothers' arms or bundled in strollers. Old people huddled against the metal sidewalk partitions or against tree trunks, facing away from the freezing northwest wind. It was the most powerful silence I had ever experienced, like roaring thunder in my ears.

Hours later the funeral cortege approached, and through teary eyes I saw a hearse draped in black and yellow rosettes. Some people in the crowd let out loud cries; others reached out their hands as if trying to stop the moving vehicle. Babies wakened by their mothers' sobbing struck the air with their fists. It must have been the greatest non-organized mourning ceremony in Chinese history, attended by more than a million people.

By the time Rainbow and I returned to the campus and joined the many others who had broken the rules, it was dark. All the gates, including the side doors normally kept open even after curfew, were locked. Now we have to pay for our disobedience, I thought; at twenty-three I am still treated like a child. Some people pounded the gates, others began to scale the high wall. Half an hour later the side door opened. As we filed past the doorman's hut we had to show our ID and have our names recorded. We were then grouped by department and in our case led to First-Hand Gao and his deputies, Master Wang and Teacher Lu, the former deputy head of the department. All three were stern-faced. Gao, seething with anger, lost no time.

"If you think I can do nothing about you, you're dead wrong," he threatened. "Wait until you graduate, young men and women. Then I hope you will remember this moment. If you don't, I'll be there to remind you and watch you shed your useless tears."

Before he dismissed us, he ordered us to hand our self-criticism to him personally the next day and await further punishment.

Here I was again, criticizing my own behavior in writing, condemning myself for something I felt I had the right to do. I had ignored Xiao Zhao's advice to drift with the stream. Rainbow told me she was not worried by Gao. She knew she would return to her unit, the Beijing Travel Bureau, after graduation. But I was deeply disturbed by Gao's open threat. Obviously our disobedience and challenge to his authority had made him lose face, and the thought of his revenge was like a dark cloud gathering over my head. I didn't tell Xiao Zhao or anyone in my family about this event.

30

BEIJING THAT SPRING WAS RIFE with fear and rumor. Most people didn't know much about the new premier, Hua Guo-feng; I had never heard of him before. The ever-informative Rainbow, whose mother and father in the Public Security Bureau knew more than most, told me that Hua had been Mao's compromise choice to ease tensions between the moderates and Jiang Qing's radicals.

The Chairman himself, I learned from Rainbow, was seriously ill, had been for several years, and was dying. It was rumored that for the past couple of years, Mao being too ill to talk, his instructions had been "whispered" to a trusted female companion who was supposedly the only person who could read his lips. His comments on Party and government documents, written in the margins — his practice for years — could hardly be deciphered because he had Parkinson's disease.

As Mao lay ill, the absurdities of the Cultural Revolution continued to pile up. The Public Security Bureau in those days was, on orders from the central government, searching the city for copies of a biography of Jiang Qing written by Roxane Witke, an American Chinese history scholar who had interviewed Jiang Qing extensively and secretly in 1972. The title was *Comrade Chiang Ch'ing*, but in Chinese it was translated as *Empress in the Red Capital*. The official line was that the biography did not exist; and that it was vicious Western propaganda against our beloved leader!

Once again there was a witch-hunt, and once again the witch-hunt pitted friends, colleagues and family against one another. This time the hunt was for "rumor." While anti–Jiang Qing graffiti appeared across the campus, criticizing her for self-revelation to a Western writer, students and teachers were called upon to inform against anyone they knew who spread rumors about the book. Numerous meetings were called. "Have you heard about the book? Where did you hear?" we were asked by nervous officials.

I was required to have a "heart-to-heart talk" with my "partner" Xiao Shi and Xiao Liu, our class Party secretary.

"Lately you have been pretty active, politically," Shi commented, referring to my trip to see the funeral cortege of Zhou En-lai.

I didn't respond.

Liu tried next. "Have you heard any rumors about our beloved comrade Jiang Qing?" — a ridiculous question, since Jiang and her book were the talk of the campus.

"Not much," I said.

"You've heard of the book, though, haven't you?"

"I heard something about a book."

"Where did you hear about it?" This was, I knew, what they were really interested in. Of course, I got all my news from Rainbow.

"I overheard something on the bus when I was on my way to the department store."

And that was the end of the conversation. Liu closed the discussion by mouthing the Party line: there was no such book, and it was just Western propaganda, a plot to smear our beloved leader.

For me this talk confirmed two things: the book did exist, and fear of Jiang Qing was deep and powerful. Since when had China paid such attention to Western propaganda? The rumor-hunting continued, and many friends and family of the more naive students were damaged. Once again, the weather became the only safe topic of discussion.

The mourning of Premier Zhou did not cease. In mid-March, weeks before *Qing Ming*, the festival to honor the dead, Beijing citizens defied government edicts by placing wreaths in Zhou's honor at the base of the Monument to the People's Heroes in Tian An Men Square. With every passing day more and more people came to the square, tens of thousands, singing, reading poems and making speeches praising Zhou's memory. In symbolic and coded words they expressed their long-pent-up hatred toward Jiang Qing and her henchmen. Each night trucks came to remove the wreaths; the next day they were replaced by new ones.

No such spontaneous mass action had occurred since the founding of the People's Republic in 1949. I wanted to take part, but before Rainbow left for home on Saturday afternoon, one day before *Qing Ming*, she warned me not to go to the square.

"Please listen to me this time, Xiao Ye," she pleaded. "Mother and Father told me that there have been plain-clothes police everywhere for days, and there are surveillance cameras all over the square. The photos, if you are in them, will haunt you all your life." Rainbow went on to say that her father hadn't been home for days, and that the militia and PLA were stationed inside the Great Hall of the People. "Something big is going to happen, Xiao Ye, and I'm scared. Stay away."

She was right. On April 5, Tian An Men Square became a battlefield. Ten thousand police, militia and soldiers clashed with the demonstrators. Thousands were beaten and hundreds were arrested. Fresh blood was splashed on the monument. The following day, the government justified the beatings and arrests with the usual rhetoric. The mass demonstrations in honor of Premier Zhou were labeled "the Tian An Men Counter-revolutionary Incidents" and Deng Xiao-ping was accused of orchestrating them.

Afterwards we were swamped with predictable political study sessions: newspaper readings and interminable "discussions," in which no one stated a personal point of view. We were forced to write personal reports that made our standpoints clear, and, like the others, I wrote what my leaders wanted to read.

When weeks later I heard that we second-year English students and our teachers were going to run some short-term classes off-campus, I welcomed the news with open arms. Tourists were coming to China in increasing numbers, but the language barrier was a problem. I heard that foreign travelers were flapping their arms to indicate that they wanted a taxi to the airport and mimicking ducks to suggest a Beijing duck restaurant. First-Hand Gao said it was our time to serve the country and the people. I wondered if he realized that because of his radical anti-learning approach to education we didn't have much to offer.

According to Gao's plan, half of us would be sent to Beijing airport to instruct flight attendants and the other half to a training school for taxi drivers. We would relocate, continue our own classes, and teach English. Rainbow was assigned to the airport and I headed off to the far northwest suburbs, an hour's bus ride, to the taxi drivers' school, a three-acre facility surrounded by tall poplar trees.

Compared to the atmosphere on campus, where I could almost smell the tension, this place, with its shady trees and blossoming wildflowers, seemed peaceful. Lao Hu, the director, was thrilled to have us there to teach his drivers English. Judging from the sparkle in his eyes, he expected miracles.

He went to great pains to ensure that our stay was as comfortable as possible. Ten of us shared a room three times bigger than our dorm (which housed six). The classrooms were spacious and bright, with newly washed walls. But what was most refreshing and rewarding was the respect and warmth offered by our students, who were eager to learn. All of them were young men in their early twenties; most had been drivers in the army.

My partner, Xiao Shi, and I were grouped with three drivers, and we gathered every afternoon for English studies. The first thing we had to teach them was how to say "Long live Chairman Mao," then "Serve the people whole-heartedly." We then moved on to more practical phrases, like "Chinese drivers don't accept tips."

I found myself enjoying the lessons, seeing others value the language I loved and had spent so much time trying to learn. I worked hard to prepare for the exercises, glad of the golden opportunity to pick up a different type of vocabulary and put aside the useless political terms fed to us at the university. In return for our hard work, Lao Hu arranged cars to take us back to the campus or to homes when needed. He also organized trips for us to such tourist spots as the Great Wall and Ming Tombs.

Each time I strolled along the flowerbeds that encircled our quarters, and past the earthenware water jars with goldfish peeping from behind the lily stems, I wondered how First-Hand Gao would react to such an "unrevolutionary" environment. According to his theory, we should all have turned into bourgeois reactionaries by now. The truth was that without the intensive political meetings and discussions that went on daily at Bei Da, everyone was minding her or his own business; even the Party members had mellowed.

31

TIME TRULY DOES FLY like an arrow, particularly when it brings fun and joy. In mid-July I booked my train ticket to Shanghai and began to count the days until my departure on the twenty-ninth, the first train available.

Two days before I was to leave, I took a walk around the taxi-school grounds after supper to get some air, for it was a typical hot Beijing summer night. Overhead a light breeze rustled in the poplars, and crickets chirruped in the dark. I pictured myself meeting Xiao Zhao at the Shanghai station, sitting around the table at home, chatting with Great-Aunt and bouncing my nephew on my knee. When I felt sleepy, I made my way back to the dorm. As I passed one of the water jars, a goldfish leapt high in the air and fell onto the flagstones where it wriggled in the dust. Hastily, I picked up the fish and dropped it back into the jar. It was then that I noticed other fish on the stones, some flipping, some lying still. But I thought no more of it.

That night I dreamt I was on the train to Shanghai. As the train pushed south, it swayed rhythmically, the soothing *click-click* of the wheels lulling me. Then the rocking of the train grew violent and screams echoed through the coach, followed by thunderous rumbles. Someone was yelling my name.

"Xiao Ye! Xiao Ye! Come out!"

The first thing I saw when I opened my eyes was a huge rent in the roof of the dorm and through it, a red sky. Then there was a booming thunderclap. I jumped from my shaking bed. The floor trembled so violently that I fell to my knees. I grabbed my trousers and shirt and made my way across the heaving floorboards to the door. As I stepped outside into a downpour, the ground pitched, throwing me headlong into a puddle. Two of my roommates, shivering in their soaking underwear, dragged me to my feet.

The sky was like an angry man, roaring with thunder, ripped with lightning. Sheets of rain whipped across the courtyard. After a few moments of screaming and running, we began to get organized. We gathered in the middle of the basketball court, away from the buildings, huddled together for warmth under blackboards that did little to keep off the fierce rain pounding from the eerily red sky.

By dawn the earth had ceased its terrible convulsions, but the rain continued to pour down. Just after first light, Lao Hu pedaled up on his bicycle, soaking wet. He told us that an earthquake had hit Beijing, Tianjin and Tangshan, a city east of Beijing.

We were allowed back into our dorm, but only to gather our belongings. Word came from the university that we should not go back there; the buildings had sustained considerable damage and were considered unsafe, especially the ones like my dorm, with its concrete-slab construction. The university hospital was jammed with the injured, most of whom had panicked and jumped out of the windows when the earthquake flung them from their sleep. The students from Beijing began to leave the taxi school for their homes.

As the day wore on, radio news confirmed that Tangshan had been at the epicenter of the quake, which registered 5.6 on the Richter scale. Looking around at the damage in Beijing, I imagined that the devastation to that other densely populated city must be horrible. Beijing residents were urged to stay calm and not to rush out to buy food to hoard at home — which only served to give them ideas.

That afternoon I decided to go to Rainbow's home, since it was near the Beijing station and I would be leaving for Shanghai the next day. Rainbow was at home with her mother. Her father and brother had been at the Bureau since the quake hit and would be there indefinitely. That night the three of us sat in the peaceful courtyard, listening to the rain on our umbrellas, talking and casting uneasy glances at the cluster of empty bottles that her mother had balanced upside down on the flagstones as a primitive early-warning device. We were all frightened, waiting for aftershocks, which, the rumors said, could be worse than the first quake. Even though electricity had been restored in the neighborhood, for some reason people were afraid to turn on their lights.

The BBC reported that the earthquake had measured 8 on the Richter scale. It also provided a lot more information on places damaged, the estimated death toll and injuries. These estimates were many times higher than the figures given out by the Chinese media, which minimized the catastrophe in every way. In fact our media were still devoting a great deal of space and time to political attacks against Deng Xiao-ping. Hearing the BBC broadcast filled me with anger. If the government could lie about the Richter scale reading, something that could be monitored in other places and the information shared internationally, what wouldn't it lie about to fit its purpose? I told myself I should be used to the lies by now.

Rainbow came along to see me off at the station, helping me with my duffle bag and a string sack bulging with watermelons I had bought that morning, the only food available at the market. We arrived an hour early because we had heard that, since the earthquake, every train heading south was jammed with passengers, with or without tickets. The square outside the station was like a refugee camp, with thousands of men, women and children sitting, lying and squatting, surrounded by bundles and bedrolls. Inside, Rainbow and I sat on the marble floor in a corner of the waiting room, chatting. Suddenly people around us jumped to their feet and streamed out the doors in panic. The windows rattled and the standing ashtray next to us clattered, although no one was near it. Before we could collect ourselves and run outside, the tremor passed. It was minor, but everyone's nerves were frayed.

My train was far behind schedule. When I finally boarded, I carefully placed the four watermelons under my seat, which, luckily, was at the window. The train was packed to capacity:

passengers without a booked seat stood in the aisles and even the washrooms.

In half an hour, the train pulled into Tianjin station, where a sea of frantic bodies surged toward the still-moving coaches. Obviously Tianjin had been hit harder than Beijing, and with so many aftershocks people feared for their lives. Shabby, and desperate to escape the city, most without luggage, they yelled and waved their arms, begging to be let in, pounding and kicking the walls and windows of the cars. I drew back as someone began to slam a rock against my window. I knew from the Great Travel that as soon as I lifted the window crazed refugees would force themselves through in a never-ending stream and the train would never leave the station. After twenty minutes of this bedlam, the train inched forward and crawled from the station.

About twenty-six hours later, at midnight, I arrived in Shanghai. I hadn't eaten a thing, nor had a drop of water, although my mind had never left the juicy watermelons beneath my seat. I hadn't dared cut one open, no matter how thirsty and hungry I was. How could I eat alone in front of such a crowd? How could four melons feed so many people? Also, as a melon lover I knew what the aftermath would be, and each trip to the washroom was a long and hard battle.

Xiao Zhao laughed when he saw my cargo. "Watermelons? You brought them all the way here?" He laughed even louder when he saw that two of them were soft and mushy.

"It's not funny," I said feebly. "I wish I had bought more so I wouldn't have had to hide them under the seat."

Great-Aunt was relieved to see me home, whole and sound. "Ah Si," she said to me, "have you realized that this is the Year of the Dragon? Since the year started, bad things have happened one after another. First Premier Zhou died, then Marshal Zhu De, and now this earthquake. I don't know if this is the end of it. It's just like your life; you never know what's going to happen next."

I wondered what she would have thought if she had known that Chairman Mao was dying.

As it had during the great famines in the early sixties, the government continued to lie about the effects of the Tangshan earthquake. And where information was absent, rumor filled the gap. People across the country were advised to closely observe animal and insect behavior because these creatures could sense impending quakes. As a result, since no city family was allowed to keep any kind of pet, there was a huge and almost permanent crowd in front of the Flower and Bird store in downtown Shanghai. The most dramatic rumor predicted that Shanghai would experience a big earthquake and, worse, the whole city would be swallowed by the resulting seismic wave. Across the city, earthquake drills were carried out. Every stall in the market outside Purple Sunshine Lane was occupied long before the sun went down by those who were afraid to sleep inside. Great-Aunt insisted my baby nephew be put into our wooden bathtub and placed under the heavy mahogany table at night. I was glad she didn't know what a tidal wave was.

But I was happy to be home. Now twenty-four, and with two years left before my graduation, I began to think about where I would live and what job I would be assigned. I still slept with Great-Aunt when I was at home, and was fully aware that when I was away she regretted the empty space in her bed.

Xiao Zhao and I spent as much time together as his shift-work at the coal docks allowed, dining with his parents or relaxing at my home under the watchful eye of Great-Aunt, who would not allow us to be alone. Like most young couples, we often took to the streets at night, where it was cooler and darkness let us pretend we were by ourselves. Seclusion was always a problem for young lovers, as social custom conspired with the realities of overcrowded living quarters to make it almost impossible to attain.

Much of our talk turned on my graduation, what kind of job I would be assigned, and where we would live.

"I hope you are assigned something in Beijing," Xiao Zhao said one evening, to my surprise. "Father and I have discussed this, and we think that foreign-language graduates will be in high demand, and you will land a high-profile job."

"But we'd have to leave Shanghai."

"Yes, but Father says he doesn't mind, as long as you can use your position to find me a job that's better than the one I have now. If that's the case, I wouldn't mind leaving Shanghai."

But I would, I thought. I had made up my mind that I would try my best to come back to the city and care for Great-Aunt, even if it meant a sacrifice. But I kept my vow to myself, reluctant to displease my fiancé and his father.

Three weeks after my summer vacation began, a telegram ordered me to return to Beijing immediately and I bade a hasty farewell to Xiao Zhao and my family. My department was forming a relief team to go to Tangshan.

32

I RUSHED BACK TO BEIJING, arriving on August 29. We were scheduled to set out for Tangshan in two weeks but no return date had been chosen — not a promising sign. Jiang Qing had visited Bei Da, calling on the students and teachers to support Tangshan and make a "meaningful contribution." First-Hand Gao couldn't wait to carry out another imperial edict handed down by the Chairman's wife, and the third-year students of the Western Languages and Literature Department once again became pawns in his game to amass political capital.

While some set about organizing food, cooking utensils and tools, I helped construct sections of what I called "rabbit hutches"; these prefabricated fiberboard dwellings were fifteen yards long, five wide and two and a half high. They had neither floor nor window, only an opening at each end. Each hutch held thirty bunks in two tiers, fifteen per side. With our own lodgings and equipment, Gao boasted that we would not "add one bit of trouble to the people of Tangshan." In this same spirit, Jiang Qing and her gang had refused aid from the United Nations and other countries: she feared that China would lose face or that spies would sneak into our country under cover of a relief effort.

Gao further emphasized that no one was allowed to bring any books or study materials — other than the *Selected Works of Mao Ze-dong*. We must, he said sternly, show our sincerity and revolutionary spirit. Listening to his ridiculous regulations, it became more and more clear to me that people like Gao were nothing but pathetic buffoons performing evil antics. I wondered whether he was consciously selling his soul to satisfy his political ambitions or whether he was just plain stupid. Did he really believe the poor victims of Tangshan would care or be hurt because we brought some books to read?

In the middle of our frantic preparations, on the afternoon prior to our departure, we were summoned again by the loudspeakers blaring all over the campus: all of us were to go to our respective dining halls to listen to an announcement of great importance. The words "great importance" had been so overused that to us they meant the opposite: some people sat around chatting or playing chess, some read, some knitted.

But this time the announcement proved to be momentous. A buzz sounded in the loudspeakers, followed by funeral music. Then a sinister and mechanical voice echoed through the dining hall: "A message to the whole Party, the whole army and people of the Motherland! The Central Committee of the Chinese Communist Party, the Standing Committee of the National People's Congress, the State Council of the People's Republic of China deeply regret to announce that our great leader, Chairman Mao Ze-dong, died at ten past midnight on the morning of September 9, 1976, in Beijing."

To me the news that our "beloved Great Helmsman" was dead was a shock, but not unexpected. Although the press had been keeping its official line that Mao was sound and healthy and had even personally taken charge of relief efforts in Tangshan, not many had been fooled. Now Mao was dead at last, like the last buddha statue removed from a temple he himself had created.

Death had touched my life so many times, but this time I didn't know how to respond. The man — almost the god — I had been taught to revere since my birth, whom I had traveled to Beijing years ago to look upon, who always seemed above the political turmoil, had also been the black hand guiding the chaos and dysfunction of the Cultural Revolution. I had never worshipped him nor would I grieve for him.

Heartbroken sobbing and quiet weeping cut into my thoughts and brought me back to reality. It reminded me that I should put on an appropriate performance. I quickly lowered my head, blew my nose and rubbed my eyes. I realized for the first time how specialized a skill acting was.

The relief mission to Tangshan was postponed: the reverent worship of our deceased leader was clearly more important than helping the suffering victims of the earthquake. One of our dining rooms was turned into a mourning hall, with paper wreaths lining the walls and black drapes hanging from the ceiling. A bier was set up at the front, covered by a Communist Party flag with its yellow crossed hammer and sickle against a red background. It was to be guarded at all times and every student would be "honored" to stand guard, wearing a PLA uniform and holding a rifle.

The idea of standing guard beside an empty coffin and pretending Mao was inside gave me goosebumps; I hoped my shift would be in the daylight. But Xiao Shi and I were slated for the eight p.m. shift two days later.

We arrived in the dining hall kitchen ten minutes early as required and each of us was given a crumpled and creased soldier's uniform. The legs of my outfit dragged on the ground; the arms of the jacket hid my hands; the cap's brim fell below my ears and blocked my sight. I rolled up the legs and sleeves and attempted to trap the cap behind my ears, then took up my position. The departing "guard" handed me a heavy old rifle, which I leaned against my ribs, not knowing the proper way to hold it.

I must have been the craziest-looking soldier in the world. To stare straight ahead and keep still was not easy, even for half an hour. My hat kept slipping down and covering my eyes. Under the pale light my attention was repeatedly drawn to the photograph of Mao on that spooky box, draped in black cloth. I wondered how a person bearing such a benevolent smile could have caused so much pain to so many people over the past two decades. The weight of hardship Mao had heaped on me and my family was enormous.

And the suffering visited upon the Chinese people was scarcely to be imagined.

The half hour passed slowly. The student who came to relieve me took one look at me and burst out laughing. He quickly slapped his palm across his mouth, conscious of the hushed reverence of the place, but his eyes danced above his hand. I handed him the gun and left quickly.

Xiao Shi criticized me as we walked back to the dorm. "How could you make such a stupid mistake! Haven't you seen enough pictures of soldiers with guns?" Then she, against her will, broke out laughing too.

Standing beside the empty coffin, I had been holding the rifle upside down, with the barrel to the floor. No wonder it had been so hard to hold in place.

33

ONE DAY AFTER THE September 18 national memorial service for Mao, Gao announced that it was time to "convert our grief to strength" and go to Tangshan.

Situated on the North China Plain almost a hundred miles southeast of Beijing, Tangshan was the capital of Hebei Province. By Chinese standards it was a relatively new city developed around its coal mines. It had burgeoned into a major industrial center, especially in steel production, after Liberation. Tangshan's rapid growth had exacerbated the disaster, for the newer buildings — notably highrise apartments — had been hastily constructed, often from giant preformed concrete slabs. What was worse, the population of 1.4 million was packed tightly into 5,000 square miles.

It had been an unusually hot night, with extreme humidity. When the first colossal shock hit at 3:42 a.m., the city of Tangshan had simply broken up and crumbled to the ground in a monumental cloud of dust and flying debris, as if virtually every building had been dynamited at the same moment by a fiendishly efficient demolition crew. This occurred within a few moments: most of the 242,419 dead had no time to run from the buildings that collapsed upon them as they slept. One in three city employees was crushed to death.

Of the 16,458 severely injured, many subsequently died, because medical aid could not get to them: the streets, filled with the crumbled remains of buildings, had disappeared. In any case, the city's biggest hospital no longer existed. An additional 360,000 were seriously hurt. In the rainy days after the first shock, rescue workers located and saved 16,400 people and dug out 70,000 bodies. These, because of the health risk they posed, were stacked and burned on the outskirts of the city. Thousands of dead were never recovered. None of this was known until years later.

Before we boarded the military trucks that would take us to Tangshan, each of us was given a braided string of garlic bulbs. "You are to eat a few cloves each day to combat diarrhea," Gao ordered.

Diarrhea! His words brought to mind my narrow escape from death when I was on the farm. I recalled the doctor's stern warning that the amoebic dysentery would recur easily under the right conditions. Would garlic, which I disliked, really help me? Gao also admonished us to keep vigilant watch on our respective "partners." No photographs were to be taken; no notes, diaries or journals kept.

I knew almost nothing of what was in store for me. During the past six weeks government news sources had fed us many articles and broadcasts about how the people of Tangshan were fighting heroically against disaster and proving themselves "masters of Nature." No unofficial visitors had been allowed into the city; none of the able-bodied residents was allowed out.

The truck's canvas roof had been rolled back, uncovering the steel support hoops and giving the ugly vehicle the appearance of a green animal with its ribs exposed. I climbed up and grabbed one of the ribs for support: packed together, we would be standing for the entire journey.

Our convoy rolled by ramshackle, makeshift shacks built by Beijing citizens. About an hour later we passed toppled walls and collapsed houses. The truck jolted slowly along until it came to a halt on the outskirts of Fengtai, a small town between Tianjin and Tangshan and the second-hardest hit. No houses had been left standing; what had been a town was now a wasteland of rubble, scattered bricks and broken roof tiles.

Although I was willing to do what I could, the more devastation I saw from the truck, the more terrified I became. What would Gao order me to do? Would I be part of a search party, combing the ruins for corpses? And what about our living conditions? People said that disease was rife after floods or earthquakes: would we inadvertently drink contaminated water?

The day had become dry and extremely hot. By now the road, ruined by the quake and inadequately repaired, was jammed with vehicles, honking and grinding their gears. Our truck crawled along in the line. Sweating in the heat, feet aching, choking with the fine yellow dust that filmed clothing and skin, I was unable to tear my eyes from the eerie landscape. Finally we stopped on the eastern edge of Tangshan. On legs weak and stiff from the long, rough ride, I climbed down.

None of my imaginings prepared me for the desolation that met my eyes. Contrary to the news reports, the angry earth's shaking had smashed the entire city to nothing. Where apartment buildings, offices, schools and factories had stood in orderly arrangement along roadways, now immense piles of rubble spilled chaotically in every direction. The floors of highrise apartments had stacked up like the sides of an accordion when the walls had fallen away. Great slabs of concrete projected at crazy angles from heaps of brick and mortar, the steel reinforcing rods twisted and bent. Here and there the side of a building remained standing, windows smashed out, roof and floors crushed. The devastation stretched into the distance; Tangshan looked like a city the morning after a carpet-bombing raid.

Of what possible use could we be, a few university students with almost no tools, only our bare hands? The hot, dry air smelled of powder and dust. Still in shock, I began to help unload supplies, setting up a kitchen and assembling our living quarters. Several hours later our "rabbit hutches" stood, eerily out of place amid the tumbled-down buildings.

We shared toilet facilities with a group of homeless residents camped in a fenced compound nearby. Three water pipes projected from the ground along a path leading between the two compounds. Adjacent to our hutches, a warehouse with damaged walls and a collapsed roof served as a wash area. Since the whole area bore signs warning people away from sites where fragments of buildings still stood, and since aftershocks continued to make the ground tremble, we washed up with unusual speed and scampered back to our quarters.

Tired from the long ride, I went to my bunk, but horrific images kept sleep away for hours. I woke up damp and freezing. In the moonlight that peeped through the gaps in the roof I could see my breath form a thick cloud. The temperature had plunged to zero. Just hours before, I had been wearing a thin cotton shirt; now I shivered in my bedding.

The next morning I dutifully chewed my first garlic clove as I squatted with the others by an open fire over which the cook stirred a big pot of cornmeal porridge. The pungent garlic made me gag. I held the remaining cloves in the palm of my hand, waiting for my gruel to wash them down whole.

We were reminded once again to march directly to our designated work site and not to leave it, then we were divided into groups of five and led through the silent moonscape of rubble, smashed buildings and clogged roads. There were no street signs or other markings.

My class was guided by a pretty young woman of about twenty, named Zhang. From talking to her I picked up information not supplied by First-Hand Gao. Our camp, half a mile from the epicenter of the quake, was formerly the industrial section of the city. Nearby, the well-known Tangshan steel mill and a large textile factory had operated. To the west had stood the cement plant and a porcelain factory, where Xiao Zhang had worked for two years. The stores, hotels and the general hospital of the Kai Luan Coal Mine Bureau, the largest in the city, had been situated in the center of town.

Xiao Zhang had been born and raised in the neighborhood where we were stationed. Her family of four lived in a single-story house of brick and wood that had miraculously survived the disaster. Her only injury was a two-inch scar on her forehead, but her uncle, who had lived in another part of the city, had been killed. Compared to most families, she told us, she felt lucky, but when she led us through the ravaged neighborhood where she had grown up, tears filled her eyes.

I asked her about the bizarre weather we were experiencing. In the days after the quake, she told me, heavy rainfall had alternated with blistering heat, driving the residents to use more water; but the water supply was contaminated, and only the arrival of medical teams prevented the rapid spread of disease. Pointing to hydro poles that remained standing at odd angles, Xiao Zhang related that a number of looters had been tied up there and left to die of exposure in the extreme heat.

Our work site was a mountain of broken cement slabs, bricks and roofing tiles. As the morning sun quickly burned off the mist, we began to sort and pile the bricks and reusable roof tiles. Soon I was soaked with perspiration, my fingers scraped raw. Occasionally I came upon a toy, a cooking pot or piece of splintered furniture — the only reminders that people had once lived here. When a grisly body part — a hand, a foot or some dust-caked hair — appeared from under the dust and rubble, I ran in fear. Sometimes the stench of buried corpses was overpowering.

We wore no masks to protect us from the dust or stench; we had no safety equipment of any kind. Each group had only one spade, one shoulder-pole and one wicker basket to move the trash. Bricks and tiles were collected by hand. By the end of the day my fingers were bleeding. I made no complaint, nor did anyone else: drawing attention to personal discomfort would seem ignoble amid such devastation. Before I left Shanghai, Great-Aunt had tucked a couple of pairs of canvas gloves into my luggage, but I was reluctant to wear them and didn't even mention them to the teacher who dressed my hands. I didn't want to be criticized for fearing hardship, which was equal to being unrevolutionary. Only after Gao was persuaded that we would soon be disabled by infection was the wearing of gloves officially approved. It turned out almost everyone had brought them but, like me, had been afraid to put them on.

A few days later while we waited, sweating and dirty, for our supper of cabbage soup and steamed buns, Xiao Zhang came by and offered to take us to visit the factory where she worked. When we had eaten, we secured permission from the Party secretary. After a twenty-minute walk skirting the ubiquitous slabs of smashed concrete and heaps of bricks, we found ourselves before a gray, single-story building, like an alien object in the middle of a wasteland. Although the factory itself had been leveled, the warehouse, built by Russians in the 1950s, stood intact, apart from broken windows.

Inside the high-ceilinged building, row upon row of stacked china plates, cups, saucers and rice bowls sat undisturbed on the undamaged cement floor. For days and nights after we had arrived, frequent aftershocks had caused more destruction and distress. And yet here under the pale and humming fluorescent tubes, the orderly rows of unharmed china presented a scene of comfort and peace so unexpected that I began to cry.

No one spoke.

I slowly lifted a plate and blew off the dust. Xiao Zhang explained that the plates were at the last stage of production. The patterns would be glued on and the plates fired one last time. Without thinking, I went through the stack and removed several broken plates, putting them aside. When I turned around I saw for the first time that there were others in the warehouse watching us — women and children sitting on their bedding, ghostly under their mosquito nets.

🌿

As the days passed, the futility of the backbreaking labor, which seemed to accomplish nothing in the midst of such widespread ruin, oppressed me greatly. The evenings were filled with political study. Worst of all, I had no idea how long we would stay. On October 1, China's National Day, we had our first day off after two weeks. I spent it catching up on my dirty laundry.

Two days later our team moved farther west, only blocks away from a ruined municipal hostel. During the lunch break I asked Xiao Shi, our group leader, for permission to take a walk around the block. I expected a refusal but she said I could go if I was accompanied by Xiao Xu, a male student: the usual "surveillance pairing."

Nevertheless, I was glad to go with Xiao Xu, a down-to-earth young man from a commune on the outskirts of Beijing, for I doubted that I would have been able to face such a dreadful scene on my own. The downtown part of the city, which was hit hardest, suffered an 80 percent death rate, mainly because of the poor-quality construction of the buildings. In this sector had stood several hostels filled with business travelers. The huge hospital with a central block of five stories and a west wing of seven had opened only months before. Except at the western end, where a few rooms hung on a thin remnant of a wall about three stories high, the entire 6,600-square-yard hospital had collapsed, strewing mountains of debris over an area larger than many football fields. Metal bed-frames, broken doors and windows and furniture poked through the rubble. I wondered how many helpless and screaming people had been crushed under the ruthless collapse. My grief turned to anger at a government that would allow such shoddy construction. All over the country buildings like this were built as a matter of course, including my dorm at Bei Da.

If I had ever resented missing classes and study time in order to come to this awful place, I now appreciated the chance to help, even though my effort was a tiny drop of water in a vast ocean. Probably this was the first time I had ever agreed with one of Gao's decisions, regardless of his true motivation.

Four days later I trudged back to our camp, sweaty and dusty, to find that Gao had been taken away in a military jeep. He hadn't even been allowed to pack his belongings. Several days after his abrupt departure, as we prepared to head out to our labor site, we were ordered to remain behind for an important announcement.

A foreboding atmosphere hung over the camp. Gossip spread like fire. Perhaps war had broken out with the Soviets. Maybe Chiang Kai-shek had attacked mainland China from his stronghold on Formosa. After ten years of the Cultural Revolution and its destruction, China was weak and ripe for attack from one quarter or another.

A thin, ascetic man from Bei Da stood on a box near the cooking fire and called for attention. "The Gang of Four," he shouted in ringing and triumphant tones, "has been smashed! They were arrested without resistance! First-Hand Gao has been relieved from his authority." He informed us that our being in Tangshan was an error, an example of Gao's sycophancy to Jiang Qing and her thugs. (I, on the other hand, had thought it the first justified interruption of our studies.) We were to return to the campus the next day. His speech contained not one word of recognition for our hard work and aid. What we deserved, according to him, was blame; we had been doing the work of the Gang. It was typical politics: the wrong had suddenly become right and the right had abruptly turned into wrong.

My joy at the fall of Jiang Qing and her millions of henchmen was tempered. My hope that this would mean the end of the terrible and destructive political movement that had begun ten years before was diluted by what I knew would be an official repudiation of my small effort in Tangshan.

In the morning, there were tearful goodbyes to Xiao Zhang and many other appreciative survivors who came to see us off. She and I promised to keep in touch. Leaving behind our hutches, cooking tent and supplies, we climbed into the trucks once more. From the back of the truck I looked at the relief teams who continued to work amidst the rubble and ruin of the flattened city. I had no doubt Tangshan would someday stand up again and be better and more modern, its devastation only a sad memory. But I was not at all certain that the destruction of the Cultural Revolution would ever be repaired.

34

BEIJING WAS IN A FESTIVE MOOD. New *da-zi-bao* were posted everywhere and people marched in the streets with banners and paper flags — rituals identical to those of the Cultural Revolution. Only the slogans and names of the vilified had been changed.

I didn't expect a triumphant return from Tangshan, but I was enraged by the cold response we received. In the eyes of those who had quickly replaced the supporters of Jiang Qing at the university, our rescue mission had merely served Jiang Qing's political ambition to take power after the death of her husband.

Day after day, week after week, I was swamped by meetings and discussions denouncing a new group of the fallen. Jiang Qing's name, and those of her many followers, with big black Xs through them, replaced the names of Deng Xiao-ping and his supporters. Every wrongful act of the past ten years was ascribed to the Gang of Four, every misconduct in the department to Gao, who had disappeared from our lives forever.

I shared the heartfelt joy of people across the country that the madness might well be behind us. However, I couldn't help but question how this group of four persons, hardly known ten years before, could have devastated a country of 900 million on their own. Had they no henchmen? Had no one but they profited from their radical policies? Their downfall had followed quickly on the heels of Mao's death. Had it really been a Gang of Five, not Four? An expression I learned at elementary school came to mind: *Shu-dao-hu-sun-san* — When the tree falls, the monkeys scatter. Only Mao's death had made it possible to move against the Four, but no one, in all the meetings and discussions I was forced to attend, was willing to touch this issue and its implications. Instead, the new leadership, headed by the new premier, announced the construction of a mausoleum in the center of Tian An Men Square to house Mao's remains. What a fraud! On the one hand the government blamed the Gang for every ill over the past decade; on the other it continued to enshrine its real leader in eternal glory and to maintain the political system that made the Cultural Revolution possible.

The political reversal sweeping the campus immediately affected my studies. We were assured that there would be no running around without direction any more, no open-door schooling, military training or visits to communes and factories. Our Tai Ping apple farming was over. To my surprise and delight, I was even allowed to read foreign literature, although most of it was abridged. Dickens's *Great Expectations* and *Hard Times* and Dreiser's *Sister Carrie* were distributed by teachers who still fluttered with fear. These books were relatively safe because they exposed the dark side of Western society. In another class, we studied *Jane Eyre* and *Rebecca*, with the inevitable political slant: Jane was a victim of the bourgeoisie and the young heroine of *Rebecca* was exploited by a rich bourgeois lady. We never talked about the romantic aspects of these books, only that everything in Western society, in Dickens's day and now, was driven by money. That these books came into the light of day at all showed the speed and extent of the changes.

The library opened it secret vaults, as it were, and made all its books available to students and teachers. Current magazines and dictionaries in foreign languages reappeared on the shelves, under warnings posted on the walls: Reference Only, or Read with Caution Against Bourgeois Perspectives.

One afternoon in early November the secretary of the department stopped me on my way to the library.

"Xiao Ye," she said, "you have a telephone message."

Someone who called herself a close relative of mine had invited me to the Qian Men Hotel at seven o'clock. The caller didn't give her name.

There must be some mistake, I thought. Since the death of my parents the term "relative" had no meaning for me. Our poverty and our orphan status had scared away most of our relatives because they feared we would rely on them financially. When the Red Guards attacked us, no one came to our aid. We had always considered ourselves on our own. So who was this relative of mine, staying in a fancy hotel reserved for the powerful and the wealthy? The hotel took its name from *qian men* — the front gate of the old walled city — and was near the south end of Tian An Men Square.

Curious but cautious, I set out on the two-hour journey to the city center, arriving half an hour early. The instructions said to meet the mystery relative at the front door of the hotel compound, for I would never be allowed in on my own. All hotels — any public building, for that matter — were surrounded by walls and no one except high officials and their guests could get past the gatekeepers.

I took up a position on the sidewalk of the busy street, across from the magnificent old structure with its overhanging roof and upturned eaves. The street was dimly lit, but through the glass doors the bright lights revealed throngs of guests. I hoped the message I had received was not a mistake, since I coveted a chance to go into a hotel for the first time in my life. At seven o'clock I crossed the street and showed the gatekeeper my telephone message, which the secretary had written out for me. He didn't even look at it.

"You expect me to fall for that old ruse?" he sneered.

I returned his insult with a level stare. "Do you think I spent two hours on the bus to try to trick you?"

He let me through, but demanded that I wait at the bottom of the wide staircase in front of the hotel so he could keep an eye on me. When I approached, I saw a rather short, gray-haired woman standing on the top step, staring at me. Judging by the evenly trimmed hair tucked behind her ears and the fashionable but oversized army coat draped over her shoulders, she was someone of importance. I had never seen her before. She couldn't be the source of the message, I concluded. I was about to leave when the woman spoke.

"Xiao Ye?"

I stopped, puzzled.

"Ah Si?"

How strange to hear my family name from unfamiliar lips. The next thing I noticed was that the gatekeeper had appeared beside me.

"It's all right, Old Comrade," the woman said. "I think she is my granddaughter Ah Si, whom I have seen only in photos."

"Oh, wonderful," the man said without enthusiasm, and returned to his post.

Grandmother? I thought. All my grandmothers were dead before I was born, and I know what my stepgrandmother looks like.

"I am your Yi Po, Ah Si." *Yi Po* means Grandmother-Aunt. "I am the younger sister of your paternal grandmother. I used to live in Qingyang, too."

"You're our rev —, er, our aunt from Jiangxi Province?" I had almost blurted out the term we usually used when talking about her, our "revolutionary aunt." She had always been a loyal and active Party member and had run away from Qingyang to escape an arranged marriage and later joined the Communist revolution.

"That's me," she said, smiling. "The Yi Po from Jiangxi, where your baby sister is."

"How is Number 5? Have you seen her recently?"

I had continued to worry about Number 5 over the past few years. Her letters were still full of depression, and my relative good fortune in getting into Bei Da had made her feel even worse.

Number 5 had mentioned in her correspondence that she had located our Yi Po and had visited her and her family in Nanchang. Yi Po's husband had been deputy governor of Jiangxi Province before the Cultural Revolution and was now on permanent sick leave with full pay. Yi Po had been restored to her leading position in the Women's Federation of the province. Although she and her husband had claimed, when asked by Number 5 to get her off the farm, that they were powerless, their three children had gone to university after spending the minimum two years working on local farms.

Their refusal to help my sister, who had been on the farm for seven years, had filled me with burning rage. I had often wished I could meet our revolutionary aunt face to face and tell her what I thought of her. But now I contained my anger and disgust. Maybe I could persuade her to help my sister. After all, things were changing.

She led me into the hotel, which was packed with representatives of government offices such as the Women's Federation, Ministry of Agriculture and Second Ministry of Machine Building, and told me they were all here for important meetings. *Bo-luan-fan-zheng* — bringing order out of chaos and reversing the wrong verdicts — was their purpose, she said, using an already outmoded and empty expression. In a huge and sumptuous dining room, filled to capacity with large round tables covered with linen cloths and plates of fragrant dishes, Yi Po chatted about her business. Awed by the opulent surroundings, I paid little attention. The diners contradicted the motto I had heard all my life, "From each according to his ability, to each according to his need." These people were wolfing down food according to the capacity of their stomachs.

After dinner Yi Po led me upstairs and introduced me to her many colleagues, telling them that I was her granddaughter and an English student at Bei Da, which irritated me greatly. I was not her granddaughter, nor would I want to be. She was using me for reflected glory; saying that I was a student at Bei Da was a way of bragging, implying that she was important and had enough *guan-xi* to get me into one of the best universities in China.

When this grand tour was over, my throat was dry and my face hurt from insincere smiling. I remained confused about Yi Po's invitation. More than that, frustration was burning me alive. We still hadn't been to her room; I was waiting until then to talk about my sister.

Yi Po announced that she had arranged to have me stay with

her for the night. I agreed. She took me to the third floor and led me into the fanciest suite I had ever seen. The vast living room was floored with polished hardwood and furnished with velvety sofas. A big television sat on a desk in one corner. Behind heavy drapes was the bedroom, with two double beds and matching tables. The handmade woolen carpet was almost as thick as my own quilt back in my cement-floored dorm.

Yi Po introduced me to her guest, a tall, strong woman about the same age. "Ah Si, this is my friend Lao Bai."

"Call me Bai Mama," the woman said in a heavy Beijing accent — a strange request to make of someone she had just met.

Yi Po asked me if I wanted to take a bath, a luxury I couldn't resist. A shower on campus, especially in cold weather, was always a great inconvenience, with long lineups, severe crowding and an uncertain water supply. Here the bathroom was spacious and spotless, with gleaming taps, a mirror and a big shining bathtub. Best of all, I could luxuriate alone in the hot soapy water.

While I bathed, I thought over how to beg Yi Po's assistance. If I had to, I would tell her that my sister suffered long, deep depressions and that I feared for her safety, even though to say so would cause Number 5 to lose face.

Half an hour later I emerged from the steamy bathroom. The two women were still chatting away, catching up on old times.

"Look at her," Yi Po said, pulling me to her side. "She resembles my sister."

I noted that Yi Po had yet to say a word about my parents, an omission that showed very bad manners. My long-dead grandmother, her sister, I knew only from a yellowed photo that the Red Guards had confiscated during the raid.

I waited and waited, stealing glances at the clock, wishing that the two women would cease their chattering. In my impatience, I began to fidget. When ten-thirty rolled around, Yi Po invited Lao Bai to stay the night in the suite. I couldn't contain myself any longer.

"How about Number 5, Yi Po?" I asked bluntly. "Now that the Gang of Four has fallen, are you going to help her? It doesn't need much effort to get her out of that dump, does it?"

I stopped myself, conscious that my last remark had been rude, and tears filled my eyes. Why couldn't I be more diplomatic? My outburst caught Lao Bai by surprise.

Yi Po patted me on the back. "Calm down, calm down," she soothed. "Your sister has been doing fine on the farm. She has visited us often and has never mentioned any problems or asked for our help. I don't understand why you should be so concerned about her."

All these lies were for Lao Bai's benefit. My sister was so desperate she had been close to suicide for a long time. But Yi Po went on to assure Lao Bai she had done her best to help Number 5, to no avail. From the way she spoke, I came to realize that I could expect no support from her. Furthermore, I was afraid I had gone too far and ruined things for Number 5. I wanted to leave, despite the late hour, but there would be no buses to the west end of the city.

Both women offered to share a bed with me but I declined. I rolled up in a quilt on the rug, as far away from them as I could get. As soon as the light of day appeared in the crack between the heavy curtains, I left without waking them.

On the bus I upbraided myself again. It would be my fault if Number 5 had to remain on the farm for the rest of her life. I cursed myself all the way back to the campus. Two days later, another phone message came, asking me to return to the hotel. I tore it to pieces. I still had no idea why our revolutionary aunt had suddenly made contact with me, or why she showed contempt for my family but interest in me, and I didn't care.

35

THE MYSTERY DEEPENED WHEN, one Saturday soon after, Lao Bai phoned me. She told me that my Yi Po had left Beijing, disappointed that I hadn't shown up at the hotel. Lao Bai seemed quite friendly, inviting me to her house to spend the weekend. She was a lonely widow, she said, and she'd appreciate the company. If I agreed she would send the ministry's car to pick me up.

I was tempted. I had heard from her chat with Yi Po that she was a widow of a high official in the railway ministry and lived in a large home in the city. I had never had a ride in a government car, and liked the idea of spending a weekend in a fine house. More than any of these temptations, there was the possibility that even if Yi Po would not help Number 5, maybe Bai Mama would.

Instead of taking me to one of the highrises along Changan Avenue where, according to Rainbow, many high-ranking officials in the government and Party lived, the ministry car turned into a *hu-tong* and stopped in front of a one-story dwelling, one of a dozen or so in a quiet neighbourhood. Each house appeared to have woven reed walls and a thatched roof, a curious kind of construction for the city, I thought. The driver led me to the door and a middle-aged maid, who introduced herself as Ah Yi showed me in and went back to the kitchen.

Bai Mama greeted me warmly, her voice deep and serious. Although she wore her short hair tucked up with pins above her ears in the anti-feminine style of high officials, she was wearing a stylish gray jacket rather than the ubiquitous Mao coat. She gave me a tour of the three-bedroom house, which boasted a living room and dining area, unheard-of luxuries in a country where most families lived in one small room and shared a kitchen. The polished hardwood floor and tiled bathroom and kitchen were beyond anything I could have imagined. I noticed the ceiling and walls were plaster, and asked her how that could be, since the house was made of wattle and straw. She laughed. The house was constructed of brick, she explained, with a tiled roof. The wattle on the outside walls and the thatch on the tiles were to keep the building cool in summer and warm in winter. That the house appeared far less glamorous than it was in reality was a bonus, she added, smiling broadly. The house's outward appearance was a sham. A high official could live in luxury while pretending otherwise.

"It fooled a university student like you," Bai Mama laughed. "It works, doesn't it?"

Over tea in the comfortable living-room Bai Mama told me about her family. Her eldest son was a career army officer who lived with his wife in Nanjing, center of one of China's ten military regions. Jian-guo, her younger son, whose name meant Build the Country, was a platoon leader in the Beijing Garrison. His posting in the eastern suburbs made it possible for him to spend some weekends at home. Jian-guo had applied to leave the army. As an officer, his departure from the forces would be different from that of an ordinary demobilized soldier. Officers were called *zhuan-ye* — career transferees, like our former First-Hand Gao — and were guaranteed a good job with the government. As a Party member, Jian-guo's future would be bright and prosperous.

Although I understood her pride in her son, Bai Mama's bragging annoyed me. She either wasn't aware of what I and the majority of people her son's age had gone through and still suffered from, or she didn't care. Whether her blindness was willful or ignorant I didn't know, but I began to regret having agreed to stay with her for the weekend to keep her company.

All the time we talked, Ah Yi was busy in the kitchen, as if preparing a banquet. Why was she taking such pains to get dinner ready for only three people? My question was answered when, to my surprise, a young man wearing a uniform walked into the room. I was sure Bai Mama had told me on the phone that she would be alone all weekend.

"How long have you been waiting, Xiao Ye?" He greeted me with a big smile.

"Waiting?" I asked, confused.

He quickly extended his hand. "I am Jian-guo, youngest son of the family. Probably Mother has told you quite a bit about me. I am glad to see you here."

"It's my honor to shake the hand of one of our beloved PLA. Obviously I don't need to tell you who I am."

Jian-guo, a year older than me, was a pleasant-looking man with a round face and rosy cheeks. His baby face made me wonder how he was able to maintain authority over his tough subordinates in the army.

After a dinner marked by impersonal small talk, Bai Mama made herself scarce watching the color TV in her bedroom. Despite our efforts to be cordial, Jian-guo and I found that our conversation was like two carts running on opposite tracks, a natural consequence of our completely different background and upbringing. The only common topic we found was hatred of the Gang of Four, particularly Jiang Qing. I realized that she was considered even more odious by high officials than by ordinary citizens, although the suffering of the latter was in my opinion more profound. Mao Ze-dong's name was never mentioned in our conversation.

I spent a sleepless night with Bai Mama. The soft mattress and weightless down quilt were luxuries completely foreign to me, and I found it strange to share a bed with someone other than Great-Aunt. After breakfast Jian-guo insisted on walking me to the bus stop. It was a cold day but the sky was clear and blue. We strolled along the *hutong* in silence for a while before he suddenly stepped in front of me.

"So, what do you think of me?" he asked eagerly.

Taken aback, I laughed. "I think you're fine."

"I really like you, you know," he rushed on, looking into my eyes. "I feel like I've known you for a long time. I understand that you will graduate in a year or so. By then I will be out of the army. You're probably concerned about where your work assignment will be. Don't worry about that. Mother could almost certainly get you a position in Beijing."

It was as if he had thrown a cup of cold water in my face. Suddenly all came into focus. I was the pawn of two matchmakers. As with so much of my life, here was a supreme irony: two genuine Communists, who supposedly shunned all feudal customs, trying to match me to this friendly young man, who all the time had thought I was aware of what was going on.

How could I have been so doltishly naive not to catch on? And how could those two old ladies treat me so? To them, matching an orphan like me with a wealthy and highly connected man like Jian-guo would be like dropping a rat into a rice bin: I would be nothing if not deliriously grateful and obedient. For their part, what would Jian-guo's family gain? Why choose me over a well-connected young woman? First, with no parents of my own to care for, I would be able to give all my attention to Jian-guo's mother; second, northerners like Bai Mama considered Shanghainese more sophisticated than local girls; and third, I was well educated.

"English is a hot major right now," Jian-guo rattled on, as if reading my mind, "and your profession is going to be in great demand. We could live with Mother here or find our own apartment after we're married. Whatever you like."

"Married? Didn't my beloved Yi Po tell you," I asked sarcastically, "that my father was a condemned capitalist and that I have inherited his contaminated blood? Weren't you informed that I have a boyfriend in Shanghai?"

Jian-guo was not fazed. "I know all that. I met your Yi Po. She told me all about your deceased parents and I feel sorry for you. But since your parents passed away so many years ago I believe that, with all the coming changes, your class background is not going to hold you back. As for your boyfriend, he is only a boyfriend, isn't he? It's not as if you are engaged."

My anger grew. Apparently Yi Po, who had refused even to ask about my deceased parents or the welfare of my siblings, had felt all right discussing them at length with strangers. Although she herself had fled an arranged marriage, she had no qualms about using me to ingratiate herself with Bai Mama, her influential comrade-in-arms.

Looking into Jian-guo's innocent, eager face, I could not be angry with him. But I was too proud even to think about acceding to a relationship with him.

"I'm sorry," I mumbled, "I don't think it would be right to throw over my boyfriend so easily." I said a hasty farewell and returned to the university.

The truth was that I felt both protected and restricted by my relationship with Xiao Zhao. In China, once you began to "see" a person, you were locked in, to the exclusion of all others of the opposite sex. There were no degrees of involvement. Everyone knew that you were a couple, and that was a clear signal to all others. As a woman tied to a man in Shanghai, I was safe from the advances of others. Most women married the first person they dated, just as my mother had done, and as all my siblings eventually would. A female considered paired would be viewed as a loose woman if she developed friendships with other men. Even those who broke up with their boyfriends were looked down upon by friends and family if they dated again right away. It was a holdover from feudal society, when a woman whose husband died was expected to remain single all her life, regardless of her age.

And yet, through my reading of Western novels, a new concept of love had begun to bud within me, no matter how much I tried to deny it. I wondered what it would be like to experience profound romantic love, uninfluenced by duty, regulations and convenience. If only love in our society was not such a mixture of feudal morality and Communist doctrine!

I didn't return Bai Mama's phone calls or go to her house when invited again. One Sunday morning two weeks later, as I was on my way to the library, I found Jian-guo waiting on the sidewalk outside our building. He wanted to talk to me — casually, was the way he put it, meaning he would not bring up the subject of our relationship. I took him up to my dorm and we sat down. I showed him my textbooks and played a Linguaphone tape for him. He showed great interest in my work, and as we talked, I grew to like him more.

I had thought long and hard over the past two weeks. If I agreed to end my relationship with Xiao Zhao and marry Jian-guo, I would have a bright, secure future, and a wonderful place to live, with no more worries about money. After a lifetime of poverty and destructive political movements, I longed for a stable and peaceful existence. And my inferiority complex was flattered that a young man such as Jian-guo was attracted to me. He seemed intelligent and thoughtful. Also I was mindful that, using his family's influence, I would be able to help all my siblings and Great-Aunt: I could almost certainly get Number 5 off that cursed farm.

But I had a boyfriend in Shanghai. I had promised not to abandon him. Although we had been apart for most of the time after I left the farm, Xiao Zhao and I did love each other. When we were together we didn't talk much about our future life as a couple, but it was evident to us and to all around us that we would share a future. Duty compelled me to stick with him.

So when I saw Jian-guo off at the front gate of the university I asked him not to come and see me any more. Hanging his head, he agreed.

36

I N THE SPRING OF 1977, my third year at Bei Da, a
young British man was assigned to teach us oral English to help
prepare us for graduation field work. This project, coordinated
by the tourist bureaus, allocated teams of two or three students to
tourist groups as guides and interpreters. Michael, as he asked us to
address him (rather than *Lao Shi* — Teacher) was a tall man in his
late twenties with a large red nose and animated face. He proudly
called himself a friend of the Chinese people and told us that his
parents owned a London bookstore that promoted Chinese books
and magazines.

Michael was actually our second foreign teacher. The first had
been an American woman who had married a Chinese doctor
named Ye. She asked us to call her Ye Ma Xi-li, a Chinese
pronunciation of her English name, Marsha. Because she and I
shared the same surname, a name uncommon in north China, she
would often pull me from my chair in class and make me dance with
her in the aisles, or swirl around by herself when I shyly declined

her invitation. I and my classmates often wondered if all Americans were so cheerful and worry-free, maybe a bit crazy. Probably, I thought, all foreigners acted like that.

But Michael turned out to be very shy and soft-spoken, polite and formal. Unlike Chinese men, he would open the door for women students, insisting that we go ahead. He thanked us for our efforts in studying, and even for wrong answers in class. Amazingly, he would apologize when he sneezed, whereas some of my classmates looked about indifferently after spitting on the floor. His behavior was new to me. I had grown up in an environment in which it seemed that, without shouting and yelling, nothing would be done, in which politeness and common courtesy were labeled phony bourgeois rubbish.

At the same time, his lessons made me aware of how inadequate our English was, particularly in speaking. I felt my own knowledge was like "boiled dumplings in a kettle" — ready to serve but impossible to get out past the neck. Michael's teaching expanded to the library and the dining room, where he gave us practical lessons. He even invited a group of us to the Friendship Hotel, where he and most foreign teachers lived. The hotel, a huge walled complex with a dozen buildings, was only four bus stops from Bei Da. There he served us tea in the British style.

I was amazed at how large his apartment was, how many books he owned, shelf after shelf of novels. He had his own tape deck and radio. But what I found most surprising was the way Michael and other foreigners acted in one another's company. They were very open with one another, freely throwing out thoughts and opinions, laughing and joking. They seemed confident and unafraid and must have thought all of us, as we shrank shyly back in our seats, a couple of us giggling with embarrassment, childish and backward. But from childhood I had learned to guard my thoughts carefully, unless I was with a close friend like Rainbow. The past ten years had taught all of us that anyone, even friends and family, might turn against us.

Not long after, I and two other women students were called to the office of the new department head, Han, who questioned us about the visit. What kind of questions had Michael asked us? Which topic was he most interested in? What answers did we give? What did the others who had gone there with us say to Michael?

At the end, he told us that Michael was reported to be looking for a Chinese wife; our visits to his residence were therefore improper and must cease, even though male students had always been present.

Department Head Han's words were alarming but didn't surprise me. Foreigners, particularly Westerners, had throughout our history never been regarded as equal to Chinese. They were treated either as masters of science and technology or as devils who had many times invaded and humiliated our country. Under Mao's regime all foreigners were pictured as enemies, even when China made alliances with them. Particularly during the Cultural Revolution, those who had contact with foreigners were mercilessly persecuted, even while some of these contacts were necessary in the work one did for the government. Chinese with relatives abroad were suspected of spying and attacked. Even after the fall of the Gang of Four, the Middle Kingdom obsession that other races were barbarians predominated. Under the revolutionary doctrine we had been taught that most foreigners were enemies of communism constantly trying to undermine us. Since foreigners lacked "socialist morality," women should remain aloof and distant to show our dignity.

The unsubtle warning from Han served its purpose. From then on, all female students stayed away from Michael and avoided being alone with him in the classroom. We knew any accusation against us would be devastating. Graduation was coming and no one wanted to ruin her chance at a good job.

Michael was banned from visiting student dorms and dining rooms. I felt very badly for him. He seemed to sense that something was wrong, but asked no questions. He had worked hard to be a good teacher, giving of himself, and his lessons helped us tremendously. His reward was to be shunned, officially declared off limits, although the university officials said nothing to him openly. Politeness forbade honesty.

A few months later I heard that Michael had married a Japanese woman at the Beijing Foreign Language Institute, so it appeared that Han's warning to us was groundless — probably a lie to prevent our becoming too friendly with a foreigner. Michael continued to teach at Bei Da, but he kept his distance from us. I didn't blame him.

The warning against foreigners stayed with me when I got my field work assignment in June, interpreting for a group of American tourists. As usual I had a surveillance partner, a female classmate. In the three days working with the Americans, she and I were glued together, refusing any offer to sit with a tourist on the bus and avoiding any possibility of being alone with a male visitor. When my carefully prepared introduction to the Summer Palace was applauded by the group, I didn't know whether to show my pride as I wanted to or present a modest demeanor as tradition demanded when facing a group of outsiders. So instead of thanking them for their compliment, I shook my head, saying, "No, no. I am not good enough."

The three-day experience with the Americans convinced me that the safest career for me would be as an English teacher where I would have no exposure to foreigners and could avoid the constant tension, surveillance and danger such exposure inevitably entailed.

That summer Xiao Zhao and I, in our effort to find time alone, discovered a place where young lovers gathered in the evenings. A new street, Zhao Jia Bang, had been constructed by filling in a creekbed in the southern outskirts of the city. The wide avenue boasted a central boulevard landscaped with flowers and tall shrubbery, and it was among the bushes that couples would stand together in the shadows, whispering, kissing and petting. The streetlights had short lives there, victims of slingshots carried by ardent suitors. For the first time in my life I noted that people were eager to mind their own business and pay no attention to what was going on only yards away from them.

Occasionally our trysts would be dispersed by city workers bearing flashlights, but when these roustabouts moved on down the long avenue, lovers would return to the shrubbery. I found these little adventures added excitement to my meetings with Xiao Zhao, except the times when, after a long bus ride, we discovered there was no room left for us on the shadowy boulevard.

When I returned to Bei Da in September 1977 after my summer vacation, the university was preparing for the restoration of nationwide exams. Deng Xiao-ping, who had been brought back to power yet one more time in July, had quickly announced that academic results would be the only criteria for accepting students to universities. This momentous decision declared an end to the era of the Worker-Peasant-Soldier students.

My feelings about this change were mixed. I admired Deng's boldness and quick resolution (his own son was a WPS student) in putting the country back in order, particularly his calling an end to political campaigns and meaningless political studies. But at the same time such a fundamental change, along with the dramatic publicity, gave me an uneasy feeling regarding my own future. I was classed as a WPS student, even though I had passed an entrance exam back on the farm. The way things went from one extreme to another, I was afraid I would be a second-class citizen now that exams had been reinstated. We WPS students would be like the children of concubines: less privileged inside the family than those born to a legally wedded wife.

My concern proved well founded. After the arrival of new students that autumn, the campus became a powder keg, with constant conflicts between the old and new students representing different political eras. WPS students were jeered at and called ignorant and undeserving beneficiaries of the hated Cultural Revolution, while the new students cast themselves as its victims. Explosive arguments filled dining halls, classrooms and the library. But once again, the master, Mao Ze-dong, was never blamed.

When the students of my year were told we would graduate early, in February, I was both relieved and anxious. In a few months my future would be determined. Was it still true that job assignments were predetermined before students darkened the door of Bei Da?

I decided to find out. One of my instructors, Teacher Nie, might help me. He was a relative of a warm-hearted woman who lived in Purple Sunshine Lane in Shanghai. A scholarly-looking man of late middle age, he was a bright and knowledgeable teacher who cared a great deal about his students. He said he would find out the answer to my question if he could. When it came, I wished I hadn't asked for it.

"Congratulations, Xiao Ye," he said. "I think I can let you know, since your dossier has already been sent there, that you have been assigned to work in the Zhong Diao Bu! You should be very proud of this assignment, for you are certainly going to have a bright and prosperous future."

I had been recruited by the secret police, the Central Investigation Bureau of the Communist Party!

I hardly heard Teacher Nie as he enthusiastically prattled on about my career. This was crazy. It must be a mistake. I, a daughter of the hated capitalist class, accused all her life of having contaminated blood and convicted on the farm for counter-revolutionary plots and sentenced to jail, was going to work in China's secret service, an agency staffed by the purest of the pure, which spied on its citizens, including government and Party officials both at home and abroad!

When I told her the incredible news, Rainbow could hardly contain her excitement. Nor could her parents, who were delighted. My lifelong uncertainty and suffering would end, they assured me, on the day I stepped into the high-walled compound called Xi Yuan.

"But why would they have chosen me of all people?" I asked Rainbow's father.

"Perhaps because you are an orphan they think you have fewer family obligations and can devote yourself entirely to the organization," he replied. "Besides, the political situation has been reversed, and many of the people who were persecuted are now acceptable."

Xi Yuan, which means West Courtyard, was the head office of the bureau, located not far from Bei Da. Most people had no idea where it was, but Rainbow's father knew about it. Xi Yuan was a large, completely self-sufficient complex of office buildings, with living quarters for employees and their families, stores, a post office and other facilities, schools and a theatre. Its military training and shooting grounds were at Nan Yuan, on the southern outskirts of Beijing.

The bureau was directly under the control of the Central Party Committee. Its three to four thousand well-trained and highly motivated devotees had been lethal weapons in the political campaigns that consolidated China's totalitarian regime and dictatorship. During the Cultural Revolution its envoys had been sent all over the country to electrify factional fighting and, disguised as Red Guards in faded uniforms or revolutionary rebels in worker's overalls, had engaged in beating, smashing and looting. Armed with a force of foreign-language professionals, the bureau also sent skilled secret agents to Chinese embassies all over the world, part of their task being surveillance of the embassy personnel themselves. I also learned from Rainbow's father that once a person was accepted into the bureau, she or he was there for life. He kept emphasizing what a plum job it was, and that I could certainly become a Party member very soon.

Did the Communists expect me to erase my miserable memories like writing from a blackboard? Did they have any idea that, to me, Party membership was not a badge of honor but a contemptible curse?

For the first time in my life I decided to take a direct part in planning my future. I could not simply refuse the assignment to the Secret Service: in China people could not choose their place of employment. Each year the State Planning Commission determined the needs of all government departments and it was the responsibility of the Ministry of Education to find people to fill the need. An individual's wishes seldom had influence unless he or she had *guan-xi*. If a university graduate refused to accept an assignment, no other job would be made available, and that meant a life of unemployment, poverty and reliance on others. In my case I would not be able to return to Shanghai to take care of Great-Aunt, my most important duty, because I would not be able to get *hu-kou* there. I knew I had to try to avoid this curse, but subtlety was required.

How could I get out of this predicament safely? I couldn't ask anyone in my family for advice, for my assignment was still a secret. So I went to visit Teacher Chen, whose gentleness and kindness had touched me three years earlier on the farm.

"I don't know what kind of advice I can offer you," she said. "I guess no harm would be done if you just tell them your concerns. They may listen to you; they may not. But at least you can say to yourself that you tried. Sometimes, though, if a person has sick parents to care for, that has a bearing on things."

I decided to go to Xi Yuan myself to get a first-hand impression. In my mind, since my personal dossier was already there, I had a right to do so. Rainbow, who thought me insane for trying to avoid a job she would have loved, agreed to come with me. She was curious. On a cold December afternoon we left the university on foot, and three-quarters of an hour later we came upon Xi Yuan. It looked like a university campus, with a main gate and side doors, but there the resemblance stopped. The walls were unusually high, there was no sign indicating the organization's title, and the gatekeeper's quarters were outside rather than inside the walls. Feeling that our every move was watched, we approached and knocked.

There were three men inside, two sitting by a small stove and one behind a desk near the window. The middle-aged man at the desk responded to our greetings with a grim face.

"Who are you? Why are you here?" he demanded. "Why are you snooping around?"

"We are looking for Zhong Diao Bu and I —" I stammered, noticing that the two men at the stove were glaring at us.

"Who told you to come here and for what business?" one of them asked.

"No one told us to come here. We were just looking."

Rainbow took over from me. "She has business here, Comrade. She is going to work here in a month or so after she graduates from Bei Da. All she wants is to talk to the person in charge of the personnel department, if that is possible."

Here I was again, despite having initiated the trip and prepared the scene many times in my mind, speechless at the crucial moment. I threw a grateful glance to Rainbow.

The man behind the desk looked shocked. He came toward me with thin smile on his face, shaking his head. "You are going to work here, as she said?"

I nodded.

"But you want to talk to someone in the personnel department?" he asked skeptically. "In all my career here I have never met a single visitor like you who wanted to meet someone inside before you are one of them."

I kept silent.

"Times must have changed," he said, handing me paper and pencil. "Write down your name and address."

He showed us to another room where we sat down on a bench. Moments later I heard him on the telephone. Nervously, I squeezed Rainbow's hand.

The man returned a few minutes later. "Comrade Ye, no one can talk to you right now. Lao Liang said if you have anything to say, you can put it in writing. He wants you to know that you shouldn't have come here in person. And don't come back again without being asked."

I was disappointed that we couldn't go inside, yet relieved, because all the things I wanted to say had flown right out of my mind. I asked the man the mailing address. He exchanged glances with his two colleagues and smiled.

"Of course not," he said. "You'll have to give the letter to me."

Well, I thought, I'll have to come back here to do that, won't I?

37

DURING THE FOLLOWING NIGHTS I devoted all my free time to preparing what I knew would be the most important letter I would ever write. In it I thanked Lao Liang for the trust placed in me by the honorable organization and for the great opportunity I had been given to serve the people and the motherland — standard expressions that came to me without effort. But I faced an insurmountable difficulty, I wrote. As a child I had always been taught that respecting the old and taking care of the weak were the bounden duties of any moral citizen. My Great-Aunt, a proletarian and childless working woman, was alone and ill, suffering from high blood pressure and arthritis, and of all my family, only I had an opportunity to look after her. After bringing up five parentless children, and now also caring for my four-year-old nephew, she herself was crying for help. I emphasized the special relationship between myself and Great-Aunt, known to everyone in the neighborhood. My approaching graduation was the only hope she could count on. Worrying about my Great-Aunt would divert my attention and interfere with my devotion to the bureau's work if I was so far away from her. Unless, I added, the bureau could help get my younger sister transferred back to Shanghai to be with her: then my problem and concern would be solved.

However rhetorical, my letter told the truth: Number 1 and Number 3 lived outside Shanghai; Number 5 was still on the farm. Number 2 had been living with Great-Aunt for years, but when he got married, a bitter gulf had opened because Great-Aunt, feeling jealous and cast aside, could not accept his wife, Dong-lan. The tension had risen so high when my brother's new wife moved into our house that Number 2 had divided the apartment in two, leaving Great-Aunt one more room beside her own. He then exchanged living quarters with another family. I was angry at my brother, not only for abandoning Great-Aunt but for cutting up our home, even though I could imagine how hard Great-Aunt must have made things for him and his wife.

Full of anxiety at my unprecedented boldness, I walked to Xi Yuan once more and handed over my letter. Meanwhile, I wrote to Xiao Zhao and asked him to inform Great-Aunt that someone might visit her or the neighborhood committee to check my claims about her. Then I waited. Weeks dragged by. After a month, still no news. In mid-February, Department Head Han announced the job allocations of all the graduates. Most were assigned to various ministries in the capital, one went back to Tibet, a couple to the capitals of other provinces. My name was not mentioned. I was the only one without a destination. That meant only one thing. My posting must have held: because I was going to the Secret Service, no one was to know.

Now I was sick with worry. My letter must have angered them, or fallen on deaf ears. Department Head Han privately confirmed my "good fortune."

Two days after my fellow graduates had left the campus, word from Xi Yuan finally came. No decision had been made. I was to leave my belongings at Bei Da and go back to Shanghai for my one-month graduation holiday before reporting to work. I boarded the train with one small bag. In it were two china cups, gifts from Xiao Zhang in Tangshan, with her surname baked on them. She told me they were among the first produced by the rebuilt factory. Tangshan was rising from the ashes.

Xiao Zhao had been thrilled to learn from my letter that I had been assigned to be a *Te Wu* — special agent; he was happy to end his days as a stevedore on the Shanghai docks and move to Beijing, where my new job would garner him an easier and much more prestigious post. I didn't tell him until I got to Shanghai that I had requested an exemption. He was devastated.

"You mean you turned down a terrific job like that? Ah Si, you're not thinking straight. Write to them immediately and tell them you've made a mistake!"

"I promised Great-Aunt that I would come back to Shanghai if I could, to take care of her. Besides, I hate the thought of working with such people."

Xiao Zhao's family, especially his father, also thought I had broken a gold rice bowl by my "hasty and thoughtless behavior." He intimated that without a job I would no longer have his permission to marry his son. He and Xiao Zhao only stopped nagging me to change my mind when I told them that, if I were to work for the secret police, my relationship with Xiao Zhao would be in jeopardy because the usual practice was that the bureau would find me a spouse from within the organization.

Great-Aunt was more supportive. She assured me that her pension could feed two mouths; if I ended up jobless and without *hu-kou*, she said, it wouldn't matter.

Three weeks dragged on, fraught with uncertainty and frustration. In one week I would have to return to Beijing and take up my new job or refuse the posting and be consigned to unemployment for the rest of my life, a burden on Great-Aunt.

Lao Luo, the retired director of the neighborhood committee, came to see us and said someone had come to ask about Great-Aunt and the condition of her health.

"It's about Ah Si's graduation, isn't it?" she asked. When she got no answer, she said to Great-Aunt, "We told the man how devoted you have been to this neighborhood and how badly you need someone to look after you. I hope we helped."

The next day I decided I could wait no longer. After breakfast I headed for the local post office, where I could make a long-distance phone call. I had decided to contact Lao Liang at the bureau and find out my fate.

All long-distance calls had to be placed by the operator. Summoning what little confidence I had, I asked for the Beijing operator, then said as firmly as I could, "Please connect me to Zhong Diao Bu — the Central Investigation Bureau of the Chinese Communist Party."

"No phone number?"

"I forgot it at home," I lied, and told her whom I wanted to talk to.

"What is your name?"

A couple of minutes later an angry male voice crackled over the line. "What on earth do you think you're doing, Xiao Ye, making a long-distance call here?"

"Is that you, Lao Liang? I'm sorry if I've done something wrong. Please forgive me for phoning you, but I am desperate to know your decision. I hope you understand."

He calmed down a little. "Of course I understand your situation. I read your letter carefully, but I hate to let you go. Listen, I have contacted the personnel department of the Municipal Government of Shanghai, a person named Fang. I don't want your talent wasted at a time when the country needs people with a good command of English."

In the pause that followed, my heart soared and the phone shook in my hand.

"But if they can't find a suitable position for you, I want you to reconsider your decision. In any event, don't call here again."

Before I could thank him, he hung up.

🌿

I could hardly wait to make my way to the Bund, where the municipal government was housed in the former Hong-Kong-Shanghai Bank building, an imposing stone structure. City Hall was guarded round the clock by two soldiers, stiffly at attention. As a child, whenever I had passed City Hall I had wished I would someday be able to go inside. I had often wondered what kind of people worked there and felt sure they were lucky.

After a long hesitation I plucked up my courage and approached one of the guards. He stared at me for a few moments before wordlessly raising his white-gloved hand, pointing to his right while maintaining a straight-ahead stare.

"Side entrance," he said.

I climbed the narrow stairs and entered a large hallway jammed with people standing around waiting to be heard. After I had registered, a receptionist directed me to a small downstairs waiting room with a tiny barred window facing the street. The benches were full. I leaned on the wall facing the stairs. Some of the people in the room appeared to be on business; they were well dressed and kept consulting their watches. From snatches of conversation I gathered that many were there to find out the resolution of long-delayed issues caused by the Cultural Revolution — rehabilitation of the living and the dead, the return of confiscated goods, money and property.

Watching the comings and goings, I felt suddenly tired, tired of waiting for others to make a decision about my past and future; tired of the battles I had had to fight in order to have a normal life. I had no idea what this Fang was like — man or woman, old or young; nor could I guess what the decision might be, or if he or she would show up at all. How am I going to break the news to Great-Aunt if I am not wanted or needed? I asked myself. And what will happen between me and Xiao Zhao if I have to return to Beijing?

"Ye Ting-xing," I heard someone call out.

A thin man in his late forties stood at the foot of the marble staircase. As I approached, he took a last drag from his cigarette and dropped it to the floor, grinding it out under his leather shoe.

"Comrade Ye Ting-xing," he said, before I could speak, "I can't give you any answer now. We haven't yet made a decision. Recently we have been swamped by all kinds of allocations and reallocations within our own jurisdiction. I hope you understand."

He sounded sincere. I nodded. He turned to go and I called him back.

"Comrade Fang," I said, "my graduation vacation is almost up, then I'll have to return to Beijing. That is what I'm trying to avoid. I want you to know that I don't mind what kind of work I do as long as I can stay in Shanghai and take care of my Great-Aunt."

The room was very quiet and I knew that everyone was eavesdropping. Fang seemed unruffled. He probably went through this a dozen times a day.

"How about coming back in two days? Let's say, ten o'clock in the morning. I hope at that time I'll be able to tell you what the settlement is." He turned away.

Outside the building, it was a typical early April day. The sun had succeeded in poking its head through the thick clouds but might disappear at any time, bringing another shower. The air was damp and heavy, the way my heart felt as I made my way along the street, loaded down with doubts and anxiety.

I walked home, deep in thought. Xiao Zhao was working the day shift at the docks and I wouldn't see him until late afternoon. Number 3 would be home in a few days with her husband, Xiao Qin, a fellow worker at her factory in Songjiang. They came into Shanghai occasionally to visit Great-Aunt and my nephew. I wished I could talk to Number 2 as I had all my life and seek his advice and comfort, but my anger at him for trading away half of our apartment to a strange family had driven me from him. I had refused to visit him in his new home and he had not come to see me. I had never imagined that, after all we had been through as a family, we would be split. What an irony that this rift, isolating Great-Aunt as it did, would provide the main excuse for my not accepting the hated job assignment with the Secret Service!

Over the next two days I counted the hours until my meeting with Lao Fang. On Friday morning, Great-Aunt offered to go to the Bund with me. She believed that if she stood beside me, white-haired and frail on her three-inch lily feet, Lao Fang's heart would be touched. I told her that by now the decision had been made and left the apartment without her, but carrying with me her best wishes.

I registered with the receptionist and, without asking for directions, descended the stairs to the waiting room like a veteran. Lao Fang showed up shortly after. He motioned me to follow him and wordlessly led me upstairs to the main floor. I dragged my feet on the steps, my heart sore, because I was sure the news was bad and that he didn't want to deliver it to me in a room where I would break down in front of others and lose face. In the hallway he turned to face me, smiling.

It was good of him to be so concerned, I thought. His traditional kind of courtesy had been lacking in China for many years. He was even smiling "apologetically."

He put out his hand.

"Congratulations, Xiao Ye. You can stay."

PART FIVE

AGAINST THE WIND
(1978–1987)

38

"STAY?" I STAMMERED.

"Your patience has been rewarded. The personnel department has decided to accept you. Come with me." Lao Fang headed toward the elevator. "I'm taking you to your office. You can start next week when your vacation is over. I'll send up the appropriate forms at that time."

We stepped into the creaking elevator and Lao Fang pushed the button for the fifth floor.

"Our department is on the third floor, yours is on the fifth," he went on.

The elevator lurched to a halt and doors clacked open. My mind bristling with questions about what office and division Lao Fang was referring to, I followed through a maze of dark hallways. Finally he stopped before a door, over which hung a wooden sign: Political Division.

"Here we are."

In the spacious, high-ceilinged office most of the desks were unoccupied. A middle-aged woman rose when we entered.

Lao Fang introduced her as Lao Yan. "Lao Yan is in charge of personnel matters for the Foreign Affairs Department of Shanghai Municipal Government," he said with a big smile.

"Welcome, Xiao Ye, to our department. We can surely use some new blood."

I shook hands with her and looked around. The room had once been grand, with hardwood floors and chestnut paneling on the walls. But the paint was stained and cracked, the wood worn and unpolished. In the corner a man sat at his desk reading intently under the light from a large iron-framed window.

After Lao Fang left, Lao Yan took me down the hall to the office of the reception division, where the bustle of activity could be heard before she opened the door. Here, in contrast to the political division, the atmosphere was electric. The air was thick with cigarette smoke that rose from a dozen or so desks. Typewriter keys clacked and phones rang against the background hum of voices. Several workers shouted into telephones, their conversations punctuated with "*Wei! Wei!*" ("Hello! Hello!") a universal habit as people tried to hear each other over the ancient telephone lines. No one in the room was anywhere near my age. Lao Yan had meant what she said when she told me I was new blood. I was ushered to a desk to meet a chubby, middle-aged man.

"Welcome, Xiao Ye, to the reception division. This is where you will work." He extended his hand. I had shaken more hands in the past half hour than in my entire life.

"Thank you very much for having me here," I said quietly, hardly able to contain my excitement.

Lao Fu was the deputy division chief, a portly, distinguished man with a double chin, well groomed and dressed — not a common sight in those days. I couldn't help but notice his "beer belly," a term I learned in my field work assignment with the American tourists. A beer belly was unusual in Chinese males.

He took me on a tour, rapidly passing on names and information. I felt like a Peking duck, force-fed with data. As he rattled on, the outlines of my new job finally took shape in my dumbfounded brain. I would work for the Reception Division of the Foreign Affairs Department of the Shanghai Municipal

Government, which was under the direct administration of the federal government. Employing more than two dozen people, my division was responsible for receiving and caring for three types of foreign dignitaries: *Guo Bin*, *Dang Bin* and *You Xie*. *Guo Bin* were state guests such as a prime minister and his or her entourage. *Dang Bin* included invitees of the Chinese Communist Party from other communist governments or parties throughout the world, for example Romanian President Ceausescu. These visitors usually stayed in guesthouses from which tourists and other foreigners were barred. *You Xie* guests usually belonged to Friendship Associations in other countries, normally non-governmental, like the Chinese-American Friendship Society.

"When would you be able to begin work, Xiao Ye?" asked Lao Fu.

"Tomorrow," I replied, for I didn't want them to change their minds.

"In that case," he said, smiling at my eagerness, "why not start now? You can go to the Jin Jiang Hotel, meet some of your colleagues and become familiar with the procedures for receiving *Guo Bin*."

"Er, sure," I answered, taken aback. I was anxious to tell Great-Aunt the good news and knew she would be more nervous with every passing moment.

"But do I look all right?" I continued. I had washed my hair and put on my best outfit, but wasn't sure if my appearance was appropriate for what I knew to be an opulent and prestigious hotel.

"You'll be fine."

After I had embarrassed myself by admitting that I didn't know where the Jin Jiang Hotel was, Lao Fu agreed to take me there. It was twenty minutes by bus from the Bund, in the former French concession, an area characterized by European-style two-story buildings the Shanghainese called *yang-fang* — foreign buildings — and streets lined with shady plane trees.

The hotel complex consisted of two sections separated by a garden, and a small auditorium in which Richard Nixon and Zhou En-lai had signed the famous Joint Communiqué between China and the U.S. in 1972. Across a tree-lined road the former French Club, equipped with an indoor swimming pool and a dance hall, had been one of Mao Ze-dong's private residences when he had visited Shanghai. After his death it had been opened to tourists. The hotel's North Building was used for regular tourists and business travelers; the South Building housed official guests and was closed to the public. In its center wing of eighteen stories, Suite 253 was the permanent office of the Foreign Affairs Department. The spacious rooms were working and sleeping quarters for those in the reception division who had guests in the hotel. The enclosed balcony was the territory of Lao Gu, secretary of the division and the eldest among us.

By this time I was dizzy with the notion that I would actually be working for an important government department in luxurious quarters. My first lesson in the advantages that attended the job came when Lao Fu and I joined others for lunch in a large dining room filled with people from the Shanghai Public Security Bureau, who were in charge of the foreign visitors' safety, and journalists from Xin Hua News Agency. The menu, written on a small blackboard, offered meatballs or chicken wings and Three Delicacy Soup. I opted for the wings. Then it struck me that I probably did not have enough money with me for such a fancy meal. When the food arrived — soup, steaming rice and a plate of four delectable-looking chicken wings on a bed of stir-fried green vegetables — I wished I had taken Great-Aunt's advice and brought more money.

Embarrassed, I gathered my courage and whispered, "Lao Fu, I don't think I can pay for this meal. I'm afraid I — "

"Don't worry about it, Xiao Ye. I have extra hotel food coupons with me. You'll get your own coupons when we get back to the office."

I then set to with gusto. Two chickens' worth of wings for me alone! I was amazed at the number of fowl killed to provide this meal. For most ordinary families, chicken was a delicacy seen only at the New Year, when the government provided one for each family at the regulated state price.

It turned out that, with the coupons provided as part of the government food subsidy in my department, and with "special" prices offered by the hotel to ingratiate itself with the officials who decided where important foreign guests would stay, my meal cost fifteen cents — in a country where the average family spent three-quarters of its income on food. At that time a bowl of noodles with no vegetable or meat bought at a food stall on a Shanghai street cost twenty cents.

I spent the afternoon in Suite 253, fascinated with everything. On a typing machine equipped with a tray of several thousand lead-cast characters, a typist was finishing the last draft of the mayor's speech for that night's banquet for the prime minister of Mali. Others filled out requisitions for limousines or hotel accommodations. There were three colored telephones: one for inside the hotel, one with an outside line, the third connected to the central government and its ministries through a three-digit number. This last was simply called the "red phone" for its vermilion color.

"Pick it up as soon as it rings and ignore everything else, including other calls," Lao Gu instructed.

I was used that afternoon as a messenger, dropping notes off at the hotel manager's office and delivering translated menus to the banquet department. Wherever I went I was greeted warmly and with respect, even though I was young and a new face. I soon learned that my department was powerful: there was no red tape, no negotiation or argument when its name was invoked.

At the end of the day I found Lao Fu and said goodbye to him.

"Why not go with Lao Liu to help him out at the banquet tonight?" he suggested, introducing me to a kind-looking gray-haired gentleman in his fifties.

"Sure," I said, for the hundredth time that day. "But I don't speak French."

"That won't be a problem. I'll put you at the workers' table with the journalists, security men, secretaries and bodyguards." Lao Liu laughed. "As far as I can see, that's the best table. No foreigners, no protocol — just eating and drinking!"

Before I left I asked Lao Gu, the secretary, to help me make a call to our neighborhood phone booth so that I could leave a message for Great-Aunt. By then, I knew, she would be worried sick. Lao Gu looked very displeased.

"Xiao Ye, never let a family member, a relative or anyone else know your whereabouts when you are dealing with foreign state leaders and important visitors!" she admonished me. "It's against regulations."

A few minutes later our car pulled into the back compound of the Shanghai Exhibition Center and stopped in front of a building that housed the city banquet hall. The center had been built by the Russians in their typical grand style: sky-high ceilings, giant crystal chandeliers and sweeping marble staircases as wide as a road. The air-conditioned banquet hall, as extensive as a football field, with a wall-to-wall vermilion carpet, was on the second floor. Nine large round tables were clustered in the center (the room could easily house thirty), each set with sparkling crystal, gleaming china and crisp linen napkins folded in the shapes of flowers or birds.

As I ate, surrounded by boisterous men and women clearly enjoying the delectable and plentiful food and liquor, I constantly reminded myself that I was not dreaming. Twenty-four hours earlier I could hardly keep a dry eye, worried that I would be sent to Beijing, forced to part with Xiao Zhao, Great-Aunt and my little nephew and do a job I loathed for the rest of my life. Now I was ending the day at a banquet in honor of a visiting head of state and Chinese officials I could previously have seen only on TV. I hardly tasted the eight courses. Nor could I clearly make out the foreign guests, as I had not brought my glasses with me. I had no idea of the content of the many speeches. I was too busy concentrating on my table manners, copying others' movements to avoid embarrassing myself. The only thing I didn't join them in were the many toasts and *gan-bei* — Bottoms up! — of *mao-tai*, the famous fiery rice liquor. My head was already swimming.

When the car dropped me off in the food market outside Purple Sunshine Lane it was past ten o'clock in the evening. Bursting with good news and stories, I ran down the lane, through our sky-well, and bounded up the stairs two at a time.

"Great-Aunt," I shouted. "I'm home, I'm home."

Doors flew open as the quiet building woke up. Neighbors gathered. Xiao Zhao, who had been waiting with Great-Aunt, met me on the stairs.

"Where have you been?" he demanded. "What happened? Everyone has been worried sick, especially your great-aunt. I tried to call City Hall, but the switchboard was closed. Why are you so late? What is the decision, after all?"

I didn't blame him for being angry. How could I possibly have anticipated the results of my simple trip downtown?

"I attended a banquet tonight," I said "held by the mayor of Shanghai for foreign friends."

"You mean the kind we see on TV?" cut in Lao Zeng, who worked in the Foreign Trade Bureau. His words reminded me that I had seen a team carrying camera equipment around.

"Yes," I said. "Probably I will be on TV tomorrow night!"

I continued up the stairs. Great-Aunt was waiting in the doorway, listening to the hubbub. She looked confused.

"Just tell me one thing, Ah Si. Are you going to stay in Shanghai or not? I don't care about banquets and TV."

I gave her a big hug. "Great-Aunt, I am staying here, staying with you. I can take care of you from now on."

Great-Aunt began to cry and later to laugh with joy. "My Ah Si is home at last," she murmured.

The neighbors crowded into our apartment, firing questions like bullets. They wanted to know details about the hotel's interior, the arrangement of the dishes on the banquet tables, how the Africans looked and talked. Was their skin really black? And what were the high officials like?

Ordinary people could not enter hotels and never met their political leaders, who kept out of the public eye, even sitting behind curtains in their chauffeured cars. In a society where there were no elections for those who led the nation, leaders were mysterious creatures. I tried to answer all their questions and wished I had brought home a menu to satisfy their curiosity, or an empty *maotai* bottle. With all the toasting that had gone on, there had been lots to spare.

All my life I had read fairy tales, and now I seemed to be living in one. I walked in and out of the old Victorian building on the waterfront, showing my new identity card and nodding to the doorkeepers. I was admitted to fancy hotels and greeted with friendly smiles. In Xiao Zhao's house I became the center of conversation at the dinner table.

I sent a telegram to Rainbow, telling her the news and asking her to send my belongings to Shanghai.

For the first week, I wore clothing I had borrowed from Number 3 until I received my special clothing allowance. It came with an admonition that it was to be spent only on outer garments, "not underwear," and a requirement that I turn in receipts in the amount of ¥120, more than two months' salary. When the news got out, through Great-Aunt's conversations in the washing area and up and down the lane, that I had received a fortune from the government to spend on clothing and didn't know what to buy, more than half a dozen female neighbors gathered in our apartment one evening, bringing with them clothing owned or borrowed. I would put on a dress or jacket, then they would appraise my appearance, all talking at once as they tried to decide whether I should buy one like it, where it had been purchased and if it was a good bargain. In China people always let others know how much they paid for things and were happy and proud when they paid less than others thought they would have to.

"Go to have your hair permed like those young women in magazines," Mrs. Zeng suggested. She had just had hers permed, or "burned," as Great-Aunt put it, "leaving her hair like an unmanageable bundle of rice straw." Before Great-Aunt could contradict Mrs. Zeng, I told her that the clothing allowance couldn't be used for hairstyling.

I appreciated my neighbors' help. As a child I had worn hand-me-downs and cast-offs and mourning clothes; when I was older I dressed like others in ill-fitting, genderless garb of "revolutionary" blue, gray or green. I knew nothing about style and had never worn good-quality clothing. At our office, Lao Li, the director, had told me that our appearance was like "front windows," the first view foreigners had of the Chinese people as a whole, a remark I found curious, since foreigners could easily walk the streets and see average shabbily-clad citizens for themselves.

Among my neighbors, talk now turned to the question of whether I should buy clothing or have it made. I myself could not imagine squandering such a huge sum of money in stores. Mrs. Yan offered to make me some, and I accepted. I asked Xiao Zhao to gather receipts from his sisters. (All of them had left their respective farms and returned home to Shanghai, thanks to their father's bribing the right people.)

I liked my job. But nothing in life is perfect. From the beginning some of my colleagues, especially the interpreters, remained aloof and treated me coldly. They thought I had acquired my position through high connections because I was taken on as a result of a phone call from Beijing. Almost all of them had been recruited either from tourism bureaus or from universities and other institutions after years of work experience.

Jealousy flared when the time came for the office draw. Interpreters and others who worked with foreign visitors often received gifts of appreciation. When a high official was given a gift, he or she usually kept it, no matter if it was a color TV or a small item. But lower-rank officials and the interpreters had to turn all gratuities — even something as small as a pen — over to Secretary Gu, who would register and store them. Twice a year, a lottery was held for these items. Shortly after I joined the reception division, there was a draw for the staff of all divisions — political, propaganda, reception. Those who resented my appointment argued that I should not be able to participate because I had not contributed to the work that produced the rewards. Lao Gu refused to listen to them. My popularity did not increase when I won the most coveted item, a watch given by the prime minister of France.

Although my job was interesting, I found I was not using my English because I spent almost all my time on the many logistical details of state visits. While my Communist masters played diplomatic games and my colleagues functioned as communication machines, I was in a whirl of detail, dealing with requests for banquet seats from Chinese officials, their spouses and secretaries, or for tickets to soirées. On some occasions I had to negotiate with discontented musicians who played at the various banquets. Except for translating menus and explaining some of the exotic dishes to guests, I never had the chance to speak English.

But I was still in Shanghai.

39

I N June of 1978 I turned twenty-six. Xiao Zhao was almost twenty-nine and his parents thought it was time for us to get married and start a family.

After three years working as a stevedore on the coal docks, Xiao Zhao had landed a position in the canteen. He still worked three shifts, rotated every two days rather than weekly, with Thursday off. (In China the work week is six days.) My hours were irregular and I often worked seven days a week, so Xiao Zhao and I did not see each other as much as we would have liked. I couldn't be with Great-Aunt as much as I would have liked either, because when I was shepherding or planning for a delegation I often had to stay at the hotel.

Even though the mandatory family-planning policy allowing only one child per couple did not come into effect until a year later, the government had for years required late marriage and late child-bearing. Marriage certificates and living quarters were refused to men and women under twenty-five and twenty-two respectively.

Xiao Zhao and I qualified for marriage, but I found I was not ready for such a commitment.

Since my return to Shanghai, not a day had passed that I did not think about Number 5 stuck on the farm. She had been there for ten years. To everyone around me I appeared capable and confident, particularly after I turned down the Secret Service posting, only to land another plum job that most people could not acquire without *guan-xi* as wide as a spider web. But deep inside I had harbored many doubts about myself and was torn apart by the decisions I had made. I had rejected Jian-guo and thus the opportunity to help Number 5 by using his family's influence. In retaliation against the system I hated, I had given up a chance at high-profile work that would have enabled me to benefit my whole family. I had achieved my goal of living with Great-Aunt and taking care of her, but had sacrificed the interests of my own siblings. I wondered if I had made the right choices, or if I had been too selfish.

But one thing I was clearly aware of: a marriage at this time would only make me feel guiltier. I told Xiao Zhao and his parents that I would prefer to wait for a while: my schedule in the new job was too busy and I had to work on my English.

There were also logistical problems. Neither Xiao Zhao's nor my family could accommodate a couple. Two of Xiao Zhao's sisters were now back from the countryside and were living with their parents. I lived with Great-Aunt and my nephew in a small two-room apartment. Xiao Zhao wanted us to marry and take one of the rooms for our own, but our apartment was also home base for my siblings when they came to Shanghai.

Most important, my pride entered into things again. I didn't want to marry and enter Xiao Zhao's family empty-handed. Although I had been supporting myself for the past ten years as a farm worker and then a student, all I had were the clothes on my back. In Great-Aunt's words, I had neither an inch of thread nor a piece of cloth as my dowry. A bride was expected to have what some Westerners call a hope chest: a stack of quilts and bedding, household utensils and so on. The quilts were homemade, after cotton rations were saved for years; many family members contributed their cotton coupons from the time a girl was young to help build up the bride's dowry, or purchased them in the black market at a much higher price.

Xiao Zhao's parents had made it clear — to everyone — that they were willing to make up for my lack of dowry and carry all the expenses of the wedding and feast. When I told Great-Aunt this she fell into a long silence.

"Ah Si," she said finally, "you are not going to walk into his family empty-handed. Your parents would never forgive me if I let that happen to you. Let us begin to put things together. Otherwise our family will lose face and it will be hard for you to hold your head up in front of his family."

I vowed to myself that I would not marry until I had exhausted every means to get Number 5 home. I visited the municipal and district bureaus that handled returns from the countryside and learned that the only way my sister could come back was poor health, certified by a doctor. The most likely to succeed in returning were those suffering from arthritis. At that time in China arthritis was a mysterious disease; it could not be diagnosed by the naked eye or detected by blood tests (unless the case was extreme and brought swollen joints). As a result the past couple of years had seen probably the highest incidence in Chinese history of arthritis among young people, especially those who wished to leave the countryside. Many of the medical certificates were handed out by doctors who had never met the patients but were familiar with *guan-xi* and bribes. Using *hou-men* — the back door — to get things was rife under communism, the philosophy that frequently reminded us to serve the people. Bribery was less endemic but not uncommon. I had always hated this way of doing things.

In any case I had access to neither of these avenues. I had no *guan-xi* with a doctor, nor did I have the money to pay a heavy bribe. I thought about approaching Xiao Zhao's parents to borrow the money, but my pride stopped me. I didn't want to be their debtor even before I became their daughter-in-law.

The solution came through my job. In the fall of that year, after I had worked for the department for almost six months, I was surprised to realize how familiar I had become with people in a number of factories, communes, schools, hospitals and other institutions qualified to receive foreigners. My frequent visits showed me how cooperative were the people who worked in these units. They were always trying to please members of my division in particular so that we would continue to bring visitors over.

At that time, work units open to foreigners were rare, and only those approved and listed in our book, prepared by the propaganda division, could accept foreign delegations. Such an establishment gained great prestige and the people who ran it acquired great face and political merit. Although many units coveted the privilege, few received it. First, the organization had to apply to our department and then its location was inspected: if it was surrounded by slums or an environment that would give China a poor image, the application was rejected. Attention to appearance was important and resulted in large-scale renovations and cleanups. Acceptance would bring government grants to set up attractive reception rooms filled with new furniture, carpets and sometimes air-conditioners — all great luxuries in China at that time. After a decade of neglect, many units applied to be "front windows." Those involved called this phenomenon "foreign affairs pushing forward domestic matters."

At that time, one of the attractions for foreigners coming to Shanghai was hospitals where "magical" acupuncture and other traditional medical techniques were practiced, so I came to know quite a few doctors who basked in the attention of foreign observers. By now I was often given full responsibility for banquet arrangements and the distribution of tickets for soirées or theatre performances arranged for the foreign delegations. For security reasons, these occasions were filled with hand-picked audiences, and the honor of being able to see foreign dignitaries while enjoying the best performances of dance teams, operas or acrobatic troupes denied to ordinary citizens was highly prized. Such tickets were far more valuable than money. And I had control of a certain number.

A discreet distribution of tickets brought me by the end of November an envelope containing a medical report and blood test featuring a high white-cell count — both bearing Number 5's name, Ye Feng-xing. Although she had never met the doctor, my younger sister was diagnosed with a severe form of arthritis, which entitled her to *bin-tui* — withdrawal from the countryside due to illness. The paperwork had the official chop on it — Zhong Shan Hospital — one of the best in Shanghai.

When I read the certificate my hands shook. The fraudulence was one crime; seeking personal gain by using my department's position and prestige was another, maybe the more severe of the two. It could cost me my career, which had barely begun. I vowed not to tell anyone, not even Xiao Zhao, for experience had taught me that a secret remained a secret only if it was kept to oneself. Besides, I was not proud of what I had done; it was the kind of action I had condemned all my life.

The next day, I sent the papers to Number 5 by registered mail.

In the days that followed I watched my colleagues closely, after they hung up the telephone and especially when some of them returned from that hospital, for a sign that I had been found out. My anxiety was eased two weeks later when I went home and found a letter from Number 5. I screamed and jumped up and down after reading it, circling around Great-Aunt with the letter in my hand. As soon as the paperwork was completed, Number 5 could come home after ten years in exile. She would regain her city *hu-kou* without any trouble. At long last a burden of guilt was off my shoulders. I looked at my parents' pictures on the wall and wished they were there to share my joy.

40

THE SAYING HAS IT that misfortune never comes singly and good news usually arrives in pairs.

After the New Year of 1979, two months after Number 5 had come home, she was assigned a job as a house painter in a repair shop run by the neighborhood committee, the only kind of work available for those returning from the countryside. Number 5 had always been quiet and withdrawn, but ten years of hardship and separation from our family had added a sharp edge to her disposition. My recent good fortune, continually bruited by neighbors and friends, did nothing to blunt her bitterness. Each morning as I dressed up to look presentable to foreign visitors and she dressed down for the paint shop, I felt her envious eyes on me.

"We both suffered," she often commented, "but your suffering has been repaid. Mine continues. Why is life so unfair?"

The phony health certificate was a sealed secret between us, for I had made her promise to tell no one. In spite of my sister's dissatisfaction with her job, I couldn't remember the last time our home had been so full of life and happiness — probably not since before my father's operation.

Late one evening in June, Number 1 walked into the apartment, surprising us all, for he was not yet due for his two-week visit. He was clearly very happy, tossing his son up in the air while he told us that he had applied for the postgraduate school of the Shanghai Ship-building Research Institute and had come to the city for the final exams. It had always saddened me that my brilliant eldest brother, so talented in music and science, should have wasted the last ten years working as a tool repair man in Guizhou Province. He had been like Number 5 and me, sent into exile. His years of engineering study at Jiao Tong University had been thrown away.

But when postgraduate schools were restored in 1978, he had looked for a way out, and when Deng Xiao-ping reconfirmed the Four Modernizations, he saw his chance. He decided to concentrate on ship building rather than on his major, automotive engineering. Shanghai had one of the biggest ship-building industries in the country, so if he was successful he would have a good chance of coming home, being with his son and being closer to his wife.

So he had studied the ship-building industry for the exams on his own, poring through every book he could get his hands on. He had passed the general exam and was now in Shanghai to write the second, more specific test. At the age of thirty-three, a father and husband separated from his wife since their marriage almost seven years earlier, Number 1 was still struggling to build a family and a new life.

History was repeating itself. Here was the Ye family once again, suffering unbearable tension, waiting all summer for the final exam results of my eldest brother, knowing full well that his entire future hung in the balance. Every time I watched Number 1 and his son, Ye Xiang, playing together I wished there was some way I could help him.

At the end of August the news came. Number 1 was accepted as one of only ten graduate students by the Ship-building Research Institute and would live at home in Purple Sunshine Lane while he attended classes. When I got home late that night I was greeted by heartfelt laughter from Great-Aunt, Number 5, Number 1 and my neighbors. Little Ye Xiang stared at us with puzzled eyes. He must have thought we had all gone crazy. He was too young to realize what this moment meant to our family. For me, then Number 5, then Number 1, our long nightmare was finally over. After ten years of separation and misery, we were home.

In the spring of 1980 my department moved into the former Polish Consulate-General compound, conveniently located across the street from the banquet hall. It was also a block away from my old high school. One of the finest premises in the city, the new location was known locally as the "white house," marked by two exquisite three-story stone buildings and surrounded with lawns and flowerbeds, rare in downtown Shanghai. There had recently been a sharp increase in foreign visitors, tourists as well as invitees, so the reception division for which I worked was split into three groups. I and eleven others formed the *Guo Bin* section and were no longer involved with guests invited by the Communist Party or those who came under the auspices of Friendship Associations except when extra help was needed, as with the delegations from North Korea headed by Kim Il-sung and from Cambodia led by Kaing Shek Leu, second man in the Pol Pot regime.

Thanks to the thoughtful Lao Gu, I received a bicycle coupon (bikes were rationed at that time), but I had no money to buy one. Xiao Zhao's father bought it for me as a betrothal gift and I accepted with deep gratitude, knowing full well it was a strong signal that it was time for Xiao Zhao and me to get married. Number 5 was home now, but there remained the problem of a place to live. The solution came, once again, through my work.

Among all the city leaders whom I met frequently in the course of my duties, I regarded Vice-Mayor Zhao as a respectable politician, different from most of his Communist colleagues. A former ambassador to Iraq and other countries, Vice-Mayor Zhao was in charge of our department. His amiable and gentle manner toward the staff, rare among men and women in his position, made me feel comfortable in his presence. It was even easy to answer some of his questions about my personal life. One evening during a casual chat after a banquet I told him that my fiancé and I were waiting for the housing department in my neighborhood to allocate living quarters to us — a common problem facing many young couples. He asked me to write him a report, detailing the size of our families' apartments, the number of occupants, our ages and so on, which he would then pass on to the municipal housing department.

I was touched by his concern. His involvement would mean that, while I would still have to enter my new husband's family empty-handed, my marriage would come much sooner than I expected, and I would get a better and bigger apartment than most. The housing distribution system, lord among all the bureaucracies, was divided into three levels: neighborhood, district and municipal. Shanghainese referred to them as shrimps, little fish and big fish. The municipal level controlled the best housing in the city, while the district picked up the leftovers and the neighborhood any crumbs that were left.

I sent in my report to Vice-Mayor Zhao a few days later. The news that such a high official was involved spread quickly up and down Purple Sunshine Lane. I was not happy about that. I felt uneasy getting an apartment through the back door, and especially about facing the young men and women I had grown up with who had been waiting for years for their turn. I should have known better than to tell Great-Aunt. Unlike my neighbors, who wanted to know everything about the visiting foreign dignitaries, from the color of their skin to their hairstyle and the way they dressed, Great-Aunt showed no interest in foreigners. Her curiosity was purely about the Chinese leaders — President Li, Premier Deng, Mayor Peng and so forth. She paid close attention to the daily newspaper readings organized by the neighborhood committee and devoured every detail. So when her Ah Si was taken under the wing of a vice-mayor, she shared the news with everyone she knew.

Great-Aunt had less enthusiasm about my becoming a bride. Her secret plan to have me and Xiao Zhao live with her had gone sour when Number 5 and Number 1 had returned home. And she was worried that she couldn't send me into my new life with a proper dowry. Because she was a single retired woman living on a small pension and was frequently asked for financial support by her relatives in the countryside, she had been unable to provide me with the six quilts required by custom.

In early November, two weeks after sending in my report, I received a phone call at work from a woman at the municipal housing bureau asking me to meet her at a downtown apartment building on busy Xizang (Tibet) Road, about twenty minutes by bike from the office. It was a five-story apartment building from the 1950s, which I had passed many times on my way to the train station. The woman led me into a unit on the first floor, a typical arrangement with two single-room apartments sharing a kitchen and a toilet. The room she showed me was about sixteen square feet, the size for a four-member family according to the guidelines. Between the front balcony and the sidewalk was a narrow strip of garden. There was also a small flowerbed in the rear of the building.

Compared to our apartment in Purple Sunshine Lane, this one seemed luxurious. It had a hardwood floor (unavailable in most new buildings) and steel windowframes. The kitchen boasted running water and a gas stove (we still burned coal); the shared washroom had a flush toilet (we still used chamber pots). The apartment was conveniently located, too, ten minutes from my home and ten to downtown. I accepted the key on the spot.

I was introduced to my new neighbors in the other room, the Lu family: two aged parents and their two grown-up children. Before she left, the woman confided that she had expected me to turn down the apartment. Most people rejected the first one, she explained, knowing that a better one would be offered next time, considering that a vice-mayor was backing the request.

With the key to the apartment in my pocket, everything suddenly seemed real: I was going to leave Great-Aunt and start a family of my own. Xiao Zhao and his father pressed me to marry soon: the New Year, the time most people preferred for a wedding, was only months away.

A week later, on a Sunday, when Number 5 and I were cleaning the house, I noticed Great-Aunt out of the corner of my eye. She was sitting down heavily on her bed with her eyes closed and her hands on her temples.

"Great-Aunt," I called from the other room, "is something wrong?"

I could barely hear her answer.

"My head," she murmured. "It feels like knives in my head."

Number 5 and I rushed into her room.

"She's so pale," Number 5 observed.

"I think we should take you to hospital," I said. Great-Aunt was sixty-eight and had suffered from high blood pressure for years. I didn't want to take any chances.

"No, no," she said softly. "Just let me lie down."

I helped her into bed and she immediately fell into a deep sleep. When I woke her for lunch she sat up in bed.

"Great-Aunt," I said quietly, "why are you holding your arm up like that?"

Her right arm was raised as if she was responding to a political slogan at a rally.

"What do you mean? I'm doing no such thing."

I held a small mirror in front of her. When she caught sight of herself, she uttered a cry of fear.

"I can't feel my arm in that position," she said. "What's wrong with me?"

I called Number 5, then ran down the lane to the public phone to call for an ambulance. In the same hospital where my mother had been diagnosed with cancer I learned that Great-Aunt had had a serious stroke, and that a spinal tap was required to determine the specific area of the brain affected. When I went into the ward she seemed to have aged suddenly. Her right eye drooped, as did the corner of her mouth. She still held her right arm up, looking oddly comical.

Number 1 and I spent the night by her side and the next day I held her hands while doctors and nurses folded her like a shrimp to perform the spinal tap. As the needle entered her spine Great-Aunt let out a fierce, haunting cry. I begged the doctor to stop.

"Do you want your aunt to live or die?" he snapped.

As the doctors worked, I wondered if her suffering was my fault, if the stroke had been brought on by stress caused by my imminent departure. Great-Aunt had repeatedly urged me to establish my home with Xiao Zhao in the second room of the family apartment.

Much as I wanted to be near her, I still felt Number 3 and Number 1 needed a home base in Shanghai, so I couldn't agree. My refusal had upset her.

The tap showed that the stroke wasn't life-threatening. My two siblings and I spent the next week with her in shifts. When she was released the doctor assured us that her arm would resume its normal function after a slow recovery.

For the first time in her life, Great-Aunt was looked after by others and we, the third generation of the Ye family, had a chance to pay back our debt for her help over the last forty years. I decided there could be no wedding until she had fully recovered.

41

IVE MONTHS LATER, on April 13, 1980, Xiao Zhao and I were married. Through his son-in-law's *guan-xi*, my father-in-law had booked a spacious dining hall at the nearby Park Hotel. My duties had taken me there many times, and I would have preferred not to have my wedding reception there, since many of the staff knew me. But I had no say in the matter: the groom's family was responsible for the wedding and reception.

Government policy allowed three days for a honeymoon, but some time before I had put in a request for three extra days, using my accumulated overtime. Xiao Zhao and I had decided to spend three days in Hangzhou, a scenic city three hours by train to the south, where he had relatives, and then go on to Wuxi so we could try to locate my parents' grave. Auntie Yi-feng said she could show us the approximate area of the grave but not the exact place. The site was still sown with crops.

My request for extra leave was refused because an American delegation was due to come to Shanghai at that time. My disappointment increased when I was criticized for making the request in the first place.

"What do you want to go to Hangzhou for," Lao Fu, who had been promoted to division chief, demanded, "climbing mountains and sailing on the lake like a tourist with nothing to do?"

And that was not the end of it. A few days later I was summoned again by Lao Fu, this time accompanied by the secretary, Lao Gu. Because of our original tight schedule of visiting two cities in six days, Xiao Zhao and I had thought it would be a good idea to fly back to Shanghai from Hangzhou and catch the train to Wuxi. Besides, neither of us had ever been in a plane and we thought it would be fun. A veteran English interpreter in our department, Lao Peng, had helped me book the plane tickets through a friend of his in the provincial tourist bureau in Hangzhou. Purchasing an air ticket was second only to climbing the sky in difficulty; ordinary people could not buy tickets because of the demand from high officials and tourist groups (who paid with much-coveted foreign currency), and special certificates were required. Unfortunately, Lao Gu took the phone call confirming my booking. A dyed-in-the-wool and ever-vigilant Communist, Lao Gu reported my "sin" of lavishness to my superior.

In his office Lao Fu accused me of bourgeois extravagance, of "throwing money away like water." The fact that it was my money did not deter his intrusiveness. Lao Gu added that in my quest for personal leisure I was taking airplane seats from legitimate officials performing their state duties. She then telephoned Lao Peng's friend in Hangzhou. When she had him on the line she handed me the phone.

"Cancel the tickets," she ordered.

Fearing more criticism for "bourgeois extravagance" if they found out that my wedding reception was to be at the Park Hotel, I told no one and invited nobody from my office. On the day of the wedding banquet I kept to my normal working day to avoid suspicion. I had learned my lesson. As Mao's famous dictum put it, a single spark could start a prairie fire, and I made this my personal proverb: a tiny carelessness could ruin my whole life.

My wedding outfit was a gray suit, a benefit of my clothing allowance. Xiao Zhao's stepmother had tried unsuccessfully to persuade me to don a red outfit. (Red is the traditional color for a wedding.) After a decade of drab hues dictated by the Cultural Revolution, I felt strange in bright clothing. Nor could I bring myself to squander money on clothing I would wear only once, so I compromised by wearing a pink sweater under my jacket. My wedding dinner was the most showy personal event I had ever been involved in, planned and paid for by my new father-in-law without consultation with me. I would have preferred a quiet family dinner such as Number 1, Number 2 and Number 3 had had. My father-in-law had booked ten tables. At one were Great-Aunt, Number 1 and his son, Number 3 and her husband, and Number 5, along with Yu-qin's younger sister. Number 2 and his wife did not come, for he and I were still angry with one another over the splitting of our apartment. The other nine tables were taken up by Xiao Zhao's relatives and by friends of his parents, many of whom I didn't know. I did notice, though, that my father-in-law had invited the rich father of a woman he had earlier planned to match with Xiao Zhao.

The dinner was an elaborate affair with ten courses. Halfway through the banquet, Xiao Zhao and I toured the tables, thanking our guests for coming and expressing appreciation for the gifts, mostly cash, that had been given to my father-in-law. I was happy but felt very much a poor country mouse, with barely enough of my relatives to fill a table among the rich friends of Xiao Zhao's family — a guest at my own wedding.

Later, in our new apartment with close friends and relatives, it seemed to me that each of them was fully aware that the only item I had brought into my new home was a rickety wooden stand Number 1 had made to hold our two-burner gas stove. He had spent three Sundays measuring, sawing and nailing from a design he had found in a borrowed book. When the last group of guests departed at midnight I gazed at our room decorated with new furniture, heaps of colorful quilts and bedding as well as other household implements beyond the reach of most young couples. I felt remote and strange standing there. Every item reminded me that it was Xiao Zhao's parents who had put it all together: I had become a debtor to them and to him. It was a burden that weighed heavily.

If I thought I would begin my marriage alone with my new husband I was mistaken, for it wasn't long after we returned from our honeymoon in Hangzhou that Hai Rui became a permanent fixture in our household.

Hai Rui was a friend of Xiao Zhao's from our days on the prison farm, but I didn't begin to know him until I started to date Xiao Zhao. He was a frequent topic of conversation among the women because of the effeminate ways that earned him the nickname Lamb. His trademark was a big woven straw bag he carried at all times, the kind of bag only women used. In his six years there Hai Rui never put a hand to farm work; instead, he acted as a housekeeper and a servant for a number of his male colleagues, cleaning the dorm, fetching water and meals for them and doing their laundry. In exchange, they covered for him and made up his quota in the fields. A year older than Xiao Zhao, Hai Rui was a fussy man who couldn't tolerate even a spot of dirt on his clothes. It was well known that he adored Xiao Zhao.

At first I didn't question Hai Rui's daily participation in our lives too much, not even when Xiao Zhao and I returned from our three-day honeymoon and found our bed made up like one in a hotel, with the quilt folded back and a square of chocolate on the pillow. Without telling me, Xiao Zhao had given his friend a key to our home. Most times when I returned from work, dinner had been prepared by Hai Rui and Xiao Zhao's laundry had been washed and hung out to dry on bamboo poles. One night I found that my laundry had been washed too, even my underwear.

I resented Hai Rui's intrusion into my household — an intrusion sanctioned by my new husband with no consultation with me. But in other people's eyes Hai Rui was a good-hearted and harmless person; my neighbors asserted that I was lucky to have such a "helpful" friend. Nevertheless, that night I expressed my misgivings to Xiao Zhao, who showed no sympathy. Instead he assured me that Hai Rui was too weak to pose a threat or to harm me. "He is just lonely and needs some company, and that is all," he said. I didn't understand what he meant, nor, initially, the meaning of the word threat, but it did remind me of an incident he had mentioned when we were on the farm. One Sunday afternoon Xiao Zhao was awakened by someone kissing him on the forehead. It was Hai Rui. Xiao Zhao told me he had slapped him and warned him never to do that again.

Although I had read the terms "homosexual" and "lesbian" in American magazines I didn't really understand them. Moreover, I believed the official government line that these practices did not exist in China. It had never occurred to me that Hai Rui was gay. However, I began to wonder why a young healthy man like Hai Rui had never had a date in his life and why he was so devoted to Xiao Zhao, and I began to ask myself, who is the real intruder, Hai Rui or me? Ever since the day I was forced to pack up my belongings and move to the prison farm I had dreamt of having a place of my own, where I wouldn't need to store my folded clothing in a pillowcase or cardboard box under a bunk, or share a bed with an aunt, a sister or a farm-mate; a place where I could arrange things according to my own will.

Reluctant to confront my husband, I decided to tackle the problem indirectly. With the help of one of Xiao Zhao's sisters I attempted to make a match for Hai Rui with a young accountant working in a children's hospital. Hai Rui at first resisted a date, but finally relented. The plan was that they would meet in a theatre near our home, see the show and then come back to our apartment, where they could have some privacy. Xiao Zhao and I would have left by then.

On the evening before Hai Rui's first date, I cleaned the house and prepared some snacks for them. The next day, just as Xiao Zhao and I were getting ready to leave, Hai Rui rushed through the door, alone, obviously irritated. He told us that, as soon as Xiao Zhao's sister had introduced them and left them at the theatre, he had said goodbye to the young woman and run off. He made it clear that he was not interested in meeting anyone again. That was the end of it. Hai Rui continued to be a third member of my household, unwanted by me but welcomed by my husband. I never did comprehend the true nature of their relationship.

42

THE REAL THIRD MEMBER of my family came to us unplanned, as the birth-control regulations would put it. Xiao Zhao and I had decided we would wait for a year before starting a family, but almost six months after our wedding, in early October, I found I was pregnant. Far from being disappointed, I was delighted. From the moment my pregnancy was confirmed I felt bonded with the new life growing inside me, and looked forward to having a little baby to care for. I soon realized the full consequence of the word unplanned, however. I was told I couldn't continue with routine checkups at the hospital designated by my work unit until I obtained permission to have a child from my neighborhood clinic. A certificate was necessary to ensure that my pregnancy was within the overall family plan of my neighborhood committee, which strictly governed the number of babies born each year.

Shortly after Xiao Zhao and I returned from Hangzhou, a woman from the committee had knocked on our door, demanding to know if we were planning to have a baby right away or were using birth control. I was annoyed at her impertinence but bit my tongue and told her we planned to wait a while. She praised our decision and departed, leaving behind a box of condoms. It was around this time that every major newspaper published an open document from the Central Committee of the Communist Party announcing the "one child/one family" policy, which carried great legal weight. I was distressed because I wouldn't be able to fulfill my dream of having five children as my mother had had, but equally I was well aware of the population crisis China was facing.

I now went to the neighborhood clinic and asked for a certificate of permission to bear a child. After a close examination of my work unit ID and my *hu-kou* book, the clerk, a woman in her thirties with a businesslike manner, checked her notebook and shook her head.

"You are not registered in the plan," she said. "I can't issue a certificate."

"What do you mean?" I demanded. "I'm pregnant. This is my first child. The only child I am going to have," I added.

"I realize that, but you are not supposed to be pregnant now."

"But I am. What do you expect me to do?"

It was a rhetorical question, but she took it literally. "You have to get an abortion. That's what we expect you to do. You can get pregnant again when you're in the plan."

"How can you say a thing like that?" I failed to curb my anger. "You sound as if you're talking about a lightswitch: turn it on when you're in the plan, turn it off if you're not. How can you be so cruel?"

I demanded to see the person in charge of the clinic or the head of the neighborhood committee. Minutes later I stood before two women in their late fifties. Sister Meng, who lived in the building next to mine, was a deputy director. She presentd a wide smile before she opened her mouth. It turned out she knew everything about me: how I got my apartment, details about my job, even that I had helped my next-door neighbors place their grown daughter in a mental hospital (one to which I sometimes took foreign visitors). Half an hour later, I left with a certificate in my hand. I knew Sister Meng had granted it not out of sympathy or because of the persuasiveness of my arguments, but because of the influence of my work unit. But I didn't care.

Both Xiao Zhao and I were thrilled, and my pregnancy developed without incident. There was no pressure to have a boy from either side of the family as there were already male heirs on both sides. My preference was for a girl.

To everyone around us, Xiao Zhao and I were a model couple. If my initial feelings toward him had been based on duty and obligation, I was in love with him by the time I got pregnant. We hardly ever raised our voices at one another. We even appeared to live harmoniously with Hai Rui, who spent almost every free moment at our place. (He lived alone in his spacious apartment, fifteen minutes away by bike, and worked as a supervisor in a factory that employed the disabled to assemble electrical components.) Every month on pay day I turned over my salary to Xiao Zhao after subtracting what I needed for food coupons. Sometimes I would ask him for money for personal items. Number 3 said to me that most women, including her, weren't so trusting. "Put some money aside," she warned me, "to protect yourself." I told her I didn't need protection; I trusted Xiao Zhao to handle money more than I did myself.

What I didn't tell her was that giving Xiao Zhao my pay (much higher than his) was my way of paying back the debt I owed him and his family for our new home furnishings and the expensive wedding. Xiao Zhao never claimed such a debt, but everything in the apartment constantly reminded me. I enjoyed the good life his parents had made possible but I also envied the joy others shared by furnishing their homes together. I often thought about how happy Number 3 and her husband were after they had bought a sofa from their mutual savings.

When I saw new underwear in my drawer and new clothes on the dresser I realized it was unnecessary to ask Xiao Zhao for extra money. When I asked him why he had bought these things rather than let me do it myself, he said I might buy the wrong things or pay too much because I didn't have much experience shopping. He began to take care of all my other needs, from hair pins to sanitary pads. My neighbors envied me my good fortune, being pampered like this. In their eyes I was a woman who had been dropped in a honey jar for so long I couldn't taste any sweets, but I could hardly agree. My hard-earned independence and dignity had been crushed by the realization that my husband thought me incapable of handling money and unworthy of the simple pleasure of shopping for personal things.

The so-called sweetness tasted sour when I visited Great-Aunt during my lunch break one day in March 1981. I was six months pregnant. Number 5 had called me the day before to say that Great-Aunt had been living on pickled vegetables for days, waiting for her next pension payment to buy fresh food. She had sent all her money to her younger brother in Chen Family Village, who had written complaining that the severe winter had killed most of the animals he had planned to sell in the spring. Great-Aunt, in her pride, refused Number 5's help.

I had not been visiting Great-Aunt as regularly as I used to because I had been experiencing fainting spells and hadn't been allowed to ride my bike for months. When I discovered her need I was unable to help, for I had almost no money in my purse. Nor could I go to the bank to withdraw money. I had no bank account.

I hated to ask Xiao Zhao for the money, but I had no choice. That night I asked him for fifty yuan, about three weeks' salary. That particular figure came to mind because Great-Aunt had given me the same amount on my wedding day, a huge amount for her. I had given it to Xiao Zhao as well as the cash gifts from my brother and sisters. He had never told me how much money had been given us at the wedding, nor had I asked.

"You'll have to wait a day or two until I can get to the bank," he said.

"I can go to make the withdrawal," I offered.

"No, no. You can't. The account is in my name."

Number 3's words rang in my ears. I was about to ask him why he hadn't set up a joint account as most couples did, but I lost my courage. Once again I was reminded that it was me and my family who needed financial help. I had felt like a dependant of Xiao Zhao and his family ever since we had been married — particularly of his generous stepmother, who had showered me with cash on my birthday and on news of my pregnancy. Living in such an unbalanced environment was bad enough; it would be much worse if I was thought to be taking advantage of it. I swallowed my words.

At work, my pregnancy further reduced my chances of keeping up my English. I was confined to office work. Apparently a rising belly didn't present a good image to foreigners. Besides, I was still the junior member of the team, so even after three years most of the paperwork and telephoning still fell to me.

Meanwhile my baby was becoming impatient. Her kicking frequently woke me up at night. Two weeks before my due date, I dragged myself home, exhausted after a long hot wait at the bus stop after work. After supper, although the baby was quiet, I felt uncomfortable. The pains came just before midnight.

Xiao Zhao and I left the apartment and stood on the street for a long time looking for a taxi. Finally we took the bus to the Luo Wan District Hospital for Women and Children, where I was examined and told that I was dilated and the baby would come within twenty-four hours. Because renovation and repairs at the hospital had reduced the number of beds, I was sent home. I spent a sleepless night, fighting the pain, frightened of what was to come.

When dawn arrived, Xiao Zhao told me he was going to work. I could hardly believe my ears.

"You're not going to stay with me?"

"I have to go, Ah Si. I have the keys to the canteen's food supplies."

They won't starve if they miss a few meals, I thought, but held my tongue. Instead I said, "What will I do if I need help?"

"The neighbors are home. I'll try to leave work early. I'm sure I'll be back before anything happens."

Minutes after he left, my water broke. I jumped from the bed in panic, my legs and nightdress soaked. It was not yet six o'clock and my neighbors were not up. The whole building was quiet. Scared and not sure what to do, I cleaned myself up, dressed hastily, grabbed the bag I had prepared the night before and left the apartment. I had to get to the hospital. It was a fifteen-minute walk along the already busy street to the closest bus stop and I was worried that I wouldn't make it. While crossing the street I spotted a taxi. Screaming at the top of my lungs and waving frantically, I ran toward the car. The driver jammed on his brakes and jumped out of the cab.

"Help me, please!" I begged him, for taxi drivers were often very arbitrary about passengers and destinations. "I must get to hospital!"

Instead of asking a lot of questions, the young man yanked open the back door, assisted me in and instructed me to lie down. After a rocky fifteen-minute ride he screeched to a stop, jumped out, ran around the car and helped me out. He refused to leave me at the hospital doorway and insisted on helping me upstairs to the registration room. Deeply touched, I asked his name and the company he worked for. He demurred, and left without saying another word.

The woman behind the desk, much less concerned about me, eyed me sternly. "Where is your family?" she asked brusquely.

"I came alone. I don't have anyone with me, not yet." The pains took my breath away. Water leaked down my legs.

"You came with no one? There are trips back and forth to make, to pay the fees, purchase special sanitary papers you will need, and — "

"Please, please take me in now," I begged. "I'm soaking wet."

"Well, why didn't you say that in the first place?" she snapped, and started calling for help.

I was carried into a room and laid on a low bed with my legs elevated. The pain was unbearable. Around me more than a dozen women moaned and yelled. I was already exhausted, unable to get a full breath between contractions. It seemed none of the nurses was interested in offering anyone help or comfort; they just stood around, talking among themselves. When one woman shrieked, "Help me! I'm in terrible pain!" a nurse shouted back, "Sister, that's what motherhood is all about. You'd better learn that now."

The poor woman next to me rolled off the narrow bed in agony and was crawling on the floor. A nurse came over to her, but instead of lending her a hand she sneered. "Stop acting stupid. Why didn't you think about this when you and your husband were having a good time?"

Her callous remark drew a burst of laughter from her colleagues. I closed my eyes in disgust.

Xiao Zhao arrived around noon and I caught sight of him on my way to the delivery room. Hai Rui was with him. The room had six beds, with a midwife's chair in one corner. Most of the beds were occupied. There were no partitions between them, no curtains, no privacy. One woman was delivering when I arrived, screaming in pain. After I was placed on a bed and the nurses were preparing me to deliver, I saw two young men in dirty white gowns walking through the room as if on a tour.

Deeply embarrassed, I asked the nurses, "What are they doing here?"

"Don't worry, they won't remember you," one said flatly. "They've seen it all before. Besides, what do you care? You'll never come back here again, will you?"

It seemed that the staff and the atmosphere existed for the sole purpose of showing that having children was an unspeakable misery, and I wondered later if all this was orchestrated to reinforce the one-baby-per-family policy.

Around two-thirty that afternoon my baby was born safe and sound. I caught only a brief glimpse of her when the nurse held her high and announced she was a girl, weighing 6 pounds, 3 ounces. She was taken away immediately according to the rules of "science and necessity," which prescribed that a mother needed rest and shouldn't see her baby for forty-eight hours. Then breast-feeding could begin. Lying there alone, waiting to be shipped back to the ward, I felt depleted and empty and wished I had my daughter to hold.

The small postnatal ward was like a university dorm, with twelve beds and a narrow aisle between them. A chamber pot had been placed in the middle of the room, which was hot and humid, and the ripe odor from the pot hung in the air. No windows were open because superstition forbade contact with fresh air or breeze after delivery. After sipping some fish soup brought to me by Xiao Zhao's stepmother, I fell into a deep sleep.

I was awakened by crying. It was dark. In the bed next to me a young woman wept bitterly. Someone turned on the lights. Thinking she was missing her baby, I tried to comfort her.

"You'll see your baby soon," I tried to soothe her.

"It's nothing like that," came a voice from across the aisle. "She had a girl and her husband is the only son in his family. No one has visited her since the baby was born. Her husband is not nice to her either."

"Please, try not to cry," I said to the young woman. "My great-aunt said it will hurt your eyesight if you cry in the month after labor." I felt stupid as soon as the words had escaped my mouth. What kind of comfort was that, telling her an old wives' tale? I fell silent, reminded once again that communism had not stamped out the feudal attitude that in all matters of reproduction the woman was to blame, and grateful that my husband's reaction to my daughter's birth was one of happiness.

After another day of waiting, I was finally given my daughter to hold. I hurriedly unwrapped the thin blanket, checking her little feet and hands. It turned out that, of the twelve of us in the room, ten had had girls. The laughing and talking while feeding our babies brought the first smile to my neighbor's face. How I hoped her smile might stay!

On the fourth day, after my stitches were removed, I asked around if anyone had been in the same waiting room as I. Four had, and they supported me in making a formal complaint to the hospital authorities. It was the first time in my life I had fought back against humiliation, and I felt good about it. The nurses lost their month's bonus.

Xiao Zhao's father had chosen Qi as the generation name for his grandchildren, so we called our daughter Qi-meng, Enlightenment.

When I came home I began, with some skepticism, the *zou-yue-zhi* — confinement following childbirth — an old custom that had survived both political movements and medical science. The strict regimen was more like a weight-loss scheme. It called for a rigid one-month bed rest, not one day more or less, despite the fact that some months have thirty days, some thirty-one and one twenty-eight. I had to wrap my forehead with a narrow cloth to retain my body heat. Disallowed were combing my hair (this caused hair loss and lifelong headache); reading or watching TV (eyesight would be damaged); brushing the teeth (roots would be injured and the teeth would fall out); a bath or shower (body heat would dissipate); and nail-clipping or a haircut (both nails and hair would turn gray). My body had to be covered at all times and protected from moving air. A sponge bath of the private parts was allowed, but only with boiled water.

The requisite diet featured eggs poached with brown sugar, twice a day, and soup, taken to encourage breast milk. I produced far too much milk for tiny Qi-meng. Here again custom competed with common sense. Instead of pouring the extra down the sink, Xiao Zhao was taught to splash it against the wall — otherwise, my milk would stop flowing altogether.

I stewed in my own sweat for the entire month of torrid heat. The moment the *zou-yue-zhi* expired I rushed to the public bathhouse two days in a row before I felt clean again. It came as no surprise that my next stop was to visit a dentist for my decaying teeth.

When my four-week maternity leave came to an end, I applied for a month's extension with a 40 percent pay cut as allowed in many factories, but my request was denied. A bout of mastitis, however, kept me away from my desk for two more weeks.

Xiao Zhao and I had to find someone to care for Qi-meng, who was less than two months old when I had to go back to work. Great-Aunt had her hands full with Ye Xiang, and Xiao Zhao's stepmother, with no children of her own, was not interested in taking care of someone else's. The neighborhood nurseries didn't take children under one year. The only solution was to ask my neighbor, Granny Zhang, for help. A housewife all her life who looked after her retired husband, aged mother-in-law and two bachelor sons, Granny Zhang finally agreed to take care of Qi-meng while I was working, with my promise that I would come home every noonhour on my bike to breast-feed her.

43

N THE FALL OF 1981 China entered its third year of Deng Xiao-ping's new economic policy, "opening doors to the outside world and invigorating the domestic economy"; but the openness was certainly within a Chinese definition. In September, a month after I went back to work, the Political Division gathered together a handful of young people in the department. The chief read us a document from the "inner circle briefing" issued by the Public Security Bureau in Beijing. A female artist named Li Shuang, accused of having an illicit affair with a French diplomat, had been arrested. Her liaison was, literally, a crime, for relationships between Chinese and foreigners were tantamount to espionage. I was used to political study sessions designed to "strengthen our immune systems against the temptations of the West," but this was the first time I had heard of the government openly interfering in an interracial relationship. It was the old practice of killing a chicken to frighten the monkeys. Li Shuang was sentenced to two years in a labor camp. The message was clear.

In the eyes of my colleagues, young people like me (I was nearly thirty) were particularly susceptible to corruption from the West. Not being a Party member, I was seen as especially vulnerable. The fact that I had never applied to join the Party made me the number-one target for scrutiny and criticism.

One day as I stood in the canteen line, a female colleague boldly brushed her finger along my eyebrows. I was speechless with surprise. She carefully examined the fingertip, then smiled at me.

"Someone at the meeting the other day mentioned that you paint your eyebrows. I just wanted to make sure."

She offered no apology. The embarrassment pushed tears into my eyes and I left the canteen without eating. Probably she thought I should have thanked her for confirming my purity.

Weeks later when I was at the airport reception hall with a number of my colleagues, waiting for a big delegation, Lao Fu's wandering eyes fastened on me, then dropped to my feet.

"What is the width of your trouser cuffs?" he asked. "They seem wider than normal. Are you wearing bellbottom pants and aping Western fashion?"

Immediately people around began a search for a tape-measure. I walked out of the hall, furious at such stupidity. I recalled my days as a child on welfare when people could stop me at any time or any place to check on what I was wearing. Now an adult and a mother, with my own job and family, I still couldn't escape this kind of degradation.

In reality, this degree of control was only a fraction of what I had to confront later when I finally began to take up interpreting in 1982, after some new graduates were brought into the office. My supervisor, Lao Peng, was my mentor. An experienced English interpreter and veteran Communist, he taught me that interpreting was not, as many people believed, simply playing a role as a language-conversion machine. I must also act as a "guard" against any indiscreet remarks made by our officials, who, as I had noticed long before, sometimes grew talkative and loose-tongued under the influence of alcohol at dinner tables. There was no validity to the notion that an interpreter simply passed on what was said without responsibility for the content of the communication. Lao Peng also indicated that when dealing with foreigners, there was no such thing as a minor matter. Everything was important and should be reported.

I also learned the intricacies of making up a reception plan for visitors. The Ministry of Foreign Affairs and Intelligence Department would supply necessary information about the purpose of each visit, the political opinions and beliefs of the guests, and information on their personal tastes or interests. I had to match the guest with a Chinese official of equal status, according to protocol. Next, I would suggest an itinerary of places to visit, keeping in mind China's political agenda as well as the delegation's interests.

For example, people who were human-rights advocates were always taken to the Shanghai Municipal Prison to meet "happy" prisoners who were shown working on paintings or sculptures in clean, well-appointed rooms. Bedding was always crisp and neat in the cells; a large wok full of delicious, nourishing food was in evidence. The host would then explain how Chinese prisoners were rehabilitated in this humane way, the implication being that a country that treated its prisoners in such an enlightened manner did not have a human-rights problem. Many foreigners were fooled by this play-acting. Similar visits to "typical" communes, factories or residential areas were staged.

Another aspect of the reception plan was the level of security to be provided, and how to "disguise" the secret police as fellow interpreters, security guards or officials. Food restrictions and appropriate accommodation rounded out the plan, which was then vetted by the division leaders before being passed up the line for final approval.

Whenever a state delegation was visiting China, whether from an ally or from a nation designated as hostile, a special team from the propaganda division was set to writing a daily report after gathering information from and interrogating the interpreters. The questions the foreigners asked, the topics they seemed interested in, the people they met, the items they purchased — everything was reported by us and duly recorded. It soon became clear that the surveillance was directed at the interpreter as well and that, in a society that still tended to kill the messenger, an interpreter was a messenger. Additional surveillance on us was kept up by the old technique of pairing — assigning at least two interpreters to one task and requiring them to report on one another as they did on the visitors.

All this put cumulative pressure on me. It was like being condemned as a counter-revolutionary on the farm and constantly watched. I was profoundly disappointed, having waited for so long, that using my English in an important job as an interpreter did not bring the satisfaction I had hoped for. I had to be cautious with every "outsider," even those invited by the Chinese government. Filling up my reports with details of our guests' every move and snippets of overheard conversation filled me with self-loathing. But if I left anything out, I could be in deep trouble.

One day, for example, I was called to the office of the propaganda division where a sour-faced official handed me a piece of paper and invited me to read it aloud and give him my comments. His false politeness did not mask his intention. Warily I read the paper, a magazine article sent to our department by the Chinese embassy in Dublin. It had been written by a former prime minister of Ireland after he and his wife had visited Shanghai a few months earlier. I had been their interpreter. In his essay the Irishman wrote about Deng Xiao-ping's new economic policy in the countryside and described his visit to a commune family outside Shanghai. When the farmer talked about the crops he grew on his private plot (as compared to his work in the communal fields) he was particularly enthusiastic.

Why hadn't I reported this "pro–private farming" tendency exhibited by the peasant? the official wanted to know. That peasant obviously required "further education" and visitors shouldn't be allowed to visit that family, and probably not that commune, any more. I said I didn't remember anyone expressing those views, or my notes would have shown it. The Irishman must have made it up, or thought he sensed a preference for private farming in the peasants' eyes. How could I be responsible for a foreigner's interpretation of things unsaid? The grim-faced official was unconvinced.

It was only after a senior official from my department who was with me during the visit confirmed my claim that I was let off without criticism and without an adverse report in my dossier. But

I learned my lesson. From then on, I dutifully recorded every detail in my notebook. When I accompanied Imelda Marcos on a midnight shopping spree through the Friendship Store (the place had to stay open until she had made her purchases), I jotted down the items she purchased as she swept along the counters — dozens of bolts of silk, box upon box of arts and crafts, stacks of specially preserved whole pigs' legs. I also noted her annoyance that none of the shoes in the store fitted her.

44

THE AGONY OF REPORTING minuscule details didn't completely cancel out the satisfaction I felt at meeting and working on behalf of people from other countries, for, after thirty years of isolation from the rest of the world, all Chinese were intensely curious about foreigners. Most of the visitors I dealt with were dignitaries, but I found them very approachable and markedly different from Chinese officials, who tended to be stiff and to stand on their dignity. Whether the foreigners were members of royal families, state leaders, high-ranking politicians or ordinary working staff who accompanied them, the vast majority were amicable and unpretentious. One time the Queen of Jordan lost a contact lens as she was about to leave the hotel. She joined us as we searched the floor for the missing lens. On another occasion Princess Sophia of Monaco thanked a store clerk when she pointed out a run in the princess's nylons.

Colonel Qaddafi of Libya presented a different sort of problem. I had been looking forward to seeing a man I had heard so much about, described as a "madman" by Western countries but considered by China a great friend among the Arab nations. In the autumn of 1982 he received a red-carpet welcome when he visited Beijing. On his way back to Libya a grand banquet was held in his honor in Shanghai, hosted by the mayor. When I arrived at the banquet hall I learned that Qaddafi had refused to attend: he had been unsatisfied with the talks in Beijing. His refusal was an unprecedented case of broken protocol. I was stationed by a phone linked directly to his hotel and reported on the progress of the transactions as various people tried to talk him out of his pique. They failed, and his place was taken by his deputy. Qaddafi cut short his visit and left the next day. At the airport, all I saw of him was the swirl of his black robe as he boarded the plane.

Almost every spring an American delegation made up of senators, congressmen and congresswomen would come to China when Congress was in recess. They always arrived on their own plane and brought their own snacks and drinks, including water to brush their teeth. I recall Senator Robert Dole coming one year, a clear-voiced and very friendly man. When my colleagues and I were invited to the delegation's reception suite for "a drink" he offered me a piece of cake. I couldn't believe my eyes. The cake had cream topping and it sat inside a tin. How was it made? I wondered. Was the topping added before the cake was sealed in or after the tin was opened?

The mayor of New York, Ed Koch, was a colorful man. One day when he was walking through the narrow streets of the old section of Shanghai, surrounded by a contingent of security guards and reporters, he spotted a street-cleaner operating a three-wheeled motorized sweeper. Koch broke away from his entourage and persuaded the man to let him drive the sweeper. Over the protests of his aide, who tried to convince him that New York garbage was much heavier than Shanghai garbage, Koch, through his Chinese host, ordered two dozen of the sweepers, to be shipped to New York. My colleagues and I spent hours on the phone trying to push the deal through. I never found out if the little Shanghai sweepers turned up in the Big Apple.

President Reagan's visit to Shanghai in the spring of 1984 was a big event, but what I remember most is the reason I spent so much time with Mrs. Schultz, wife of the secretary of state. An official from the American Consulate in Shanghai had warned us to schedule Mrs. Reagan and Mrs. Schultz in different places at different times, as they didn't get along. I found Mrs. Schultz a kind and friendly woman as I walked with her in the garden of the Shanghai Music Academy and attended concerts with her. I later understood what the American official had meant when, in a casual debriefing, the interpreter for the First Lady complained about Mrs. Reagan's imperious manner. She always made sure to be in front of a camera and was sometimes rude to the interpreter.

In the spring of 1983 I was assigned to arrange a visit by David Lange, head of New Zealand's Labour Party. In my reception plan I had written that Lange would in all likelihood be elected as the next prime minister, so he should be assigned a high-ranking Chinese official to accompany him, as protocol demanded. When my plan was returned I was informed that my prediction was not valid as it was based only on polls and shouldn't be taken seriously. I, not a government official, was going to be Lange's guide.

I learned a great deal from Lange: how the political system worked in his and other democratic countries and his views on international affairs. He was a big man and full of humor. He told me once that, if he hadn't had an operation to remove fat from his belly, he would have needed the whole back seat of the sedan for himself.

(Lange became prime minister of New Zealand in 1984. When he returned to Shanghai on his state visit in the fall of the same year, he asked for me. I was by then studying at the Foreign Affairs College in Beijing and although I could easily have met him when he went there, he was told that I was unavailable — by the same official who had informed me that the polls predicting Lange's election were not valid.)

Lange's three-day visit had a deep and lasting effect on my life. I started to shift my interest from English literature to political systems, and to the history, economy and culture of the countries that sent visitors to China. I realized how inadequate my interpretation was without this kind of knowledge, and it was one of the reasons I decided to apply for a two-year postgraduate program of international studies at the Foreign Affairs College.

There were other reasons too. One of them was unpleasant and humiliating sexual harassment from my supervisor, Lao Peng. When I began the job I had been warned by a female colleague that Lao Peng might come after me. I was young and, according to her, attractive. When we were alone in the office he would touch my arms or shoulders in what I thought was a friendly way, but he made no further advances.

I admired Lao Peng's abilities and experience and appreciated the way he helped me. Once, when I was still new at interpreting and protocol, he and I worked with reporters who were part of the delegation of the president of Pakistan. One evening we had to accompany them to the telegraph office on the Bund, the only place from which foreign journalists could send telexes. The reporters were drunk and became rude and abusive. I tried to keep calm, worried that in defending myself I would make them angrier and cause an incident, but their attacks became sexual and they eventually cornered me. Luckily, Lao Peng walked into the room at that moment. He shoved the reporters away from me, took me to a car and sent me back to the hotel. At a meeting the next day, he suggested that female interpreters not be assigned to work late hours with male foreigners, and from then on my evening assignments were mainly with women visitors.

During that autumn British prime minister Margaret Thatcher visited Shanghai, and I was chosen to read the English translation of the mayor's speech at the banquet because those in my office thought my English had a "British sound." Lao Peng was kind enough to spend time coaching me so that I would read the speech fluently and without error.

But the following May my illusions about my mentor were broken when, finding himself alone with me in the office suite of the Jin Jiang Hotel, he grabbed me and kissed me. As I struggled to get free, he forced his tongue into my mouth. Finally I broke away and ran from the room, my mind in a whirl. What had I done, I wondered, to encourage that kind of behavior? I was afraid to face him, but when I saw him again only half an hour later he acted as if nothing had happened. I had been a fighter all my life, but when it came to this issue I was a chicken. He was a powerful and highly respected man in the department and I did not have the courage to confront him.

If I had not admired him, if he had not helped me so much, it would have been easy for me to hate him. But I didn't; I was just afraid to be with him. In my reception plans I made sure that, in suggesting the official who would be responsible for my assignment, I avoided him. But he was the deputy division chief and he would often change my suggestion and put down his own name.

In the fall of 1983 Lao Peng was invited to lecture for three months at the newly opened tourist college in Shanghai. I welcomed a lengthy respite, but while he was away I received an envelope addressed to me at the office in his handwriting. Inside there was no letter, just a few typewritten pages. I began to read, then threw them down with disgust. The pages described several detailed sex scenes. Shaking violently, I tore the pages to bits so no one would ever see them. Years later I learned they were copied from *Lady Chatterley's Lover*.

Lao Peng dropped into the office the day after and talked to me in a matter-of-fact way as if nothing had occurred. I felt cheap and ashamed. I knew I couldn't tell anyone about his harassment, for there was no defence from the wrath of a powerful official. But I could try to leave the office if an opportunity arose.

In addition to being afraid of Lao Peng and heartily sick of the pressure of surveillance, I was worn out from the demands of my job. I was constantly on call, often working seven days a week, sometimes ten or twelve hours a day. Sometimes I would wave goodbye to one group at the train station then rush straight to the airport to greet another one. The wear and tear on my nerves and concentration was immense. Once I spent a long afternoon at the Shanghai Research Institute of International Relations interpreting for an American delegation. The main topic of conversation was the Watergate incident. After that I went directly to meet Robert McFarlane and his wife. As he was said to be involved in the scandal, I was instructed by my boss not to mention Watergate at all. It was difficult sometimes to keep things straight.

I was also under increasing pressure to join the Party. To say that I hated the Party that had destroyed my family and ruined my youth would be a great understatement. But to be promoted and trusted in any organization, Party membership was required. A person had to apply for membership (less than 5 percent of the population were Party members) and normally had to go through a long vetting process, sometimes for years, that did not exclude currying favor with Party-member colleagues who could help the application. Many bought gifts and did favors for Party members and became obsequious in their presence. Party membership was supposed to be a privilege and an honor, and propaganda always reminded us that a member was automatically a loyal, trustworthy and honest person. My life had proven this was far from true.

During my tenure in Shanghai, a number of opportunities arose to study in foreign countries. I would have loved to be chosen, but only Party members were eligible. I would always remain a junior and not completely trusted member of the staff as long as I refused to apply for membership. Still, I couldn't bring myself to do so, not even when Number 1 joined as part of his promotion to economic development manager of Daishan Island, where he had agreed to live in order to be reunited with his wife and son after eleven years. He was made an "instant member" when he was promoted.

While I was debating the idea of applying to study in Beijing I was held back by the fact that I would not be able to take Qi-meng with me, because students were required to live in dorms shared by three or four women. I felt guilty even thinking about leaving her for two years. But what made up my mind was my husband.

Xiao Zhao told me one night at dinner that he had been accepted by the Party. I was speechless. He hadn't even told me he had applied. After all the long talks we had had about our suffering on the farm, the attacks on his parents during the Cultural Revolution, the humiliation of my parents and family, he had gone and joined the Communist Party. Xiao Zhao tried to mollify me, saying that he needed the membership to get a better job, but after that night we never spoke of it again. For the first time since I had been married I felt lost, betrayed by the person I had loved and trusted with my life.

My decision to apply to go to Beijing shocked everybody.

"Ah Si," wrote Number 1, "drinking more bottles of ink won't help you improve your position. You are sitting on a chair which many people would die to occupy. What you need now is political advancement." His own education, for which he had fought so hard, had little to do with his present job.

Great-Aunt responded as I expected.

Number 5 had married the previous year. She and her husband Xiao Yao had met on the farm, and after their wedding he joined her in Purple Sunshine Lane. I now had no worries about leaving Great-Aunt, but when I told her my plans she groaned, "Why are you so unsatisfied, Ah Si? Why can't you settle down like everyone else in the family? They don't have even half of what you've gained. Make me understand. At least try to."

When my explanations, which did not include my experience with Lao Peng or my disaffection with my husband, failed to move her, she resorted to her usual trick.

"I can accept why you would leave me, a useless old woman, but what about your poor little daughter?"

The Foreign Affairs College described itself as the cradle of Chinese diplomats. It was run jointly by the Ministries of Education and Foreign Affairs. The two-year program to begin in September was open to English interpreters across the country, from those at the foreign affairs departments at city and provincial levels to those from the ministry itself. A wide range of courses was provided: world history, world economy, political economy, English literature, and simultaneous interpreting.

In July, when Qi-meng was three, my application was accepted. I would receive my salary while at the college but only if I signed a contract guaranteeing that I would continue to work for my department following the completion of my studies. On my own initiative I arranged to have one quarter of my pay sent to me each month and the rest to Xiao Zhao.

Granny Zhang, our neighbor, who had looked after Qi-meng during the day, could not keep her for twenty-four hours. Her husband suffered from heart disease and her mother-in-law required care. Although Xiao Zhao was then working on regular day shift, he felt he couldn't care for Qi-meng by himself, reflecting the standard Chinese attitude that children's care was the province of women. Usually a child's grandparents could be enlisted, but Xiao Zhao's parents were still not interested in taking care of my daughter. Hai Rui was not an option for me, regardless of his openly expressed delight that I would be leaving and even though he kept coming to our apartment every day after work to eat with us. He had assured me that he would take good care of Qi-meng, probably better than me, for I wasn't always around when needed. He continued to do Xiao Zhao's and Qi-meng's laundry on occasion; often he cooked supper — an arrangement I continued to dislike but could do nothing about because Xiao Zhao found it convenient and would not discuss it. I knew that Hai Rui saw my leaving for Beijing as paving the way for a more permanent presence in my family and I was determined to oppose him.

So I looked around for a boarding kindergarten. Once again, the prestige of my work unit helped. I was able to enroll Qi-meng in a school run by the navy. Most of the teachers were family members of the servicemen. Xiao Zhao and I took her there a week before I left so she could become used to the place. We played with her in the courtyard and, when it was time to go, rushed out of the gate. The loud cry flying over the wall haunted me the rest of the week until I picked her up on the weekend. When I looked for her on Monday morning to take her back, I found her hiding under Granny Zhang's bed.

I missed my lovely daughter already, even before I left. If Xiao Zhao had said he would be lonely without me and had asked me to change my mind, I would have done so. But it didn't happen, and I was not surprised. Although everyone thought my going to Foreign Affairs College was a career move, I wanted to be away from Xiao Zhao, at least for a while, and I hoped that my absence would rekindle the love I had held for him. I had entered marriage thinking that living together and having a child would bring us even closer, but slowly the opposite had happened. I found myself keeping thoughts inside instead of sharing them with him; holding back the expression of opinions instead of stating them freely — especially on political matters. We never seemed to laugh any more. We were no longer partners. If I couldn't share pent-up feelings with my own husband, who else could I turn to? A deep fear had grown within me, a dread of loneliness.

I recalled a conversation we had had early in our marriage when I had complimented Xiao Zhao for being an obedient and filial son, so strong was his sense of duty to his father and stepmother.

"It's true, Ah Si," he had replied, "on my care-list, you are third, after Father and Stepmother."

Stung by his confession, for I had never imagined that he felt this way, I retorted, "Well, it's a good thing my parents are dead, otherwise you'd be third for me as well!"

Where on his care-list would I find my name now? I wondered as I packed for my trip.

With many conflicting thoughts in my mind, I boarded the train to return to the city I had left with relief six years before.

45

BEIJING HADN'T CHANGED much in the past six years. The Foreign Affairs College, an exclusive institution for training China's diplomats, was located in the west of the city, near the zoo. One four-story structure housed dorms, lecture halls, language labs, classrooms and offices while the surrounding buildings of red brick were mainly residences for teachers and their families, including foreign teachers on short-term contract. The campus was enclosed by a wall, with a main gate and porter. With fewer than two hundred students, the college had begun to offer courses to outside groups like mine to earn extra revenue.

There were about forty students in my program, half from the ministry, the remainder from its departments at city and provincial levels. Most of us were married, with children back home; all were required to live on campus. I was allocated a small dormitory room shared with two other women.

The first order of business was to divide the group according to ability. Two American women teachers, Miss Potucek and Miss

Jones, gave us an oral and a written exam. I was assigned to Class One, the advanced group, comprised mainly of ministry people. From the day the classes were divided, the ministry bunch looked down on the others, who in turn swore revenge, muttering that when the ministry people came into their jurisdictions in the future, they would give them a hard time. I and three other "outsiders" who had been put in Class One were squeezed between the two factions. What a way to start a new school!

Although we were all adults, our class was organized and controlled according to the regular policy. We had a Party secretary and a monitor chosen by the college to lead us and liaise with the school authorities.

In spite of the regulations about residence during the week, the Beijing students went home whenever they could. Since I was staying with two of them I had my dorm to myself most of the time. After six years of hectic running around, I enjoyed the relative peace and quiet of college life, especially on weekends. I missed Qimeng terribly, but was shocked to find I didn't miss Xiao Zhao at all.

My two American teachers had taught in other countries before coming to China. At our political study meeting we learned that they were missionaries. We were warned to guard against them and to report any attempt to proselytize. Here was another irony. All my life I had been taught that missionaries had served imperialist foreign governments in the first wave of cultural invasion, yet the college had taken Potucek and Jones on because it did not have to pay them. The missionary society handled their salaries and expenses.

Both women were in their thirties. Jones was always well groomed, with carefully applied makeup. Potucek looked the opposite, plain and unadorned, her hair cut short like a man's. They were in charge of our oral English classes and organized interesting but not necessarily realistic lessons for us, simulating shopping in an American supermarket and working in an American-style kitchen set up temporarily in the classroom. At that time China did not have supermarkets such as they described, and most households shared a kitchen with other families, cooking on coal stoves. Nevertheless I enjoyed their classes, which opened a window for me to glimpse the daily life of an American family, along with social and cultural concepts. They made no attempt to bring religious propaganda to class.

Everything went smoothly until one week before Christmas, when they invited all of us to a party in our classroom. They taught us to sing Christmas songs and play games. Before we left, each of us received a present, along with an explanation that the American custom was to open a present right away, not take it home and open it privately, as a Chinese person would do. I found myself holding a brand-new New Testament, about the same size as Chairman Mao's famous Red Book. When I looked around, I saw that all of us had been given identical gifts. As far as I knew, the Bible topped the list of forbidden books, and customs agents and the post office were always on the lookout for them. Trouble was sure to follow.

Class Party Secretary Yang announced the end of the Christmas gathering. A few hours later he called a meeting in the same place and was joined by the vice-president of the college, Jiang. We were asked to bring along the Bibles and hand them over. A few of us, including some Party members, arrived and reported that they had misplaced their Christmas presents. I was one of these careless people. I didn't have any strong feelings about the Bible, nor was I an advocate of freedom of religion. My defiance was purely toward the college's attitude that it could tyrannize us, and toward the contradiction of an institution of higher learning showing fear of words that might undermine their power.

Despite the Bible episode, I enjoyed my classes, and the semester passed quickly. I returned to Shanghai for the winter break, excited by the prospect of seeing my daughter and spending as much time with her as I could in the next two weeks. When Xiao Zhao met me at the train station, it became clear to me that I had not really missed him since September, and the hope that my feeling for him would be refreshed was unfulfilled. I was not surprised to learn that Hai Rui had been with him every day, washing and cleaning and making sure Xiao Zhao's supper was ready for him when he got home from work. What did surprise me was that knowing this did not bother me as much as I would have thought. It seemed clear to me now that my love for Xiao Zhao had slipped away, and with it my dream of an intimacy of spirit.

I visited Great-Aunt and my two sisters, glad to find that Number 5 seemed content with her new husband and Great-Aunt was in good health. When I got back to Beijing, Rainbow met me at the train station, just as in the old days.

Rainbow was married now, but had no child yet. She had left the tourist bureau a few years earlier for a better job at the Population Census Bureau of the State Council. She told me the bureau had some documents in English from United Nations conferences on world population that needed to be translated into Chinese. Would I be interested in my spare time? The pay would be generous.

I accepted and was thrilled to discover how right she was: seven hours of burning the midnight oil producing two thousand Chinese characters earned me almost a month's salary. The documents kept coming and I was like a fully wound spring, churning out translations. But my moonlighting was soon raised at the meeting of Party members. In a "heart-to-heart" talk with Party member Xiao Yin — which meant her butting into my business — I was told that since I was receiving my salary while attending school, I was allowed to do only school work. I should spend my free time helping classmates who had fallen behind or reading Marx and Lenin and improving my understanding of communism. I knew this so-called advice was a coverup for "red eye disease," the jealousy of my classmates of my proficiency in English, and the consequent opportunity to earn extra money. Xiao Yin also offered me her unsolicited counsel that being at the college offered a great chance to apply for Party membership. The few others in my class who were not members had already started the process.

Her efforts succeeded in one respect: I changed my moonlighting schedule. Sometimes I worked at Rainbow's house, sometimes in the dorm behind my locked door when my roommates had gone home. This subterfuge reminded me of my days at Bei Da when I had been forced to hide my politically incorrect studies.

The new semester also brought us a new teacher, for Jones had not had her contract renewed. I never learned why. Her replacement was an Englishman named O'Neill, a bookish and pleasant young man with his narrow face half covered by a large beard. His bashful smile came easily and his classes were fun and challenging, as we were often involved in serious discussions based on the British newspaper he brought to class.

The only problem was, he smelled. His body odor was so strong that we often opened the classroom windows before he arrived and left the door open to create a cross-breeze even on cold winter days. But as soon as he entered the room, he would take off his coat, close the door and shut the windows, trapping us again.

The class monitor called a special meeting. We didn't know whether O'Neill smelled because he didn't regularly wash his clothing, or himself, or either. We did know that the foreign teachers' apartments were equipped with running water.

"Why don't you guys have a 'heart-to-heart' talk with him?" I joked. "Or take him to the public bathhouse?" Nobody laughed.

During the ensuing discussion, which I found highly amusing, we decided that the only face- (and nose-) saving solution was to take turns sitting at the front. Whether O'Neill found it curious that each day different faces looked up at him I don't know. He never said anything, but he remained friendly and helpful — and smelly. At the end of that year he returned to England to finish his PhD.

With all of my time occupied by studies and moonlighting, the school year quickly came to an end. Before I left that summer, I learned that the Foreign Affairs Office of the Chinese People's Congress needed a female interpreter for an Australian parliamentary delegation visiting Beijing, Shenyang, Xi'an, Shanghai and Guangzhou. If I agreed to help out, I could leave the tour at Shanghai and my travel home would be paid for.

Throughout the trip everyone, politicians, their spouses and members of their entourage, treated me warmly and as an equal. This touched me deeply. On the evening after we flew to Shanghai, the Australians wanted to visit the Peace Hotel because they had heard about an old jazz band that performed there. While listening to the music, the senator from Queensland, Mr. Sheil, invited me to dance with him. I did. Back at the Jin Jiang Hotel, Lao Fu roundly criticized me, pointing out sarcastically that dancing with a foreigner was not part of my job description. I should have declined Sheil's invitation firmly, he said.

On the day of their departure, the Australians gave me a shopping bag that contained a woolen coat and a blouse for my daughter. I appreciated their gift, but told them I was not allowed to accept personal presents. I bade them goodbye and left their suite. Not long afterwards, I got a phone call from Mrs. Sheil, asking me to meet her downstairs as she would like to do some last-minute shopping. In the store she pressed a parcel wrapped in plain brown paper upon me.

"We all want your daughter to have this, Miss Ye," she said. "Please accept it. No one will know. Take it as a gift from the stubborn Australians!"

Outside, Mrs. Sheil laughed all the way back to our car, as if she had just accomplished a secret spy mission.

That night I hugged and kissed my daughter, then triumphantly presented Xiao Zhao with a thick bundle of ¥10 bills; I had accumulated the equivalent of a year's salary. It was my way of making up for being away from home, unable to take care of Qi-meng. It was money I had earned independently.

After six years of marriage I still had no bank account of my own. More than once I had suggested to Xiao Zhao that he open a joint account, but he had never done so. He kept full control of our finances and I never knew how much money we had saved. But I had decided that, by the time I finished at the college, I would have paid back what I felt I owed to him and his family. Then I would open my own account.

I was glad to be home again and tried to get along with Xiao Zhao. I had let the matter of his Party membership fade; there was no other choice. That month was the happiest in my life because I spent every day with Qi-meng, taking her to see Great-Aunt, walking in the park and just being together. Qi-meng was a beautiful girl and, as I watched her play with other children, I wished she could have a sibling so she would not miss me so much when I was away.

My wish was answered in a cruel way. When my period didn't come at the end of August I began to worry. At the neighborhood clinic, my fears were confirmed. I was pregnant. The doctor informed me that I should have an abortion immediately and left me alone, sitting on a long wooden bench.

It was an old story, known in every household. Poor-quality condoms had by then caused every woman in Xiao Zhao's and my family to have at least one abortion. Some women were urged to have their tubes tied as soon as their first child was born, with a bonus of one extra week's paid leave. Most refused, fearing that, if something happened to their only child, they could never have another. Some also hoped that the government might change its policy after a few years. But it was obligatory to have an IUD put in if a woman became pregnant a second time. Ever since Number 3 had got hers, she told me, her periods had become a monthly nightmare, with horrible pain and heavy blood flow.

I was distraught. I wished I could keep my baby, but I knew the consequences too well. The immediate result would be the loss of my job and the end of my studies. Xiao Zhao would suffer too. He would likely be kicked out of the Party and would never receive a promotion for the rest of his life. But the real victims would be Qi-meng and the new baby. Qi-meng would be a second-class citizen, denied good schools, branded as a child of an "illegal family" and forced to the back of lineups for everything from schools to medical treatments. My second child would have the life of an outcast — no *hu-kou*, no ration coupons, no medical care, possibly no schooling, and certainly no access to higher education.

I had many sleepless nights. Despite my clear knowledge of reality, I couldn't bear the thought of having an abortion. Xiao Zhao was a great comfort to me, staying awake with me and talking it through. Such compassion was not typical, but I knew he blamed himself for my misery. I was glad that Qi-meng was back at boarding school. I couldn't have faced her, knowing I was about to destroy her little brother or sister.

Finally Xiao Zhao and I went to the same hospital where Qi-meng had been born. I was astonished to see the long lineup to register for an abortion. Most in the line were couples; all looked somber. The waiting room was unusually quiet. When my turn came, I was told that I had to wait a week. On the way out I overheard a young woman tell her husband the date and time of her procedure: the same day as me, fifteen minutes later. I was numb with disbelief. How many abortions did this hospital perform, I wondered, each day and each year? I covered my mouth with my hand to hide my crying, and Xiao Zhao attempted unsuccessfully to comfort me as we left the hospital.

I tried to be reasonable and calm in the following days, but the reality made me miserable. I had no appetite because, in a strange way, I felt that eating well would give my baby false hopes. As a kid I recalled being told by a neighbor that prisoners condemned to death were treated nicely the night before the execution, given a good meal and even some wine, for our tradition said that a hungry ghost would never achieve final rest. What would happen to the ghost of my new baby?

After a week of sleeplessness and inability to eat, I went to the hospital and was shown into a waiting room with six beds occupied by nervous women in blue gowns. One after another we were called into the operating room. When my turn came I saw a surgical table in the middle of the room surrounded by half a dozen people chatting as if they were at a picnic. I did not know what the procedure entailed and was not told. Sick with fright, I climbed up onto the table as ordered and they began.

When it was over, I was sent back to the waiting room for a half-hour rest, feeling hollow and depressed. As I was signing out, the nurse said to me, "There will be no trips back here for you. Everything has been taken care of."

Only then did I realize the IUD had been inserted. My consent was neither asked for nor required. The IUD would cause me the same problems as it had Number 3. The kind used in China had no string attached and so could not be removed except through surgery. They were meant to be permanent.

It seemed even my body was subject to state policy.

46

WHEN I RETURNED TO the college a week late, I kept the reason to myself, making up a story about stomach problems. My two roommates noticed my unusual quietness and may have guessed my problem, for they tried to console me. I hoped that my wounds would heal with time.

Xiao Wang, my desk-mate from Beijing, tried to cheer me up. "At least our new teacher, Bill, doesn't smell like O'Neill did!"

I laughed for the first time since I had lost my baby. She went on to say that the students enjoyed this Canadian teacher's class, which was different from the Americans' or O'Neill's.

Bill, as he liked to be called, was a thin, dark, youthful man with a ready wit. From the very beginning, when I introduced myself and explained (untruthfully) why I was late in arriving, I liked the way he conducted his lessons. Instead of sitting down and starting the business of grammar and reading right away, as the other foreign teachers did, he opened the lesson with a ten-minute discussion, beginning, "What's new?" On my first day back I was surprised to see how everyone, including those usually silent, was eager to join the discussion. Apparently Bill had set up a procedure whereby each day someone was "on the spot" to bring up a topic — from the newspaper or from personal life. Then the class would join in. It was good practice for oral English, and it lifted the seriousness of the classroom. I could see how relaxed everyone was; even some ordinarily stiff Party members didn't want to be left out. Bill had a keen sense of humor and seemed to enjoy every minute of the class.

But one day, shortly after I rejoined my classmates, a Beijing student, Xiao Chi, went too far. When Bill asked, "What's new?" Chi told a horrible story that was going around his neighborhood. A restaurant owner had been arrested for killing young girls from outside Beijing who had come to the capital to seek under-the-table work. The grisly murderer had disposed of their bodies by chopping them up and using them to fill the dumplings he sold in his establishment.

Immediately a pall fell over the class. Bill looked stunned. But he was not as shocked as we. The report was bad enough, but telling it to a foreigner was worse. China regarded murder as something that should be kept secret because it would cause the Chinese, who boasted one of the oldest civilizations on earth, to lose face. One of our proverbs says that domestic shame should never be known outside the family. In those days hardly any murder cases were reported in the newspaper, especially one as gruesome as this. It wasn't hard to predict that we would be called for a meeting as soon as the class ended and Bill left the room.

After he had made a self-criticism in front of the class, Chi was sternly rebuked by the department head as well as his fellow students for his lack of vigilance and for failing to "distinguish between us and them." We should always remember that foreigners were to be distrusted and never, ever taken into one's confidence. And that was not the end of it. Department Head Feng warned us that Bill was, as reported in his dossier, known for his casual style of teaching that put his students at ease and encouraged them to talk. This information had been noted when he had taught at the Harbin University of Science and Technology a few years before. Feng made it sound as if, in allowing his students to use English in real-life conversations, Bill was doing espionage work.

When the general meeting was over, the Party members stayed behind for another one, since Chi was a Party member. I was exasperated by all of this. The skill of drawing students close to him would have been a good quality if Bill were Chinese but, because he was not, he was suspected of ulterior motives. Despite all these warnings, the Canadian remained popular with his students.

Throughout the autumn I worked hard at my studies, with great enjoyment. Immediately after the New Year of 1986, Rainbow left for the Soviet Union to attend a short-term program on population census, sponsored by the United Nations. She would be away for six months. Before leaving she arranged for me to replace her as English tutor for the employees of her bureau, adding that, with her gone, I would lock myself up inside the college all the time if I had no other interests.

In the past months I had found great comfort in talking to Rainbow whenever I had the chance to go to her apartment. Although it had been ten years since the end of the Cultural Revolution I still didn't feel comfortable expressing my opinions or sharing my thoughts with my classmates. With Rainbow gone, I had no one to talk to. Gradually I found it was easier for me to put things down in my journal. Bill had given us an assignment that required us to write a certain number of journal entries each week, then he would collect our journals, read them and make written corrections and suggestions. I found myself writing more and more, telling about myself, looking forward to the return of my assignment. I felt I could trust him and that my thoughts would be safe with him. Each time my journal was returned I read his comments eagerly, then tore up the pages so no one else would see them.

I found that my teacher was a good listener, with understanding but without doctrine. He never asked intrusive or political questions as most foreigners did. On one occasion he indicated that I could go to his office to have a chat and practice my spoken English as other students did, but I was reluctant. I didn't want to be seen alone with him. He was a married man and I was a married woman, and even to be accused of impropriety would be devastating. The case of Li Shuang had not been forgotten.

One spring day, Bill asked me to stay behind for a moment after class to talk about my assignment. It turned out that he wanted to ask me privately if I would be interested in tutoring English to the daughter of a family friend, a woman from Hong Kong named Eleanor who occasionally had business dealings in China. She and her daughter lived in a compound near the college. The girl was thirteen, attending middle school, and her mother wanted her to have extra English lessons a couple of times a week.

"You can think about it and let me know," he suggested. "You're welcome to come to our apartment tonight to meet them."

I had already met Bill's wife and would see her from time to time on campus. I knew his three children well because they came to the weekly college video shows. When I met Eleanor and her daughter Rowena I liked them immediately and committed to the English lessons.

Thus my days were full. I was either buried in my school books or teaching in Rainbow's bureau or tutoring Rowena. I came and went on Rainbow's bicycle and told no one my whereabouts. I made sure that I didn't miss any classes, assignments or political study meetings, even if I sometimes had to miss my supper. But doubts and questions were written on certain faces, especially those of the Party officials. They wanted to know my every move off campus. The only one who shared my secret was my teacher, Bill, and I didn't hide from him my pleasure at keeping the busybodies and nosy colleagues in the dark.

I started to visit him in his office, despite my misgivings about doing so, when I ran into problems with Rowena's lessons. I always left the door ajar and spoke to him in a voice higher than my normal volume so that others could hear me. Bill sat in his chair and listened attentively, seldom giving his personal advice, but letting me find a solution by talking the problem out.

I found myself going to see him more and more and beginning to talk about different things, from my tutoring to my readings in English literature and sometimes about college and classroom politics. Only then did I come to realize what a talker I was, and I was amazed that I had so many things to tell an outsider. His frankness and intelligence were refreshing and helped me to express myself both more and better. We became good friends.

But one night in May, when I was alone in my room, I realized that I was very attracted to Bill. The sudden revelation terrified me. I was a wife and mother.

From then on I tried to avoid Bill, even eye contact in class. At night I awoke crying from nightmares in which I was sent back to the prison farm and Qi-meng was taken away from me forever. So when I received a letter from Xiao Zhao saying that he was thinking of a five-day trip to Beijing, using his accumulated overtime, I replied by telegram, urging him to come as soon as possible.

My husband and daughter arrived two weeks later. And Hai Rui was with them.

I met them at the train station and held my daughter in the taxi all the way to the campus, still haunted by my nightmares. My roommates had offered us the use of the dorm so that Xiao Zhao and Qi-meng wouldn't have to stay in the rooms the college held for visitors. I had also spoken with all my teachers, including Bill, asking permission to miss classes for a few days.

Throughout the week I was tortured by guilt and shame. My family and I spent each day visiting Beijing's many attractions, always with Hai Rui tagging along. At night I held Qi-meng in my arms until both of us fell asleep, then Xiao Zhao would awaken me to move over to his bed. After he fell asleep, I would return to Qi-meng for the rest of the night.

After my family and Hai Rui left for Shanghai, I continued to avoid Bill. School was coming to an end; I would graduate in a month or so. I decided to quit my two teaching jobs at the end of June so that I could concentrate on my exams. But it was hard to avoid him; I saw him every day in class, or talking with students in the hallway, and it took all my self-discipline to keep myself from speaking to him.

Then one day two of my classmates asked me a favor. Bill's two eldest children were returning to Canada early and he had asked if one of my two classmates could come with him to the airport to interpret for him in case there were any problems. By then it was well known that Bill was not getting along with the Foreign Affairs Office of the college and, being Party members, Hu and Chi did not want to be seen to help him. They asked me if I would go instead. I agreed. I told myself I felt indebted to him because he had got me the job teaching Rowena. The truth was, I wanted to be with him, even for a short time.

Days later he asked me to meet him in his office after supper. I almost refused, but said I would if I had time. When I arrived, we made small talk for a few moments, then Bill smiled and said, "Happy Birthday, Leaf," placing a gift on the coffee table between us.

He had called me Leaf after the first day, when I explained the meaning of my surname in English.

"In the West it's the custom to give a birthday present to someone you care about," he added. "And you have to open it now — that's a custom, too."

It was a novel, *Sons and Lovers* by D.H. Lawrence, one of Bill's favorite writers.

No one had ever given me a birthday present; it was not our tradition. Bill knew I loved to read and was well aware of how hard it was to get novels like this in China. I was very moved by his thoughtfulness and thanked him by shaking his hand.

"Come on," he said. "We're friends, Leaf." And he gave me a hug.

My heart was pounding, even though I knew no one could see us. But it felt so good being close to him.

We sat and talked for a long time. I asked him if he missed his two kids and he said that he did. All of us knew he loved his children very much. When I remarked that now, however, he and his wife would have more time to go places together, his face clouded.

"No, I don't think so," he murmured sadly. "We . . . don't get along very well any more. We've slept in separate rooms for a couple of years now."

I was surprised that he was telling me such an intimate thing, a proud man like him, and I didn't know how to respond.

"Anyway, let's not ruin your birthday party!" he said with false cheer. "How about more tea?"

After a while, I left his office, having agreed to go downtown with him the next day to help him purchase a carpet to send home to his parents.

We met at the bus stop because it might mean trouble for me if we were seen leaving the campus together. We went to Liu Li Chang, a famous shopping area south of Tian An Men Square. It was an oppressively hot day, and after Bill had bought a carpet we strolled around, making silly jokes about the oddly dressed tourists.

In the taxi, Bill suggested we go to the Beijing Hotel to get a cold drink.

"There is something I need to tell you," he said nervously.

The air-conditioned bar in the lobby was like an oasis after the sweltering heat of the streets. It was half empty and we found a table at the back. Bill bought a beer for himself and an orange drink for me and we attacked our drinks in silence. In the carpet store, where Bill had to arrange to have the carpet shipped to Toronto, I had been back in my element, dealing with clerks and red tape the way I so often had in Shanghai on behalf of visitors. But in the bar, sitting face to face with him, I was suddenly out of words.

"Leaf, I want to tell you something," he murmured. "I've been struggling with a decision for weeks, wondering whether to say anything. But since you're going home in a few days and I won't see you again, I decided I have to say it. I'm in love with you."

His words were like thunder in my ears. I stared at the table top. I was recalling my nightmares, and was acutely conscious that I was in a public place with a foreigner.

"I hope you won't think badly of me," Bill went on, turning his empty glass round and round on the table top.

"I love you too, Bill," I whispered. "But it's wrong, it's so wrong."

I looked up at him. His face betrayed surprise: he had not realized my feelings for him.

"Listen," he said quietly after a few moments, "there is nothing wrong with loving someone. We didn't chase or seduce each other. We fell in love without meaning to. I didn't realize . . . maybe I shouldn't have said anything."

We were silent a long time, then he suggested, "Let's have dinner here. Our first and last meal together."

We ate in the hotel dining room. My thoughts spun around and I could hardly taste the food. On the bus back to the campus, Bill stood beside me. We didn't speak. When we neared the college we alighted at different stops and entered by different gates.

47

ALONE IN MY DORM that night, the scene in the hotel kept running through my mind like replaying a videotape. It was the kind of love I had read about, but had not thought was real, not in my life anyway. There had been no kiss, no physical expression of any kind. Because it had happened at the wrong time and in the wrong place, our love could never come true. And it was twice forbidden — a love between two married people, and between a Chinese and a foreigner. But I was glad that we had opened our hearts to each other. There would be no regret for the rest of my life, even though I would never see him again.

My mind was a sea of confusion as I tried to prepare for my exams. I didn't see much of Bill. Something my friend Xiao Wang had said to me a few weeks before kept coming to mind. She had told me she sensed Bill was attracted to me and she quoted the familiar proverb: *yi-shi-zu-cheng-qing-gu-hen* — One slip may cause lasting sorrow.

"You are not so stupid as to make such an error at the expense of your career, your family and your daughter. You two live in totally different worlds."

"Don't be ridiculous, Xiao Wang," I had scoffed. "You and your imagination."

Her comment had been based on nothing but her intuition, but the proverb was apt. Even though Bill and I had so much in common, we were supposed to treat each other as aliens, were not allowed to think the same and feel the same. I had to face reality. And I had to be careful. If she had noticed something, maybe others had too.

I arranged to leave for Shanghai as soon as I could, ahead of schedule, and I moved off campus to spend my last few days at Rainbow's apartment. She was surprised, but didn't ask me anything and I volunteered nothing. I couldn't even share my secret with my best friend of many years. Falling in love with another man was not something I could be proud of.

I didn't say goodbye to Bill when I left the college. I thought that was for the best, to keep a beautiful memory. But I could neither eat nor sleep well. Alone in Rainbow's apartment all day, I felt the time drag. When she and her husband were home I had to put a smile on my face and pretend nothing was wrong. I was going mad trying not to think of Bill.

The day before I was to leave Beijing, I went to a public telephone and dialed the Foreign Affairs College. Bill picked up the phone when the switchboard operator put me through to his extension. He was surprised to hear from me. He understood why I had left the college early, he said, but he wished he could see me again. Our conversation was full of long pauses; we both felt forlorn and didn't know what to say.

The old lady who was in charge of the public telephone had been eyeing me ever since I had switched to speaking English. During one of our conversation's pauses she rapped her fist on the desk.

"Talk Chinese! You are Chinese, aren't you?" she snarled. "Who are you talking to? Why have you stopped talking so suddenly?"

She wouldn't let me alone. I covered the mouthpiece and, summoning all my patience, politely said to her that I was talking to a person who spoke only English.

"In that case, you shouldn't talk to that person at all. How can I know that you are not saying something you shouldn't?"

She stood up then, with a determined look on her face. Quickly I told Bill that I wanted to see him too, once more.

Bill told me that his wife was out of the city with some other teachers and he was alone with his six-year-old boy. "Come for supper," he said. "It will be the last time we ever meet."

That night, after dark, I entered the college compound by the side gate and climbed up the unlighted staircase to the fifth floor of the teachers' residence building. Bill's son was already asleep in bed. Bill had a meal ready, but neither one of us could eat much. We sat and talked, holding hands, hanging on to every moment. The tea cups stayed untouched and grew cold.

Finally I had to leave. Bill gave me a thick envelope and asked me to read the letter it contained in the train next day. We embraced, both of us in tears. We kissed each other long and hard, then I disappeared down the dark narrow stairs without looking back.

Rainbow and her husband saw me off at the train station the next day. Depressed, I tried to make small talk with them but found myself restlessly searching the crowds, hoping that Bill had ignored my warning not to come, yet at the same time afraid he would turn up. Finally my train was announced. I said goodbye and boarded the train that would take me back to reality. In my purse was Bill's letter, which I had been looking forward to since the night before.

The saying goes that coincidence makes good stories. Before the train pulled out, I noticed a familiar face in the hard-seat car. It was one of Xiao Zhao's older brothers, who had been in Beijing on business. He quickly negotiated a change of seats so that he sat opposite me by the window and within a few moments had filled our tea cups, opened a bag of roasted peanuts, spilled a few candies onto the table top and brought out a deck of cards.

"What a lucky coincidence," he said. "Now the twenty-hour trip will pass more quickly."

My favorite among Xiao Zhao's siblings, Second Brother was a chubby middle-aged man with an open, friendly face. Ordinarily I would have welcomed his company, but I had Bill's letter waiting in my handbag and I wanted to read it in private. We played game after game of cards. I lost almost all of them, despite the urgings and advice of my seatmates. After a couple of hours the dinner carts rolled through the car, pushed by attendants selling boxed meals, wine and snacks. I bought a bottle of rice wine for my brother-in-law. My false generosity produced the desired result. By the time the ten-o'clock news was blasting from the speakers, he was sound asleep, lolled against his seat back.

I tore the envelope open. There were six double-sided pages of handwriting, written like a diary over the past couple of days. Tears welled in my eyes. Bill was a writer as well as a teacher. He had published his first novel that spring, and he expressed himself very movingly. One of the entries had been written while he watched Pavarotti's concert from the Great Hall of the People on television and it told how he had held me in his mind as he listened to one of Puccini's great arias.

"What are you reading, Xiao Ye?"

I looked up to find my brother-in-law staring at me. I had no idea how long he had been watching. He reached over and snatched the pages from my hand.

"Hey, this isn't Chinese. What is it?" he exclaimed, waking up the other passengers. "Why are you crying?"

"Lower your voice!" I urged him. I stood up and took the letter from his hand. "What are you getting excited about? It's just a story written by my teacher. It's very emotional."

He laughed, still under the influence of the wine. "I've heard foreigners are good at making movies but I had no idea they can write well too. What's it about? Why don't you translate it for me?"

His request was backed up by our fellow passengers. I wished I had bought him two bottles of liquor.

"It's a story about a young woman who was sent to work in Heilongjiang Province during the Cultural Revolution," I said. "Ready?"

And I began to make up a tale, trying hard to make it as boring as possible. One of the passengers soon complained that he had heard enough sad stories to last him a lifetime and went off to sleep. Soon I had lulled everyone into a trance. I then stuffed the letter into my purse and took up the card game again with my brother-in-law.

Xiao Zhao and Qi-meng were at the station to greet me. My daughter had turned five that summer; she looked healthy and felt heavy in my arms. I was glad to see them both, relieved to be home and back to my normal life. I would have a month off before I had to report to the department.

I was not happy to find Hai Rui in our apartment when we got home. When Xiao Zhao had taken the afternoon off work to meet me, Hai Rui had done the same — to clean our apartment. After the long trip from Beijing, I watched Hai Rui fussing in the kitchen and noticed how close and natural Qi-meng was with him.

That evening, after Qi-meng was in bed, I raised the issue with Xiao Zhao. "I feel like a stranger in my own home with Hai Rui around," I said. "Qi-meng listens to him before she listens to me! Don't I have any say in what goes on in this family?"

I knew he would not want Hai Rui's presence in our lives reduced, but I was unprepared for his vehemence.

"Now you have crossed the bridge so it's time to burn it," he replied, his eyes flashing. "It was Hai Rui who offered help whenever Qi-meng and I needed it. You were too far away. All three of us owe him a lot, that's what I think. Besides, what do you think our neighbors will say if we abandon Hai Rui? And have you thought about our daughter's feelings?"

I had realized that my being away from my husband and daughter, seeking "endless advancement" by furthering my studies, was a frequent topic of gossip among my neighbors, and now my husband was throwing it in my face. They did not know the real reasons why I had gone to Beijing, but they were unanimous in their praise of Hai Rui and the help he had proffered.

After seven years of marriage and striving to cancel my debt by turning over my pay to Xiao Zhao, I had finally begun to feel free financially. Now, according to my husband, I was deeply in debt to Hai Rui, who had intruded into my family's life — very successfully — without my once being consulted, and the only way I could pay that debt was to keep my mouth shut. It was a bitter pill to swallow, and it drove the wedge deeper between Xiao Zhao and me.

Nevertheless, I was glad to have August free. It was the most unbearable month in Shanghai, with hot and humid weather. It was the only month when I welcomed rain to break the heat. But sometimes the rain arrived with a violent typhoon.

I wanted to be near my daughter, so I canceled Qi-meng's boarding school and registered her for September, when I would be returning to work, in a day-care center run by the neighborhood committee. I could drop her off each morning on my way to work, but, because of my irregular hours, couldn't pick her up. Although Xiao Zhao was able to perform that duty as he was off shift work, he insisted that Hai Rui could do it. This angered me, but I kept silent. I didn't want more conflict so soon after my return home.

I found that I could not forget Bill as I wanted to. In the hot afternoons, when Qi-meng was taking her nap, I would get out his letter and reread it. I found myself attached to his words, his thoughts, his love and understanding. Then I would look at my little girl sleeping soundly and feel deep pangs of guilt. It was over between us, I kept telling myself; we would never see each other again. But I couldn't bring myself to tear up his letter.

Two weeks later my intended peaceful month with my family was cut short by a telephone call to the local phone booth from my department. The message asked me to report immediately. The caller had not given a reason or left his or her name. That was typical.

I asked my neighbor to watch Qi-meng and took off on my bike. As I pedaled through the muggy streets, I tried to think what the emergency could be. At the gate, I was told to go not to my own office but to the political division.

I began to panic. Everything about this spelled trouble: ordered back in the middle of a vacation to report to what I called the "brain-washing division." There could be only one reason: somehow my relationship with Bill had been discovered in Beijing and passed on to my department. Maybe the nasty old lady at the public phone booth near Rainbow's apartment had chased me down; or the staff in the Beijing Hotel had overheard Bill and me that day; or one of my many nosy fellow students at the college had spotted me visiting his apartment that last night.

Although I was steaming hot from my rapid bike ride I felt a cold chill when I stood outside the political division on the third floor. I wondered if they would arrest me immediately or give me a chance to explain. Would they let me see my daughter once more before they took me away?

"Come in, Xiao Ye!" someone called cheerfully from inside the room.

Stay calm, I told myself. Inside I met Lao Liu, the deputy chief of the division. He smiled warmly and with a firm handshake welcomed me back, congratulating me on behalf of the department for my outstanding achievement. He had seen my marks sent by the Foreign Affairs College.

He beamed. "We have received great reports from the college and we're very proud of you."

I was so relieved I forgot for a moment the mystery of the hasty summons.

Lao Liu soon provided the answer. "In two weeks, Mayor Wang is taking a ten-day trip to San Francisco, Vancouver and Hong Kong, and the department has decided to send you along as his interpreter. I was told to inform you immediately as there will be a great deal of preparation. You should contact the 'Sister Cities' division as soon as you can."

Mayor Wang was in fact the ex-mayor, retired for several years, but still using his outdated title. I reported to the division that had been set up to liaise with Shanghai's many twin cities throughout the world. There Lao Kang, the section chief, a middle-aged woman with an adequate but not remarkable command of English, informed me that she, Mayor Wang and I would accompany the Shanghai men's basketball team, who were visiting San Francisco as part of a cultural exchange. When the basketball team flew back, the three of us would continue on to Expo in Vancouver, then stop in Hong Kong, where Mayor Wang would hold several business meetings.

I was surprised at this assignment. Until then I had seen many of my colleagues given the chance to travel or study abroad, but all were Party members, and I had been told more than once that my "political awareness" was not yet developed; I had not even applied to join the Party. I could only assume that high marks from the prestigious Foreign Affairs College conferred "political awareness." At any rate, here I was, trusted — not fully, perhaps, since it was clear that Lao Kang had been "paired" with me and would, as a loyal Party member, keep an eye on me. The news was overwhelming. Everyone was impressed. Not only was I going abroad, but I was going with a high official, and not to some third-world country, but to capitalist Canada, Hong Kong and the United States, places everyone yearned to visit.

The last two weeks of my "holiday" were a hectic round of telexes to our destinations, shopping trips for gifts for the mayor to distribute, better clothes for myself (as ordered by my office) and travel documents, including a green "service" passport. This last was a novelty: Chinese citizens were not allowed to have passports. Those traveling abroad were issued passports, but they were taken away after they returned home.

I was excited at the prospect of stepping on foreign soil for the first time in my life, completely unaware of how the winds of change were about to snatch me up yet again.

48

AFTER A SEEMINGLY interminable thirteen-hour flight to San Francisco via Hong Kong, during which I couldn't sleep a wink, I began my day's work immediately, for Mayor Wang was waiting for me in his hotel. San Francisco was damp and cold after the steaming weather in Hong Kong. By noon the fog had moved off and on our way to an official lunch I was shocked to see the downtown streets populated by people who looked as if they were on their way to the beach. Women and girls especially seemed to be wearing so little; some were barely covering themselves properly.

I lost count of the meetings, meals, teas and talks during which I translated all that day and into the evening. At midnight Lao Kang and I went to the home of an American couple who belonged to the American Society of Friendship with China and had offered to put us up. Early the next morning I rushed downtown to the mayor's hotel and then to the Canadian Consulate to arrange for our visas for Canada. When I got back, Nancy, our hostess, took one look at me and told me that I needed some sleep. She promised to wake me in plenty of time for me to take up my translation duties at the dinner Mayor Feinstein of San Francisco was hosting for Mayor Wang. I fell asleep within minutes of lying down.

What happened next convinced me that there is such a thing as Fate.

Nancy's concern and thoughtfulness turned into a disaster: that same afternoon she received a phone call from a friend and left the house, apparently forgetting me and her promise to wake me up. When I did open my eyes, it was past six o'clock. I was horribly late. I ran out of the house in a panic, looking for a taxi.

When I got to the hotel, my party had departed. The note left for me said they had grown tired of waiting; neither instructions nor the location of the banquet were included. The missing information was sharp criticism, I knew, and discipline would follow. On the second day of my mission I had botched my job entirely. There was no one I could call to find out where the dinner was being held; according to protocol, meeting places were not public knowledge. I stood in the hotel lobby, scared and lost.

While rooting around in my pocket for a quarter to call Nancy's house, I found a business card given me the day before by a Chinese-American who lived in the city. Perhaps he had heard where the dinner was. In desperation I phoned him. He did not know the location, but suggested I go to the stadium where the basketball game was being played. Maybe someone connected with the Chinese team would know.

What kind of interpreter are you? I asked myself in the taxi. Once in the stadium, having failed to locate anyone who could help me, I found a corner and sat down alone, away from the players and coach, despondent and homesick. I wished I was home with Qimeng and Xiao Zhao; even the thought of Hai Rui's presence was less repellent. I had never played basketball in my life and I had no idea what was going on in front of me. When half-time came, my train of thought was interrupted by Xiao Yuan, the Shanghai team's interpreter.

"Xiao Ye, a reporter here wants to talk to you," he said in Chinese.

Beside Xiao Yuan was a Westerner, a heavy man of medium height with a huge black beard and horn-rimmed glasses. He held a pad and pen in his hands.

"I answered some of his questions but it seems he wants to ask you some more," Xiao Yuan went on. "I have to get back to the players."

What was going on? How did this reporter know I was here? I wasn't even supposed to be at the game in the first place. And why talk to me? I was Mayor Wang's interpreter. I had nothing to do with the team and didn't know a basket ball from a dumpling. Then a cold thought struck me. Had he found out that I had failed to show up at the dinner and tracked me down to write an embarrassing and face-losing report: "Interpreter Prefers Basketball to Dinner with Feinstein"?

"What do you want to know?" I asked him.

Xiao Yuan had been keeping an eye on me since he resumed his seat, but the reporter stepped between us — purposely, I noticed.

"Miss Ye," he said quietly. "My name is Tom. I'm not a reporter. I'm a cousin of Bill, your Canadian teacher."

He sounded nervous. As he spoke, he scribbled on his pad, as if making notes.

Unlike the strange, broad-shouldered man before me, I was so confused I couldn't frame a proper sentence. And I was scared.

While alone in the mayor's suite that morning, waiting for him to finish breakfast in the dining room, I had telephoned Bill's house in Ontario, amazed at how easy it was to place a call more than halfway across a continent. All I wanted was to hear his voice. His wife answered the phone. When I had identified myself and asked for Bill she told me tensely that she knew what was going on between me and her husband. Before she could say more, I had hung up, mortified that Bill had told her about me and embarrassed by her abrupt manner.

I knew that in English "cousin" could refer to someone on either side of the family. Was this strange man, Tom, Bill's wife's cousin? Had he come to make trouble for me, to expose me as Bill's secret lover?

He seemed to sense my nervousness. He pulled a photo from his breast pocket and laid it on top of the pad. It showed Bill's two older children, whom I'd helped see off at the Beijing airport the summer before. I nodded my head, acknowledging them.

"Listen," Tom said. "I came here to look for you because Bill called and asked me to try to find you and give you a message. By coincidence I live near here. He wants you to call him. That's all."

I felt silly about my overreaction and smiled in apology. Tom wrote down a telephone number and, shielding his actions, tore the strip of paper from his pad and gave it to me. It was the same number I had dialed earlier that day.

"I can't call him," I said, unwilling to face the embarrassment again. "Please tell him that."

I had to repeat myself at least three times, for Tom wouldn't accept my answer. "At least tell me where you're staying so he can call you," he insisted.

I did so, just as Xiao Yuan came toward us. Tom wrote down the number and quickly closed his pad, then gave me a warm handshake and thanked me loudly for the interview.

I sat there for the rest of the game, lost in thought. Unlike Great-Aunt, I had never been much of a believer in Fate, but what happened that night was surely nothing but Fate. Tom had been able to find me only because I was in the wrong place.

When I was dropped off at Nancy's later, I steeled myself for Lao Kang's wrath. But Nancy had reached her first, explaining that my missing the dinner was all her fault. She was going to say as much to Mayor Wang the next day, she assured us both. I was relieved that Lao Kang confined her criticism to a quiet scowl.

Her mood was not improved when Nancy told me half an hour later as Lao Kang and I were getting into our beds that I had a telephone call from someone who said he was my Canadian teacher. I could take the call in the living room.

"Who is this teacher, Xiao Ye?" Lao Kang demanded in Chinese. "How could he know you are here?"

"He was my teacher at the Foreign Affairs College," I said, quickly leaving the bedroom.

I attempted to sound cheerful as I spoke to Bill, for I knew Lao Kang would be doing her best to listen. I told Bill about the trip, our reception, my impressions of the city — its emptiness, compared to the human sea of Shanghai, its cleanliness, its abundance of stylish automobiles and attractive architecture — talking loudly for Lao Kang's benefit. But I had to cut the call short.

"How did your teacher know Nancy's phone number?" Lao Kang demanded as soon as I entered the bedroom.

"Because I gave him her name in a letter when I told him about this trip. It was on the business card you gave me in Shanghai, remember? It's easy to get someone's phone number in North America if you know the name and the city."

My answer was quick and logical and came from the knowledge I had gained while reading the telephone directory in the hotel. The next morning Nancy confirmed what I'd said when Lao Kang, who seemed to relish her job as my watcher, asked about finding someone's phone number.

"Oh yes, Miss Ye is perfectly right," she said, much to my relief.

If the scenery and the cleanliness of San Francisco were a delight, Vancouver, at least the area around the Pan-Pacific Hotel with its huge, fanlike architecture, was a fairy-land on earth. Expo '86 stretched my imagination with its incredible feats of science and technology, especially the Cinesphere, where I tried to hide from the moving train on the screen as it hurtled straight at me. Totally amazed, I wondered how life could be so different on the other side of the Pacific.

Bill called me that evening, as he had promised — he managed to track me down at the hotel — and the evening after that. Lao Kang was as vigilant as ever, wanting to know after the first call why my teacher was "constantly" phoning me. I explained that dealing with Westerners had taught me they were as addicted to the telephone as we were to rice, and she seemed satisfied.

On the second evening I took advantage of a luxury provided by the fancy hotel — a bathroom telephone. I took Bill's call there, turning on the bath water to hide my words. Lao Kang was none the wiser.

I felt miserable when the plane took off from Vancouver. I was leaving Canada, where Bill lived, a free and sane country as I had learned in my two-day stay. When I had said goodbye to Bill in Beijing about a month before, I had never thought I'd be in contact with him again. Nor did he, and that was why, as he explained on the phone, he had told his wife about me when she asked him again and again what was bothering him.

In Hong Kong I managed to speak with him again. When I boarded the plane for China, I believed in our love more than ever, even if we couldn't love each other in any conventional way. I no longer worried about the discipline that might await me in Shanghai. I didn't trust the promises made to me and Nancy over my missing the banquet, but I didn't care that much any more, because I had discovered that neither Bill nor I wanted to give up our love. Since the death of my parents, he was the first person — including Xiao Zhao and all my family members — who would fight for me as he promised. Even the thought of him made me feel good and without fear.

49

BILL AND I HAD AGREED during our last telephone conversation that we would write to one another, and I suggested we employ a guerrilla warfare technique: he would send his mail alternately to my home and my office to minimize any attention his letters might arouse. I would send my letters to his school in Barrie, Ontario, to keep up the pretense that we were teacher and student corresponding for old time's sake. Whenever possible, Bill sent letters to Eleanor in Hong Kong, asking her or a colleague to post them on their next trip to China.

When dealing with overseas mail, the word censorship was an understatement in those days: the government made no attempt to hide the fact that outgoing and incoming correspondence was routinely opened and read without the receiver's knowledge. The mail sent to my office might be exempt but, once it arrived, it was scrutinized by the politically correct and the nosy. We were always questioned about letters received from abroad, and had to turn them over if requested. A love relationship with a foreigner was still forbidden to anyone in the general population; for a woman in a sensitive job like mine, it was a crime.

I had once received in the mail a copy of *Gone with the Wind* from an Australian visitor for whom I had interpreted. Even though I had no idea this generous but unsolicited gift was being sent to me, I was criticized on three fronts: first, for "requesting" a gift; second, for receiving corrupt bourgeois literature; third, for receiving a love story from a man, and a foreign man at that. The book was confiscated. There was no such concept as personal property in China under the *Gong Chan Dang* — "Share Property Party."

In this context, corresponding with a foreigner whom I loved and who loved me presented, to say the least, certain challenges. To avoid scrutiny, I volunteered to fetch the mail from the gatekeeper as soon as it arrived. In this way I could pocket Bill's letters before they got to my office. I mailed mine from different post offices, with no return address. Each time I received a letter from Bill I would carefully examine the envelope to see if it had been steamed open; sometimes I could tell, but I knew from my own training that the procedure didn't usually leave much trace. Both of us recorded the date of our most recent letter to the other so we would know if it had gone astray.

Certainly there was no intimate language in our letters under those circumstances, but one time, under the pretense of sending me song lyrics to improve my English, Bill inserted in the middle of songs stanzas written by him, to tell me how he felt about me and how he missed me. I now felt sure I would have made a good secret agent, even though I had turned down the opportunity after my graduation from Beijing University.

Meanwhile, several welcome changes occurred at work. To my great relief, Lao Peng retired. There would be no more harassment from him. He was replaced by Lao Jun, a kindly, down-to-earth man back from four years' diplomatic service in Africa. Given three new younger staff in the office and my two years of postgraduate studies, I found myself no longer among the junior ranks. Lao Jun placed a great deal of trust in me, but as Party secretary he urged me more than once to hand in my application to join the Communist

Party. Each time I declined politely, assuring him I would give the matter deep and serious thought.

My return to work in the department was soon filled with preparations for the visit of the Queen of England, who was scheduled to visit Shanghai with Prince Philip in the autumn of 1986, her first trip to China. Months before her arrival, the issue of her accommodation became a hot topic. It seemed every hotel of note in the city wanted to host the Queen and her party, from the well-established Jin Jiang Hotel to new joint-venture houses like the Sheraton, to prestigious guesthouses like the Xi Jiao — the West Suburb Guesthouse, which had been another of Mao's residences when he stayed in Shanghai. For days, I and others in my division went on inspection tours, scrutinizing lodgings and being plied with sumptuous meals and gifts to help us make our decision. The Xi Jiao Guesthouse, a large estate with several villa-style buildings and expansive lawns and gardens, won the competition.

Several days in advance of the Queen herself, the royal yacht Britannia arrived. The yacht's band leader offered to give a concert and I was chosen to be the emcee. On the evening of the performance I went to the stadium where the band was to play. It was only when I reached the door that I realized this was the very place I had stood eighteen years before, waiting with Teacher Chen for the bus to carry me away to the prison farm. Now there were no colorful banners floating in the breeze, no revolutionary songs blaring from the loudspeakers, no cries from families about to be separated. Later I introduced the selections played by the band, and the stadium that brought bitter memories was filled with glorious music.

I had tried — and failed — to put aside my feelings for Bill, to accept the reality that I had a husband, family and career. I had kept asking myself if it was possible to love two men at the same time, but more and more I realized that my feelings toward Xiao Zhao had become more obligation and duty than love, and I also knew I had never felt for him what I did for Bill, had never experienced a passion like that in my life. Bill was the one person in the world from whom I didn't need to hide anything. But he was gone.

Or so I thought. At the end of October, he wrote to say that he wanted to fly to Shanghai on his Christmas break, but that he wouldn't book his ticket until I told him my decision: should he come or not? His letter caused me many sleepless nights, but in the end I decided that, for the first time, I was going to do something different. I had always gone along with rules and regulations, meeting the standards of others. I wrote to Bill with a big yes.

A month later I was reminded of the expression "Trouble is my middle name," for I got into a political mess again. In November demonstrations burst out in Shanghai, initiated by university students demanding political reform. Some of their posters were so brave as to call for an end to the Communist Party's monopoly on power, an end to totalitarianism, and the initiation of a multi-party system. This was ironic because Shanghainese were often called "cowards" by other Chinese because of their perceived lack of involvement in political issues after Liberation. The demonstrations filled major streets, blocked traffic, clogged access to city hall and filled the People's Square in the evenings. As always the crowds were sprinkled with plain-clothes police. When it looked as if workers might join in, the authorities acted quickly to prevent a major confrontation.

One evening I took Qi-meng to the People's Square to see what all the fuss was about. I had frequently been a target of political movements; this time I felt moved to observe.

"It's not a good idea," Xiao Zhao said. "There could be trouble."

"They're only students," I replied. "We're not marching in the street, we're taking a walk. What harm is there in that?"

Reluctantly, Xiao Zhao came with us.

The square, about twenty minutes' walk from our apartment, was filled with well-behaved and well-organized groups conducting discussions and debates or listening to speeches. It was all very civilized and calm, with no drums, gongs or shouted slogans — nothing like the movements of my youth. Xiao Zhao was relieved, and relaxed a little. With Qi-meng perched on her father's shoulders we walked among the groups, listening to the discussions.

Hours later, at about eleven o'clock, police and militia began to move into the crowd, breaking up the gathering.

"Go home," they urged. "It's getting late. Go home and have a good sleep so you won't miss work tomorrow."

Their tone was that of concerned parents. One policewoman even asked me, "Why did you bring your child to something like this?"

I didn't answer her. I hoped this demonstration would encourage reform and mark the beginning of an era where Qi-meng could grow up more freely and peacefully than I had.

The very next day Lao Jun took me aside for a private talk. Days earlier, he told me, I had been seen walking with student demonstrators.

"I didn't say anything to you then," he said. "But now I have learned that you were seen in People's Square last night."

"What do you mean, walking with student demonstrators?" I asked indignantly. "I was caught in the traffic on my way home and was waiting at an intersection while the parade passed. As for last night, what's wrong with curiosity? How could a stroll in the square with my family be a political act?"

"Xiao Ye, listen," Lao Jun urged in a quiet voice. "You don't want to earn a reputation as a student sympathizer. The government has repeatedly warned against that. Be wise. And join the Party. That is where your talent will be fully used."

His kind and polite words were a clear warning.

The outbreak of demonstrations across the country that winter gave the old guard the opportunity to clean house, remove those who were soft on demonstrators, and tighten their grip on ordinary citizens. There were bold-faced warnings on the front pages of the major newspapers claiming that supporting the Four Modernizations was not enough: all Chinese should help in combating "spiritual pollution." I and a dozen or so colleagues from the department were sent for a two-week political study session in the International Club where we were organized into groups to read documents, editorials and policy papers — and of course to discuss them whole-heartedly.

How ironic that Bill should arrive a week afterwards, in the midst of a second campaign, the "battle against Yellow Pollution"

— Western influence and its decadent lifestyle. The increased divorce rate in China, shown by recently published statistics, was cited as an example of socialist ethics being eroded. Like virtually every other "bad thing" in China, this was blamed on Western influence and the inevitable corruption of morals that came with it.

I had planned to meet Bill at the airport but members of my office would be there receiving a delegation, so I went directly to the Sheraton Hotel. I showed my department ID to the gatekeeper and shook hands formally with Bill, watched by many pairs of eyes. As we waited for the elevator, Bill pointed out several video cameras trained on us. I had heard and read many "triumphant" reports resulting from raids on hotels like the Sheraton. A number of men and women were behind bars, called prostitutes by the papers, pilloried for destroying China's reputation in front of the world.

As in our letters over the past months, we showed great restraint in his hotel room. We were aware of the danger of being intimate and we sat and talked, looking out at the traffic far below on the ill-lit street. We were constantly interrupted by inquisitive hotel staff, knocking on the door, bringing first a fresh thermos bottle, then teabags, then cups, then, not long after, an offer to turn down the bed. It was obvious to me that the time to leave had come. It was past ten o'clock, the curfew set by the city Security Bureau governing Chinese visitors to all hotels open to foreigners.

The next day, using accumulated overtime, I asked Lao Jun for the day off so that I could pay a visit to my Canadian teacher. I willingly provided Bill's name and the hotel, knowing full well that Lao Jun would check on me, find out I'd told him the truth, and drop the matter. I was right. During his six-day visit to the city, Bill kept on the move, changing hotels four times so that I would not be seen visiting the same hotel day after day. When he left a hotel, he was required to give his next stop. He would name a hotel where he had no intention of staying, take a taxi there, wait a bit, then take another one to his real destination.

I saw him as much as possible, once for almost an entire day, other times for an hour or two at a time. One night before he left he asked me if I had thought about going abroad to study. Both of us knew what he meant. A Chinese could not even have a passport, much less leave the country. The only way I could go abroad was for study. I told him yes, I wanted to be with him and I wanted to leave China. But I didn't say that it would be next to impossible for me. Going to another country to study was for people with powerful parents or connections or overseas relatives — and for people with the correct political attitude. Almost all the English interpreters in my department except me had been sent "outside" at government expense to study; but I was still not a Party member and my political incidents made matters worse.

The only way I could study in Canada was if a university accepted me with free tuition and room and board — in other words, a huge scholarship. Private sponsorship was not acceptable to my work unit. Both Bill and I knew that it was virtually hopeless.

After Bill left, I fell ill with a high fever. Days and nights I woke up soaking wet from nightmares or painful longing for Bill and his love. I felt more strongly than ever that my feelings for him were something no one could take away from me.

Bill didn't waste any time. I soon received letters from two universities in Toronto describing their graduate studies programs. Each information kit contained a cost-of-living budget for foreign students. My worst fears were confirmed. More than $15,000 were required. So it was impossible, and that was that. I put the letters away and went on with my daily routine, keeping myself busy, trying to forget.

50

O F ALL THE EVENTS in my interpreting career and of all the kings, queens, presidents, government officials and other dignitaries I met, the most memorable was the Crown Prince of Thailand.

His advance team came early in 1987, just after the New Year; the prince was scheduled to arrive in the spring. Since intercourse between the Thais and Chinese was carried on in English, I was assigned to the party. The prince was a polite but arrogant man about my age, who liked to run every day for exercise. Huai Hai Park, near the Jin Jiang Hotel, had to be cleared of people and surrounded by guards. A walkie-talkie in my hand, I ran with him and his security team.

One afternoon, when we had returned to the hotel panting from the run, I met two clerks from the Shanghai Arts and Crafts Trade Fair who had come to collect payment for items the prince had purchased the day before. I led them to the prince's suite and knocked on the door. The door swung open and I found myself staring at the top of a bald head.

It was an old man, a servant of the prince, and he was on his knees. Shocked by this comical apparition, I took a step back. Inside the suite, servants dressed in loose clothing were passing back and forth across the corridor, all of them on their knees. Showing the invoice, I told the doorman I had come about payment and asked to speak to the chief liaison officer, whom I knew from the advance team.

A great deal of talk ensued, all of it in Thai, between the kneeling figures. I heard the voices of the officer and the prince but could not see them. Then the old man waved me to come in. I took a step forward and he shook his head violently, jabbing his finger toward the floor and pulling at my sleeve. He wanted me to enter on my knees.

Chinese do not kneel any more, I thought; the *kou-tou* went out with Liberation. I also imagined myself thumping awkwardly down the corridor and could barely repress a smile. I shook my head, stepped back from the door, handing the invoice to the old man, and left.

Because of what had happened on the Queen's yacht the autumn before I had no worries that I had caused an international incident by refusing to kneel. The Queen was to hold a reception aboard the Britannia and the British delegation had sent out notices with the invitations, describing the appropriate protocol since, in their eyes at least, the Britannia was British territory. Among the rules laid down was one stating that women guests must wear floor-length dresses and must curtsy as the Queen greeted them.

Lao Li, head of our department, told us that we should not curtsy before the Queen. "The ship may be British," he had observed, "but it is floating in Chinese waters, and the Chinese do not curtsy."

❦

The setback in his hopes to help me come to Canada was devastating to Bill, who didn't know where to turn to come up with the money required of foreign students. He felt even worse when I wrote to inform him of another obstacle. It didn't matter if he had the money: my department would never let me go if I was funded by an individual Canadian.

Because of the increased number of Chinese studying abroad, the government had set out a two-tiered system. One included *gong-fei* students, those who were sponsored by the government. Their expenses were covered either by their work units (that is, the government) or under sponsorship from a foreign government through its cultural exchange or educational programs. *Zhi-fei* students were self-supported, but even so they were under government control. They had to prove they had a satisfactory scholarship or support from a direct relative. Private sponsorship by a foreigner or distant relative was not allowed.

These rules were designed to block attempts by those who would "sell anything from their soul to their body" to gain sponsorship from rotten foreigners, or by those who would engage in espionage activities in return for financial help. Since almost all *gong-fei* students were the children of high officials and the *zhi-fei* required help from rich relatives, the system, as always, worked against ordinary people.

A few weeks after the New Year, Bill wrote to me, telling me that one wall had been broken down. He had contacted York University in Toronto and found someone willing to help. In mid-February I received a letter from Dr. Lumsden, Master of Norman Bethune College, inviting me to spend a year at York as a visiting scholar studying English literature. I would be allowed to audit classes free, but I could not receive credits.

I was overwhelmed by the news. But there was still the problem of living expenses, not to mention the cost of travel. I thought briefly of my two step-uncles in Taiwan, but I didn't even know their names or where they were. Besides, any dealings with Taiwanese would bring trouble.

So far I had told no one about my hopes, nor did I speak about Dr. Lumsden's letter. Strangely enough, that night I found myself less irritated by Hai Rui's casual and possessive manner in our home. I had always regarded myself as a fighter but I had withdrawn from the battle to have the kind of family life I wanted.

A week later I had another letter from Bill. With it was a scholarship application from the Ontario Educators' Scholarship for Studies in the Humanities (O.E.S.S.H.). My hands shook as I read the general information and the guidelines. The scholarship seemed perfect for me, aimed to "encourage and assist students from under-developed and less-developed nations who wish to undertake studies related to Western Culture in the Canadian context at an institution of higher learning in Ontario (Canada). Applicants who are 'sponsored' by teachers and educators within Ontario will receive priority but such 'sponsorship' is not necessary," it concluded. I read the regulations twice and realized that I met all the criteria and had the advantage of Bill's sponsorship, for he had been an Ontario high-school teacher for years.

With a growing sense that hopelessness might be fading, I began to write the essay required for the application. I worked on it for days, typing and polishing, and finally sent it away.

In March, the Canadian governor-general, Jeanne Sauvé came to Shanghai, bringing the only delegation I had experienced for whom French and English interpreters worked as a team, Canada being officially a bilingual country. Compared with the Americans, the Canadian delegations, large or small, appeared to be more tolerant and less demanding. To put it simply, they presented us with no headaches.

However, when Governor-General Sauvé's group was about to leave, the first secretary of the Canadian Embassy in Beijing, a man called Wilson, told me in a panic that he had left the electrical cord for his typewriter in the hotel. Their plane would be leaving soon, he said, and he knew he couldn't find a similar cord in China. Could I help him?

I called the hotel and asked them to search for the cord, put it in a taxi and rush it to me at the airport. We knew the governor-general would not delay her departure for an electric cord, but it seemed worth a try. The taxi raced onto the tarmac as the passengers were boarding. Clutching the cord in my hand, I dashed to the foot of the stairway into the plane just as it was about to be separated from the aircraft. Mr. Wilson ran out onto the stairs, took the cord, kissed me loudly on my cheek and told me to contact him if ever I needed a favor.

I knew I would be upbraided for the kiss, and steeled myself for Lao Fu's harsh words as I descended the stairs to join the officials waving goodbye. But before Lao Fu could begin his criticism, Mayor Jiang praised me for helping Wilson, adding that kissing on the cheek was equivalent to a handshake in the West. Lao Fu kept quiet.

Mayor Jiang Zhe-min went on to become one of the most powerful men in China. And I was to have the opportunity to ask Wilson to return the favor.

In remarkably short order, the answer from the scholarship committee came back — a thin envelope from Ontario. I was afraid to open it. I took a deep breath and withdrew the single sheet of paper. A letter from the scholarship's chairperson, William Talbot informed me that my application for financial assistance had been approved to a total of $6,500, the amount stipulated by the Canadian government for living expenses. Should I need a travel grant, I could apply for that also. The letter confirmed that "should the Canadian government raise this requirement, your grant will be increased accordingly" — a well-considered statement as it turned out, since it quelled the queasiness of my superiors who claimed that inflation in Western countries was on the rise.

Almost breathless with excitement, I presented the news and the letter to Lao Fu and was immediately criticized for applying for the scholarship in secret. The matter would have to be discussed at a higher level, he said, among the five top officials of the department (four of whom had children or nephews and nieces studying or living abroad). I was the first person from my office to have the chance to become a *zhi-fei* student, assisted by a scholarship gained through my own effort.

I went home and stiffened myself to tell Xiao Zhao and Hai Rui the news that I might have a real chance of going to Canada. To my shock, both of them hailed my sudden news. Hai Rui, who had been beside himself with delight when I had applied to the Foreign Affairs College two and a half years earlier, jumped from his chair and threw his arms wide with happiness.

"Don't worry about Qi-meng," he said eagerly. "She was fine when you were away last time and things will be even better now, because she's older. As a matter of fact, in my personal opinion, she behaved better when you weren't around."

I turned to Xiao Zhao. As usual, he was indifferent to Hai Rui's rudeness. Nor did he show any grief that I might be leaving him again.

"That's great," he said. "You can be our pioneer and gain permanent residence in Canada. Then I'll bring Qi-meng and Hai Rui to join you when you've established yourself. I've heard that life in Canada is one of the best in the world, much easier than any of us can imagine."

The next day, with great misgivings, I went to the director's office to find out if they had made a decision about me, and discovered that my scholarship was under investigation. The department was sending a telex to the Chinese Embassy in Ottawa to check the background of the O.E.S.S.H. to see if it had any Taiwan connection! Deputy Director Zhu said this was necessary because the Taiwan government often tried to recruit Chinese students to spy for them by offering them scholarships. I tried to suppress my outrage. It was a good thing I hadn't sought help from my Taiwanese step-uncles.

At the end of March the required documents arrived for my visa application. Everything seemed to be falling into place but, as usual, red tape was still in abundance.

In the meantime, I decided to get my house in order before I left China. Two things had to be done. One was to use my department's connections to effect Xiao Zhao's transfer from the coal-dock canteen to the Harbor Bureau office, a goal he had been working on for a long time, buying gifts, holding dinners for the right people and being as politically correct as possible in his role as a new Party member. Upon my return from San Francisco I had been to a few banquets held for Americans from that city, particularly having to do with harbor matters, and I had interpreted for officials from the Shanghai Harbor Bureau. I went to see the deputy director, told him about Xiao Zhao and asked for his help. Two weeks later, Xiao Zhao's transfer was completed.

My second goal was to visit my parents' grave. A couple of months before, my mother's sister, Auntie Yi-feng, had written to tell me that she had finally reached an accommodation with the family who was farming the land where my parents were buried. For a down payment of ¥200 and a fee of ¥100 every year thereafter we would be allowed to locate and remound their grave. The extortionate sum was to compensate the farmer for the crops he would lose.

It had been twenty-five years since Father's burial, twenty-two since my mother's, and I still felt guilty because I hadn't forced my way off the train in Wuxi during the Great Travel in 1966. So my two sisters and I decided to go to Qingyang for the *Qing Ming* festival in the spring of 1987. Xiao Zhao didn't want to come — he said he shouldn't leave his new job. I didn't care, as long as Qi-meng came along. I wanted my daughter to pay her respects to her grandparents and to remember the place where her grandparents and great-grandparents had come from.

Qingyang hadn't changed much — still the same dirt road through town, flanked by the same tired-looking buildings. Grandfather's house and store had been replaced by a brand-new two-story brick theatre. I wondered if my grandparents' ashes were buried underneath.

We left town and headed for Wang Family Village where Auntie Yi-feng lived, cutting across country by walking single file along the narrow paddy dikes. Tears came to my eyes as I remembered Mother's insistence on taking the roads rather than the dikes back to Qingyang after I had almost drowned in the river one winter day when I was a little girl. How I wished I could tell her that I was a mother myself now.

I was burdened with secrets that I couldn't share even with my two sisters, although we had gone through so much together over the years. I couldn't imagine their reaction if I told them that there was a good chance I would leave my marriage with Xiao Zhao and stay in Canada for the rest of my life. No one knew about my relationship with Bill. We three daughters hardly talked about our married lives. We had been brought up the way our mothers and grandmothers had: you married the first person you dated and you stuck with the marriage whether it worked out or not, particularly after you had children. The newspapers might report the increase in the divorce rate, but none of us knew anyone who had broken up her marriage. I wondered what my sisters would think of me if I told them I was willing to try for my own freedom at the price of not seeing Qi-meng for a while.

With my Auntie Yi-feng as guide, we found the newly mounded grave near the canal, surrounded by green vegetables with yellow blossoms. Staring at the smooth mud surface of the tumulus, I wished my two parents could hear me and help me in my confusion. All their children had survived a bitter sea of human disasters and their Ah Si, Number 4, was ready to spread her wings. I held Qi-meng tightly and promised myself that, as soon as I could save enough money to send to Auntie Yi-feng, a tall gravestone would stand here again.

That night my sisters and I sat in bed with my aunt, and, with my daughter sleeping beside me, we talked until dawn broke in the east. It was during that long talk that I heard for the first time about the marriage of my parents, the ups and downs of their lives, and how Great-Aunt came into the family — the kind of thing traditionally kept from the younger generation. I brushed a strand of hair from Qi-meng's damp forehead and thought, No one but me is going tell my story to my daughter. More than anything I wanted to ensure that Qi-meng would not live the kind of life I had. My going to Canada could be a big step in that direction.

51

ABOUT A MONTH LATER the so-called scholarship investigation came to an end when the Chinese Consulate in Toronto telexed our department that there were innumerable scholarships in Canada and it was not possible to investigate them all. Lao Jun told me that everything seemed all right, but final approval still had not been given.

"Xiao Ye, I want to help you, and I'm telling you that things will go easier for you if you show your desire to join the Party."

I handed in my application the next day.

A week after the May Day celebration I was called in to see Director Zhu. She asked me to take a seat and handed me the document of approval for my going to Canada. I was so relieved I felt numb. After formally urging me to study hard and not to let the department down, she went on to ask me circumspectly if I could help her niece win the O.E.S.S.H. scholarship the next year. She would have a résumé ready to take with me, she said. Her tone and manner were quite different from a few weeks earlier when she had been concerned that the scholarship might be a Taiwanese plot.

Great-Aunt's response to my plans was predictable. "Why do you want to go to a country that Mrs. Yan tells me doesn't even share day and night with us?" she asked. "All your life, you wanted to be with your family. Why the change?" She looked straight into my eyes. "Is there anything wrong between you and Xiao Zhao? And what will happen with Qi-meng? She has been left in the hands of two men for too long and she needs you, Ah Si."

Her words stung. I wished I could open my troubles and my fears to her, the way I had when I was a little girl. But that had ended the moment I was sent to the prison farm. She never knew, nor did anyone in my family, not even Xiao Zhao, the details of my interrogation there and my attempted suicide. What's the use of telling her my secrets now? I asked myself. And how could I possibly reveal my reasons for wanting to leave the country and live in Canada?

If my department had reluctantly granted me permission to go abroad to study, various officials from different divisions made sure, in typical bureaucratic fashion, to *chuan-xiao-xie* — fit me with small shoes, that is, make things difficult for me.

In the next few weeks I was like a bee in the wind, buzzing back and forth between office, home and Shanghai Number One People's Hospital. I had medical checks from forehead to toenails, lined up for hours to have numerous squares on numerous forms filled in, walked from room to room to have myself pressed, squeezed or hammered on the joints — all to satisfy two governments. Canada wanted above all to make sure I was not pregnant; China wanted to be certain I didn't have syphilis, a disgraceful disease that would cause my country to lose face.

Where was my plane ticket? I was asked. No ticket, no passport. And make sure the ticket is round-trip, to prove you are coming back as scheduled, I was admonished. The passport came, but almost too late to get a visa in time. I contacted Mr. Wilson at the Canadian Embassy in Beijing. Luckily he remembered the electric typewriter cord and expedited the visa.

Finally everything was in order. But the small shoes still pinched.

I was called yet again into the political division and informed that I would have to sign a contract with my department, which represented the government. The contract stipulated that, if I failed to return at the end of one year, I would be fined ¥25,000 — more than twenty-six years' salary! Lao Liu let it slip that this was the first contract of its kind ever in my department, designed especially for me because I was not a Party member, even though I had now applied.

"How did you come up with this amount?" I asked, too angry to keep my mouth shut. "Is the figure based on a certain formula?"

"What difference does it make?" Lao Liu smiled. "It's just the number that came to mind. It's meaningless, isn't it? Just theory, because you're coming back — we all are sure about that. I could have put down one million."

I left as quickly as I could before he changed his mind.

My signature was not sufficient, of course. A close family member had to cosign. That night, after Hai Rui had left, I told Xiao Zhao about the contract.

"I don't think it would be wise for me to sign, Ah Si," he said, to my amazement. "First, you know very well that the fine would mean that all my savings would be taken away; the government might even go after my parents' new apartment. Also, if I sign, I might not be able to come to Canada myself."

I didn't bother to remind him that at least half of his savings had been built up with my contributions.

"Why not ask one of your sisters?" he went on. "They are your blood relations, and most of all they have very little money —"

I stopped him before he went any further and took off on my bike to my real home.

Great-Aunt immediately offered to go with me to the court and "put down her finger" — give a fingerprint, since she could not write. I explained to her that she couldn't because only a blood relative was allowed.

Number 5 said quietly, "I'll meet you at the district court office tomorrow at two o'clock when I get off work. Ah Si, my husband and I don't have much money, nor any property. If the time comes, the government can take what it wants. We've been through it before. Besides, I don't think the Communists will throw us out on the street."

Later, as I was leaving, she drew me aside and said, "Ah Si, don't worry. If it were not for you I would still be on the farm, with no husband and no daughter."

The next day, after we had signed the contract and stood outside the district courthouse, she held my hands. Referring again to my helping her escape the farm, she said, "I feel so much better now, Ah Si, being able, for the first time in my life, to help you."

I did not realize until later, when I had had time to go over her words to me, that she had sensed I wasn't coming back.

On the thirteenth day of August 1987, I woke for the last time in my apartment, with my little girl in my arms. It was a hot, sticky day already. Number 3 had arrived the night before and we had sat up most of the night, but not talked much. In the morning we said goodbye; she had to leave early to catch the bus to Songjiang.

Hai Rui suggested he take Qi-meng to a park to make the parting easier, so I said goodbye to her in our home.

"I'll see you soon," I kept telling her, wiping away her tears and holding back my own. It seemed she was the only one of the three who didn't want me to go.

After boarding the Canadian Airlines jet I looked out the window at Shanghai, and recalled my last meeting with Great-Aunt. I had gone to see her after registering Qi-meng in a neighborhood elementary school — a long and involved process. When I told Great-Aunt I had finally managed to put Qi-meng into the only nearby school that provided lunch for the students, she held my hands in hers for a long, long time. Tears streamed from her wrinkled eyes.

"Ah Si, you are ready to fly away for a long, long time, aren't you?"

She didn't wait for my answer. "Don't tell me. You don't need to. All I want is for you to know these two things. I will be waiting here for you. And, Ah Si, whatever good comes to you, you deserve it, especially happiness."

I kept nodding my head, crying with her. I couldn't speak. I didn't know how to explain why her little girl, whom she had taken care of since she was ten months old and who had returned to her after ten years' separation, was leaving again for a long time. Sitting with her in the room we had shared all my life, watching Qi-meng play with Number 5's daughter, Lin-lin, I tried my best to comfort this old, white-haired woman who had devoted her life to a family not of her blood.

Qi-meng and I spent the last few days with Great-Aunt, the three of us sleeping in the same bed. With her blessing in my heart, I didn't feel quite so guilty about leaving my daughter. It was clear now that I was going to do something no one in my family had ever done. Great-Aunt had always said I was different from the others.

As I prepared to leave her for the last time, Great-Aunt took me aside.

"Ah Si, don't you worry about me and your daughter. You didn't have a mother's love as you were growing up, but she did. Don't feel bad. When she is older Qi-meng will understand that she is lucky to have a mother like you."

To my surprise, she grabbed me and hugged me, holding me in her arms, the first time in my life she had shown such emotion. Then she hobbled to her room and closed the door.

As I descended the stairs holding Qi-meng's hand, and walked down Purple Sunshine Lane, I reflected on Great-Aunt's words, that I had grown up without a mother's love. She was wrong.

EPILOGUE

As I write this, Bill and I are together.

I began my new life at thirty-five years of age, when most people had long since settled down, full of uncertainty: while I had no doubts about what I had left behind, I was not at all sure about what might come. I had known Bill such a short time. I knew he loved me and I loved him, but I was also painfully aware that love is tested by circumstance. Would his parents accept me, a stranger from a different race and culture, and treat me well? Would his children accept me? Could I adapt to a society so vastly different from my own, despite its obvious attractions? Could I find work so that I would not be a burden to anyone?

And what would happen if I suffered another failure? How could I go back to China, to Xiao Zhao, to my unhappy life?

But the transition has not been as difficult as I thought it might. The first time I walked into a grocery store in Toronto I began to weep, stunned by the quantity of food and the sheer volume of items standing on the shelves. I was speechless when I realized that no ration coupons were required.

In my classes at York University, it took me a long time to join in the discussions. I found myself holding my breath when others expressed themselves freely, challenging the teachers, even criticizing the government and well-known politicians.

It was shortly after Bill met me at the airport in Toronto that I learned the scholarship I had won was his invention, that the mailing address was his sister's home, and that the chairperson of the fund who wrote to congratulate me was his best friend — a teacher whose signature, so boldly written with a black felt-tip pen, had left my Communist leaders with no doubts about the scholarship's authenticity. The money had come from Bill's book royalties. He could not have let me know that the scholarship was tailored to one person for fear that the mail readers would find out. (The documents concerning the scholarship are reproduced in the Appendix.)

When news finally reached my department, two years later, that I would not return to China, Number 5 was called to appear in court. She didn't obey the summons. When I asked her what had happened, she said, "Nothing, Ah Si. Don't worry about it."

As I promised myself, a new gravestone is now standing in front of my parents' burial mound beside the canal near Qingyang. I sincerely hope it will never be toppled again, the sort of hope shared not only by Chinese people but by people around the world, for a standing gravestone is a symbol of stability.

I never saw Great-Aunt again after I left Shanghai that hot August day. She died in May 1989, shortly after she had returned to live out her days in Chen Family Village. I was informed of her death two weeks after the fact. I often wonder if she knew all along the dilemma I faced when she told me that Qi-meng was lucky to have a mother like me. How I wish Great-Aunt were still alive so that I could tell her how wrong she was when she said I grew up without a mother's love. All my life, either living at home or torn away from it, I had always had her love, a love no less than any mother would give.

Her ashes are buried in Chen Family Village, the place from which she had been exiled because she was seen as a woman cursed with bad luck. I hope she realized before she died that the girl she had said would have a hard life because she was born in the year of the dragon had finally escaped from hardship.

When I broke with Xiao Zhao, he took revenge and made our daughter his pawn. That a woman who had dutifully handed him nearly every cent she earned and worn the clothes he bought for her since the day they were married had turned her back on him was more than he could take. Qi-meng is not allowed to visit any of my family members, nor are they permitted any contact with her. All of my mail to her is returned torn to shreds.

I went back to China as a Canadian citizen in July 1994 to see her. When he heard I was in the city, Hai Rui stormed into Number 5's apartment, the place where I grew up, and demanded that she warn me to stop trying to find out where Qi-meng was. Ah Si would never see her daughter again, he said.

I went to the summer school where I knew Qi-meng was attending English lessons. She was not there, and the teachers had not heard of her. It was only when a student heard my daughter's nickname, Meng-meng, and said she knew her, that I found Qi-meng did go to that school, but her father had changed her name so that I couldn't trace her.

For three days in a row I went to Xizang Road, to the apartment building where I lived while married, and stood across the road, hoping for a glimpse of my daughter. I didn't dare knock on the door because Xiao Zhao had told my relatives that if I came to see her in my former home he would beat up both me and Qi-meng. On the third day, I saw her standing on the front balcony. I waved. She saw me and ran inside. A few minutes later, Xiao Zhao came out, looking for me. Then he and Qi-meng got on their bicycles and pedaled away. As I ran along the sidewalk behind her I recalled the day so long ago when Number 1 sprinted frantically beside the bus that would take me to the prison farm, stretching out his hand and calling my name. Before I could reach her, Qi-meng followed her father around a corner and was swallowed up by the traffic.

I had not seen her for seven years. She was a tall, slender, beautiful girl.

Afterwards, Xiao Zhao moved, leaving no forwarding address. When a friend made enquiries at the local police station, I learned that Xiao Zhao had bribed someone there to erase certain information from our file. The record now shows that I was a single woman living alone in that apartment before I emigrated to Canada. It was as if the home I had shared with my husband, my daughter — and Hai Rui — had never existed.

Great-Aunt had always complained that I was destined for a life of struggle and pain. She was right. But with her love and support, with the help, sometimes, of others, and with my own determination I have survived the bitter wind. I am free now. No one looks over my shoulder; no one reports my activities to Party officials. I need no one's permission to travel to one place or another. I can think my own thoughts and speak out, and I can write. Shortly after I began this book, my recurring nightmare, in which I am told my mother has run away to an island to avoid me, ceased. I have one more very difficult obstacle to overcome: to re-establish myself in my daughter's life, so that one day she too may be free.

Orillia, August 1996

APPENDIX

The invented scholarship

(see pages 368–371 and page 379)

ONTARIO EDUCATORS' SCHOLARSHIP

for STUDIES in the HUMANITIES

Information

Regulations

Application Form

1987

GENERAL INFORMATION

The Ontario Educators' Scholarship for Studies in the Humanities was established in 1986 to encourage and assist students from under-developed and less-developed nations who wish to undertake studies directly related to Western culture in the Canadian context at an institution of higher learning in Ontario (Canada).

The principle goal of the scholarship is to promote knowledge of Canadian culture and its place in the fabric of Western culture. For this reason, scholarship assistance is limited to applicants whose field of studies is within the broad scope of the Humanities rather than the Sciences, Engineering, Mathematics, etc.

While the majority of contributors to the scholarship fund are teachers and educators, contributions are also made by editors, publishers, business persons and others.

Applicants who are "sponsored" by teachers and educators within Ontario will receive priority, but such "sponsorship" is not a necessity.

GENERAL REGULATIONS

1. Any student from an under-developed or less-developed nation may apply.

2. The applicant must be enrolled in or must have been accepted by a university or community college of applied arts and technology in Ontario (Canada). Proof of acceptance to the university or CAAT should accompany the application form.

3. The field of study must be within the Humanities -- e.g. the Arts, Language, History, etc. Applicants whose major field is Mathematics, Engineering, Science etc. are not eligible.

4. Applicants must submit a TOEFL score (on official form) OR a letter of recommendation from the applicant's teacher or former teacher whose first language is English and who can attest to the candidates competence in spoken AND written English.

5. The scholarship provides funds for tuition and/or living expenses at an amount to be determined by the scholarship committee and in a manner to be determined by the committee.

6. The scholarship is for one year's study, but may be extended to two years at the discretion of the committee.

7. All decisions reached by the committee are final. Unsuccessful candidates are encouraged to reapply for the following year.

8. Applications must be post marked no later than February 28th of the year in which the applicant wishes to begin his/her studies.

9. Mail applications to: The Ontario Educators' Scholarship for Studies in the Humanities, c/o 3 Bartley Drive, Rural Route 3, Caledon East, Ontario, Canada L0N 1E0.

the Ontario Educators' Scholarship for Studies in the Humanities

APPLICATION FORM

Please print or type.

* applicant's name (in English) .... Ye Tingxing ....

* (in native language) .... 叶 婷 行 ....

* address .... Room 105, 312 Xizhuang Road (N), Shanghai, People's Republic of

China
....

* country of birth...... China ...... citizenship..... Chinese ......

* date of birth.. 28/6/52 ...... sex... F... occupation. English Interpreter ....

* marital status (circle one) single (married) divorced

* languages spoken other than English ....

* name of college or university you will attend ... Bethune College, York University ...

* course or area of study. English literature. level (graduate or undergraduate)..........

* education and schools attended:

1. secondary school...... Shanghai ....from... 1964 to. 1968.
   Beijing University 1974-1978
   Foreign Affairs College 1984-1986
2. college or university.......................................from..... .....to..........

3. field of study and specialization . English language & English literature;
   foreign affairs courses

4. degree(s) held ...... B.A. ....

_____

_____

5. TOEFL score.......... date........OR name and address of referee. . .Recommendation by .

Mr. William Bell, #11 Neywash Street, Orillia Ontario, Canada L3V 1x1
. . . .

* work experience, if any . . . I have been working as an oral English interpreter .

in the State Guest Section of Foreign Affairs Office of Shanghai Municipality
. . . .

for about nine years.
. . . .

* present employer's name and address. . . Foreign Affairs Office of Shanghai . . . . . .

Municipal People's Government, 1418 Nanjing Road (W), Shanghai,
. . . .

People's Republic of China

* PLEASE COMPLETE THIS PART ON A SEPARATE PIECE OF PAPER.

Please describe, in 250 words or less, your reasons for choosing your field of study and

for selecting Canada as a place to study. Your "essay" should be in your own words

and should be printed or typed. The competence in English displayed will have a direct

bearing on your chances of acceptance.

ONTARIO EDUCATORS'
SCHOLARSHIP
FOR STUDIES in the HUMANITIES
c/o # 3 BARTLEY DRIVE
CALEDON EAST, ONTARIO
CANADA L0N 1E0

1987.02.24

Ms Ye Ting-xing
Office of Foreign Affairs
Shanghai Municipal People's Government
1418 Nanjing Road
Shanghai, China

Dear Ms Ye Ting-xing,

The Board of Governors of O.E.S.S.H. is very pleased to inform you that your application for financial assistance to study English Literature at York University in Toronto has been approved.

The grant for living expenses will equal the sum required for the acquisition of a Students' Visa -- as of this writing, $6,500 (Canadian). Should the Canadian Government increase this amount, your grant will be increased accordingly. In the near future, this money will be deposited in a bank account in your name at a bank in Toronto. If there is a particular bank you would prefer, please inform us at your convenience.

Please note that these funds are not transferrable outside Canada and are intended to be used by you for living expenses only. Should you require assistance for travel expenses, you may apply separately. The fund occasionally grants such requests, but only under exceptional circumstances.

For visa purposes, proof of financial support will be sent to you upon request.

Please accept our congratulations. We wish you success in your studies. If we can help you in any way as you prepare to come to Toronto, please do not hesitate to call upon us.

Sincerely,

William Talbot,
Chairperson, O.E.S.S.H.

cc: William E. Bell, Sponsor

ONTARIO EDUCATORS' SCHOLARSHIP for STUDIES in the HUMANITIES

c/o #2 Bartley Drive, Caledon East, Ont. L0N 1E0

1987.03.10

Visa Office
Consulate of the Government
of Canada
Shanghai, China

Re: Ms Ye Ting-xing

To Whom it May Concern,

This letter is to inform you that Ms Ye Ting-xing, Interpreter with the Shanghai Municipal People's Government, #1418 Nanjing Rd. W., whose home address is room 105, #312 Xizhuang Rd., N., Shanghai, has been awarded a scholarship by the Ontario Educators' Scholarship for Studies in the Humanities.

This scholarship will support Ms Ye's studies in Literature as a Visiting Scholar at York University, Toronto, under the guidance of Dr. Lumsden, Master of Norman Bethune College, for a period of one year, commencing September, 1987.

Funds will be deposited in a bank account in Toronto in Ms Ye's name.

The scholarship will cover living expenses (room and board) either in the university residence or in quarters of Ms Ye's choosing; travel expenses within Ontario, including travel to and from York University from her residence; text books and other materials; spending money; and medical insurance -- up to an amount not exceeding $8,000 (Canadian). Travel expenses to and from Canada and tuition fees are not covered by this scholarship.

We hope you will render to Ms Ye any assistance necessary in the acquisition of her student's visa. If we can be of any further help, please do not hesitate to call on us.

Sincerely,

William M. K. Talbot